Mary's Place in
Christian Dialogue

Mary's Place in Christian Dialogue

edited by
Alberic Stacpoole, O.S.B.
M.C., M.A., F.R.Hist.S.

Morehouse-Barlow Co., Inc.
Wilton, Connecticut 06897

Cover illustration:
Our Lady of Czestochowa, the black Madonna of Jasna Gora

The original was brought to Czestochowa in 1378 by a governor of a south-east province — which would account for the Byzantine influence in the painting.
After its defacement in 1430, a new copy was made by a Krakow artist, under royal patronage — the memory of the violent defacement of the original being retained in the two long scars on the right cheek. The ikon became a symbol of protection in wars, till King John Casimir solemnly declared the Madonna to be 'Queen of Poland'.
It was brought finally to the mountain of Jasna Gora (the 'luminous mountain') where it rests today as a symbol of Poland's perpetual protection through the intercession of the Blessed Virgin. Every summer, huge pilgrimages from all over Poland, and now also from many other countries, come to pray at the foot of Jasna Gora.

Published in Great Britain 1982
St Paul Publications
Middlegreen, Slough SL3 6BT, England

Published in the United States 1983
Morehouse-Barlow Co., Inc.
78 Danbury Road
Wilton, Connecticut 06897

ISBN 0-8192-1333-0

Printed in the United States of America

Contents

Foreword by the Editor   vii
Foreword by Eric W. Kemp, Mervyn A. Alexander, Gordon S.
   Wakefield   viii
The Marian Section of 'The Final Report' (ARCIC)   ix
Introduction   xi

  I. ECUMENICAL   1

    An Ecumenical Future for Roman Catholic Theology
    of Mary
    Donal Flanagan   3

    The Evangelical Mary
    John de Satgé   25

    Mary as an Ecumenical Problem
    J. A. Ross Mackenzie   34

  II. SCRIPTURAL   43

    The Blessed Virgin Mary in the Bible
    Ralph Russell   45

    Bible and Tradition in regard to the
    Blessed Virgin Mary
    John de Satgé – John McHugh   51

  III. THEOLOGICAL   61

    Mary and Right Belief in Christ
    Eric Kemp   63

    The Relation that exists between the
    Holy Spirit and Mary
    Léon Josef Suenens   69

    The Holy Spirit and Mary
    Alan Clark   79

  IV. DOCTRINAL   89

    The Mother of God
    Eric L. Mascall   91

    Immaculate Conception
    John Macquarrie   98

    The Assumption
    John Saward   108

    The Immaculate Conception, the
    Assumption and Reunion
    Edward Yarnold   125

V. THE PROTESTANT TRADITION 131

Embodiment of Unmerited Grace
Eric W. Gritsch 133

From Dysfunction to Disbelief
Donald G. Dawe 142

The Virgin Mary in Methodism
Gordon S. Wakefield 151

Mary: An Evangelical Viewpoint
Keith Weston 158

VI. OTHER TRADITIONS: CHRISTIAN
AND NON-CHRISTIAN 167

The Mother of God in Orthodox Theology
and Devotion
Kallistos Ware 169

Mary in Syriac Tradition
Sebastian Brock 182

A Woman in Israel
Nicholas de Lange 192

Mary in Islam
R. J. McCarthy 202

VII. HISTORICAL 215

The English Tradition of the Doctrine of the
Immaculate Conception
Alberic Stacpoole 217

Cardinal Newman's Teaching about the
Blessed Virgin Mary
Charles Stephen Dessain 232

Pope Pius XII and the Blessed
Virgin Mary
H. E. Cardinale 248

VIII. DEVOTIONAL 261

Intercession
Gordon S. Wakefield 263

Living Lourdes
A. G. C. King 271

FOREWORD

HIS HOLINESS POPE JOHN PAUL II
AND THE ECUMENICAL SOCIETY OF THE
BLESSED VIRGIN MARY

The Holy Father, it is well known, is devoted to the Blessed Virgin. Any doubt of that would be dispelled by perceiving the M (for *Maria*) put upon his coat of arms in face of heraldic purists' protests. As Karol Wojtyla, appointed a bishop in Krakow in July 1958, he has naturally led many diocesan pilgrimages to the great protectress of Poland, the black Madonna of Czestochowa, whose famous painting is revered there in the monastery of Jasna Gora within the diocese of Krakow. As a bishop he has preached there on many occasions, rarely forgoing the Feast of the Queen of Poland (3rd May). There in 1977 he stressed that Our Lady was Queen of all Poles, at home, abroad and in exile. There in 1978, he observed that in four years time (1982) Poland would celebrate the sixth centenary of the arrival of the mysterious painting at Jasna Gora; and, invoking the Evangelist's account of the crucifixion, he recalled the words 'Behold your mother', calling on all to become spiritual sons of Mary, Mother of our Saviour who is also our brother. In late May 1979, he was back in Poland as Pope, relating the Polish experience to the passion of Christ, and ended by saying: 'All that in the hands of the Mother of God, at the foot of the Cross on Calvary and in the upper room of Pentecost'. He spent three days at Czestochowa, his first sermon there lasting almost an hour, being devoted to Mary's role in Polish history and present life: 'She is present in some strange way, Poles becoming used to bringing their problems to Jasna Gora, to tell their mother everything'. Taking his farewell of the Madonna of Jasna Gora, the Holy Father said: 'I surrender myself to your maternal servitude of love; I surrender to you the Church as a whole'.

Such a Pontiff has naturally shown interest in our Ecumenical Society of the Blessed Virgin Mary. Indeed, until his life was radically changed by his being shot in St Peter's Square, there was a strong hope that he would write an Introduction to this collection of Marian papers. As it is, it cannot be. But a second-best is to use the text of his blessing upon our 1979 International Conference at Westminster. On that occasion he sent a signed letter to the Cardinal, our Co-President, quoting *Lumen Gentium* 68 & 69 initially, and *Redemptor Hominis* 22 in the ultimate paragraph:

'In its teaching on Our Lady and the Church, the Second Vatican Council presented Mary as "a sign of certain hope and comfort to the pilgrim People of God", and prayed "that she, who aided the beginnings of the Church by her prayers, may now ... intercede before

vii

her son in the fellowship of all the saints, until all families of people ... may be happily gathered together in peace and harmony into one People of God, for the glory of the Most Holy and undivided Trinity". Between the Mother of the Church and our present work for the unity of the Church there is a close and important link.'

'Mary "was included in the history of salvation and of the Church's mission from the very beginning ... Accordingly, we who form today's generation of disciples of Christ all wish to unite ourselves with her in a special way. We do so with all attachment to our ancient tradition and also with full respect and love for the members of all the Christian communities". I gladly bless the work of ... the Ecumenical Society of the Blessed Virgin Mary and pray that it will bring nearer the achievement of that unity for which Christ prayed.'

FOREWORD
BY THE EXECUTIVE CO-CHAIRMEN OF THE ESBVM

What is presented here is a cross-section of the work of a remarkable society, the Ecumenical Society of the Blessed Virgin Mary. It was the surprising and courageous idea of the founder, Martin Gillett, to bring together Christians of different traditions to discuss the place of Mary in faith and devotion. In the early days few people could see any future for such an enterprise, but the Society has survived and flourished.

From the beginning there has been active participation by members of the main Christian traditions, as this selection of papers bears witness. It has been possible to create an atmosphere of friendship in which the most controversial issues can be discussed. Each speaker can share his views in complete frankness. There have been moments of shock, bewilderment and hurt, but these too are part of the experience of growth.

It was soon brought home to us that in a serious discussion of the place of Mary we were not dealing with a peripheral subject. In the course of our meetings all the central Christian doctrines come under scrutiny. We have also been led into many highways and byways of art, history, literature and science! More than ever we are convinced that Mary represents a way forward in ecumenical relations.

Martin Gillett died on St George's Day, 1980. As part of the many tributes paid to him we feel that it is fitting to offer to a wider public these papers which were first given at meetings of the Society which he founded. We believe that they are a valuable contribution to the cause that he had so much at heart.

+ Eric W. Kemp, Bishop of Chichester
+ Mervyn A, Alexander, Bishop of Clifton
  Gordon S. Wakefield, Principal of Queen's College, Birmingham

THE MARIAN SECTION 'THE FINAL REPORT' OF THE ANGLICAN/ROMAN CATHOLIC INTERNATIONAL COMMISSION

The ARCIC 'Final Report' deals essentially with the papacy, under four sections. The fourth, taking up a half of the whole, concerns Infallibility. The two Marian definitions, the Immaculate Conception (1854) and the Assumption (1950), provide a strong illustration for reactions by many Anglicans to infallible dogmas promulgated by the Bishop of Rome apart from a synod or council since the separation of the two Communions; Section 30 continues:

> Anglicans and Roman Catholics can agree in much of the truth that these two dogmas are designed to affirm. We agree that there can be but one mediator between God and man, Jesus Christ, and reject any interpretation of the role of Mary which obscures this affirmation. We agree in recognizing that Christian understanding of Mary is inseparably linked with the doctrines of Christ and of the Church. We agree in recognizing the grace and unique vocation of Mary. Mother of God Incarnate (*Theotokos*), in observing her festivals, and in according her honour in the communion of saints. We agree that she was prepared by divine grace to be the mother of our Redeemer, by whom she herself was redeemed and received into glory. We further agree in recognizing in Mary a model of holiness, obedience and faith for all Christians. We accept that it is possible to regard her as a prophetic figure of the Church of God before as well as after the Incarnation. Nevertheless the dogmas of the Immaculate Conception and the Assumption raise a special problem for those Anglicans who do not consider that the precise definitions given by these dogmas are sufficiently supported by Scripture. For many Anglicans the teaching authority of the bishop of Rome, independent of a council, is not recommended by the fact that through it these Marian doctrines were proclaimed as dogmas binding on all the faithful. Anglicans would also ask whether, in any future union between our two Churches, they would be required to subscribe to such dogmatic statements. One consequence of our separation has been a tendency for Anglicans and Roman Catholics alike to exaggerate the importance of the Marian dogmas in themselves at the expense of other truths more closely related to the foundation of the Christian faith.

The acceptances, followed by the caveats above, are all rounded out in some measure in the papers that follow below. There it may be seen how the Marian definitions emerged and how soundly based they are in biblical theology. From there it may be judged whether Anglicans and Roman Catholics alike were not right to 'exaggerate the importance of Marian dogmas'; and whether this has indeed been at the expense – or to the considerable enrichment – of other truths.

INTRODUCTION

She is the favourite daughter of the Father and the temple of the Holy Spirit. She far surpasses all other creatures, in heaven and on earth. However, because she belongs to the offspring of Adam she is one with all human beings in their need for salvation. Indeed she is clearly the mother of the members of Christ.

Lumen Gentium VIII 53

Instead of being a cause of division amongst us, Christian reflections on the role of the Virgin Mary should be a cause of rejoicing and a source of prayer.

Max Thurian, Frère de Taizé

The ecumenical movement, taking its name from a Greek word *oicumene*, meaning all who form the community of man, nevertheless begins and ends in God himself, in the oneness of God in his creation. It expresses itself primarily in the common prayer of all Christians in so far as they can share their *communicatio in sacris*—common belief and baptism, common service of Christ, common scriptures (if not interpretation of them), common religio-cultural tradition. It has rightly been said that the love of Christians, in pursuit of the Gospel teaching, is the *fruitio* which is the 'realised ecumenism' of the God-given unity that is his Church.

It is strange then to find our Blessed Lady, Mary, the Mother of her Son Jesus the Christ, a central subject of ecumenical devotion in a Society founded to her name. Strange, because the theology surrounding her name and office has tended to separate religious men rather than unite them; and the exaggerated devotions that sprang up down the years have sealed that separation. When Lord Halifax and the Abbé Portal sought grounds for reunion, they chose to begin with the subject of Orders. When the Anglican/Roman Catholic International Commission sought common doctrinal ground, they began with the Eucharist. And yet it was a visionary in Martin Gillett who, finding the Blessed Virgin a stone of stumbling in the 1960s, chose to endeavour to make her a foundation stone to reunion for the 1970s.

Like Newman before him, Martin Gillett began as an Anglican, becoming a deacon in the Church of England. Like him, he ended as an honoured Catholic, being created in 1975 a Knight Commander of the Order of St Gregory. The heart of his life work had been devotion to the Blessed Virgin, in writing, lecturing and promoting Marian shrines. In honour of the 1950 Holy Year which saw the promulgation of the doctrine of the Assumption of the Blessed Virgin, for instance, he was invited to give a dozen talks on Radio Vatican upon national shrines of Our Lady. Two decades later he was to become the effective founding figure of the Ecumenical Society of the Blessed Virgin Mary (ESBVM).

Today that Society has flourished in some strength for over twelve years. Its present Co-Presidents are Cardinal Basil Hume (from 1976) and Archbishop Robert Runcie (from 1980). Its Co-Chairmen include Catholic and Anglican prelates and senior ministers from the Methodist tradition; and Orthodox prelates have also been identified with its work. Besides its activities in Britain and Ireland, it has a thriving 'chapter' in the United States; at the invitation of Cardinal Baum of Washington, Martin Gillett flew out two years before he died in 1980 to be present at the inauguration. The Society's activities culminate in a series of international conferences/congresses held every two years in such places as Birmingham or Canterbury, to which some of Christendom's leading Marian scholars are asked to deliver papers that are subsequently published.

At other times, meetings are held in the ten branches of Britain and Ireland, or in the United States; and annual one-day national conferences are held in London. By degrees, over a decade of fruitful study and prayer, a steady flow of not undistinguished papers have been brought to the Society's corporate consciousness by being printed for internal circulation as pamphlets or broadsheets. While the Congress papers have been published after the events as a set of collections (and are not here republished, despite the remarkable quality of many of those papers), the less 'eventful' papers of the Society's current activity, which deserve a wider record than they have yet received, remain to be put together to remind us all of how far we have come towards reunion at least in Marian matters in the decade of the 1970s.

If the seventies have witnessed any remarkable progress in ecumenism in the English speaking world, surely it has been largely in three areas: at the parish and pastoral level, a breaking down of prejudices and learning to pray together; at the doctrinal level, the three Agreed Statements on Eucharist, Ministry and Authority (ARCIC); and at the devotional level, the pursuit of Marian reunion in great measure through the ESBVM. Mariology has been and remains a subject upon which wide gulfs between Christian traditions are yet to be bridged. The following is a fair indication of that: when at the end of April 1977 Dr Donald Coggan visited Pope Paul at the Vatican to renew the ties between the two Churches of Rome and Canterbury, he was characteristically candid about the issues which still divide these two communions. He described the doctrines of the Immaculate Conception (1854) and the Assumption (1950) of the Blessed Virgin Mary as 'still presenting great difficulties for Anglicans'.

Perhaps, in the light of the papers that follow, we should pursue further the fact of doctrinal division and its extent, since it leaves Churches beyond immediate prospect of reunion. Let us take the Church of Scotland for example. When its General Assembly met in May 1977, just after the Canterbury/Rome visit, it considered a 12,000 word document from its Panel on Doctrine which concluded that most Catholic teaching on Mary, Mother of Jesus, cannot be justified from evidence in the New Testament: 'The Roman Catholic Church associates Mary very closely with Christ himself, seeing her as sinless, as our heavenly intercessor and even ascribing to her such titles as "Mediatrix" and "Queen of Heaven". There is no doubt that Mary holds a unique place as the Mother of Jesus, but the Church of Scotland believes that the greater part of Roman Catholic teaching cannot be justified from the evidence of the New Testament and that it tends to obscure the uniqueness of Christ himself—a tendency which seems very apparent in popular Roman Catholic devotion to Mary.'

The quotation taken from the Panel on Doctrine comes from *Part III: Fundamental Differences*. In justice we should also quote from *Part IV: Particular Issues—Mary and the Saints* (sect. 32). 'Criticism of the Roman Catholic cult of Mary and the saints often concentrates on the most superstitious aspects of some types of popular Roman Catholic piety. In fairness, the Church of Scotland has to recognise that the Roman Catholic Church is itself critical of many of these excesses; and in particular that the Second Vatican Council spoke very sharply against them. It is rather to the official position, as stated by the Council, that we must refer here. In general, it is this: Christ is the one mediator between God and mankind. However, just as here on earth Christians share in the ministry of Christ to each other, so too do Mary and the saints in heaven. They can therefore be offered a kind of worship, called *douleia*, or "service" (which is different from *latreia*, the worship which can be offered to God alone), and asked for their support and intercession on behalf of ourselves and others. This support and intercession is not some extra or independent activity of their own apart from Christ, but rather their participation in his ministry for us; and it is understood to strengthen rather than weaken the bond between Christ and ourselves'. Accepting the communion of saints in Christ, the Church of Scotland cannot go so far as the Catholic Church 'in allowing prayer to Mary and the saints. The Church of Scotland does not believe that we are united to Christ through Mary and the saints, but rather that it is through Christ that we and all the saints are one. It does not believe that others, however holy, are more approachable than Christ or in any way closer to us than he. Accordingly it holds that Christian faith and hope and worship must be grounded and focussed upon Christ himself, and not diverted in any other direction. Any such diversion, however well intentioned, is not consistent with a proper recognition of his unique centrality.' The point is good: it requires a very careful answer—and the resolution of the issue needs to be widely broadcast.

Steadily down the years the ecumenical dialogue generated by the Society's meetings has been providing fair answers; and they are to be judged by the collection brought together here, fairly evenly divided under eight representative headings that largely compose the corpus of Christian study. It is a source of pride to the Society's members that so rich a series of proceedings has accrued that from it this selection can be made without touching the papers from the international events and without exhausting the reservoir. Indeed a second such volume—though perhaps less rich in all—might well be put together from that same reservoir.

It may be apposite here to sketch in the titles of the more significant papers delivered at the Society's international Conferences/Congresses. At the first, held at Coloma College, West Wickham, in April 1971, among the papers read were: "The reticence of the bible tradition of the Blessed Virgin Mary" by Alan Richardson, the Dean of York; "The theological life of the Blessed Virgin Mary according to Vatican II" by Mgr Philip Delhaye, Dean of the Louvain Theological Faculty and since brought into the Curia; and "The place of the Blessed Virgin in a secular society" by Fr F.M. Jelly OP of the Washington Dominican house of studies. At the second Conference, held at Newman College, Birmingham, in Easter Week 1973, among the papers read were: "Systematic theology of the Blessed Virgin in relation to exegesis" by the Carmelite theologian Fr Eamon Carroll of the Catholic University of America; "Mary in Midrash and Mary in fact " by Duncan Derrett, a London professor of Oriental law; "Mary in the communion of saints" by the Abbé René Laurentin of Angers University, Vice President of the French Society of Marian Studies; "Luther's Commentary on the Magnificat" by Fr Donal Flanagan, Professor of Dogmatic Theology at Maynooth; and "The woman clothed with the sun" by Fr John McHugh, lecturer in Scripture at Ushaw College and Durham University. At the third Conference, held at Selly Oak College, Birmingham, in Easter Week 1975, among the papers read were: "Predestination and Mary" by Dr Alasdair Heron of the Department of Christian Dogmatics, University of Edinburgh: "The impact of family structure on personality, with particular reference to Our Lady on Christ" by Dr Jack Dominian of the Department of Psychological Medicine at the Central Middlesex Hospital; "The Divine and feminine" by Rev John McQuarrie, Lady Margaret Professor of Divinity at Oxford; "Mary in the Lucan Infancy narrative" by Rev Marie Isaacs of Heythrop College, University of London; "Born of the Virgin Mary" by Rt Rev. Alan Clark, Bishop of Elmham and President of the RC Ecumenical Commission; "The Grace of Christ in Mary" by Rev. Edward Yarnold SJ, Senior Tutor of Campion Hall, Oxford; "The theme of Eve and Mary in early Christian thought" by Rev. Dr John A. Ross Mackenzie, Dickinson Professor of Church History at Union Theological Seminary, Virginia, USA; and "The true devotion to the Blessed Virgin", again by Fr John McHugh.

An International Ecumenical Conference was again called at Selly Oak, Birmingham, for Easter Week 1977, but the response was not strong and it failed to mature. The most promising paper from it was "Motherhood in Jewish thought" by Rabbi Louis Jacobs of the New London Synagogue. So the fourth Conference was held at the Westminster Cathedral Conference Centre and at St Mary the Virgin, Oxford, in late September 1979, and among the papers read were: "What Zwingli taught" by Rev. Professor Walter Hollenweger, Professor of Mission in the University of Birmingham; "Calvin and the Calvinists on Mary" again by Professor Ross Mackenzie; "Links between the spirituality of the middle ages and the English Reformation" by Rev. Dr B.R. White, Principal of Regents Park College, Oxford; "Continuity of Tradition in the Colonial States of America" by Fr Alban Maguire OFM of the Franciscan Providence Province, USA (printed as "Mary in America: a tradition continued"); "The Virgin Mary in modern reformed theology" by Rev. Donald Dawe, a Presbyterian minister and Professor of Theology at the Union Theological Seminary, Virginia, USA, and President of the American chapter of ESBVM; "Mary the bearer of Christian unity" again by Fr Frederick Jelly OP; and (at Oxford) "The development of Newman's Marian thought and devotion" by Rev. Dr Roderick Strange of the Oxford Catholic Chaplaincy. The fifth Congress was held at Christ Church College, Canterbury, in mid September 1981, and among the papers read were "The Blessed Virgin and the Holy Spirit" by Cardinal Leon Josef Suenens of Belgium; "The New Eve" again by Fr John McHugh; "Mary in Russian literature" by Rev. Professor Dmitry Grigorieff of Georgetown University, Washington, DC; "The concrete meaning of Mary's motherhood" again by Fr Frederick Jelly OP; "The dogma of the Assumption in ecumenical perspective" again by Rev. Donald Dawe; "Mary, the Jewish Woman" by Dr Geza Vermes of the Department of Oriental Studies, Oxford; "Honouring the Virgin Mary: A Reformed perspective" again by Dr Ross Mackenzie; and finally "Pluralism on Mary in the bible and today" again by Abbé René Laurentin. The proceedings of the last three of these international gatherings will have been published in either a Supplement of THE WAY or an issue of ONE IN CHRIST: some of the papers of the first two Conferences were issued among the Society's own current pamphlets to its members.

There are essentially two ways to edit a collection of scholarly papers. The first is to impose a uniform pattern of presentation, particularly in relation to the use of footnotes and support material, spelling (defence/defense, etc.) and punctuation (capital letters, etc.). The second is to leave the writers to answer for themselves in their own manner, the editor doing just a little coordinative tidying up. I have chosen the latter, which should please the writers and interest the readers.

I have made a short introduction to each section, and then given the credentials of each writer according to his affiliation and appointment at the time of writing. In ecumenical affairs that seems the proper conduct; thinkers change, not only their minds but their offices and sometimes even their clerical state. They should be described as at the time that they declared their Marian beliefs in print; this I have tried to do, without an eye to the ironies of hindsight. If one was later converted to another tradition, if one left his *ordo* for the lay state, or if another laid down his scholarship for a pastoral calling, that is all regarded as belonging to the future at the time of writing and so goes without comment. Suffice it to say that all our contributors are servants of the Blessed Virgin, not in herself but as Mother of God, to whom be the glory and the honour and the worship.

> 'Now to that face which most resembles Christ
> Lift up thy gaze; its radiance alone
> can grant to thee the power to look on Christ.'
> I looked, and on that countenance there shone
> such bliss, bestowed by sacred minds who soar
> —for this created—through that lofty zone,
> that nothing I had looked on heretofore
> had held me breathless in such wonderment,
> or unto God such close a likeness bore.   (Canto 32)

> The eyes which God doth love and reverence,
> gazing on him who prayed, to us made plain
> how prayers, devoutly prayed, her joy enhance.
> Unto the eternal light she raised them then:
> no eye of living creature could aspire
> to penetrate so fixedly therein.   (Canto 33)
>   Dante, *Paradiso*

8 September 1981
Feast of the Birthday of the BVM
A.J.S.
St Benet's Hall, Oxford

I
ECUMENICAL

It is right to begin where the work of the Society is found, in the problems of inter-tradition dialogue. It is equally right, when dealing with ecumenical matters, to keep papers in strict sequence; since nuances of acceptance are changing always significantly and sometimes rapidly, and the theological climate needs to be seen in sequence. So the following papers are printed sequentially.

The first was delivered in Easter Week 1971 at the first International Conference at Coloma College, Kent, by the Professor of Theology, St Patrick's College, Maynooth, Eire. It surveys Marian dialogue in the years from Pio Nono to the digestion of the Second Vatican Council, and particularly the Barthian reaction.

The second was read to a meeting of the Society at St Marylebone parish church on 10 February 1976 by a former Canon Residentiary of Sheffield who has since become a fulltime writer. His books include *Mary and the Christian Gospel*, *Christ and the Human Perspective*, and *Peter and the Single Church* (all published by SPCK). This paper complements his first book.

The third was given to a one-day conference of the Society at the Oblate College, Washington DC, on 29 April 1976, by the Professor of Church History, Union Theological Seminary, Richmond, Virginia, USA. He has since been given an award by the Catholic University of America for promoting interest in Mary the Mother of Christ. He is a Presbyterian theologian, who is now Senior Minister of First Presbyterian Church in Gainesville, Florida.

An Ecumenical Future
for Roman Catholic Theology
of Mary

REV. DONAL FLANAGAN, D.D.

The title of this paper will no doubt appear rash to many people even to some within the Roman Catholic communion. For there are some people within Roman Catholicism itself who do not see that mariology has anything to offer in the area of ecumenism. I, personally, most strongly reject this view for I believe that Catholic Mariology has a significant, even irreplaceable contribution to make to the ecumenical debate. And I think that this already emerges from a critical examination of mariology past and present. And it is with this I propose to begin.

Before facing up to the basic question should we be silent about Mary in ecumenical discussion or should we face the facts, it is necessary to have some appreciation of how things were with regard to Catholic devotion to and doctrine about the Mother of God before the second Vatican Council. This is the context in which the Council itself treated of Our Lady. It is only if we know something of this preconciliar situation and the history which stands behind it that we can appreciate the ecumenical progress which came through the Council on the one hand and the legitimacy of those Protestant fears which the Conciliar document had in mind on the other.

May I say at this point that in using the terms 'Catholic' and 'Protestant' I am obviously oversimplifying a very complex situation. I am trying to describe perhaps two main lines of approach to Mary found in our Christian Churches in their broad outlines.

A Protestant View of the Division

Robert McAfee Brown in his recent book, *The Ecumenical Revolution*, writes:

> "Next to the papacy, Mariology is the area of greatest theological division between Catholics and Protestants. The problem centres on the most recent papal pronouncements, the dogma of the Immaculate Conception of Mary, so that she was freed from the taint of original sin and the dogma of the Assumption of the Virgin into Heaven immediately after her death".[1]

Brown continues by underlining particular difficulties about these doctrines on Mary from among the many which Protestants felt before

3

Vatican II. Protestants were concerned at the apparent *centrality* of these truths in the faith and life of the Roman Church. The ever-increasing attention given to Mary in Roman Catholicism struck them as necessarily bringing with it the danger of an eclipse of Christ, even ultimately of his displacement. Protestants felt this danger to be more real in that they saw it as the product of an unchecked (and uncheckable?) process of 'development', which seemed to be independent in some strange way of the objective and recorded data of revelation. The definitions of the Immaculate Conception and the Assumption (for which, in their view, there appeared no Scriptual warrant) seemed to rest ultimately on a decision of the *magisterium* of the Church, which gave as its justification for these two definitions its own authority and the faith of the Church, evident in a long standing tradition. These definitions and particularly their apparent lack of relation to Scripture seemed to many Protestant Christians to leave open the possibility or even to indicate the likelihood that the Roman Church would proceed ultimately to the solemn declaration of the co-redemptive function of Mary thus finally committing herself to a dogmatic assertion not merely unsupported by the New Testament but directly and clearly contrary to its most fundamental assertion of One Mediator (1 *Tim* 2, 5-6).

These very fears themselves indicate how wide the gap was between most Catholic mariological thinkers and their Protestant brethren before the Second Vatican Council. There was on the Catholic side an unjustifiable lack of concern with the legitimate fears of Protestant Christians. To put it bluntly, Protestants were often written down as 'enemies of the Madonna', and their pointed questions to mariologists simply ignored.

On the Protestant side, it must be said also, there was a certain perhaps over-shrill defence of the centrality of Christ and the significance of the Scriptures, as if Catholics did not accept these things also as basic to their faith. The fatal *Christ or Mary* dilemma designed as a polemical anti-Catholic weapon succeeded only in leading Protestants astray about Catholics attitudes to Mary and in cutting them off from authentic Marian elements in their own Protestant tradition.

Up to the Council the doctrinal confrontation of Protestant and Catholic in regard to Mary was polemical in extreme. McAfee Brown speaking of the Assumption definition as it appears to Protestants writes:

> "the dogma of the Assumption represents simultaneously the one completely unambiguous exercise of the prerogative of papal infallibility and that portion of Catholic theology that seems at the farthest remove from the New Testament".[2]

Catholics must face the fact. The Assumption definition appeared and appears to many Protestants as an arbitrary exercise of a not biblically sustainable papal infallibility. This exercise seems to be directed to giving a position of central significance to a peripheral truth, on which in any case, Scripture is totally silent. This peripheral truth is declared to be a truth necessary for salvation.

The type of misunderstanding instanced above extends to every single area of marian doctrine and devotion.

The history of marian theology since Trent shows all the evidence of a marian apartheid. The Mary of Catholic doctrine and devotion gradually becomes a figure quite foreign to Protestants. Catholicism gives her greater and greater prominence and Protestants, in many Reformation traditions, reply, almost instinctively, by playing down Mary.

Our division about Mary a product of history

From a sixteenth century Reformation to the present day we can study and see a gradual growing apart of Christians on the subject of Mary. This is a highly complicated phenomenon which has a whole series of different and interrelated causes. It is, by no means, a simple theological disagreement between scholars, nor was it ever such.

The earliest Protestant Reformers Martin Luther and Huldrich Zwingli initially rejected very decisively some undoubted abuses and false ideas which were being propagated in the marian devotional forms current in popular piety in the early sixteenth century. They quickly enough, however, came to reject for various reasons the cult of the saints, including Mary, as such. Catholic controversialists reacted strongly to this attack and tended to play down the abuses, even as the Lutheran, Zwinglian and slightly later the Calvinist polemic in particular, tended to play them up.

The Reformation, in regard to Mary and devotion to her, first set out to curb excesses, but quickly passed to a rejection of marian devotion as a matter of principle and within a decade of Luther's first great commentaries it had produced its own new and recognisable Protestant understanding of the Mother of God and her relation to the salvation of men.

Even as Christians of the Reformation traditions played down Mary because they felt she had been given a much too prominent place in late medieval piety, so Catholics concentrated on her more and more. Mariology, or the study and defence of the privileges of Mary emerged fully as an inner-catholic discipline.

Mariology appears in Roman Catholicism increasingly as a special branch of theology with special rules. It seems to develop theologically according to an inner dynamic of its own. It gradually asserts itself as the 'Catholic' section of theology in the minds of some and Mary comes to be seen more and more in much popular piety as the typical Catholic devotional figure. Devotion to her comes to be emphasised as the hallmark of the devout Catholic.

The Second Vatican Council recalled the theology of Mary from the isolation in which it had developed since the Council of Trent. It called upon it to realign itself with the doctrine of the Church, that is to return to the situation which had prevailed through so much of the Church's history, where Mary was seen in the Church and the Church in Mary.

The post Tridentine period saw the development of a one-sided doctrine of Mary in which her uniqueness is emphasised at the expense of her common kinship with us. Vatican II ended this imbalance in both mariology and ecclesiology. It did so for mariology by replacing Mary in an ecclesial context. Mary in the Church focussed attention on the inwardness of the mystery of the Church, so that ecclesiology too was assisted to overcome its onesidedness.

The need for a polemical response in post-Tridentine Catholic theology influenced more than mariology and ecclesiology. It made itself felt also and particularly in the doctrine of grace. It is correct, it seems, to view mariological developments in the line of the Immaculate Conception and Assumption as the working out in personal terms of an anti-Reformation polemical theological anthropology and doctrine of grace. There is a much closer link than we, perhaps, imagined between the decree *de Justificatione* of Trent and these marian doctrines. The same preoccupation with created grace is evident in both cases, the same anxiety to state the real intrinsic difference grace makes to man.

The fact that the Indwelling Spirit is barely mentioned in the Tridentine theology of justification is paralleled rather exactly by the rarity of mention of him in the marian doctrinal developments.

The centuries following the Council of Trent (1545-1563) saw the gradual erosion of Protestant faith and practice in regard to Mary. This was paralleled and mutually influenced by, while also influencing in turn, a one-sided unbalanced development of marian theology and devotion within Roman Catholicism. The long estrangement continued.

The nineteenth and in particular our own century saw what has become known as the marian movement make its appearance. In this movement we can observe a series of high points in a certain kind of Catholic affirmation of Mary and a cause of that most extreme Protestant reserve in regard to Mary evidenced in the attitude of many Protestants to Mary in the middle years of this century.

The Marian Movement

The remote causes of the modern marian movement which we have seen reach its climax may be sought as far back as the seventeenth century. The first half of the nineteenth century saw its emergence as a recognizable general trend in the Church. Its culmination in the reign of Pius XII (1939-1958) will have to be described in some detail, for this provides the immediate backdrop to the mariological understanding of

Vatican II and the statement it has given us. This crest itself, however, was prepared by a slowly-gathering wave which reaches back over five pontificates to the third decade of the nineteenth century.

The dialogue of popular piety, theological effort and official encouragement which characterizes the marian movement of the nineteenth and the first half of the twentieth century might be said to have begun in 1831 with the revelation to St. Catherine Labouré of the miraculous medal, a devotion soon approved and widely popular among the faithful.

The mid-nineteenth century saw the supremely significant definition of the Immaculate Conception in 1854, poised between the turbid uncertainty of the vision of La Salette (1846) and the crystal clarity of Lourdes (1858) and its untutored witness. In this definition for the first time a pope pronounced finally on a doctrine which was not in dispute in the Church, thus engaging the power of his teaching office in favour of a marian truth and giving the Church its first marian definition in more than 1,200 years.

The seventies of the century saw further marian apparitions at Pontmain, France, in 1870, and at Knock, Ireland, in 1879.

In the eighteen eighties came the publication of the epoch-making mariology of M. J. Scheeben of Cologne—a book which set new standards and in its emphasis on Mary's inner relation to the Church took up a theme long lost sight of.

Leo XIII, Pope from 1879-1903, gave a great impetus to the marian movement by his encyclicals which emphasized Mary's intercessory power. In these he constantly, year after year hammered home the value of prayer to Mary, particularly the rosary. It was during the pontificate of Leo XIII that the marian congress, later to become such a typical feature of the movement, made its first appearance.

Pius X's most significant marian statement was his encyclical *Ad diem illum* on the fiftieth anniversary of the Immaculate Conception. Benedict XV did not issue a special marian encyclical but his *en passant* statements on Mary's role in redemption—which have been over-used by many mariologists—cannot exactly be called reserved. 1917 saw the foundation by Fr. Maximilian Kolbe of the Militia of the Immaculate Conception, the first of the modern marian mass-movements with 2,000,000 members. This same year saw the apparition at Fatima.

In 1921 Cardinal Mercier re-opened his efforts to secure a definition of Mary's mediation, securing later from Pius XI the institution of a feast whose celebration would be granted to any diocese which would request it. And this same year saw the foundation of the Legion of Mary in Dublin.

Mercier, who had persuaded Pius XI to set up three commissions to study the definability of the doctrine of the mediation of Mary, was himself in this way responsible for a new impetus given to marian studies, particularly studies on the mediation. Articles and studies began to appear in ever larger numbers; they also began to reveal an increasing scholarly quality. This movement of studies continuing through the nineteen twenties led in the thirties to the foundation of the first national societies of marian studies in Belgium (1931) and in France (1935).

Parallel to this, encouraging the ever-growing movement of marian piety, came the further apparitions of Beauraing (1932) and Banneaux (1933) while the older shrines such as Lourdes continued year by year to draw their pilgrims.

It is vital to note that these apparitions which are an important element in modern marian piety tend to give it a particular stamp. They emphasize strongly our Lady and her great intercessory power. Indeed, it seems they tend to make Catholic piety as a whole more marian in cast. So that one can say, I believe, that in our day as never before devotional practices to the Blessed Virgin Mary seem to have become the typical form of Roman Catholic popular piety.

But this is slightly to anticipate for we must now turn to the climactic pontificate—that of Pius XII.

PIUS XII (1939–1958)

Even when the popes from Pius IX to XI did not directly speak on marian doctrine they often gave an impetus to the marian movement in other ways. But in comparison with Pius XII these pontifical interventions seem small and insignificant. They were nonetheless preparing the ground for that absolutely astonishing upsurge of devotional practice, doctrinal effort and papal support for both which were such a marked feature of his pontificate and which anyone who has lived through it hardly has to have described to him in detail. With Pius XII the enthusiastic mariologist's dream of an "Age of Mary" seemed to have become a reality.

The pontificate of Pius XII, particularly in its latter years (1950-58), represents the high point of the Marian movement of the nineteenth and early twentieth century. The recorded statements of this pope on the Blessed Virgin outbulk the combined contributions of his five predecessors. Pope Pius XII engaged himself with discretion, it is true, but heavily on the side of the marian movement. And while he took occasion to point out the dangers, and the need for a solid theological approach, there is no doubt that without his support and encouragement the ever greater manifestations of marian piety simply could not have taken place. In the years 1950 to 1958 we find a mounting crescendo of marian enthusiasm.

Pius XII defined the Assumption in 1950. This year saw the first great International Marian Congress meet in Rome itself—its theme *Alma Socia Christi*. The Marian Year 1954, the centenary of the definition of the Immaculate Conception, saw the second International

Marian Congress held again in Rome—the theme this time: *Virgo Immaculata.* The Pope himself issued in this year also the encyclical *Ad Coeli Reginam* proclaiming Mary's Queenship.

The third International Marian Congress was held at Lourdes in 1958—the theme this time: *Maria et Ecclesia.* This theme already is a portent of the future.

These doctrinal and devotional gatherings turned out colossal series of Proceedings, e.g. Lourdes 1958, 16 vols., including one volume of over six hundred pages. The years 1948-57 saw an average production of one thousand "scientific" contributions on marian theology per year reach the overworked theologian. This production was partly due to the official magisterium which kept up a continuous flow of marian commentary, partly due to the ever more frequently recurring marian congresses which on regional national and international levels reached the astronomical total of 43 in the year 1954.

Pius XII, however, did not begin his marian activity in 1950. To name only two earlier and very significant steps. Already in 1942 he had consecrated the world to the Immaculate Heart of Mary. In the next year, 1943, he had produced the theologically compact and complete marian appendix which he added to his encyclical on the Church of that year.

This pope expressed himself again and again on the theme of Mary. And to this constant encouragement popular devotion and theological effort responded. The Blessed Virgin gained more and more prominence in the minds of the faithful. Devotional practices, public acts, meetings, writings, institutes, libraries—all these devoted to honouring her and extolling (typical word!) her privileges—multiplied.

Those of us who are old enough to remember the pontificate of Pius XII will have no difficulty in agreeing that we live to-day in a changed mariological climate. The statement of the second Vatican Council on Our Lady compared with any of the later marian statements of Pope Pius XII shows a sharp change of emphasis in our presentation of Mary. This change, however, should not make us forget that an examination of mariology up to the second Vatican Council gives no clue that it has an ecumenical future.

Silence about Mary or facing the facts?

With such a past which is it best to do in the interests of ecumenism, observe a discreet silence about Mary or to boldly face up to the considerable differences which divide us?

I believe that the second is the proper course. Silence about Mary now when one has spoken so gladly and so often of her in the past runs the risk of being misconstrued. There still exist between us *gross* misunderstandings of sincerely held views and attitudes about Mary which are an abrasive element making all ecumenical communication more difficult. These must be faced. Marian truths cannot be pushed to one side because there are no such things as isolated Christian truths which concern Mary alone. All truths about Mary are expressions of aspects of the mystery of Christ and his Church, of the mystery of God's saving presence in and with man, and the form this takes. They are not pieces of Christian information, which have no relevance to our understanding and living of our Salvation.

The clearest proof, however, that facing the difficulties is the right attitude is provided by the eighth chapter of *Lumen Gentium*, the Dogmatic Constitution on the Church of the Second Vatican Council.

The Ecumenical Significance of Lumen Gentium, Ch. 8

When the Bishops of the world were confronted at the Council with the problem we are discussing, I feel there must have been some temptation to pass over Mary in silence. In view of the situation, this might have seemed the wiser and more reasonable course. It was not adopted. Instead, calmly facing the difficulties in what was admittedly a highly sensitive area the Council produced a genuine increase in ecumenical understanding through the considered and courageous document it published.

Chapter Eight of *Lumen Gentium* is very obviously ecumenical in intent. Thus, it sets out to speak biblically, avoids extreme positions and phraseology, and deliberately situates the ecumenically difficult title "mediatrix" in a historical row of titles, thus showing it to be one among many and to be understood within this very venerable tradition. The ecumenical concern of the document can be seen most markedly in the great care it takes to emphasize the Unique Mediator, Jesus Christ, and to say categorically that if the title "mediatrix" is applied to Mary, it can only be understood in a sense that no way takes away from or adds to the dignity or the effectiveness of the one mediator, Christ.

The document further makes specific mention of the duty of theologians and preachers to avoid anything which could lead their separated brethren or any other person into error about the Church's teaching on our Blessed Lady.

The special attention it pays to points in which misunderstandings could arise, and the conscious effort it makes to relate its teachings to Holy Scripture have not gone unnoticed, and its seriousness of purpose in seeking to overcome the imbalance from which Catholic Mariology suffered before Vatican II as well as its deliberate return to the richness of the patristic authors on Mary has impressed those who do not belong to the Roman Church.

The nervousness with which non-Roman Christians often approach the subject of Mary is something we must reckon with. This document in writing in major ecumenical emphases explicitly has quite obviously listened to and learned from Protestant fears.

10

The Second Vatican Council engaged in a critical examination of the Church's marian conscience and it tried to give an objective account of what it found there. The Council was a disappointment to many; to some it said too little, but to many others it said too much. It did, however, provide genuine indications for the future of marian theology. There is in the conciliar documents a profoundly important starting point for ecumenical dialogue about Mary and her place in Christian belief and Christian life.

Some Catholics got quite a surprise when the Second Vatican Council did not produce the kind of the extreme marian document they were hoping for. The Council went back into the Catholic marian tradition to discover and restate for our day, some traditional Catholic insights. The balance of the schema on Mary, which became chapter 8 of *Lumen Gentium* is due to this recall of traditional ecclesio-marial material. This chapter surprised not merely some Catholics, but some Protestants as well.

McAfee Brown writing of the chapter notes that it has lifted the ecumenical discussion to a new level.

> "Catholics", he writes, "have gone a first mile in trying to re-establish theological *rapport* on this issue, Protestants have an obligation to go a second mile in opening themselves to an examination with their Catholic brethren of what the New Testament says about the place of Mary in Christian faith, and then trying to understand how Catholics can be led beyond that direct evidence to further affirmations that clearly mean so much to them in interpreting the signs of God's loving concern for his children".[3]

McAfee Brown clearly welcomes ecumenical dialogue about Mary and he is in this a welcome change from the hesitant stances of some Roman Catholic ecumenists.

Chapter Eight of *Lumen Gentium* is a document of ecumenical significance for, perhaps, a more basic reason than any named so far. It is ecumenical because in it we find a forthright statement of basic marian positions to which the Roman Catholic Church has committed herself. When all due allowance has been made for the effects of history and polemics, when new emphases and new perspectives have been introduced it remains necessary to avoid the greatest hazard of all—a purely verbal agreement.

It is an ecumenical service to remove misunderstandings which unnecessarily divide but it is an even more important service to clarify the positions we hold so that we can see, if we are divided, why we are and what exactly it is that divides us.

Mariology and Christian Anthropology

It is reasonable to wish to begin ecumenical discussion with the great soteriological truths where differing interpretations divide us. To post-

11

pone the discussion of difficulties about Mary can be justified as the avoiding at the beginning of an area in which over years of separation very strong feelings have grown up, an area in which many non-theological factors are at work, an area of great sensitiveness.

It must be clear however that the ecumenical discussion cannot start in the implied agreement that the truths which concern Mary are in some way optional.

There must be constant purging of theological and devotional dross which disfigures Mary's image in order to keep arriving at a proper appreciation of 'the handmaid of the Lord' (*Lk*. 1:38). This critical approach does not mean the abandoning of devotion to Mary or of marian theology. It makes very much greater demands on the theologian who writes about Mary than the half-reflecting repetition of formulae and their 'proving'. The theologian's duty is not to defend any system or formula or school opinion but to honestly report his understanding of what revelation tells us of her mission and her person. He cannot remain silent about her in the ecumenical discussion. Because revelation speaks of her not marginally but in a very close and unbreakable connection with the work of our salvation so must the theologian. Silence would be unecumenical because dishonest.

Yet some Catholics appear to regard keeping a discreet silence on what concerns the Mother of God as the most ecumenical posture possible. This attitude although wrong is understandable in as much as mariological writings and marian devotional forms have in the past, to say the least, sometimes needed correction.

On the other hand, there are Catholics who appear to be convinced that the constant preaching of Mary *à l'outré* will somehow bring about the acceptance by all Christians of the theological account of her given by those Catholic theologians who are called maximalists.

The theologian who writes about Mary must be clear that in this demesne quantity is neither a problem nor an aim. He is not trying to say as little possible about Our Lady or as much as possible about her. He is rather trying to talk about salvation—and to present Mary as she whom God saves and calls to a unique task. The basic themes of marian theology are those of soteriology. Marian theology is in its root the recounting of Mary's salvation by God and a description of the form which this salvation took. It is not a special part of theology which concerns itself with Mary in isolation.

The realization of this fact is very important for the ecumenical dialogue. This is the basic reason why marian theology cannot be left out of consideration in the discussions between the Churches—because its basic questions are the great questions about the form God's salvation takes in the world. The basic things that the Church has said about salvation in Mary she has affirmed in other terms at other times of us all.

The difficulty with mariology is not the Assumption as such though

12

this could undoubtedly have been better presented at the time of its definition. Nor is it any other single marian truth in itself. The mariological difficulty is basically the theology of salvation implied in each and all of these truths. God, man, sin, salvation, grace—these fundamental truths run together and are thrown into the sharpest focus in the theology of Mary. And this is the real root of our differences. The problem which lies at the base of our mariological difficulties is not an exclusively mariological one but a theological and anthropological one, a problem in the nature of divine salvation.

It is an illusion to think that there is a separate and separable marian problem. It is ultimately not because the Immaculate Conception and the Assumption speak of Mary that they pose an ecumenical problem but because of what they affirm by implication about the nature of human salvation.

Protestants must examine their own tradition back to its roots to see if they can find there marian insights which have fallen from view. Catholics must do the same.

It is only by consciously attempting to speak the entire truth to one another from a fuller and fuller understanding of each tradition that real ecumenical understanding can come. To refuse to discuss mariology from the beginning in the ecumenical dialogue is like trying to discuss the Roman Catholic doctrine of the Church without mentioning the highly evolved doctrine of the papacy, which is part and parcel of Catholic ecclesiology.

It should be added that the ecumenical dialogue of Protestant and Catholic must not shun the problems raised by some Reformation Christians, who see marian doctrine and devotion as a frightening and reprehensible 'humanizing' of Christianity, which destroys its basic character of Gospel of God.[4] The problems raised here are absolutely fundamental ones, and this explains the fierce concern which is often expressed.

In a comment on the well-known anti-marian polemical work of Giovanni Miegge, a German reviewer writes:

"The original theocentric and christocentric character of Christianity is "humanized", and that means that, in the last analysis Christianity takes on the character of a way of self-redemption. Miegge sees modern Catholicism on this dangerous road, from which one can only depart by a decisive return from Mary to Christ."[5]

A further Protestant comment on Roman Catholic mariology speaks of "a final levelling out of theology in which the Christian character of this theology disappears more and more in face of a generalized *religio humana*. What remains is Man, the *homo cooperator* who emerges in the person of Mary and takes over."[6]

These are admittedly very extreme positions but they represent a segment of Protestant opinion which is by no means negligible. For Protestants in this line of thinking marianism is simply paganism

13

dressed up, an affront to the saving God, and a typical product of the mind of the unsaved creature.

Karl Barth's Criticism of Roman Catholic Mariology

The rejection of the Roman Catholic understanding of Mary which is characteristic of so much of the tradition of the Reformation finds in Karl Barth what is, perhaps, its clearest expression. The reasons for the rejection are made quite plain by him. It is precisely because of what it is understood to say about God's salvation that mariology as understood in the Roman Catholic Church cannot have a place in evangelical Christianity. It is because Roman Catholicism, as is revealed most clearly in its mariology, is a doctrine of human self-sufficiency in regard to salvation that Protestant Christians must reject it so decisively.

Barth's criticism of Roman Catholicism fixes on marian dogma as "the critical central dogma of the Roman Catholic Church." Surveying Roman Catholicism and its doctrine of Mary from the standpoint of Reformed Christianity, Barth had the following severe words to say:

"We reject Mariology, (1) because it is an arbitrary innovation in the face of scripture and the early Church, and (2) because this innovation consists essentially in a falsification of Christian truth. We must now touch briefly on these points. Our best procedure is to take the actual explanation of Marian dogma attempted by Catholic theology and let it speak for, i.e., against, itself. Scheeben op. cit. p. 456 quotes with approval the antiphon from the third nocturn in the *Commune festorum B. Mariae V.* in the *Brev. Rom.*, an anonymous saying of the 8th century, in which Mary is addressed thus: *Cunctas haereses sola interemisti in universo mundo.* However this may have been intended at the time, if it is a satisfactory expression of Roman Catholic systematics (and we have reason to believe that this is the case), it means that Marian dogma is neither more nor less than the critical, central dogma of the Roman Catholic Church, the dogma from the standpoint of which all their important positions are to be regarded and by which they stand or fall. It is a profoundly based fact that for the popular consciousness, Catholic or Protestant, there is probably no Reformed position which has proved so illuminating even to a child as the simple No uttered from the standpoint of Reformed knowledge in answer to the whole doctrine and worship of Mary, an answer which in every circumstance must be uttered inexorably. In the doctrine and worship of Mary there is disclosed the one heresy of the Roman Catholic Church which explains all the rest. The 'mother of God' of Roman Catholic Marian dogma is quite simply the principle, type and essence of the human creature co-operating servantlike *(ministerialiter)* in its own redemption on the basis of prevenient grace, and to that extent the principle, type and essence of the Church.

Roman Catholic dogmatics has every reason to insist with Thomas Aquinas *(S. theol. III qu. 25 art. 5 sed contra)* that *mater Dei est pura creatura.* Not only its delimitation against heathen parallels, but everything

14

else that it can say positively in Mariology, depends upon the fact that in spite of her infinite dignity, in spite of her incomparable privileges, and in spite, nay because of her co-operation in redemption, Mary is not a goddess and does not belong to the sphere of being of the triune God, but, compared with Him, belongs wholly to the creaturely, indeed to the earthly, human sphere. It is as a creature that her dignity, her privileges, her work of co-operation, and with it the central, systematic place and function mentioned above, are attributed to her. The decisive act by which she acquires her dignity and her privileges, and on the basis of which she is capable of the co-operation, is not merely that physically she is the mother of God, but that there is a bridal relation to God which accompanies the motherhood, expressed in the words: *Ecce ancilla Domini, fiat mihi secundum verbum tuum.* In this believing acquiescence in the promise made to her she proves that she is disposed to possess the grace of the motherhood in question. She desires the positive receptivity required (Scheeben, op. cit. p. 489 ff.). *Beata Virgo dicitur meruisse portare Dominum omnium non quia meruit ipsum incarnari, sed quia meruit ex gratia sibi data illum puritatis et sanctitatis gradum, ut congrue possit esse mater Dei* (Thomas Aquinas, *S. theol.* III qu. 2 art. 11 ad. 3). But this definition of Mary's *meritum* fairly describes the way in which according to Roman Catholic doctrine the human creature in general may acquire a *meritum*, and what this consists of. Man is capable, by prevenient grace, of preparing himself for genuine sanctifying grace, by uttering this *fiat*. The creature blessed in virtue of its acquiescence is the proper object of Mariology."[7]

He states very clearly the attitude an Evangelical Christian must take:

"The Evangelical statement of faith which we must set against Marian dogma is thus the very same as must be maintained against the Roman Catholic doctrine of grace and the Church. Jesus Christ, the Word of God, exists, reigns and rules in as sovereign a way within the created world as He does from eternity with the Father, no doubt over and in man, no doubt in his Church and by it, but in such a way that at every point He is always Himself the Lord, and man, like the Church, can give honour only to Him and never, however indirectly, to himself as well. There can be no thought of any reciprocity or mutual efficacy even with the most careful precautions. Faith in particular is not an act of reciprocity, but the act of renouncing all reciprocity, the act of acknowledging the one Mediator, beside whom there is no other. Revelation and reconciliation are irreversibly, indivisibly and exclusively God's work. Thus the problem to which the Roman Catholic doctrine of grace and the Church, to which Mariology in particular is the so-called answer, i.e., the problem of creaturely co-operation in God's revelation and reconciliation, is at once a spurious problem, the sole answer to which can be false doctrines. *Quid est creaturam loco creatoris ponere, si hoc non est?* With this question of early Protestant polemic (F. Turrettini, *De necessaria secessione nostra ab ecclesia Romana*, 1678, Disp. 2, 16) we too must protest against Mariology as such."[8]

A comment from the well-known Barthian scholar, Professor G. C. Berkouwer seems in order here:

"Barth does no injustice here to Roman Catholic mariology. The central function of Mary in redemption is to be the mediatrix of grace. He correctly points out that it is natural for Roman Catholic dogma to emphasise—with Thomas—that Mary is a *creature* and in *that* capacity takes her place in salvation *via* human cooperation. It is true that this cooperation is not autonomous for it takes place against the background of grace, but against this background the cooperation is *real*. According to Barth the Reformation was wholly right in reacting to this only with an angry No and we are called to continue this protest even more insistently today, now that the evolution of mariology in the 19th century (1854) and in the 20th century (1950) has made the meaning of this cooperation even clearer than it was in earlier centuries."[9]

Berkouwer adds by way of specific comment on the definition of the Immaculate Conception,

"We do not wish to forget here that the encyclical *Ineffabilis Deus* of 1854 accentuates the background of grace in the words '*intuitu meritorum Jesu Christi.*' This accentuation certainly belongs to the whole of Roman Catholic mariology but it is far from guaranteeing the freedom and the sovereignty of grace."[10]

Some Considerations on Barth and on the Roman Catholic Position

Barth is fundamentally right in saying clearly that mariological doctrines and the doctrine of grace are essentially interrelated. This is true not merely in Roman Catholicism; it is also true in Reformation Christianity as a glance at the Lutheran classic, *A Commentary on the Magnificat* which Luther produced in the years 1520-21 will show. In this work we can clearly see the impact of Luther's new thinking on grace making itself felt in his treatment of Mary.

But Catholicism (and in particular the Council of Trent) is far from wishing to propose or defend any teaching which does not guarantee the freedom and sovereignty of grace. Trent, in fact, showed itself very anxious to rule out any suggestion that salvation is something within the power of any creature to provide.[11] This concern is basic to Roman Catholicism, which accepts fully the Lordship of Jesus Christ, the Word of God.

Trent (and all Roman Catholicism too) is concerned to uphold the view that man is not destroyed or corrupted by sin. He remains even as sinner fundamentally perfectible. But by God not by man. It affirms further that man, even though weakened and injured by sin can be renewed by grace, that he can be and is taken up into a relationship of true and real collaboration with the living God in grace.

There is, however, no work of man which does not have its root, origin and continuing effectiveness in God's free grace. This is ultimately why it can have significance for salvation.

Barth's polemic against Catholic mariology (and the Catholic doctrine of grace) in so far as it is directed against a doctrine of self-salvation is unnecessary. In so far as it represents an attack on the integrity of the human, even after sin, it must be rejected as wrong.

Human freedom cannot substitute for grace but neither can grace for human freedom. It is neither necessary nor useful to exalt grace by depreciating the human in its freedom.

The classic Reformation formulations *sola scriptura, sola gratia, solus Christus, solus Deus* are often enough invoked against Catholic marian doctrine and devotion. In this negative interpretation they confront us with impossible dilemmas like Bible or Church, grace or freedom, Christ or Mary, God or man.

I think it very necessary to point out that such a negative interpretation is not necessarily the best defence of the true sovereignty of God, of his grace and his word.

Paradoxical as it might seem the best defence of what these principles affirm when they are understood positively—the *primacy* of God, Christ and grace—is an adequate doctrine of the human in salvation in its true creatural autonomy and perfectibility.

The marian doctrines of Roman Catholicism represent an attempt at such a doctrine. They are a firm defence of the creatural and relative autonomy of man and of his perfectibility by God's power.

They do not deny the primacy of grace, the uniqueness of Christ, the sovereignty of God but rather affirm these the more forcibly by situating them at a profounder level.

Man is not God's rival. He is simply that nothingness which is by God's gift, his partner.

The very basic reason for the constant opposition which Catholic marian teaching encounters from theologians in the Reformation tradition is that it runs hard up against the Reformation conception of the relation God/creature, more exactly God/sinful creature.

The question about man the sinner is a question about man and a question about God. To this basic question we find in Catholic and Reformation theology mutually exclusive answers and through the various theological developments on both sides certain basic theological affirmations remain constant. From Protestant first principles the kind of salvation we affirm is not possible. Within their terms it cannot be described as salvation at all; it smacks rather of human self-justification. From Catholic first principles the kind of salvation Protestants affirm cannot within our terms be described as salvation at all. It smacks rather of the wilfulness of an arbitrary God who seems to have no real contact with his creation although Creator, for his saving activity somehow leaves man untouched in the core of his being.

The Catholic understanding of salvation affirms not merely a certain human reality which survives as good in the sinner, it sees the relationship of saving God and sinful man as a real true co-operation, a work achieved by God in man with man, *in nobis sed non sine nobis.*

Vatican II pointed out unambiguously in the title it gave to chapter eight of the Church Constitution that Mary belongs in the mystery of Christ and she belongs in the mystery of the Church.

The great periods of Christian theology had an instinctive grasp of this fact. The Fathers saw the Church mirrored in Mary and Mary in the Church. And both were meaningless apart from the Lord Jesus. In the profounder, more mystical strain in our own western theological tradition right up to the Reformation these profound insights into the mystery of human salvation never faded entirely from view.

What for generations of Christians were mutually complementary, mutually clarifying truths we unfortunately seem to have come to view today as truths in competition. The impossibly isolated and one-sided way in which mariology and ecclesiology have developed in our own western latin tradition since the sixteenth century is responsible for this. And following on this undesirable development we have seen not merely the separation of Mary and the Church but in response to the demands of religious polemic a setting of Christ against the Church, and even against Mary. If Vatican II had only recalled mariologists to traditional insights on the relation of Christ, Mary, and the Church it would have deserved well of them.

Mariological progress after the Council would seem to demand necessarily that the mutual implications of the truths of revelation about Christ, the Church and Mary be worked out in more and more detail in a way which they will be acceptable to all Christians. The centrality of Christ and the secondary and derivative character of the truths about the Church and about Mary must be made plain.

This is a formidable challenge posed by Vatican II, and it can hardly be said to have been successfully taken up by mariology in the last five years. It is a task which has not always been faced up to as it ought to have been by those with the best ecumenical intentions. It is not possible to jettison the 'analogy of faith' in favour of a 'hierarchy of Christian truths' for this latter does not mean that some Christian truths are negotiable others not, though it sometimes appears to be taken in this way. No Christian truth is negotiable if the Church has committed herself to it in the way she has committed herself to the dogmas of the Immaculate Conception and Assumption. We can re-think them, re-situate them, but we cannot re-interpret them into their direct contraries. If the place of mariology within Christian theology is properly grasped and the mutual interrelation of Christology, ecclesiology and mariology is clearly seen these so-called 'marian' truths appear for what they fundamentally are: truths about the nature of Christian salvation, as salvation in and through Christ and his community, not just doctrinal information about Mary. They represent in theological terms, not embarrassing pietism posing as theology but true gains in the field of the doctrines of christian anthropology and eschatology which we ignore to our loss.

Mariology is basically a theology about salvation. It is not at its deepest level a doctrinal treatment of Mary as a saving figure; it is fundamentally viewed, a doctrine of man being saved and becoming through the gift of God the free collaborator of God the Saviour.

The marian doctrines of the Roman Catholic Church represent her clearest statements on human perfectibility by the grace of God and on the actual involvement of man in the work of God's salvation.

This is why they must be taken very seriously. This is why they must be the object of serious ecumenical thought.

The Incarnation and The Human

Roman Catholic theologians cannot help noticing the verve with which many theologians in the tradition of the Reformation react against marian theology as the affirmation of the human. Yves Congar writes:

"We have again and again the impression that for Protestant theology everything which is attributed to man not from himself but even through God's gift of grace, is removed from God's sovereignty as though God were Lord only on the condition that He alone exists."[12]

Roman Catholicism can and does recognise the force and vigour with which Christians in the tradition of the Reformation have given their witness to God's word, to God's grace, to Christ and to God. Christians in the tradition of the Reformation feel with a particular sensitiveness the need to emphasise these truths.

Their Reformation forefathers lived in an age when the word of God sometimes appeared entangled in and bound by the traditions of men; when the grace of God often appeared to be dependent on the works of men; when the uniqueness of the merciful Lord Jesus sometimes appeared obscured by the figure of his Mother.

It is beyond doubt that the century of the Reformation needed to be recalled to an understanding of God as God. It needed to have a clear emphasis placed on salvation as of God not of man. It needed to have a clear distinction made between the word of God and the words of men. It needed to realise once more how far the human element can adulterate the gospel as this is understood and lived in the world.

The Reformation Fathers had to make a very determined attempt to correct the situation which confronted them. Their commitment to try to keep God's salvation from contamination seems to have carried them as far as a certain refusal of the human which cannot be justified.

Roman Catholics on the other hand have in their doctrines about Mary committed themselves clearly to an affirmation of the human as God's creation and the mode and vehicle of his salvation.

I think it can fairly be said that the Roman Catholic position taken in our statements about Mary is one which demands some courage. It is, in fact, a position of risk which has exposed and exposes us to pretty massive attack. It is a position which is open to misunderstanding. It is a position which is not seldom misunderstood as the assertion of man in place of God or as somehow the assertion of Man as against God.

But the necessary risk we take of defending the 'humanum', the human element as an inalienable part of God's salvation is not a matter of free choice. It is forced upon us by our understanding of the doctrine of the Incarnation itself.

The implications of God becoming man do not stop short at the humanity of Jesus Christ. The Incarnation says something about man as such, about the character of man and the human as that in and through which God reveals himself, in and through which he works.

No marian doctrine makes such an extreme statement about the possibilities of the human, about man as the basic fact recorded by John the evangelist: "And the Word was made flesh."[13]

Mary is today even as at Ephesus a witness to the Incarnation. Then she was a pointer to its truly historical reality—one Jesus Christ who is God. Today she must be seen as indicating the full implications of the Incarnation for our understanding of being human.

There is an insidious temptation to view the human as perfect in Jesus Christ and somehow corrupt in all its other manifestations. This is not the message of the triumph of creation.

Christians in the tradition of the Reformation must put themselves the question: Does the Incarnation say something specific about Christ only? or about man? If so, what does it say?

The Human and the work of the Spirit

We have concentrated a great deal of attention on marian doctrines as expressions of Roman Catholic anthropology or doctrine of man but this is not the whole picture. To present Mary as the affirmation of the human in its perfectibility and in its creatural autonomy and to stop there is to paint only half the picture. The most important point is as yet unmentioned.

Our Christian doctrine about the possibilities of man and his involvement in salvation is not complete and self-enclosed. Indeed to speak about the perfectibility of man is already to speak of the work of the Spirit, God's Holy Spirit. To speak of the involvement of the human in salvation is to speak of the Spirit at work.

We touch here on the marian theme which is of the greatest ecumenical significance today—the relation of Mary to the Holy Spirit.

The doctrine of the Holy Spirit, active in the Church, as bond of Christ and the Christian, as *the* Sanctifier, as *the* Intercessor[14] is the context within which all Catholic reflection on Mary and her part in our salvation must be placed. It is alas! a context still to be supplied by theologians for we suffer in Roman Catholicism today from a woefully underdeveloped doctrine of the Holy Spirit, not to mention, in consequence of this, an attitude of great reserve, if not positive suspicion of manifestations of the Spirit's presence which are not immediately related to our present authority structure.

The absence of such a doctrine is a major reason for the disproportionate development of mariology within Roman Catholicism since the Reformation period, if not even earlier. It is also a notable *lacuna* in *Lumen Gentium*, chapter 8.

We must frankly say to our brethren in the tradition of the Reformation that we need to and are prepared to relativize our view of Mary by setting Roman Catholic teaching and devotional practice concerning her clearly in a pneumatological context, in the perspective of the Holy Spirit. It is a context which should never have been missing. Mary is she whom and through whom Christ's Spirit sanctifies.

Laurentin speaks of the Council as calling the theology of Mary to assume an anthropological orientation and a pneumatological orientation i.e. to recognise itself as a doctrine of man and as a doctrine of the work of the Spirit in man.[15] The Council recalled and underlined the traditional role of Mary as Eve. In the Church tradition, in patristic and early medieval times at least, Eve was 'Woman', an all-embracing creatural figure appearing in many guises but always as over against the divine, the place or mode of the Spirit's operation, the human, the purely human as capable of assumption by God to be the instrument of his power, the transparent humility but not nothingness (against Luther) of the creature. It was losing sight of this basic marian fact which made for charges of marian triumphalism. This insight must control how we state Mary's relationship to the Church and demands a strong affirmation of a mysterious yet not total identification of these two temples of the Spirit. The Assumption in this perspective appears not as 'a jewel in the Madonna's crown' but as God's saving work in and for man, a work which shows us the end of the development intended by God for the 'Woman' i.e. his creature. It illustrates clearly the possibilities of glory which are given in creation itself by providing a living example of glory realised.

The Assumption leads naturally to a consideration of Mary in the communion of the saints. Mary assumed belongs in the communion of the saints, for an anthropological understanding of the Assumption leads us directly into the theological assertion of the communion of saints. Mary's destiny was to participate in the salvation of man as an active and free agent and this is essentially the collective destiny of all. Her intercession is the fulfilment of the potential of the human as receiver of grace. Man by grace is made a saved fellow-worker of God. There is no purely passive salvation or grace. Mary's intercession should therefore be seen first in and with the Church's intercession under the general heading of man's involvement in the work of salvation. This reaches its peak as active concern and effective involvement in sanctifying others as God's helper.

Mary's role in the redemptive work of her Son so often very inadequately presented, must be viewed anthropologically as essentially man's involvement to the limits of his possibilities in the work of human salvation. Here the great traditional themes of marian theology, like Mary's faith, the *'loco totius naturae'* theme of St. Thomas fit in. Man, creature of God, assumes a collaborative role with God who is the primary and only ultimate cause of all salvation. The figure of the Woman sums up this creatural receptive-creativity of man.

The theology of Mary must engage in a critical self-analysis to distinguish the solid gains of the post Tridentine development from those hyper-refinements which are now seen to be of no great theological significance, to be in fact a series of blind alleys.

This self-analysis is best carried out under the headings (1) the theology of Mary—a doctrine of man (2) the theology of Mary—a doctrine of the Holy Spirit. A critical approach to its own development since Trent under these headings is the best way to provide the theology of Mary with a solid grasp of where it is now. This knowledge is of the utmost importance to mariology for its ecumenical future.

These headings provide two broad perspectives within which marian theology must be placed in systematic theological relationship with other elements of the theological synthesis. This work of theological integration called for by the Council is a *sine qua non* for any future theological consideration of Mary and is a first necessary step towards real ecumenical dialogue about Mary.

Personally, I feel that there is a certain danger that quite superficial considerations may in all good faith, focus ecumenical attention away from Mary. I would consider this quite mistaken. I believe in fact that the two major headings under which I have suggested our theology of Mary re-examine itself and re-organize itself, provide excellent avenues along which to attempt an ecumenical meeting.

A re-examination of mariology as a Catholic anthropology or instance of the doctrine of grace would underscore the point often overlooked that Mary's uniqueness is a uniqueness, among the children of Adam, not apart from them; it would also pinpoint the precise understanding of personal salvation to which Catholics are committed, not merely in mariology but across the board and allow differences on this point if they are found to exist, to be located in the context where they most fundamentally belong.

A re-examination of mariology under the rubric 'a doctrine of the Holy Spirit in action' would let Catholics see the narrowness of the Marian development in the Catholic tradition since Trent and the danger of misunderstanding this constantly gives rise to. It would force them to restate their entire doctrine of Mary's role in the salvation of men in the fuller and more biblical context of a doctrine of the Spirit.

This would remove the possibility of the dilemma Christ or Mary once and for all.

Protestants for their part would be helped to read the Church's marian concern as an attempt to give expression to a Christian truth very dear to Reformation thinking, the doctrine of the Spirit who sanctifies. This emphasis on the Spirit would help also to bridge the gap which tragically exists even about Mary between Western and some Eastern Christians.

I would personally attach great significance to the ecumenical task which immediately and obviously awaits marian theology. I cannot see any possible future for mariology in which such a theological enterprise will not loom very large.

The lucan presentation of Mary as the humble (ταπείνος) Woman overshadowed by the Spirit that Christ might be formed is indeed an approach rich in ecumenical possibilities.

We can learn much in this renewal of our devotional practices and attitudes and of our theologies from our separated brethren.

I think they in their turn must try to appreciate our concern to defend the human in its divinely given integrity. For it is the place and mode of the Spirit's operation.

Christ is not found apart from his Spirit. And His Sanctifying Spirit does not disdain to use the human in all its manifestations as the vehicle of the power of his love.

Conclusion

Mary is sometimes discussed as if she were simply a divisive factor among Christians. This radical over-simplification is to be placed on a level with the naive assumption that fervent prayer to Our Lady within the straight jacket of the nineteenth century forms in which it has come to us combined with a constant underlining of every aspect of the marian phenomenon as it has historically emerged within Catholicism particularly in the last 100 years, will work the miracle of ending Christian disunity.

There is a sense in which Mary is an obstacle to Christian unity. She is not so in herself, but in our defective understanding of her role in salvation and in our inadequate or misleading presentation of this.

It is, on the other hand, absolutely certain that no doctrinal unity can be achieved apart from Mary. For it is not possible to accept a separation of Christ from the human and religious situation which by God's choice served as the matrix for Christ and the Christian Church. Christ the Lord did not drop down from heaven, he was born of a woman, (*Gal.* 4.4). The faith of the Church is necessarily anchored in history and Mary is the great guarantee which prevents the scandal of the particularity of the Incarnation being abolished. She is also the guarantee of the reality of human salvation, the affirmation that grace reaches down into the roots of man's being and makes him holy and just before God, even now.

It is because Christian unity cannot be bought at the price of excluding Mary that the Council Fathers single out for special mention the place Our Lady holds in the belief and devotion of some non-Roman Christians. The Christians of the East have always honoured her in a special way from very early times and have been responsible for the real beginning of her widespread veneration in the Church, by the irreplaceable significance in the scheme of salvation they asserted for her at the Council of Ephesus.

It is not only eastern Christians however who venerate Mary. There is found among members of the Church of England also a tradition of veneration of her, which is matched in continental Lutheranism. The working out of an ecumenical understanding of the Mother of the Lord and her place in Salvation can best begin with discussion between those traditions which already venerate her and have some understanding of her role in salvation. It must be expected that Catholic scholars will better recognise the strengths and weaknesses of their own theological tradition when given an opportunity to view Mary through the eyes of another Christian tradition.

Mary in the belief of the Roman Catholic Church has a care for all men. She is the Mother of the Saviour of all. She is *the Woman*, chosen by the Father of All to share in freedom in the realization of his purpose that all might be one,—one people of God in Christ for the glory of the most holy and undivided Trinity.

NOTES

[1] p. 298. Dr. Brown's statement that the dogma of the Assumption relates this to her death needs to be qualified. The definition deliberately left open the question of Mary's death, even though it is unquestionably the more commonly held view in the marian tradition.

[2] op. cit., p. 298, note 22.

[3] op. cit., p. 300.

[4] v.g. G. Miegge. *The Virgin Mary*. London, Lutterworth Press, 1955. (engl. tr.).

[5] H. H. Wold, *Pastoralblaetter* 2 (1965), 128.

[6] G. Maron, *Evangelische Theologie* 22 (1962), 410.

[7] K. Barth, *Church Dogmatics* I, 2 pp. 143-44 (engl. tr.).

[8] op. cit., p. 146.

[9] G. C. Berkouwer, *The Triumph of Grace in the Theology of Karl Barth*, London, Paternoster Press, 1956, p. 175-6.

[10] op. cit., p. 178, note 37.

[11] Denzinger-Schoenmetzer. *Enchiridion Symbolorum* cet. Ed. 34. 1521-2 Cf. 1551-53.

[12] Y. M-J. Congar, *Begegnung de Christen* (Festschrift O. Karrer). Stuttgart/Frankfurt/M. 1959, 421.

[13] Jn. 1, 14.

[14] Rom. 8, 26-27.

[15] *Court traitè sur la Vierge Marie*. Paris, Lethielleux, 1967, p. 98.

The Evangelical Mary

REV. JOHN DE SATGÉ, M.A.

I

Early on August 19th 1662 there died a giant among men: Blaise Pascal: mathematician, scientist, theologian, apologist. The next day, after the funeral, his will was opened. Emile Cailliet describes the scene in his most perceptive study, *The Clue to Pascal.* As the man of law began to read it, this profession of faith stood forth:

> First, as a good Christian, Catholic, Apostolic, Roman, the suppliant has recommended and recommends his soul to God, whom through the merits of the precious blood of our Saviour and Redeemer Jesus Christ may it please Him to pardon his faults and to join his soul, when it shall leave this world, to the number of the blessed, imploring to this end the intercessions of the glorious Virgin Mary and all the saints of Paradise.

"Let the most strictly evangelical Protestants," Emile Cailliet continues (p. 113f)

> measure with a glance the abyss which separates them from the most holy, most intelligent, the least scholastic, and the most audacious Catholic student of the Bible, and the most reverent before the Sacred Word who ever lived under God's great sky. Never was a Roman Catholic nearer evangelical Protestantism, nor farther away. In this supreme antinomy is summed up for us the secret of Pascal and of his anguish.

The abyss which so impressed Cailliet is caused no doubt by Pascal's dependence not only on the merits of his Redeemer's blood but also on the intercession of the Virgin and the saints. For Cailliet and for most Protestants such behaviour is an infinitely tragic version of the man who wore a belt in case his braces should break. It revealed a lack of assurance of salvation which in turn sprang from inadequate theology of redemption. The antimony Cailliet found is that of a man who continued to live loyally within a religious obedience which denied his own deepest convictions.

We may turn to another reformed scholar, Professor Franz Leenhardt of Geneva, for a more positive interpretation of Pascal's antinomy. Leenhardt's book *Two Biblical Faiths* has not received in this country the attention which it deserves, partly perhaps because its English title is so much less expressive than the original *La Parole et le Buisson de Feu.* He attempts to do justice to the Christian integrity of Catholic as well as Protestant ways by seeing them as developed stages in two different traditions of obedience to God.

Protestantism whose chief constituent is, according to Leenhardt, God's spoken word goes back to Abraham who rose up and left everything in obedience to the divine command. It was an obedience shown by faith only, unbacked by the sight of any divine guarantee; even God's name was only revealed later. The Abrahamic champion under the New Covenant was, of course, St. Paul, from whom essentially derive those dynamics which at the Reformation broke out of the Catholic synthesis.

The Catholic system looks for its prototype to Moses, no less faithful in his obedience than Abraham, though in a different style: fortified by the identification which he demanded and won from God before defying the Egyptians, backed by his intercessors, his work fulfilled in the Law which bound the life of faith together with a network of detailed obedience. The New Testament exemplar was, of course, St. Peter. The chief constituent is the Divine Presence.

We return briefly to Pascal. Cailliet, viewing him in a strictly Abrahamic perspective, cannot but see the recourse to our Lady as a belt-and-braces operation with all its implications of defective faith. Leenhardt, leaning over from the Abrahamic position to look along the Mosaic perspective, sees how naturally the emphasis on God's Presence leads to a stress on Transcendence which has far-reaching consequences for the proper approach to God.

"If it is only a detail," writes Leenhardt,

> it is none the less a significant detail that the catholic believer speaks to God with greater reverence than does the protestant. Protestant prayer is more familiar, more direct, more spontaneous; it makes its requests in the second person. Catholic prayer is more liturgical; the personal element is less apparent in it; adoration and contemplation occupy a far greater place. It normally likes to use intermediaries, which help the soul to approach God and to overcome obstacles which would hinder the granting of prayer; such intermediaries are the intercession of the saints, the intercession of the church, and, above all, the intercession of the mediatrix of all graces, the Blessed Virgin Mary. (p. 103)

Leenhardt goes on to point out a striking contrast between the intercessionary styles of Abraham and Moses to be seen in two Old Testament incidents (*Gen.* 18, *Ex.* 32.)

Leenhardt reminds us that many failures of comprehension between separated Christians could be avoided by seeing how differently the same matter appears when viewed in different perspectives. But perhaps his chief service to the cause of Christian unity is to show what solid foundations both catholic and protestant ways of thought and devotion have in Biblical experience. There is no ground for either to doubt the Christian authenticity or propriety of the other.

But of course, Leenhardt goes on, neither tradition has been fully true to its inheritance; both suffer from distortions, deviations, deformities. Let each sort itself out, dive into its own past and renew itself at the springs of its own integrity. Let Catholicism be more Mosaic and Protestantism more Abrahamic. When both are fully extended, conditions will be right for worthwhile dialogue. Meanwhile beware of premature entanglement, Protestantism garnished with catholic sauce, Catholicism lightly flavoured with protestant spice. "We are not asked today to eat tomorrow's bread," Leenhardt warns, "but to pray that our daily bread may be granted us." (p. 116).

II

I take Leenhardt's warning very seriously, indeed personally. For am I not in danger of doing precisely what he warns against when I say that, for its own good, evangelical Christianity needs a far more positive relationship with our Lord's mother and with all the saints than it has normally encouraged? But let me state my case.

My first point is that a proper relationship with our Lord's mother safeguards the conditions essential for evangelical religion, the heart of which is to know Christ as your Saviour.

There have been so many parodies of 'the old-time religion' and indeed evangelicals can so easily cheapen their beliefs that thoughtful people go to great lengths to express their convictions in terms which are fresh and intelligible to those who do not share them. But every authentic presentation must embody in some form or another the two elements expressed classically by the terms 'receiving Christ' and 'walking with Christ'. These terms relate to a personal, individual, experience, but they have an inescapable social corollary; for a relationship with Christ implies a relationship with everyone in a similar position.

Logicians will point out that relationships thus described are of quite another order from those experienced in everyday life, a comment to which evangelicals will enthusiastically assent. Such descriptions are essentially theological—that is, they are about God and about human life and its setting in the universe as these matters connect with Him. Evangelicals are not happy with a Christianity presented exclusively in terms of this present life.

Indeed, how could they be, unless all they live by is mere words, metaphor, hyperbole? The evangelical faith in Christ is 'religion' in the proper sense, that which binds you to God; and it depends entirely on the fact that God is the 'Living One', free from the limitations of time and space. Of Christ, it insists at least that He shares in that freedom, for how else could He be 'received' by countless people in different places at the same time, at different times and at times which overlap? And of human beings, evangelical religion assumes that they have about them that which is capable of 'receiving' the divine Presence thus communicated. "Behold, I stand at the door and knock", says the exalted Christ in a passage (*Rev.* 3.20) which is at the heart of evangelical spirituality. "If any man hears my voice and opens the door, I will come in and eat with him and he with me."

These are stupendous claims and evangelicals must take care that familiarity does not cheapen them. They speak of an intimate re-

27

lationship; but that relationship is with the eternal God the Creator of all that is: made possible through the sacrifice of His only-begotten Son: made effective through the power of the all-holy Spirit. It is an awesome intimacy.

If evangelical religion is not to be merely metaphor or sentiment or coziness, it must say things about the Saviour which mean that though He is fully human and our Brother, He is a great deal more besides. And those are the very things that lead us to call his mother the Mother of God. The things which Catholics say about Mary safeguard the things which Evangelicals say about her Son.

III

All we have said so far is that Evangelical religion and Marian devotion arise from the same fundamentals in traditional theology. They are natural allies against so-called radical interpretations of the Faith which eliminate all supernatural elements. It seems desirable to underline this obvious matter to indicate in advance that the more exciting and indeed heady views which I am about to put forward have their roots in solid and sober theology.

We are now to consider a range of issues where Marian devotion goes beyond the common limits of Evangelical religion. The usual evangelical view is that Marian devotion distorts and falsifies the pure lines of belief as the Scriptures draw them. I believe that while that can be the case, there is no necessary reason why it should be; if it is, the particular Marian devotion will have become distorted. Proper Marian devotion, on the contrary, opens up further reaches of experience to the searching and the succour of the Gospel.

Most apparently we see this to be the case in the several matters involved in the universal human experience of death.

Christians of all persuasions deplore the conspiracy of silence with which our society surrounds the fact of death. Yet by no means all Christians are persuaded that there is personal life beyond death, and of those who are, the evangelicals often have little to say that will make sense to the bereaved.

An unhappy family situation which I came across a good many years ago now comes to mind. A solid Church family, elderly parents, their one child a grown-up son still living at home: all highly educated, cultured, artistic. The father died and the mother came to me some weeks later in great distress; the son seemed to be avoiding her and was no comfort in the hour of need. On investigation it turned out that the son had no comfort to give since he believed that his father, whose religion was not evangelical in expression, was in Hell. His mother wished to pray for her dead husband; the son believed any such activity, however humanly understandable, to be both futile and wrong.

An extreme case perhaps, but it would not be hard to find a parallel.

28

It is a view which can find support from contemporary Anglican theologians. Thus J. A. Motyer, the Principal of an Anglican Theological College, writes: "The dead are either in paradise where they do not need our prayers or else are under divine judgement in which case our prayers are of no avail." (*After Death*, p. 59). He describes the relation between the living and the departed in the Communion of Saints by an analogy with that between Christians in one part of the world and their missionary friends elsewhere. But at one point, he says, the analogy breaks down: the living do not pray for the departed.

It is a view which accompanies a total denial of Purgatory. Protestants are here following the Reformers who believed that the whole elaborate mediaeval teaching in this field was entirely without scriptural warrant, was based on a sub-christian view of Redemption and could only lead people astray. It must therefore be cut out of Church teaching root and branch.

I have long believed such wholesale condemnation to be far too sweeping. Some purgatorial state after death seems essential, for who but the rarest of Christian souls could bear the beatific vision without at least some measure of training? Heaven must have its ante-chamber or the divine mercy lacks imagination.

More recently I have come to think of that ante-chamber in much closer connection with this present life. If one gives due weight to the teaching in the Fourth Gospel that eternal life begins with belief in Jesus here and now, then all those who abide in the Vine are necessarily involved with each other most fully. The onus of proof is on those who would limit the degree of involvement. It seems likely therefore that Mr. Motyer is wrong to rule out mutual prayer between those in this life and beyond it.

To my surprise and even dismay I have found myself becoming more favourably disposed towards at least the idea behind Roman Catholic teaching on Indulgences and the Treasury of Merit. Investigating with some caution an area marked on all Protestant maps 'Danger! Keep Out', I have been relieved to find a note of restraint in responsible Catholic teaching today. Karl Rahner, for instance, in the article on Indulgences in his *Encyclopaedia of Theology*, is most careful to guard against crude presentations which might have appealed to an earlier age but which are likely to give offence today. The "Treasury of the Church", he insists, is not a Bank account where indulgences serve as cheques, but

> the salvific will of God, which aims at bringing all men to perfect charity. And such charity includes reparation and the elimination of 'the punishments for sin', since this salvific will exists as centred on the redemption wrought by Christ and the holiness of the whole Church which depends on this redemption but is also present through it. And this holiness implies a dynamism which tends to the perfect charity which eliminates all the consequences of sin in every member of the Church. (p. 709a)

29

Not easy to follow; but I think that at the end of it my difficulties are more stylistic than theological!

The Reformers disliked the whole affair because even where the system was not in practice abused, it smacked of salvation by human merit; and only the merits of Christ allowed any human being to be accepted in the divine Presence. Modern objections are more radical, for they centre on the notion of 'merit' itself, with its judicial overtones and its hint of a mathematic of pass or failure; it is altogether too impersonal a concept. But are those undesirable overtones necessarily to be heard? Two considerations make me doubt it.

First, an extension of a point already made, this range of catholic teaching removes the limits on Christian concern. We are all "members of one another", as St. Paul taught; the joys and sufferings, the failures and the excellencies, of one belong to all. "No man is an island": John Donne's great image of the human continent speaks most compellingly in an age where community has largely given way to the isolation of the crowd. However crudely, even undesirably, they may have formerly been presented, Indulgences and the Treasury of Merit in themselves mean that the concerns of love spread out through time as well as space, the generations bound together in that 'bundle of life' which is Christ, the whole Christ, head and members. To insist that such concern ends with an individual's death makes it trivial.

My second consideration concerns the proper nature of Grace. Protestants in their wonder at divine grace have sometimes spoken of it as if it were a juggernaut trampling over human effort. Evangelists bent on arousing a sense of sin have so spoken of human corruption as to make one wonder whether God knew what He was doing to save such worthless creatures.

Mankind indeed cannot pull itself up by its own shoestrings; the evangelical cliché is true. All is of grace. But, "Graciousness by definition cannot pauperize", to borrow a striking phase of Professor C. F. D. Moule (*The Parish Communion Today* (1962) p. 84). Grace is the offer of sonship, not of serfdom. Grace calls out the truly human qualities hitherto paralysed by evil within and without. Grace recognises unsuspected worth and releases hidden potential.

Mary is above all 'full of grace': kecharitōmenē, the graced one. The Lord was with her. The Annunciation was an awe-inspiring experience but not a crushing one. Mary's spirit strengthened by the divine favour rose to the challenge. Be it done unto me according to thy word. She was indeed one of the Lord's poor whom the Psalmist celebrated, but she was in no way pauperised. The exultant vigour of *Magnificat* can hardly be confused with the fawning attitude of the pauper on permanent charity. In that respect also, she is the mother of us all.

So it was by reflecting upon the Lord's mother, by honouring her among her son's people and coming to see her as Mother, I found her prayers which I requested throwing light into corners of human experience which had hitherto been dark. And, contrary to what the polemic of centuries said, my devotion did not lead to diminished trust in Christ but to an enhanced understanding of what it means to acknowledge Him as the Lord of all Time.

IV

There will no doubt be those who believe that in accepting devotion to our Lady as I have, I have thereby sold out the Reformation; whether they approve or not will depend on their own position. I do not propose to plead either Guilty or Not Guilty, for I am not persuaded that it is that sort of thing. But, clearly what I have just said does have its bearing both on the history and on the present divided state of Christendom. I am going therefore to make certain observations which explore a little an area which I will call, perhaps grandiloquently, the philosophy of Christian Reunion.

First, a distinction between two different attitudes to be found among evangelicals approaching these matters. There are those who value the Reformation heritage and its confessional positions for the safe lodging which they provide for evangelical religion. And there are those who value Reformation confessions in a more absolute sense, finding in them an authentic statement of divine revelation, so that to depart from those proportions of the faith is to apostatise. For convenience in this discussion I call the first type the 'Relative Protestant' and the second type the 'Absolute Protestant' (I am, of course, thinking in theological, not political or sociological, terms). Relative Protestants believe that evangelical religion was preserved at a time of extreme danger by the Reformation positions, but that it may well exist in its integrity within other frameworks of theology. Absolute Protestants see an integral relationship between evangelical religion and protestant theology.

If you have followed me thus far, you will not be surprised to hear that I line up with the first group, not the second; my protestantism is relative, not absolute. If evangelical religion can exist in another theological frame, I have no special concern for protestant theology.

A second factor is the presence of evangelical religion within the Catholic Church before the Reformation and in the Roman Catholic Church since. The last twenty years have seen something of a revival in articulate, scholarly, conservative Protestantism. Its growth must give some disquiet to the ecumenical enthusiast. But there are encouraging signs, among them the generous recognition of evangelical elements to be found in surprising places.

Take for example a small book entitled *The Evangelical Renaissance*. Its author, Donald G. Bloesch, appears to be an American Calvinist of Conservative but not Fundamentalist outlook; the book is dedicated to Professor John A. Mackay of Princeton, New Jersey, and it carries a foreword by John R. W. Stott, which implies respectability in conservative evangelical Anglican circles. It carries lengthy and careful appreciations of Karl Barth and of the Pietist tradition, Lutheran, Moravian and Methodist, both unusual features in a study from such a source. Apart from the Early Fathers, Saints Bernard of Clairvaux, Francis of Assisi, Thomas Aquinas, Catherine of Siena, Teresa of Avila, and John of the Cross are among those commended for genuinely evangelical elements in their teaching, though several of them come in also for criticism on other grounds. Of modern Catholics, Bloesch has appreciative words for Hans Küng, Louis Bouyer, Josef Gieselmann and Raymond Brown, among others.

Evangelical elements appear on such a scale within the Catholic Church that one is surprised at Cailliet's surprise at finding them in Pascal. It seems likely, too, that Leenhardt's division between Abrahamic and Mosaic traditions is overdone. It is not a matter of alternative spiritual ways existing in separate integrity. There are too many interactions between them, and have been from the earliest times. A striking development of recent years is the renewed Catholic emphasis on the Word, according to Leenhardt the chief constituent of the other tradition.

The Mosaic-Petrine tradition by its very nature demands a structured organisation. The Abrahamic-Pauline has no such essential requirement. Therefore a convenient model for thinking about the relation between the two is to fit the Pauline inside the Petrine. It would be going too far to call evangelical religion the soul and catholic order the body but it is less misleading than a model of two parallel, independent structures. At all events the two belong together; they complement each other and, apart, each of them is incomplete.

A third and most obvious factor is, of course, the 'new look' that has come over Catholic theology since the second Vatican Council. I cannot imagine myself saying the things that I have said tonight, for example, without the eighth chapter of the Constitution *De Ecclesia*; and even after that I should not go to the lengths I have done with such confidence had it not been for the papal exhortation *Marialis Cultus* two years ago.

One must speak cautiously here. The teaching of the Church has not changed, one will be told; though to an outsider it looks as if it has. In reality, I suppose, it has been clarified. Theologians have listened to Protestant objections in a spirit of self-criticism; the result is that, without compromising their beliefs, Catholics have managed to present them in such a way as to remove unnecessary obstacles. Here and there they may even have gained something from Protestants in the process. Certainly some of the Protestant objections may be seen to have been illusory. I remember at the time of the Council discussing Rome's new look with a very senior and respected Anglican theologian. I was young and must have been over-enthusiastic. He looked at me quizzically.

"Do you really think the leopard can change his spots?" he asked. But I had started to wonder whether the animal in question really was a leopard.

Considerations such as these lead me to think that where I am questioning the hard-won positions of the Reformation, I am not so much betraying the Reformation as saying that its work is accomplished. Speaking, as for the sake of brevity I have done throughout this paper, purely in terms of Western christendom, I would say that evangelical religion only has to exist in special structures when something has gone wrong with the Catholic Church. If its existence is threatened it may have to go outside. But the gates of Hell do not prevail even in the tragedy of schism. Its presence outside becomes sooner or later in the good purpose of the Spirit a spur to quicken the Catholic conscience into renewal. Once the Catholic Church has reordered its house, the time for protest is past and the evangelical should go home as soon as may be. I believe that, in Marian matters at least, that point has been reached. The task before those who believe as I do is to help our fellow-heirs of the Reformation appreciate that which they had previously denied.

V

I have taken the title 'the Evangelical Mary' to refer to the effect which a new devotion to her has had upon the Christian outlook of one evangelical. I have not mentioned except in passing the theological reasons which led me to this position, for I have set them out at length in my book *Mary and the Christian Gospel*, to which I suppose this paper is a footnote.

It seems to me that our Lady stands in the life of her Son's people as a gracious hostess, making one free of large rooms which hitherto had been closed or dark and forbidding. She is supremely fitted to do this, being wholly one of us and wholly yielded to God, the Mother of God who through grace is the daughter of her Son. May evangelicals who rejoice in her Son's Gospel take their proper share in calling her 'blessed', who accepted so fully that grace by which they live.

Mary as an Ecumenical Problem

REV. DR. J. A. ROSS MACKENZIE, M.A., Ph.D., T.L.

Robert McAfee Brown has described one of the marks of the contemporary ecumenical revolution as the movement "from diatribe to dialogue." Those who want to continue in the dialogue, to keep talking, as it were, will be helped by some of the recent discussion between Christians and Marxists about dialogue and its philosophy. For instance, Dominique Dubarle of the Institut Catholique gives the name "first kind of dialogue" to discussion which aims at intellectual agreement on the basis of evidence open to all and making it possible in principle to establish true knowledge. This first kind of dialogue is a conversation between several speakers but directed towards a "monologue in unison" once unanimity in the truth has been reached. The religious convictions which clashed at the crisis of the Reformation made this kind of dialogue impossible. Convictions which are grounded on freely chosen beliefs and which vary from individual to individual produce an intellectual and spiritual multiplicity in which no one conviction can claim predominance. Unanimity could not be restored in human society by the victorious predominance of one doctrine over all the rest.

Dubarle goes on to define a second kind of dialogue: human conversation where spiritual convictions confront one another. In this second kind of dialogue the action and thought of each of those taking part refers to a consciousness freely and differently established. This kind of dialogue becomes possible only when time has started to do its work amongst those who are separated, and experience has shown that when this second kind of dialogue is begun it has three kinds of objective. The first seeks to remove grave matters of dispute still outstanding on either side. The second involves defining those domains in which interests are found to coincide. The third allows the possibility that each side may bring to the other new resources of vitality and progress even on the plane of the convictions in which they differ.[1] This essay seeks to make a contribution to the conversation where convictions about Mary confront one another—the dialogue that becomes possible when the time is ripe.

Some Matters of Dispute Still Outstanding

In August, 1547, one hundred and twenty prisoners sailed in French galleys for the coast of Normandy. Amongst the prisoners was John Knox himself, and for nineteen months he experienced a captivity described by his biographer, P. Hume Brown, as one of "unutterable horror." With several of his companions Knox was converted into a galley-slave. Only once or twice in the whole of his writings did he later refer to these months of suffering; but when he did, the depth of his pain was evident. One of the incidents which he relates describes how he and his companions were forced to do reverence to a statue of the Blessed Virgin:

> Soon after the arrival at Nantes, their great *Salve* was sung, and a glorious painted Lady was brought in to be kissed and amongst others, was presented to one of the Scottishmen then chained. He gently said, "Trouble me not; such an idol is accursed; and therefore I will not touch it." The Patron and the Arguesyn (Lieutenant), with two officers, having the chief charge of all such matters, said, "Thou shalt handle it"; and so they violently thrust it to his face, and put it betwix his hands; who seeing the extremity, took the idol, and advisedly looking about, he cast it in the river, and said, "Let our Lady now save herself: she is light enough; let her learn to swim." After that was no Scottish man urged with that idolatry.[2]

It is hardly surprising that from the time of Knox Protestants in Scotland have regarded the figure of Mary in a Catholic church as an idol, and Catholic veneration of Mary as an activity forbidden in the Ten Commandments. "After that was no Scottish man urged with that idolatry" has remained a firm conviction in Presbyterian faith and spirituality. And when Presbyterians settled and flourished in the New World, that principle of faith and practice remained. If we can use legal terminology, Mary was formally separated from Protestant worship and prayer in the sixteenth century; in the twentieth century the divorce is complete. Even the singing of the *Magnificat* caused the Puritans to have scruples, and if they gave up saying the Apostles' Creed, it was not only because of the offensive adjective "Catholic", but also because of the mention of the Virgin.

Sociologists draw a distinction between an espoused theory—what a group officially holds—and a pragmatic theory—what it actually believes and acts on. The espoused theory of Mary expressed in the confessional documents and catechisms of the Reformed churches is, by any measurement, both biblical and at least formally loyal to ancient definitions. Whatever may be true in Protestant churches today, none of the Reformers or their immediate successors questioned the biblical foundation of the two phrases of the ancient creeds, that Christ was "conceived by the Holy Spirit, born of the Virgin Mary." Calvin, like Luther and Zwingli, taught the perpetual virginity of Mary. The early Reformers even applied, though with some reticence, the title Theotokos to Mary, because, as Riissen wrote, "she bore him who is also God." Lutherans and Calvinists were in agreement that Mary's own prophecy—"all generations will call me blessed"—was constantly being fulfilled in the church. Calvin called on his followers to venerate and praise her as the teacher who instructs them in her Son's com-

35

mands. Even as late as 1655, the year of Milton's famous sonnet, the Waldensians in their Confession stated that the most holy Virgin and the glorified saints are "blessed and worthy both of praise and imitation," the Virgin herself being designated "blessed among women."

The pragmatic theory of Mary was quite different. She was an easily identified symbol of "Catholicism"—increasingly a pejorative term for Protestants after the sixteenth century—and therefore of all that the Reformers rejected. Whatever other characteristics it may have had, the Reformation was a movement of religious renewal. The Reformers wanted to recall the church to its true centre—to Christ, to his gospel, to the dominical sacraments, to "the freedom of the Christian," and so on. It was not Catholicism that they rejected, but Romanism—and by that they meant such things as the *sacro egoismo* of a church which appeared to identify truth with its own understanding of truth. They meant papal claims of universal jurisdiction and they meant the mass, and resolutely they repudiated both ecclesiological divinization and sacramental divinization on the grounds of Christ's sole Lordship in his church. But though it was Romanism rather than Catholicism that the Reformers rejected, in practice the two ideas were easily assimilated to each other, and Mary—even the Mary of the Bible and of the primitive faith—was extruded in the process.

If the first objective of dialogue is to remove grave matters of dispute, we need to become aware of the emotional history that underlies the theological history of the Protestant and Reformed churches. The almost complete obliteration of the cult of Mary amongst the Protestant churches and their severe restriction of any doctrine about Mary or any piety centred on Mary to the lines of faith and conduct permitted by scripture have both been justified, in Protestant understanding, on the basis of scripture. But there is more than an intellectual understanding involved. The very naming of Mary arouses powerful feelings of antipathy still amongst many Protestants. Feelings of resistance and even anger are aroused by language such as "Queen of Heaven", or "Mediatrix of all graces," and devotional practices familiar in shrines in the United States and Europe leave many Protestants shaking their heads and wondering if the gulf between Catholic and Protestant can ever be bridged.

It is no less important for Catholics to ask Protestants why there also remains a gulf between their espoused and their pragmatic theory about Mary. No doubt, much in medieval and later Catholic devotion to Mary was unbiblical and a deviation from the faith of the earliest Christians. She is neither mediator nor redeemer in the univocal sense in which Christ is both Mediator and Redeemer. It is in Christ not in Mary that all are made alive—"by a man came also the resurrection of the dead", and the particularity and scandal of the Christian faith is that the one through whom that resurrection came is Christ and no other.

Nevertheless, the Reformed and Protestant churches have also to remember the heart of their own appeal in the sixteenth century. The call of Christ is a call to *metanoia*. To be true to the Reformation does not mean to echo in our day the legitimate protests of Luther and Calvin and those who came after them. "No Popery" and "No Mariolatry" may make popular battle cries, but to be truly "reformed" does not mean to be like the generals who are always fighting the last war. It means to listen afresh to the Word of God as a reality higher than any of our traditions, as that which judges us and our past, and calls us into a new future. A re-examination of the meaning of Mary may well form part of this larger *metanoia* which Protestants, at their best, have always sought.

Domains in Which Interests Coincide

The question that Luther asked in the monastery was whether or not he could believe that God was gracious. The larger context within which he asked the question included the notorious venality of the indulgence traffic. In 1476 Pope Sixtus IV had asserted that indulgences for the dead are of benefit to them, and by the beginning of the sixteenth century, as Gordon Rupp pointed out, indulgences had become a holy business so complex as to demand the superintendence of the Fugger banking house. In an essay on indulgences published in 1969 Karl Rahner sounded a severely muted note, and he spoke of diminishing interest in indulgences and of the need for "prudently restricted" efforts in the practice. Here is one of the areas in which, by and large, the Roman Catholic Church has come to agree with the concerns of the reformers.

Another, and a more positive, area is the whole understanding of what reformation means in the life of the church. For centuries the churches of the Reformation took as their watchword the motto, *ecclesia reformata semper reformanda*. This means, in part at least, that the church must concentrate continually on the Word of God, acknowledging its primacy over the whole shape and direction of its life. But here again is a domain in which the interests of Catholics and Protestants alike coincide. To quote (with strong endorsement) Hans Küng: "In so far as the church is deformed, she has to be re-formed—*ecclesia reformanda*—and in so far as the church is constantly, repeatedly deformed, she has to be constantly, repeatedly reformed, *ecclesia semper reformanda*."[3]

Is the question of Mary also one about which a later generation of theologians will speak of "diminishing interest", and devotion of any kind to Mary a practice which will become "prudently restricted"? On the contrary, Mary may well come to be one of the crucial domains in which Catholic and Protestant interests coincide. What is happening to us, that we treat people and things as we do? That, certainly is the crucial question of our time; and all theological reflection today is done against a horizon that includes the holocaust of the 1940's, the opening of the age of nuclear warfare at Hiroshima, and the struggles for human liberation for which the third world provides many but by no means all of the symbols. In such a time as this the question of Mary takes on new significance.

Thus, for instance, to talk today about Mary is to face head-on the economic and social implications of the Magnificat. The question posed by that song is precisely, Where does God range himself? And the witness of that song is that God "has come to the help of Israel his servant, mindful of his mercy." Mary was one of the *anawim*, one of the poor of the land. The word of the gospel is that God calls all human beings to a fulfilment of which Christ is the disclosure, the means, and the end. And it is a fulfilment that involves the whole of life, technical, political, and economic.

If, then, we are going to talk about Mary, the conversation must include those who are purposefully involved in the issue of human liberation. In the eloquent words of a black sister:

> Gifted beyond all
> that can be thought of or desired,
>   black women
> were in the mind of Yahweh
>   when he chose Mary.[4]

To say that God has come to the help of Israel his servant means that when black people, or women, or the oppressed, or just plain, needy, questing human beings say Yes to their humanity by affirming their blackness, or their womanhood, or their manhood, or their dignity, we see that their affirmation—their "Yes", "Let it be!"—is an expression amongst us of God's reconciling act in Jesus Christ. Mary for all of these is a sign that it is the gentle of spirit who *have* the earth for their possession; and in the global struggles of which Viet-Nam, Watergate, and Middle East oil are immediate symbols, Mary is a sign of contradiction, precisely as the one who bears witness to a future that is of God's making and not ours.

New Resources of Progress on the Plane of Differing Conviction

In his eloquent meditation on survival in the death camps, Terrence des Pres spoke of what the survivors had to face in these places of death: "And finally there is this: in extremity, the bare possibility of survival is not enough. There must also be a move beyond despair and self-pity to that fierce determination which survivors call up in themselves."[5] Confronted by the landscape of disaster in places like Auschwitz, Hiroshima, or the obliterated earth of Indo-China, what can I believe about goodness or about providence? In the conditions of

38

our extremity we are asking again the question of Luther: What does it mean to live by faith?

The churches in the United States are busy. Most of the major religious bodies have undergone structural changes; parishes have been updated; the liturgy renewed; hymnals rewritten; new educational alignments made; and steps taken towards organic union. But a small voice is heard at the back of our minds: What does it all matter? Where is God? If the Messiah has already come, why, as in Albert Camus' city under siege, has the plague become the normal condition? We have adapted ourselves to the plagues of war, hunger, and the final solution. These monstrous things, crushing out life, are part of the show.

Faith, as the writer of Hebrews understood it, is that fierce determination which lets us "keep firm in the hope we profess, because the one who made the promise is faithful." (Heb. 10:23) Remember this, the writer continued: "You and I are not the sort of people who draw back." (Heb. 10:39) Even on the plane of the convictions in which we differ, is it possible that each of us, reflecting on the meaning of faith, the Spirit, and prayer, may bring to the other new resources of vitality and progress?

For the unknown writer of the letter to the Hebrews, faith characteristically means "faithfulness", "constancy in faith". As Christ himself proved his faithfulness to the one who appointed him, so Christians are bidden to remember that they are the sort who keep faithful. But faith in the "victim world" in which we live is often merely a cheerful, facetious and resourceful optimism. In the New Testament it is focused on God, and supremely on what God has done in Jesus Christ. Faith, in the phrase of Karl Barth, discovers that this man is God.

How, and how slowly, and with what pondering Mary came to this faith is hidden from us. But she shows us still what it means to keep firm, because the one who made the promise is faithful; and that promise, as the Magnificat shows with more gentleness than the fiery appeal of the Communist Manifesto will be embodied in a revolution of political and economic consequences. To be in communion with Mary means that we have within the family one who shows us what it means not to draw back when God addresses us, what it means to listen to the Word of God, to take it into our life, our body, our body politic, to cherish that Word, and to give that Word, to share it, for the life of the world.

In the plague-ridden city of Oran the people despair, become selfish and mean. That is our world. "I've got mine—you get yours." Against that enemy there is no way to act. But at the beginning of the Good News about Jesus Christ there is a breakthrough—an anthropologically significant breakthrough. In Mary's willingness to receive God's Word and to give birth to God's Word the life that we had lost is recovered: not, I've got mine, you get yours, but, What I received from the Lord I pass on in turn to you. Mary's receiving and her giving of the Word of God brings us Christ—that is the breakthrough—the Christ who alone bears our sufferings and carries our plagues, who brings us to the kingdom, and makes us, in the phrase of 2 Peter "able to share the divine nature". John Calvin did not often yield to lyricism in his New Testament Commentaries, but in his reflection on the implications of that text he could not stop himself: " The fact that God makes himself ours so that all his possessions become in a sense ours is a grace the magnitude of which our minds can never fully grasp."[6]

What can it mean for those of us who do not either want to be out of communion with Calvin to learn, as he himself expressed it, "to praise the holy Virgin?"

Calvin himself liked to return to the faith and teaching of the early church: "Not every age or place has men like Athanasius, Basil, Cyril, and such vindicators of true doctrine," he wrote in the Institutes. These were the writers who brought, as he saw, to its fullest expression the orthodox tradition of redemption, that is, the doctrine of redemption in its biblical form. Can Athanasius, Basil, and Cyril help the Protestant churches to discern again the fullness of our faith?

There is clear evidence that late in the fourth century an anaphora of the type of Basil of Caesarea was in use in the Coptic church. In its general structure the anaphora may quite possibly be the work of the great Cappadocian Father. Since Basil and Athanasius died within six years of one another, we may conjecture that the Coptic church, a conservative church liturgically, used this liturgy, or something close to it, by the end of Athanasius' life. There is a presumably earlier fragment of the anaphora in which the following petition is included in the intercessions:

> Remember, O Lord, ... especially the holy and glorious Mother of God, Mary ever-Virgin; by her prayers have mercy on us all, and save us for the sake of the holy Name, which we invoke.

In its position, after the consecration, this prayer is both impressive and significant. In a revealing phrase Metropolitan Anthony Bloom says, concerning prayer for the dead, "The living are related to the dead for whom they pray. In the dead we no longer belong completely to this world, in us the dead still belong to history."[7] In remembering the holy and glorious Theotokos, the Alexandrian church—if, indeed, it used this prayer—rejoiced with Mary in the reality of salvation. Such a liturgical prayer implies a recognition of Mary's part in the work of salvation. The church does pray for Mary: "Remember, O Lord, Mary ever-Virgin." In doing so it reveals, in the phrase of Bengel, an eighteenth century Lutheran scholar, that Mary is to be seen as the daughter of grace, not as the mother of grace: for she too is saved only by the loving-kindness of the Word. A future development of ecumenical liturgy may well be this glad recalling of Mary as the sign of salvation.

NOTES

[1] Dominique Dubarle, "Dialogue and Its Philosophy," in *Concurrence*, no. 1 (1969), p. 8.

[2] P. Hume Brown, *John Knox: A Biography*, p. 84. London: Adam and Charles Black, 1895.

[3] Hans Küng, *The Council, Reform and Reunion*, p. 51. London and New York: Sheed and Ward, 1961.

[4] Source unknown.

[5] Terrence des Pres, *The Survivor: An Anatomy of Life in the Death Camps*, p. 7. New York: Oxford University Press, 1976.

[6] John Calvin, Commentary on the Second Epistle of Peter, 1:4, in *Calvin's Commentaries: The First and Second Epistles of St. Peter*, tr. William B. Johnston, p. 330. Edinburgh and London: Oliver and Boyd, 1963.

[7] Bloom, Anthony, and LeFebvre, Georges, *Courage to Pray*, p. 60. London: Darton, Longman & Todd, 1973.

II
SCRIPTURAL

Mary's presence in Scripture initially seems at least jejune. But when it is seen as a whole, and her part is drawn out from every intimation, it dawns on us that she pervades the pages of God's word. She is, so to say, present *passim*, from Genesis to the Book of Revelation.

The first paper was read to the Society by a monk of Downside on 14 June 1967. Dom Ralph was one of the co-founders and strongest supporters in early days. This is the earliest paper we have on record.

The second is a dialogue between two regular contributors to the Society's work, followed by comments from a panel of theologians. It occurred at a one-day conference held at Regent's Park, London, at the Convent of the Sisters of the Sacred Heart, on 1 October 1977.

The Blessed Virgin Mary in the Bible

The Scriptural Basis of Ecumenical Dialogue

DOM RALPH RUSSELL, O.S.B., D.D.

Writing ecumenically about Mary the Mother of Jesus soon makes it evident that she cannot be considered in the abstract. For everything is related to her divine Son, and she is wholly and continually related to him. Therefore the great biblical themes make their appearance: the word of God, Old Testament prophecy, the Holy Spirit, the incarnation itself, the kingdom of God and its demands, Calvary, the redemption, the resurrection, the Church. The mistake rejected by the Council fathers at Vatican II was to take Mary in isolation. She should be thought of along with these scriptural themes and others: patristic, liturgical, sociological, psychological, and then we shall not frighten off some who have valuable contributions to make from their own backgrounds, such as devotion to the Word of God.

To speak of Mary from a scriptural basis, we must try *to see things as Scripture sees them*. This disarms fears: the fears of Protestants that skeletons are hidden in the Roman Catholic traditions' cupboard, and the fears of Roman Catholics that ecumenism will somehow degrade the Mother of God. Such fears had influence for a time at the Second Vatican Council, and are still with us.

But Scripture must be seen as a whole. The Holy Spirit who inspired it means it to be seen in entirety. Then the 'Woman' in Genesis will be answered by the Woman in the Book of Revelation (ch. 12), the Fall will go with the Annunciation, Adam with Christ (cf. St Paul), Eve with Mary. This is the way the earliest fathers saw Scripture and if we look through their eyes we shall not be tempted to think that the Bible has little to say about Mary's place in the work of her divine Son, the one redeemer. Another way of approach is to ask what is the central event to which all salvation history builds up? St Paul answers that: 'When the time had fully come, God sent forth his Son, born of woman' (Gal. 4:4). What more has Scripture to tell us about this?

The Old Testament prophets, struggling, against the spirit of proud self-sufficiency, to shift attention from man to God, had spoken of the *anawim,* the humble and lowly people, who 'leant upon the Lord, the holy one of Israel, in truth' (Is. 10:20). They were not necessarily poor as a class, for David was one, but they usually were. They were conscious of their need for God, ready to wait and serve, with the trusting love of a child for their saviour. This is the meaning of the 'poor' in the Isaian passage which Jesus applies to himself: 'The Spirit of the Lord is upon me, because he has anointed me to preach good news to the poor' (Luke 4:18; Is. 61:1); and the first of the Beatitudes is 'Blessed are the poor in spirit' (Matt. 5:3; cf. Luke 6:20). The flower of the poor and humble of the Lord is the 'handmaid of the Lord' who said 'let it be to me according to your word', and 'he has regarded the low estate of his handmaiden' (Luke 1:38, 48).

From *other Old Testament themes*, provided they are read with the traditional Jewish and Christian interpretations, there emerges the figure of the woman, mother of the redeemer. There is Matthew's interpretation of Isaiah: 'All this took place to fulfil what the Lord had spoken by the prophet: "Behold a virgin shall conceive and bear a son" ' (Matt. 1:22 ff.; Is. 7:14). There is Genesis 3:15, the enmity between the woman and the serpent, her seed and his seed, of which more later. There is the prophetic figure of the Daughter of Sion. This takes us to St Luke and *the Annunciation*.

The angel says to Mary: 'Hail full of grace' (or 'O favoured one'), 'the Lord is with you'. And then 'Do not be afraid, Mary, for you have favour (or "grace") with God. And behold you will conceive in your womb and bear a son, and you shall call his name Jesus' (Yahweh-Saviour) (Luke 1:28–31). The Old Testament background to this is Zephaniah 3:14–17: 'Sing aloud, O daughter of Sion ... The Lord is in your midst ... Do not fear, O Sion, the Lord your God is in your midst (your womb), a warrior who gives victory'. So in Luke 'hail' means 'rejoice' with messianic joy' and Mary, 'favoured one' or 'full of grace' is seen as the Daughter of Sion, who realizes the hopes and longings of Israel's history, and in a more wonderful way the Lord will be in her midst. The angel goes on, in the words of the prophecy of Nathan, to tell her that her Son will be the Messiah, and when Mary asks 'How shall this be, because I have no husband?' he explains: 'Holy Spirit will come upon you, and power of the most high will overshadow you. Therefore the child to be born will be called holy, Son of God' (Luke 1:32–35). 'Overshadow' refers to the Shekinah, the cloud of God's presence which went with the Israelites in the desert, filled the temple of Solomon, appeared at the transfiguration and the ascension, and according to Israelite tradition, covered with its shadow the Ark of the Covenant (cf. Exod. 40:35). Thus Mary, like the Ark, becomes God's resting place on earth. 'Son of God' is a messianic title, but its full meaning will be gradually unfolded, and gradually also Christian faith will come to see what it means to be God's Mother. Mary's humble answer, 'Behold I am the handmaid of the Lord; let it be to me according to your word', is an unhesitating acceptance of her place in God's redemptive plan. This is what the second century fathers saw, together with its consequences for salvation: 'The knot of Eve's disobedience', says Irenaeus, 'was untied by Mary's obedience' and 'in her obedience, Mary became the cause of salvation for herself and for the whole human race' (*Adv. Haer.* 3, 22, 4; PG 7, 959). Everything is in relation to her Son, the divine redeemer, but here is the point about Mary, stressed by Vatican II (*De Ecclesia*, 56), where ecumenical dialogue can begin. One can add that 'favoured' or 'full of grace', suggests that she had been endowed by God with gifts, dependent upon 'God my saviour' (Luke 1:47) which fitted her for her great work of bringing into the world 'the very life who renews all things'. This the Greek fathers especially develop and the Council cites a number of them in the desire to open a dialogue here, especially with the Orthodox, about the Immaculate Conception viewed from the Greek standpoint as fullness of grace.

There is time only to notice a few points from *the rest of the infancy narrative*. The Magnificat's 'all generations shall call me blessed' is a good starting point for discussing whether honour should be paid to Mary. The stories of the shepherds and the Magi show her with her Son before men. She and Joseph are evidently poor (Luke 2:7, 24); her future sorrows are foretold: 'a sword will pierce through your own soul also' (Luke 2:35) and the twice repeated 'Mary kept all these words in her heart' (19, 51), suggests that she was the ultimate source for Luke's account.

The Finding in the Temple brings us to the saying of Jesus: 'How is it that you sought me? Did you not know that I must be in my Father's house', or 'be busy with my Father's affairs' (J.B., Luke 2:49). This is the first of his declarations of independence, starting at the age of twelve, though thereafter 'he was subject to them'.

Other declarations of this sort have been used by Protestants to diminish Mary, and avoided or soft-pedalled by Roman Catholics. On one occasion Jesus asks 'who are my mother and my brethren', 'and looking around on those who sit about him', says 'here are my mother and my brothers: Whoever does the will of God is my brother and sister and mother' (Mark 3:33 ff.); on another, he replies to the woman who cried out 'blessed is the womb that bore you', 'rather, blessed are those who hear the Word of God and keep it' (Luke 11:27 ff.). Vatican II has brought out these texts, adding that they exalt the kingdom above the natural claims of flesh and blood and that Mary has to progress in the pilgrimage of faith. At the same time Luke, that careful writer, has already said twice that Mary did 'keep all these words in her heart' (Luke 2:19, 51). St John carries things to his own deep level. Really the central and deepest thought about Mary is contained in 'the Word was made flesh'. Indeed St John's prologue seems to have St Luke's infancy narrative in mind. 'There was a man sent from God whose name was John' looks like a summary of what Luke has to say on the Baptist, 'his own received him not' while having of course a wider meaning, may have come from 'there was no room for them at the inn' and 'children of God who are born, *not* of blood, *nor* of the will of the flesh, *nor* of the will of man, but of God' (even if we do not take the other reading, 'who is born', referring directly to Christ), probably by its very emphasis is bringing out that the birth of the children of God is like the virginal birth of God's own Son. 1 John has more to say about those who are children of God being like the divine Son.

The links between Cana and Calvary suggest, as the *Jerusalem Bible* notes, a whole Marian theology. At the marriage feast at Cana, starting point of Jesus's public life, 'the Mother of Jesus was there'. The wine failed. Mary's kindly eye doubtless noticed the distress of the young bride and bridegroom. She said to Jesus: 'They have no wine'. Commentators discuss whether or not she was asking for a miracle. Vatican II will not take sides and says simply 'she was moved with pity and called forth with her plea the beginning of signs of Jesus the Messiah'. Jesus answers: 'Woman, what to me and to you? My hour has not yet come.' 'Woman' is a strange form of address from a son to his mother; we shall meet it again (19:26; cf. 4:21; 20:15). 'What to me and to you' in the Bible always means 'what have you to do with me over this matter'. It is another declaration of independence (cf. John 7:1–9). But the implication is that when his 'hour' has come, and 'hour' in St John is the hour of his passion and glorification, it will be different. Yet Mary knows he will do something now for the young couple and says to the servants 'do whatever he tells you'. Then he works the great messianic sign of water turned into abundant wine at a marriage, and his disciples believe in him (John 2:1–11).

Now *Calvary*, the end of Jesus's life, is linked with the Cana scene by a repetition of key words. John's Gospel is full of such meaningful inclusions (e.g. 1:1 linked with 20:28; 1:29 with 19:36; 9:1 ff. with 9:41). To Cana's 'the mother of Jesus ⋯ Woman ⋯ My hour' corresponds 'Standing by the cross of Jesus were his *mother* ... When Jesus saw his mother and the disciple whom he loved standing near, he said to his mother "*Woman*, behold your son". Then he said to the disciple "Behold your mother". And from that *hour* the disciple took her to his own' (RSV 'home') (John 19:26 f.).

John records five episodes at the cross: the title, proclaiming Jesus as King of the Jews, the parting of his garments and casting of lots on his tunic, this one, 'I thirst', and the piercing of his side, no bone being broken. The other four fulfil prophecies which converge upon Calvary (cf. Ps. 21:19; 69:21; Exod. 12:46; Zech. 12:10); and our passage would also appear to refer to prophecy, because John continues: 'After this, Jesus knowing that all was not completed', and 'completed' would ordinarily refer to the fulfilment of his Father's will expressed in prophecy. What prophecy? The key word 'Woman' takes us back to Genesis 3:15—'I will put enmity between you (the serpent) and the woman, and between your seed and her seed. He shall bruise your head and you shall bruise his heel'. The combat between the woman and her seed (man, and ultimately Christ) against the devil and his seed ('you are of your father the devil' [John 8:44]), culminates on the cross. Then 'the ruler of this world is cast down' and Jesus 'lifted up from the earth, draws all men to himself (John 12:31 f.). Standing by the redeemer, the second Adam, is his mother, the second Eve.

'Woman, behold your son' and to the beloved disciple 'behold your mother'. Distinguished Anglican scholars (Hoskyns, Lightfoot), besides some Roman Catholics, suggest that in a text to which St John attaches such importance on Calvary more is involved than *simply* asking the disciple to look after his mother. For one thing, it is his mother whom Jesus addresses first. Then in Genesis 3:20 we find 'Adam called the name of his wife (same word as "woman") Eve, because she was the mother of all the living', and in a moment John's Gospel by mention of a 'garden' (John 19:41, cf. 20:15) will hint at the new creation. The beloved disciple is real, but like other figures in the Gospel (e.g. Nicodemus), he is also representative. For all the disciples are beloved, as are all who keep Jesus's commandments (14:21). Is there, then, here a scriptural basis for understanding that Jesus gives them to Mary as sons and Mary to them as their Mother? It is certainly worth investigating, though the Second Vatican Council, following its principle of leaving disputed points to be worked out, simply reproduces the bare text.

'I will put enmity between you (the serpent) and the woman, and between your seed and her seed' (Gen. 3:15). In Revelation (Apoc.) 12, we find again 'a woman, clothed with the sun, and the moon (symbol of mutability) under her feet' and 'a great dragon' (the 'ancient serpent', v. 9). Is the woman a symbol for womankind, or the Church of the Old and New Testaments, or *the* Daughter of Sion, or all of them? In early centuries she was thought to be simply the Church, but it is increasingly recognized that John's symbols are polyvalent and that Mary can hardly be out of mind. She bears in pain (cf. Gen. 3:16—anticipation of Calvary?) a male child, 'one who is to rule all the nations with a rod of iron' (this is certainly the Messiah, Ps. 2:9); the dragon tries to devour him (? Herod, but the cross too) but he is 'caught up to God and to his throne' (? all converges to the ascension). The woman flees from the dragon into the wilderness where she has a 'place prepared by God' (the same words as in John 14:2 'I go to prepare a place for you'). Eventually the dragon goes off to 'make war on *the rest of her seed* who keep the commandments of God and bear testimony to Jesus' (i.e. the Christians). Have we here scriptural elements for the relationship between Mary and the Church developed by the fathers and the Second Vatican Council, and, although the Council does not use it, is there a hint of the assumption? I end this with a query. Let us examine the Bible together again.

In all this have we conveyed—or missed—the divine charm which shines through Mary from her divine Son? 'When the voice of your greeting came to my ears, the babe in my womb leaped for joy' (Luke 1:44). Our relationship to the Mother of Christ Jesus must be one of love.

Bible and Tradition in regard to the Blessed Virgin Mary

REV. JOHN DE SATGÉ, M.A.
REV. JOHN McHUGH, D.D., L.S.S.

I. STATEMENT AGREED BETWEEN THE SPEAKERS

1. The period when the controversies between Catholic and Protestant about our Lord's Mother were crystallised, from the Reformation to the mid-Nineteenth Century, was one where all but a few of the controversialists were agreed on one basic principle: all dogmatic statements must be found, at least implicitly, in Scripture. There were minor differences over just what the term 'Scripture' included; the Anglicans, for instance, refused to accept the books known as Apocrypha as authorities for doctrine, valuable as they were for edification. But otherwise, Old and New Testaments were common property.

2. The debate between Catholic and Protestant was therefore a matter of deciding what the Bible really taught. A classical example may be seen in the endless disputes about the sacrificial nature of the Holy Eucharist. It must be noted, however, that both sides were agreed on the basic principle of interpretation: it was taken for granted that the words attributed to our Lord by the evangelists were actually spoken by Him, and all the debate concentrated on their meaning. For almost three centuries after the Reformation, this was the style of debate between Catholic and Protestant; and when Catholics appealed to Tradition, with very few exceptions, they meant that the teaching of the Roman Church expounded the true interpretation of Scripture, not that there was an unwritten source of doctrine which could add to what was contained in the Bible.

3. Since about 1850 there has been far wider divergence.

3.1 After the definition of the Immaculate Conception in 1854, some Roman Catholic theologians, perceiving the weakness of the biblical justification offered in support of the Dogma, began to claim that the doctrine, though unwitnessed in the Bible, had been handed down from apostolic times by unwritten, oral tradition. Many Protestants assumed the admission to be true and assailed the Roman Catholic Church as one which had not merely misinterpreted the Scriptures, but had wilfully and explicitly departed from them. Similar arguments and charges followed the definition in 1950 of our Lady's Assumption.

3.2 Another factor of major importance was the impact of modern biblical criticism. Protestant theologians generally accepted critical methods in approaching the Scriptures some 50 years before their Catholic colleagues did. There was thus a considerable period, roughly 1900–1950, when basic differences in methodology made it hard for Catholic and Protestant to engage in debate at any depth. Part of the difficulty in ecumenical dialogue now is that many people are as yet unfamiliar with modern techniques of biblical study.

Yet those techniques are no longer a matter of dispute between the Churches. Today's two speakers both accept a critical approach; and by that they mean:

1. We take each Bible writing on its own merits, trying from the evidence of its form and content to see what particular purpose it served when it was originally written and heard. We compare it with other writings both inside the Bible and, where relevant, outside. In other words, we must understand the original meaning of each document against its own historical background before we apply it to any later Christian situation.

2. We believe that, while each separate Bible writing is as it has come to be by thoroughly human means, it has done so under the controlling hand of the Spirit; and that it takes its place in the total body of writings which we call the Bible under the same controlling hand, thus forming the 'canon' or measuring-stick of Scripture. It is, we believe, proper to use one part of the Canon to interpret another and to look across them all to find a 'general sense' to which each different part supplies its distinctive nuance. (In honesty we should add that many scholars do not accept as readily as we do the integrity of the Canon, and its authority.)

IIA. STANDARD OBJECTIONS OF THE REFORMED TRADITIONS TO ROMAN CATHOLIC MARIAN DOGMAS

John de Satgé

The striking extent of this agreement means that Marian issues may be discussed ecumenically in quite a new spirit. Realism reminds us how new that spirit is. Until the Second Vatican Council the Roman Church appeared to the outsider to be caught up in an expansion of Marian doctrine which was isolating it progressively from all other Christians. The varying emotions with which many of us greeted the proclamation of the Dogma of the Assumption in 1950 cannot but have some effect on our attitudes today.

There are of course two dogmas to consider. That of the Immaculate Conception proclaimed in 1854 teaches that 'the Blessed Virgin Mary, at the first instant of her conception, by a singular privilege and grace of the omnipotent God, in consideration of the merits of Jesus Christ the Saviour of mankind, was preserved free from all stain of original sin.' The dogma of the Assumption teaches that 'the immaculate Mother of God, the ever-Virgin Mary, when the course of her earthly life was run, was assumed in body and soul to heavenly glory.' That is all; neither the explanations which support the proclamation, nor of course the imagery of countless artists, are matters required for belief.

Protestant reactions are of two kinds. Eastern Orthodox and Anglo-Catholic objections have often been technical, rejecting not the substance of the beliefs but their new status as dogmas binding on the faithful. Most Protestants, however, rejected the teachings themselves; though frequently less attention has been paid to the dogmas themselves than to the underlying 'cultus' of Mary from which they were seen to spring. That cultus is objectionable on four counts. It is contrary to the Scriptures. It is a doctrinal distortion. It is a religious disaster. It is a non-Christian phenomenon best explained by comparative religion and (morbid) psychology. The last three counts only concern us now.

Doctrinally, it is alleged, Marian cultus is no true consequence of Christ's Incarnation. For the Catholic Mary is no longer the Mary of the Gospels. Rather, she personifies the human striving to win salvation by human effort. From sinless beginning to final glory, the Catholic Mary expresses that human pride which cannot accept its own sinfulness and total need of grace. It is thus in the doctrinal area of Grace and Justification, not of Incarnation, that the theological battle of Mary should be fought.

The religious objection follows. The Biblical Mary was the handmaid of the Lord. The Catholic Mary is the enemy of the salvation which He died to achieve. The cult of Mary is disastrous because it blocks the true way to God through Christ alone. Protestants are not convinced by the Catholic distinction between *Latria*, worship that belongs to God alone, and *dulia*, the veneration of holy people with its intensive form *hyperdulia* reserved for the Virgin only. It is not enough to prevent idolatry.

But the Marian cultus is not Christian at all. Four historical factors strengthen the conviction already reached for doctrinal reasons that the Catholic Mary is not Mary of the Gospels but an intruder, the mother-goddess of ancient pagan religions. 1. The late date of any Marian cultus: the really early Church managed without it. 2. The dubious orthodoxy of those circles where attention was first paid to Mary. 3. The ease with which the cult of Mary has taken over shrines anciently sacred to heathen divinities. 4. The links connecting the expanding Marian cultus of the Middle Ages with the growing emphasis on celibacy. Does the emphasis on a female object of devotion, taught mainly by a celibate priesthood, not indicate a measure of psychological compensation?

IIB. STANDARD ROMAN CATHOLIC REPLIES

John McHugh

I think John de Satgé has given a very fair and very accurate account of the standard objection to Catholic Marian dogmas. And following his lead, I am going to lay aside for the moment the question which principally concerns us today, namely, the scriptural basis for these doctrines. Let me take his other points in order.

Dogmatically, Marian development is a distortion. The first thing to be said is that, from the Protestant point of view, it *is* a distortion. That is, if one starts by assuming that the Lutheran and Calvinistic doctrine of justification is true, then obviously the doctrine of the Immaculate Conception is appalling heresy. But if one starts by assuming that the Council of Trent (not the Reformers) was right on justification, the case is altered. For the fundamental difference between Catholic and Protestant is to be found in the different interpretations of 'justification'. For the Protestant, it means that a veil is drawn over our sins; for the Catholic, it means that God's power transforms our nature *in this life*. Consequently, the Catholic sees in Mary this power at its fullest. It is seen preserving her, by the merits of her Son, from every being affected by original sin; and once her earthly life is over, bestowing upon her the fullness of heavenly glory. Mary is certainly seen as a creature, but a creature in whom we see manifested the *fullness* of grace.

Religiously, it is dangerous. The first thing to be said is that there certainly have been, still are, and probably always will be, abuses in Marian devotion. And these are to be condemned, not defended or explained away. I would only add that, as a general rule, not sufficient attention is paid to the many interventions of Popes across the centuries which censure irregularities in Marian devotion. And it is not only Protestants who pay insufficient attention to them; R.C.'s are the worst offenders. It is sad to note, for example, how little attention has been paid to *Marialis Cultus* in recent years. Outside this Society, one hardly hears of it. [Apostolic Exhortation *Marialis Cultus*, 'To Honour Mary', 2 February 1974. Transl. CTS.]

The second remark is connected with what I said about Catholic doctrine on justification. God wills us to be saved, and to work out our salvation, as members of one body, the Church (cf. St. Paul passim). Praying for one another in this life is normal for Christians. Deep in the Catholic consciousness is the conviction that the faithful departed do not cease from prayer, least of all when they stand before the throne of God. And here Mary must be in a privileged position. And though a person deeply conscious of his own weakness may find it psychologically difficult to identify with Christ in glory, because he is God, he may find it psychologically easy to ask Mary to intercede on his behalf because she *as a creature* is on his side of the divide between God and his creatures. (Similarly, he finds it psychologically easy to imagine St. Peter turning a sympathetic ear to his prayer.)

As a phenomenon, it is best explained in terms of comparative religion and (morbid) psychology. It is true that especially around the shores of the Mediterranean, the earliest cult of Mary and the places of particular devotion are closely connected with centres where a mother-goddess was revered in pagan times (e.g. Ephesus, but also the Lebanon). The question is, *whether* this old pagan cult has been *too lightly* baptized. Personally, I think it was a stroke of genius, to interpret the aspirations of simple people as a (divinely inspired) *praeparatio evangelica*, and to use the figure of Mary as virgin and mother in order to purge the old shrines of their grosser characteristics.

But is this *Christian?* There can be no doubt that down the ages the Catholic tradition has emphasized the virginity of the Lord's mother, and that this has at times (some would say all too often) led to a depreciation of the holiness of sex within marriage. But it is important to remember what a terrible battle the Christian Church had to wage against the worship of Venus; it was not, and it is not, easy to prevent the worship of sex. And such worship inevitably leads to the degradation of women, from the temples of Corinth to the preoccupation with youthful female beauty in our own day. Properly understood, the presentation of Mary as *both* virgin *and* mother strikes a psychological balance that is needed in every age.

IIIA. SCRIPTURE, TRADITION AND THE MARIAN TEXTS

John de Satgé

'The determination to express Marian doctrine under the control of Scripture is one for which all who have the reunion of Christendom at heart will be deeply grateful.' That is as true now as when I said it at an early meeting of our society, in 1967. Ten years later it is also true that the use of Scripture in *Lumen Gentium* VIII, the Marian section of Vatican II's Constitution on The Church, needs explanation before it will win ecumenical acceptance. I greatly welcome therefore this opportunity to press Fr. McHugh for comment on crucial matters raised in two passages to which for convenience I will limit myself; they are typical of many others.

The first problem is the relation of doctrine to Scripture. *Lumen Gentium* (LG) n. 58 contains a classic example: 'Thus the Blessed Virgin advanced in her pilgrimage of faith, and loyally persevered in union with her Son unto the cross. There she stood, in keeping with the divine plan, (cf. Jn. 19.25), suffering grievously with her only-begotten Son. There she united herself with a maternal heart to his sacrifice, and lovingly consented to the immolation of this Victim which she herself had brought forth. Finally, the same Christ Jesus dying on the cross gave her as mother to his disciple. This he did when he said "Woman, behold thy son" (Jn. 19.26–7).'

The first verse cited in support says simply 'But standing by the cross of Jesus were his mother, and his mother's sister, Mary the wife of Clopas, and Mary Magdalene.' LG ignores the other women and adds five things about the mother's interior disposition.

1. Mary suffered grievously—and so would any normal mother. We may accept that addition on the authority of human experience. No problem.

2. Her son was 'only-begotten'. Is that note purely honorific? If so it adds nothing but spoils the powerful restraint of the Gospel account. Or is it theological—referring to controversies over the so-called 'Brothers of the Lord'; or reflecting Jn. 1.14? Or does it merely underline the mother's grief?

3. LG asserts that Mary's presence was 'in keeping with the divine plan'. The comment underlines an element especially prominent in St John's Gospel and is thus very appropriate.

4. LG's 'Finally, the same Christ Jesus dying on the cross gave her as mother to his disciple' simply re-states the Gospel.

5. But the real problem lies in the words: 'There she united herself with a maternal heart ··· which she had brought forth'. Before that can be accepted as a proper comment on St John's text, we must know the principles of interpretation which lie behind it. Most emphatically, it is not to be found in that text itself.

If that problem concerns the relation between doctrine and scripture, my second problem is over the relation between history and what may perhaps be called 'metahistory'. It is posed acutely in a passage from LG 62: '(The) maternity of Mary in the order of grace began with the consent which she gave in faith at the Annunciation and sustained unwavering beneath the cross; it lasts until the eternal fulfilment of all the elect. Taken up into heaven, she did not lay aside this saving role, but by her constant intercession continues to bring us the gifts of eternal salvation.'

1. By connecting Annunciation and the cross, LG 'teams up' St Luke with St John, for St John has no Annunciation and St Luke does not mention Mary's presence at the cross. No texts are cited and the biblical authority is evidently that of the Canon of Scripture as a whole. Satisfactory treatment of our problem will therefore involve discussion of the post-NT Church, of Tradition and of the work of the Holy Spirit through the events of history.

2. 'The maternity will last until the eternal fulfilment of all the elect' goes well beyond any scriptural passage. Is it an inference made after considering the total scriptural testimony? We have again reached the border between doctrinal and scriptural statements.

3. 'Taken up into heaven ... gifts of eternal salvation'. I am inter-

ested in that event 'taken up into heaven'. What sort of event is it? It seems of a different kind from the others referred to in the paragraph—the Annunciation, the standing by the cross. They at least are in the NT narrative. In that narrative they are at least presented as historical—events that happened in the same way that you came into this room. Or were they events of that sort? It might be that discussion of how we interpret those NT events will throw some light on 'taken up into heaven'.

IIIB. REPLY

John McHugh

May I deal ever so briefly with John de Satgé's remark about *Lumen Gentium* n. 58, not in order to dismiss them lightly, but simply because I think he is right on all counts. I concede the whole case. The Vatican Council does make its argument by drawing upon other texts of St John, and other books of Scripture, to throw light on the scene at the foot of the cross. Like John de Satgé, I consider this to be a legitimate procedure, though both of us would have to admit that not all scholars and not all members of our own Churches would be as happy with the method as we are.

Space prevents me developing a similar answer on Lumen Gentium n. 62, but may I end with a counter-question? I was surprised to find so much attention paid to *Lumen Gentium*, for I had expected rather queries about the dogmas proclaimed in 1854 and 1950. These seem to me to make greater difficulties. It is interesting, however, to note that what the Reformed Churches find most difficult is the assignment of a 'mediatory' role to Mary, whereas I think most Roman Catholics would have expected the major difficulties to arise from the doctrines of the Immaculate Conception and the Assumption. In RC thinking, these loom much larger than the (not yet defined or adequately worked out) idea of 'mediation'.

Now if we had time to discuss either or both of these doctrines, I should start by assuming that post-biblical tradition is a legitimate development of Scripture, and then try to trace a path from NT times to the present day. This is in fact a most difficult academic exercise, and each would merit a day's discussion on its own. But for the Assumption, may I refer readers to John Saward's excellent paper published by the ESBVM last year? [See Doctrinal section, below for full text.] And for the Immaculate Conception, may I simply hint that we have not yet fully learned to perceive and to interpret the wealth of doctrine contained in the picture-language of the early Fathers? Phrases like 'children of Adam' and 'the new Eve' are familiar to us, but our formalized and abstract way of talking theology in the West has not yet developed to a point where we can express well in propositions the unformalized and concrete vision of truth that the early Fathers encapsulated in these simple phrases.

IV. CONTRIBUTIONS BY THE PANELLISTS

Reverend Dr Marcus Ward

If among Methodists there had been on this theme a deafening silence, it was in no way due to disregard for the Virgin Mother of the Lord of the Church but to the implicit feeling that this was a Roman 'thing' and so, dangerous to touch! Now in the blander ecumenical climate many Methodists were finding it possible to make explicit their reverence and gratitude. But problems remain, especially the question whether proper Marian devotion *must* require assent to the Marian dogmas. It would seem, for example, that the phrase in the definition of the Immaculate Conception 'preserved from the stain of original sin' is far too ambiguous to bear the weight laid upon it, indeed that in tradition in 1977 quite other conclusions are tenable. Standing firmly, as we do, on the basis of Scripture and the historic Creeds, we ask, what more is needed than the full and rich evidence of Scripture for a true Marian devotion.

Reverend Anthony Barker, SM

It would seem to me, as a Catholic priest and member of a Marian Congregation (Society of Mary or Marist Fathers), that understanding of Mary and the Church go hand in hand. There is a sense in which Bible, Tradition and Church are all one. The Church, ever contemplative, ponders the Word in Bible and the lived experience of her day-to-day life as she transmits to others the fruits of her self-understanding, the whole Christ—head and members. As a living Body the Church, under the guidance of the Spirit, achieves ever deeper consciousness of herself and her mission, the begetting of the Word of God in the minds and hearts and limbs of men. In this Mary is the model or type—an idea which stems, I understand, from St Irenaeus. Whilst it is valuable to study the Marian texts of *Lumen Gentium*, it is important to place chapter 8 in its full context—as it is important to place Mary within her context, which is the Church. In this way both the doctrines and the dogmas of the Immaculate Conception and Assumption present little difficulty to me, for they are part of the life of the Church in her fullness; that is, over the centuries, she discovers in her contemplation of Mary a greater self-understanding, a deeper consciousness that expresses itself in defined dogma, attending to the 'signs of the times'.

May one suggest then that, at the root of the differences of opinions between Catholic and Protestant, lies a radically different attitude to the Church? In this, true devotion to Mary, a devotion that is spelled out in action, can be the means, under grace and the Holy Spirit overshadowing, whereby the ecumenical endeavour can be achieved.

The Venerable G.B. Timms, Archdeacon of Hackney

The NT is the earliest 'tradition', and was accorded particular authority because it is the nearest to the Christ-event. It was 'canonised' to secure the tradition against heresy and false tradition, e.g., the apocryphal gospels. So it is a standard against which later formulations of doctrine have to be checked. Defined dogma exists to safeguard the original deposit of faith, to which the NT bears witness. What is it in the NT witness which the two Marian dogmas safeguard?

The wording of the dogma of the Immaculate Conception I find difficult because it assumes that we know what is meant by 'the stain of original sin'. I find that a difficulty because we no longer accept the Adam and Eve story as historical, on which it appears to be based. If the dogma really means that our Lady was 'sinless', perhaps I could accept it; though I do think that there are passages in the NT which imply that her spiritual vision was not unclouded. As far as the Assumption is concerned, I can accept it if it does not necessarily imply that her mortal body did not see corruption; though I think that the title is perhaps unfortunate, and that a more neutral one would be better.

But finally I ask, What *are* the truths of the NT witness which these two dogmas are held to safeguard to such a degree, that the dogmas warrant being declared to be part of *essential* Christian belief? That, to me, is the fundamental question to which I feel the need of an answer.

Reverend Edward Yarnold, SJ

(1) One must be careful about asserting that Mary is the one example of the absolute triumph of grace in a human life, 'our tainted nature's solitary boast'. It is Jesus who is the summit of human moral achievement. His human nature was full of grace, and 'from that fullness we have all received' (Jn 1.16). Aquinas called this 'the grace of the Head'. Yet Jesus expressed in his human nature his divine relationship with his Father; therefore although he experienced temptation (moral struggle?), he could not sin. In Mary we have for our encouragement the fullness of grace in one who is not God, and therefore whose holiness and sinlessness is of a different order from that of her Son.

(2) It seems a mistake to seek agreement now about the way the Immaculate Conception and the Assumption can be definable articles of faith. Let us penetrate together their meaning, and only then shall we see how they relate to essential Christian faith.

(3) The modern danger for large sections of the Roman Catholic Church is not excessive Marian devotion, but almost total neglect of it.

Roman Catholics need to join people from other traditions in the search for true devotion to Our Lady.

Canon E.L. Mascall, King's College, London

It has been objected that to argue from the Virginal Conception of Jesus (i.e. that Jesus had no human father) to the Immaculate Conception of Mary (i.e. that Mary was conceived without original sin) must be fallacious, since it would carry the implication that Mary's mother Anne also was immaculately conceived, and Anne's mother also, and so on through the female line back to Eve, the mother of all living, and this is plainly preposterous. This, however, does not follow. If the *virginal* conception of an offspring implied the *virginal* conception of its parent, an indefinite retrosequence of *virginal* conceptions would have preceded any actual *virginal* conception as a logical necessity. And if the *immaculate* conception of an offspring implied the *immaculate* conception of its parent, an indefinite retrosequence of *immaculate* conceptions would have preceded any actual *immaculate* conception as a logical necessity. But in this case neither of these premises has been asserted. What, it is said, has been asserted is that the *virginal* conception of the offspring (Jesus) implies the *immaculate* conception of the parent (Mary), and from this no retrosequence logically arises.

I doubt whether in fact any responsible Mariologist would affirm a relationship of strict necessity between the Virginal Conception of Jesus and the Immaculate Conception of Mary, rather than a relationship of great appropriateness (*maxima convenientia*). And the starting-point would be less the simple fact of virginal conception, considered in isolation, than its place as a highly important element in the whole cosmological and soteriological fabric of Christology.

III
THEOLOGICAL

It is interesting to notice how often theologians turn to poetry to express their argument, once unfolded. Interesting too is it to see how often the Spirit of God is brought into the discussion of Mariology. It is as if Mary's calling overleaps the constraints of formal theology.

The first address was given after the Society's Annual General Meeting in London on 3 March 1975 by the Bishop of Chichester, who is also Executive Co-Chairman of the Society. His beginning with Newman and Keble reminds us that he was formerly a Fellow of Exeter College, Oxford, before becoming Dean of Worcester.

The second address was given at the first of the society's International Conferences, at Coloma College, Kent, in Easter Week of 1971 by the Cardinal of Belgium, Archbishop of Malines. He became a bishop, Auxiliary of Malines in 1945. His several publications include *Mary, the Mother of God* (1959). He returned to the subject of this address at the fifth International Congress at Canterbury in September 1981, again being the Society's guest of honour.

The third address was delivered in Wells Cathedral at the Wells Festival of the Society, on 12 June 1976 by the Bishop of East Anglia, who was also Co-President of the Anglican/Roman Catholic International Commission—for this work he and Archbishop McAdoo were awarded the Lambeth Cross, in September 1981.

Mary and Right Belief in Christ

RT. REV. ERIC KEMP, D.D.

There is a well-known passage in the first chapter of Newman's *Apologia* in which he writes of the influence of John Keble in transforming two great intellectual principles that he had learned from Butler's *Analogy*. The first of these two principles is not easily summarised and I am not concerned with it this evening. The second is that Probability is the guide to life. Newman writes that the danger of this doctrine is that it destroys in some minds the possibility of absolute certainty, and he goes on to say:

> "I considered that Mr Keble met this difficulty by ascribing the firmness of assent which we give to religious doctrine, not to the probabilities which introduced it, but to the living power of faith and love which accepted it. In matters of religion, he seemed to say, it is not merely probability which makes us intellectually certain, but probability as it is put to account by faith and love. It is faith and love which give to probability a force which it has not in itself. Faith and love are directed towards an Object; in the vision of that Object they live; it is that Object, received in faith and love, which renders it reasonable to take probability as sufficient for internal conviction. Thus the argument from Probability, in the matter of religion, became an argument from Personality, which in fact is one form of the argument from Authority." (p. 19)

Among the letters of R. W. Church, Dean of St. Paul's, is one written in answer to a problem put to him on behalf of a lady who was in some perplexity about her faith. Towards the end of the letter we find Church giving a development of Butler's similar thought which Newman had learned from Keble, but giving it in what might be described as a more explicit form. The heart of what he had been asked seemed to be the problem of the existence of suffering and he writes of the difficulty of giving any answer to that problem. Then he says:

> Of course this is only Butler again; it is only vagueness and platitude. Every one knows it. But not only I cannot get beyond it, but I cannot imagine any one doing so. And then it comes to the old story: here are facts and phenomena on both sides, some leading to belief, some to unbelief; and we human creatures, with our affection, our hopes and wishes and our wills, stand, as it were, solicited by either set of facts. The facts which witness to the goodness and the love of God are clear and undeniable; they are not got rid of by the presence and certainty of other facts, which seem of an opposite kind; only the co-existence of the two contraries is perplexing. And then comes the question which shall have the decisive governing influence on wills and lives? You must, by the necessity of your existence, trust one set of appearances; which will you trust? Our Lord

came among us not to clear up the perplexity, but to show us which side to take." *(Life and Letters,* pp. 275f)

That letter was written in 1879, and Newman was writing of 1827/28, so that there is about fifty years between them, a half century of intellectual torment for religiously minded people, a time in which friends were parted and the faith of many was shattered. The marks of this are perhaps to be seen in Church's words and in that pregnant sentence "Our Lord came among us not to clear up the perplexity, but to show us which side to take". There is a contrast with the rather more abstract and philosophical language of Newman. Newman's phrase: "Faith and love are directed towards an Object" have become "Jesus Christ shows us which side to choose". The half century of torment has, as it were, focussed the attention of the believer more upon the Person of Jesus whose human life among us shows us the true way.

In the case of R. W. Church we know that his theology was thoroughly orthodox, but we also know that that period of the nineteenth century saw the beginnings of a concentration upon the Jesus of history which has made of the Christ no more than an inspired prophet, and which while attending to his life and sufferings has abandoned belief in the triumph of the Resurrection. The line runs from Strauss and Renan to "Jesus Christ Superstar"—the love of the humanity of Jesus to the neglect or exclusion of his Godhead.

I would like now to take you back from Newman and Church some nine hundred years to a period which is roughly the century and a half following the Norman Conquest. This too was a time of intellectual travail. It begins with the powerful and yet calm treatises of St. Anselm, comparable perhaps in their spirit to the writings of Newman, and then moves into the intellectual ferment called by historians the Twelfth-Century Renaissance, the period of the questionings of Abelard and the passionate treatises of St. Bernard, of the early stages of scholasticism with its challenge to authority, of the beginnings of heresy— all in an atmosphere of violence, religious and secular.

Many students of the religious thought of this period have noted the development during it of devotion to the humanity of the Lord, with increasing attention to his sufferings and death upon the cross. As Sir Richard Southern has put it, "The imaginative following of the details of the earthly life of Jesus, and especially of the sufferings of the Cross, became part of a programme of progress from carnal to spiritual love."

St. Bernard is a key figure in this development, and one of those characters most difficult to assess. Dr. Prestige, sympathetic to him in many ways, nevertheless writes, contrasting St. Francis with him: "Bernard could never have been called Christ's troubadour, but rather his hardy and loving vassal, devoted to his Lord with passionate attachment, but readier to die with him than to assist Him in raising Lazarus from the dead." Edmund Bishop's judgment was considerably harsher: "As we look at St. Bernard's *Life* as he actually *lived* it, his activities as a whole and what they involved, I can conceive nothing (except secularity) more alien from the idea and spirit of Cistercianism; even his activity in writing, and his correspondence first of all, are not merely alien, but even antagonistic to the conception of Citeaux". (Downside Review lii,1935,221). The difficulty of reconciling a man's public career with the expressions of his spirit is a not uncommon one and happily it is not necessary for my present purpose to attempt to resolve it in the case of St. Bernard, for the point I wish to make is simply that of the new direction that he helped to give to spirituality. I quote Dr. Prestige again:

> "Bernard sees the cross as the constraining revelation of divine love. His meditation on it is profoundly moving. Familiar as we are to-day with such conceptions as he expressed, it is hard to realise that practically nothing even remotely resembling them was known before the twelfth century, and that Bernard, in creating a type of piety which has intensely influenced all subsequent Christian devotion, was uttering thoughts far nearer to those of Isaac Watts, the Independent minister who published in 1707 the hymn 'When I survey the wondrous cross', than to Athanasius or Augustine. He seems to peer through Christ's wounds as through windows to watch the beating of His heart. This feeling for Christ as love's tortured victim in something altogether new."   (*Fathers and Heretics*, p.387)

The artistic expression of this development is also well-known but I must nevertheless mention it. Until the late eleventh century the most powerful representations of the crucifixion had emphasized the divine power at work in the struggle against evil. In Sir Richard Southern's book *The Making of the Middle Ages* are pictures of two Danish crucifixes. One, of about 1050–1100, shows the Christ as a young warrior, robed and crowned, with head erect and eyes open. The other, about a century later, shows the head still crowned but it is bowed, the eyes are closed, the upper part of the body is naked, the development is well on the way to the realism with which we are familiar. Nearly thirty years ago on a visit to the National Museum in Copenhagen I observed this development in a series of medieval crucifixes over precisely that period, and I suspect that it could be connected with the penetration of Cistercian influence into Denmark at an early date.

This particular artistic development is, as I said, well known and has often been described, but Southern draws attention to another and parallel field of representation which is less well-known. It will be simplest if I quote his words:

> "The transformation of the theme of the Virgin and Child was a natural corollary to the transformation of the theme of the Crucifixion. In the eleventh century, the West had long been familiar with the Child seated as if enthroned on his Mother's knee, holding up his right hand in benediction and, in his left, clasping a Book, the symbol of wisdom, or an orb, the symbol of dominion. This conception persisted and was never abandoned, but it was joined by many other forms which expressed the more intimate

65

inclinations of later medieval piety, such as the laughing Child, the Child playing with an apple or a ball, the Child caressing its Mother, or the Child being fed from its Mother's breast".
                                                                                    (p.238)

He refers to a picture in an early Cistercian lectionary as illustrating this, but comments that "rich though the artist is in suggestion, he has not learnt to express the pathos with which already the pupils of St. Anselm, and later those of St. Bernard, approached the subject of his illustration. Considered as human beings, his central figures are not quite at ease in their new attitudes: the Child about to feed still raises his hand in benediction and still clasps his Book; the Mother gazes on the world with a detached dignity, and the proffered breast causes no interruption in the folds of her dress." He then contrasts with this a carving done at Liège in the late twelfth century and known as "The Madonna of Dom Rupert", saying: "Sixty or seventy years later it was just this maternal tenderness which the artist of The 'Madonna of Dom Rupert' set out to portray. The Mother has lost her remoteness; the Child has laid down the symbols of his wisdom and authority. Only the inscription from Ezekiel round the border discloses the hidden divinity; all else is humanity, frailty and love." (p.240) In a few years from that carving we have the devotion of the Crib, so much promoted by St. Francis.

Reverence for Our Lady is as old as the Fathers of the Church, but in the medieval period of which I have been speaking it acquires a new impetus and expansion. This is the time of Richelde's foundation of the chapel at Walsingham and of the great developments of the pilgrimages to the shrines at Chartres, Rocamadour and elsewhere. As we know, this devotion took exaggerated forms. We remember the crude satire of Erasmus's visit to Walsingham, when he was shown the heavenly Milk of the Blessed Virgin, "Oh mother most imitative of her Son! He has left us so much of his Blood upon earth; she so much Milk, as it is scarcely credible should have belonged to a single woman with one child, even if the infant had taken none of it!" (p.21) And yet I have been wondering, as I wrote this paper, whether this fervent devotion to our Lady did not, with all its excesses, in a providential way provide a necessary counterbalance to the exaggerated devotion to the humanity of her Son, recalling perpetually, as the Virgin Birth must do, his divine origin.

I am the more moved to this reflection by re-reading after a long time a book which has, I think, never been as well known as it deserves, the Bampton Lectures given in 1922 by Dr Leighton Pullan under the title of *Religion since the Reformation*, a very remarkable survey of religious thought and teaching over some four hundred years. It is in many respects a depressing book as it shows so clearly the spiritual and intellectual impoverishment which afflicted a divided Christendom and whose fullest effects were felt in the 18th and 19th centuries. Pullan has many severe things to say about events in the Roman Catholic Church in the period 1700 to 1854 and especially about the disastrous place of importance accorded to the teaching of St. Alphonsus Liguori but his severest words are reserved for the chapter on aspects of Lutheranism and Calvinism since 1700. He writes with a certain sympathy of the outlook of Herder, Schiller and Goethe and with praise of the intentions of Schleiermacher of whom he says that "His real work and his great work was to teach, and to teach from the heart, that the Christian religion was and is created by the impression which the Person of Christ produced and still produces in and through the Christian community" (p.183). Ritschl he regards as continuing the work of Schleiermacher. "But", Pullan writes, "even according to the most generous criticism the message of both of them falls short of the glory of the message of the New Testament. The religious importance of Christ's pre-existence, of His eternal reciprocal relationship with the Father and His exaltation and present life in heaven is put aside ... Neither Schleiermacher nor Ritschl adequately understood the religious value of the doctrine of the Incarnation." (p.185) An account follows of the work of Strauss, Baur and Harnack of whom Pullan says that "Like Luther he extols the 'Gospel'; but by the 'Gospel' he means his own mutilated version of certain parts of the New Testament". Pullan's summing up of his survey is in these devastating words: "I have ventured to speak strongly about some existing corruptions in the Church of Rome. But having so spoken, I say that the meanest Roman chapel in England is nearer to God than the finest temple where they preach any sham German Jesus" (p.190).

We have returned to the century from which we set out and I am reminded that in the last years of Schleiermacher's life John Keble, whose influence on Newman I have already mentioned, was writing these lines:

> Ave Maria! thou whose name
> All but adoring love may claim,
> Yet may we reach thy shrine;
> For He, thy Son and Saviour, vows
> To crown all lowly lofty brows
> With love and joy like thine.

This is one verse of the poem of sixty lines set in *The Christian Year* for the Annunciation of the Blessed Virgin Mary. It reminds us that for many in England that cleaving to Jesus as our teacher and guide amid the perplexities of life, of which R.W. Church wrote, was against a background of love and veneration for the Mother of Jesus, just as we have seen in the Middle Ages a devotion to the humanity and suffering of Jesus accompanied by love and devotion, albeit excessive, to his Mother. There is a striking contrast to the contemporary developments in conventional Protestantism.

Natural caution makes me hesitate to draw the lesson too sharply, but there is I think a prima facie case for saying that devotion to our Lady is a corrective against the dangers inherent in a concentration of devotion on the humanity of her son. The only reason for devotion to the Mother is that her Son is divine, and Marian devotion is a safeguard for the doctrine of the deity of Christ.

At the beginning of this paper I mentioned the musical "Jesus Christ Superstar". That, by its authors' own confession contains no teaching of the deity of Christ. It ends with the death, there is no resurrection. "Godspell" too ends with the death, though resurrection is felt by many to be implicit in the music with which it closes. Neither, as it seems to me, comes nearly as close to an explicit message of triumph over death as the closing scene of "Hair" with its chorus of "Let the sun shine in", but that is perhaps a personal impression. What had not occurred to me until I started to write this paper is the absence of the Mother of Jesus from both "Godspell" and "Jesus Christ Superstar" and her replacement as, so to speak, the female interest, by Mary Magdalene who cannot be in anything like the same way a witness to the deity of Jesus.

"Godspell", more than "Jesus Christ Superstar", represents the Jesus cult of to-day and the words of Dean Church might well be applied to its message: "Jesus Christ came among us not to clear up the perplexity but to show us which side to take". Perhaps the most remembered of its songs will be the adaptation of that great thirteenth century prayer to the humanity of Jesus, the prayer of St. Richard of Chichester. But if there is any lesson to be drawn from the history that I have tried to sketch, it is that the modern Jesus cult needs to be accompanied by a renewal of devotion to his Mother, reminding us of his Godhead, if it is to be soundly and safely based. The promotion of that renewal should be a matter of prayer and thought on the part of this Society.

The Relation that exists between the Holy Spirit and Mary

H.E. CARDINAL LÉON JOSEF SUENENS, Ph.D., D.D.

At the opening of the International Theological Congress in September 1970, I said: "I do not know any more than you when the hour of the rediscovery of unity will strike. I think that the Christians of my generation are doomed like Moses to see only a glimmer of the Promised Land. But if I read the signs of the times aright, we may believe that this return of all Christians to a visible unity is coming closer. The star which led the Magi to Bethlehem is already a light in the sky of ecumenism. The pilgrims towards unity are again on the way, they all advance, but sometimes the star is hidden and they have to check up on the road they have taken and consult their map. But everything indicates that they are not far from Bethlehem."

And I added: "Perhaps, like the Magi, they, too, will together see the Mother first, then the Child. It would be difficult to imagine a reunion of disunited children in their common home without their finding the Mother standing on the doorstep to receive them and to lead them to the Lord."

In pronouncing these words, I thought of the Congress which brings us together at this time (1971): it is already, in itself, a sign of hope, a symbol, an anticipation. It appears to me as a ray of light at daybreak: night has not yet completely disappeared and the mist still hangs over us but the ray of light on the horizon gives us a glimpse of the brightness of the dawn.

The second reason for joy is the theme of my conference: the relationship that exists between the Holy Spirit and Mary. Not only is this theme fruitful in itself, but, even more, it offers the opportunity to clarify perhaps some ambiguities which obscure ecumenical dialogue and block the road toward unity. For it is precisely on this point that misunderstandings among christians of different traditions rest.

The difficulty of understanding one another concerning the place held by the Holy Spirit and Mary, respectively, has been clearly outlined in an article by Elie Gibson.[1] She writes: "It is possibly as difficult for Catholics to understand what Protestants believe about the Holy Spirit as it is for Protestants to understand what Catholics believe about Mary. When I first began reading Catholic periodicals and books, I was puzzled and offended by caricatures of our views regarding the Holy Spirit, more than by anything else. The Catholic consensus seemed to be that we glorify human impulses and judgments, attributing them to the inspiration of the Third Person of the Trinity. This is a travesty of the Protestant position ... When I began the study of Catholic theology, wherever I expected to find an exposition of the doctrine of the Holy Spirit I found Mary. What Protestants universally attribute to the action of the Holy Spirit was attributed to Mary."

Among Christian non-catholics, it is not unusual to meet a feeling of uneasiness as regards certain statements or expressions concerning the Blessed Virgin. These statements seem to have a common fault in their eyes: that of substituting Mary for the Holy Spirit, of attributing to the Blessed Virgin that which belongs, in fact, to the Holy Spirit or in any case, that which belongs to Him by absolute priority. One notes such expressions as:

—to Jesus through Mary
—Mary forms Christ in us
—Mary is the link between us and Christ
—Mary is associated with the redemption
—Mary is the mediatrix of grace.

In such expressions, one would object that it is precisely the role of the Holy Spirit to lead us to Jesus, to form Christ in us, to unite us to him, that the Holy Spirit has cooperated in an unique way in redemption and that if Christ alone is mediator, it belongs to the Spirit to assist us and promote our return to the Father through Christ.

All this invites us to give the precision necessary in order that the hierarchy of truths be maintained, and that the Holy Spirit should have his real place of priority, which allows us to place these expressions about Mary in their context, bestowed and in dependence upon the Holy Spirit.

This reproach of "substitution", of screening the Holy Spirit to the profit of Mary cannot leave us indifferent and we cannot bypass it. One can find this same reaction among various Protestant as well as Catholic writers.[2] It is a fact that, historically, Latin Mariology was highly developed at a time when pneumatology was failing. Often, at the Council, the oriental fathers insisted on the necessity of accentuating the role of the Holy Spirit.

After having noted the opposing views on the subject, Elie Gibson continues her exposé trying to find the way out from this deadlock, and she outlines an approach in terms which invite reflection: "Within Protestantism, the divine Presence of the Holy Spirit is recognized by the holiness engendered whether this be in personality, forms of action, or developments in church life. Does the Catholic, perhaps, finding these effects more visible in Mary than anywhere else, glorify the Holy Spirit by praising what has been accomplished in her? If Mary's life is a first fruit of an anticipatory abiding action of the Holy Spirit in the Church, in contrast to the temporary activity of the Spirit of the Lord in prophetic utterance in the Old Testament, this might help to explain to Protestants the priority give to her in the Catholic Church. Perhaps the Scheme on the Church will make the relationship of the Holy Spirit to Mary clearer. But as the matter has stood in the past, here again, the human figure has appeared to eclipse the divine Person."

As we have just said, we also believe, on our part, that it is necessary to stress the absolute priority of the Holy Spirit, of the sanctifying Spirit, and then to show Mary as the sanctified *par excellence*, in an incomparable way, and as the humble woman whom the Holy Spirit overshadowed in an uniquely profound way.

In order to be seen as she really is, Mary must appear to us as a real creature privileged by the Spirit, as his most outstanding success, always as the result of the action of the Spirit, living under his inspiration and his dependence. It is in this perspective that we would like to think of her in order to situate her better in relation to the Spirit and to situate ourselves better, according to her example and in spiritual communion with her, in our own adherence to the Holy Spirit.

I. The Relation of the Holy Spirit and Mary in function of Herself

Let us consider, first of all, the fundamental relationship between the Holy Spirit and Mary which is at the very heart of the mystery of Incarnation. We wish to stay, as much as possible, in the domain of faith and not to enter into theological controversies on the aspects derived from this mystery. We would simply like to try to express the meaning of our Marian devotion such as it appears to us and such as we live it in the Roman Catholic tradition. During the course of the exposé it will be well to remember above all that my purpose is not to make any polemical argument but to bear witness. It is not easy to define the relation of the Holy Spirit and Mary by reason of the ineffable character of the action of the Holy Spirit in her: no human terms can grasp the mystery of the Incarnation.

A. The Holy Spirit will overshadow You

Holy Scripture relates how when Moses came to Mount Horeb he saw the angel of God revealed to him under the form of a flame of fire breaking forth from a bush. As he looked, he saw that although the bush was burning it was not being consumed, and he wished to approach nearer in order to examine the phenomenon; but God called to him from the centre of the bush and thus commanded him: "Do not come nearer; rather take the shoes from thy feet, thou are standing on holy ground."

Tradition has compared Mary to that bush, which, although on fire, was not destroyed. Having become a mother without ceasing to be a Virgin, she bore within her that flame of fire that is the living God, and the presence of the Spirit in Mary made her, as it were, a living sanctuary, a holy place, not to be approached save with infinite respect and after having stripped ourselves of ideas that are too human.

The biblical word which causes us to penetrate the mystery of the covenant between the Spirit and Mary is that of St Luke: "*The Holy Spirit will come upon you, and the power of the Most High will over-shadow you.*" (Luke 1,35).

At the hour of the Annunciation, in prelude to the Incarnation and the unique mediation of Christ, she is the connecting link between heaven and earth. One might say, the Holy Spirit is the love of God which comes to us, in its ultimate form, as the Messenger of the Father and of the Son. Mary is the most pure human love expressed in a creature, who is only a creature, and who is raised by the Spirit in His encounter with her.

Jesus Christ is the focus point of the covenant, the meeting of a double love, the divine one, the human one. Obviously, we stammer: we are at the heart of the mystery of the Incarnation. "The Holy Spirit will come upon thee, and the power of the most High will overshadow thee." To understand these words fully, we must consider them in a Biblical setting, with all the echoes they must have evoked in a Jewish girl brought up on the Old Testament.

For every believer in the Old Covenant, the Holy Spirit, the Spirit of the Lord, meant Jahweh, the Lord himself. He is the same Spirit, who as Isaiah proclaimed would rest upon Emmanuel and who came upon other chosen people in the Old Testament. "The power of the most High will overshadow thee". This overshadowing reminds us of the cloud which symbolized the veiled presence of God among the chosen people. We read in Exodus: "When all was done, a cloud covered the tabernacle, and it was filled with the brightness of the Lord's presence, nor could Moses enter the tabernacle ... so thick the cloud that spread all about it, so radiant was the Lord's majesty; all was wrapped in cloud."

As we know, the glory of God means nothing else than God himself; it was in a cloud that that glory appeared to the Jews in the wilderness, as it was in a cloud that he spoke to Moses. That cloud is mentioned again in the account of the dedication of the Temple at Jerusalem: "So the ark that bears witness of the Lord's covenant was borne by the priest to the place designed for it ... And with that the whole of the Lord's House was wreathed in cloud, lost in that cloud, the priests could not wait upon the Lord with his accustomed service; his own glory was there, filling his own house."

And we recognize it once more in the account of the Transfiguration on Mount Tabor, where we read: "And even as he said it, a cloud formed, overshadowing them; they saw the others disappear into the cloud and were terrified. And a voice came from the cloud: 'This is my beloved Son; Listen then, to Him' ". Hence, she who was listening to the message must have realized that the same "glory of God" which had filled the tabernacle and the Temple was to rest upon her and in her. This was the proclamation of a mysterious feast of the dedication which would take place within her, as in a living temple.

That divine presence which of old had hovered over the tabernacle, and so filled it that Moses was unable to enter, and had subsequently dwelt in the Temple at Jerusalem or, more strictly speaking, in the most secret sanctuary of that Temple—the Holy of Holies—that presence which was finally to consecrate the symbolical temple of the Messianic era, the angel Gabriel tells her is to become, as it were, present in her virgin womb, and to transform her into a living Holy of Holies. That divine presence which from her childhood she had been taught to venerate in one single spot on earth, there, whither only the High Priest might enter and then only once a year, upon the great Day of Atonement, she learns from the angel, she is now to adore within herself.

B. Be it done unto me according to your word

Whereas we see the Holy Spirit descend upon her, it is necessary to understand that the Holy Spirit is at work in the very heart of Mary's response. Her "fiat" rises from the depth of her liberty, but this supremely free response is itself the work of divine grace. The free and active co-operation of Mary is wholly nourished with, and steeped in, the Love which effects in her "the will and the deed". She remains completely receptive to God's action in the very impulse of her freely consenting liberty. It is not she who takes the initiative: it is God who raises her towards Himself, it is God who gives her the unheard of grace of this complete gift of herself. Maurice Zundel's beautiful verse about God's generosity is fulfilled in her to an infinitely greater degree than in any of us:

What He gives He gives truly,
What He demands He gives again,
What He receives He gives twice.

Let us not fear to exaggerate her rôle at God's expense, as though it was not fitting that God, the first Cause, should associate His free creatures with His work, thus giving to secondary causes the power of collaboration in the divine plan, and of thus becoming better. God acts as God, as a God infinitely good, when He makes us sharers of His power, and capable of good. Thus He creates freedom in us and His grace gives us in depth our freedom.

Yet it is surely to God's glory that He should call His creature to His service and give him part in His overflowing generosity, that God in His absolute independence might consent to be dependent. Is this a reversal of values? Is it inconceivable that God, by the archangel Gabriel, should require Mary's consent? Is it beneath Him to await her answer? Is it not rather an example of matchless delicacy?

Never did a creature receive more decisive magnificent or triumphant a grace than Mary. Yet never did human freedom remain more inviolate. The angel bowed before Mary as a sign of God's respect for her. Mary bowed low before Gabriel's message, and her whole being trembled in veneration for God. This fiat, a masterpiece of divine grace and human liberty, a mystery of prevenient grace, which surrendered Mary to the will of God is, for reasons never to be equalled, "the finest transport of an unfettered love".

This collaboration in Mary's faith harmonizes perfectly with the initiative of the Holy Spirit. In the witness of the New Testament, it is at the source of faith (*2 Corinthians* 4,13; *1 Corinthians* 2,10–14; *Ephesians* 3,16–17; *John* 3,4–12; *1 John* 5,5–8); besides, in the Old Testament, it is also that which kept alive the faithful expectation of the people by prophetic word. Thus there is no opposition, but on the contrary, a reciprocal implication between the action of the Holy Spirit and the faith of Mary which is totally the fruit of his action while remaining a completely human and free act. It is there that the general dialectic of grace and faith is found. Moreover, as Catholic theology affirms, Mary's faith and its consequences in the history of salvation can only be a grace merited by Christ and communicated in the Spirit.

II. Relation of the Holy Spirit and Mary in function of us

The union of the Holy Spirit and Mary, which the Holy Scripture reveals to us, may not be seen only from the outside as if it involved only Mary. We have to seize all the dimensions.

A. This union of the Holy Spirit and Mary concerns us all

With every fibre of her being, she is the *fiat mihi secundum verbum tuum* that her lips pronounced. That is her only desire: to be utterly at the disposal of the Holy Spirit, acquiescent to His Will wholeheartedly collaborating and corresponding with His work. Ungrudgingly she gives herself up to the Holy Spirit.

But by the same impulse she gives us up with herself to the action of God. For it is not in her personal name only that Mary has answered. St Thomas tells us that her assent was given "loco totius humanae naturae", in the name of the whole human race. In her Amen resound all the amens which will rise from earth into heaven. At this unique moment mankind welcomes in Mary its Saviour and accepts the offered Union.

B. This union lasts for ever

From what has been said, we can reflect now on the place and the part of Mary in the history of salvation. She is the one who, in faith, eminently accepts the coming of the Messiah by entering the service of his coming as the one who will be the mother of the Messiah. By doing this she summarizes in herself the whole expectation and the hopeful faith of the Old Testament. She is above all others the one who, in the community of those saved by the power of the Holy Spirit in the faith of our Lord Jesus, links the Old to the New Testament. Of course, this link is performed in the proper meaning of the word, in the person of Jesus of Nazareth himself. This initiative, here as always, comes from Christ; but it is in the logic of the divine plans to involve the faith of men in the history of salvation and it is there that Mary, as the mother of the Saviour, plays a part obviously unique.

The human nature of Jesus of Nazareth has come to us through Her, by Her faith, and in this way, the salvation performed in the history of this human nature comes also to us by Her, as a result of the action of the Holy Spirit in herself.

There is not only at the outset a dependence of God in relation to Mary, established in complete independence, but Jesus himself has wanted to emphasize it during his life. By free choice, Jesus will live in complete dependence on his mother first during nine months, afterwards he will be obedient to Her during thirty years. These facts in themselves are worth volumes and may not be discounted by reference to texts which are difficult to interpret. We have only to read the Gospel. It is in proximity with her that the Holy Spirit will sanctify the forerunner and Elisabeth will be filled with graces. It is through Her that the shepherds and the kings will discover the Messiah. It is from Her that Simeon and Ann will welcome the One who was desired by the nations. It is by Her prayer that the first miracle will be accomplished in Cana. It is thanks to Her that humanity at the foot of the cross confirms the redeeming sacrifice that Jesus has accomplished with the collaboration of the Spirit. It is in union with Her that the Holy Spirit is transmitted to the apostles and that the Church is born on the morning of Pentecost.

How could we believe that this mysterious union does not yet last today? The conclusive events of the history of salvation may not be considered as simply past. It is obvious for the human nature of the Lord himself: is it not the meaning of the affirmation of the kerygma of the Resurrection that the Lord, by his human nature, remains present to His Church through the action of the Spirit to be the source of every grace? It is through the human nature of Jesus of Nazareth that God still today grants us every grace by the Spirit.

By virtue of this identity of the Jesus of faith with the Jesus of history, by taking thus the affirmation of the Incarnation seriously, we may say that Mary remains the "Mother of the Saviour" or the Mother of the Incarnate Word, according to the affirmation of Ephesus. The graces we receive today, since they come to us through the human nature of her Son, continue to involve her original fiat under the influence of the Holy Spirit. But as any personal reality, this original *fiat* may not be considered as simply past: the faith of Mary has not remained at this original acceptance, it has developed in faith in spite of the Cross, in the faith in the Resurrection, till it lights up in the Vision, till the Lord comes back at the end of time. Our relation to the original fiat of Mary therefore involves, it seems to me, not only a relation to an event in the past but also to a personal actual reality. To receive grace in the Holy Spirit through the mediation of the human nature of Christ, is not only to be in relation with the past fiat of Mary, but, in consequence, to be today in relation with her, as she is filled with the Holy Spirit in glory and entirely turned towards the Father by her Son. Is it not the meaning of the "communion of saints" to assert that, if the human nature of Christ remains the source of every grace, the history of salvation is never simply past, and that, in consequence, we are in relation with the faith,—today developed into the Vision—of all those who have there played a part?

We may not isolate Mary in the communion of the saints. If we believe in the triumphant Church, we believe that the saints live in Christ, in intercommunion among them and with us. There is exchange, sharing, reciprocity: each will play a part in proportion to his vocation, to his election. Mary, mother of Christ, cannot "not play" a unique part in this communion which unites the redeemed round the throne of the Lamb. She remains for ever the one who has received the Word of God and has integrated Him in the human race. She remains for ever the one who made the link, the one who adheres to the Spirit, the one who has lived in her soul and in her body, the communion with the Spirit.

It is there that for us this spiritual step takes root which so many saints have if not described, at least lived and that we call to share the mind of Mary, to join ourselves to her to receive in a better way the Holy Spirit. Her actual part is not situated in the line of the communication of graces; it is the Holy Spirit who is and remains the messenger of the Father through the Son. She is not in the line of mediation conceived that way. But she is situated in the line of our answer. In union with her, and following her example, Mary helps us to receive the Spirit and to live under his dependence. She invites us by her existence in advanced glorified, to progress in joy and with confidence. The Council has said about Mary that she is the sign of confidence for the people of God on the way.

C. This union is entirely Christocentric

This union of the Holy Spirit and of Mary *is directed only to one finality*, it has only one purpose: *to join us more intimately to Christ himself*.

That the mission of the Spirit is such, who would doubt about that? He comes to us as the living Promise of the Son, to extend and finish his task. Christ has merited everything for us by his passion which has saved the world; but he has applied everything to us by the Spirit. The Spirit's mission is above all Christocentric. It is the same, at her level and through the grace itself of the Spirit in her, with Mary. Mary is inseparable from her Son. With all her being she reaches out to Him. All devotion to Mary leads to Jesus, as a river flows into the sea. Mary's sole and constant thought is contained in the words she spoke to the servants at Cana: "Whatsoever He shall say unto you, do ye". She has no other message. She is not only Christocentric, she is the foremost Christian.

Moreover it is important to understand that this Spirit, who fills her, is and remains always the Spirit of Her Son. He is the one who "christianizes" Mary at a degree which we can not even perceive. She is the Christian woman above all, the "Christified" by superabundance. In her the Holy Spirit realises his masterpiece. She is his achievement and his splendour. "Woman! above all women glorified, Our tainted nature's solitary boast ..." (Wordsworth). Mary, the creature closest to God, belongs more than anyone else to Christ—*nos autem Christi*—to an unfathomable degree. She is entire submission to Him, a clear transparency. "*Riguardo ormai nella faccia ch'a Cristo più s'assomiglia: che la sua chiarezza sola ti può disporre a veder Cristo*". "Behold now", sang Dante, "the face most like Christ's because its brightness alone can prepare you to see Christ".

Why is it that our fellow-Christians so often persist in thinking of her as a barrier? The more a soul belongs to God, the closer is it united to God. The more a soul is united to God, the more it unites other souls to Him. Our reservations and diffidence in loving Mary fully for fear of showing insufficient reverence to our Lord, prove our fundamental misunderstanding of what she is. "It is the rôle of the Blessed Virgin to lead us surely to Jesus Christ, just as it is the rôle of Jesus Christ to lead us surely to the eternal Father", wrote St Louis-Marie de Montfort.

Here we are at the heart of the mystery of God; it upsets all our narrow systems, our timid calculations and wrecks our neatly-made divisions and compartments; we enter a world of mutual sincerity, of absolute disinterestedness and of luminous communion.

This is the domain of the Mother of God. That is why St Pius X was able to write: "There is no more certain or quicker way to unite men to Jesus Christ than Mary, and to obtain through Jesus Christ that perfect adoption of sons which makes us holy and without stain before God ... No one in the world has known Jesus as she has, no one is a better master or better guide to the knowledge of Jesus. It follows from this ... that in uniting men to Jesus no one is of greater value than she."

In proportion as our union with Mary increases, not only will she put into our hearts the dispositions which she has taken from Jesus, but she will give us her own heart with which to love Him. This is her only thought and her only purpose. To give Jesus to every soul and to the whole world is still the only ambition of this incomparable mother. Let us unite ourselves with her: her limitless love for Jesus will become ours. We shall thus reach a transformation of the soul, an identification with Christ, which will make us think, feel, act and will as He does. Then, and only then, will Mary's task be completed when she can say (with greater justice than St Paul): "My little children of whom I am in labour again, until Christ be formed in you." (*Galatians* 4,19). That labour will be no other than our birth into heaven.

NOTES

[1] Mrs Elie Gibson, *Mary and the Protestant Mind*, in *Review for Religious*, Vol. 24, no. 3, May 1965.

[2] Cfr. R. Laurentin, in *Nouvelle Revue Théologique, Esprit Saint et théologie mariale*, p. 26–27, January 1967, T. 89 *(New Theological Review, The Holy Spirit and Marian Theology)*.

The Holy Spirit and Mary

RT. REV. ALAN CLARK, D.D.

In offering you my reflections on a theme of such grandeur, I would begin by reminding you of the prayer of Erasmus, the friend of St Thomas More, acknowledged by all as one of the greatest figures of his time. A man of deep piety, he composed this prayer while visiting the Shrine of Our Lady at Walsingham:

> "May your Son grant that in the imitation of your own holiness, we may also be made capable by the grace of the Holy Spirit of conceiving the Lord Jesus in the depths of our souls; and that once conceived, we may never lose him".

This is our prayer, too, and its theological and doctrinal roots are the source of my own meditation on the mystery which, from the moment of her conception, embraced the person of Mary, the mystery of the work of the Holy Spirit.

But first let me plan out the scene in which the emerging doctrine will find its clearest and most satisfying development. I take as my starting point the startling and vivid statement of St Athanasius:

> "The Word took flesh in order that we could receive the Holy Spirit."

The second coming of God into the world, in the Person of the Holy Spirit, is the reason for the first coming, in the Person of the Son, Jesus Christ of Nazareth. For God has come twice, not once, and all attempts to penetrate the meaning of the historical events, recorded in the Gospels, which reveal God's purposes in His comings, will find unnecessary restraint if the perspective of Athanasius is not firmly maintained. This perspective will influence our consideration of Mary and her relationships which form the material of our various doctrinal affirmations concerning her person and her work within the salvific plan of God. In fact, if we are to be led into the vision of the totality of the Revelation of God in Christ, we need to people the stage of our mind with five '*personae*': God, Christ, the Spirit, Mary and the Church. To study part of one of the actors in the drama, or even two, without remembering the interlocking parts of the others, risks distorting the whole. At the same time, method requires a certain humility, and in developing the precise theme of today's subject the risk has to be prudently taken of isolating two of the figures in the drama of God's love for His creatures – creatures whom He has made His sons and daughters by the gift of the Holy Spirit.

A second restriction must also be accepted – that the theme is too big, the horizons too wide, to be encompassed in so short a lecture.

Certain positions, however, must be explored in order that you, in prayer and meditation, can enter into the joy of the total vision. Of these, naturally, the first must concern the Holy Spirit. How do we understand the Creator God, the Advocate, the Sanctifier to whom this age belongs? How does He enter into the work of Jesus who is Lord and Christ? How does He overshadow both Son and Mother? How did the Church come to "isolate" His Person within the Triune God revealed to us in Christ? No, this is not a list of questions finding answers (a theological enterprise outside my scope and beyond my competence) but rather searchings into the Christian experience which the Creeds and particularly the Eastern Tradition have voiced in vigorous affirmations and hymned in majestic poetry.

The second area of our search for understanding concerns Mary as the one whom the Holy Spirit sanctified. The contention must be stringently upheld that this work of the Spirit was progressive – a process of growth and development in the heart and mind of Mary herself – a series of santifications. Like her Son, Mary had to grow in wisdom and grace. Given her total humanity, it could not be otherwise.

The conclusion of the paper will be like an unfinished painting, unfinished because here – in the environment of the Holy Spirit – more than anywhere else, we see as in a glass, darkly, in faith, in undiminished hope, and in the longings of charity. Christian attitudes outstrip their theological expression. No single person can execute with competent artistry the scene before our present eyes, in this last quarter of the twentieth century, where Mary is gathering together her sons and daughters who have, with typical stupidity, gone wandering off and are really trying to find enough courage to come home. Here, within the Ecumenical Society, we all experience her loving but stringent guidance.

1. Who is the Holy Spirit?

It is important to remember from the very beginning of our searchings that the understanding of the Holy Spirit as a *Person*, as someone distinct though fully God, is a comparatively late development. Not until the fourth century was a certain clarity achieved in the Church's articulation of the extensive doctrine concerning the Spirit which forms so much of the New Testament writing. It was as though a considerable length of time was needed for Christians to voice their convictions that in order to speak of God, they had to speak in a three-fold way which nevertheless would not attack the substantial unity of the Godhead while disclosing the distinction of the Persons. Augustine, for example, had little liking for the term 'person' but accepted it as the only alternative to a dangerous silence. The experience of the presence of the Holy Spirit was too strong, too undeniable to be left unspoken, unformulated. As Professor Maurice Wiles notes so well: "the emergence of the Holy Spirit was grounded in the early Church's experience of the transforming power over human life that they (the early Christians) discovered in their fellowship, in the name of Jesus, their risen Lord". [*Christian Believing*, SPCK 1976, Pg. 129]

But this experience, however new, however overwhelming in its intensity, is not discontinuous with the developing awareness of the Spirit in both the Old and, of course, the New Testaments. For our purposes some limited information is necessary but it is strictly limited. The Hebrews understood the 'spirit' as a *material* reality, as the privileged environment in which God in His power meets man in his feebleness. The 'spirit' is an environment and of this world, never a divinity even though given to God's elect. It is the source of life on earth, renewing the life of the man of flesh in his material world. It is the spirit of renewal, transforming Samuel, Saul, the kings, the prophets. Elisha has a double spirit, Ezechiel sees into a realm of the spirit which creates the totally new. The spirit is a vital force, like the wind, like the air breathed by man, energising the puny resources of human nature. In the prophets the vehicle of the spirit is the word, the communication of God in power and proclamation. Indeed, by the time we enter the New Testament period there is a vivid awareness of the action of the Spirit as a universal, life-giving, *salvific* intervention.

But in the New Testament writings themselves we encounter "the new" with such intensity that the prehistory of the Spirit needs the reminders of the Gospel writers for us to perceive the continuity with the earlier Testament. The word "Spirit" (*Pneuma*) occurs three hundred and seventy-five times in the New Testament. It is no exaggeration to say that the New Testament is dominated by the Spirit. The world, with His coming, is possessed by the Spirit, and the Christian family becomes a "possessed people". The analogy of "wind" almost completely disappears in the face of an emerging understanding of the mystery of the new creation (Pauline) and the mystery of man's re-birth (Johannine). God's transforming power, released by the victory of Christ and His vindication before the Father, is no material force, but a new environment engulfing the whole of creation but finding its area of entrance in the heart and mind of man. Light and love are its dominant characteristics. This power attacks the constituents of human life, bruising the spirit of man in the ground of his human existence, searching out inmost thoughts and the unspoken strivings of love. It is in this apex of the human spirit that the Pneuma of God operates with transcendent force.

But who is the first to receive the Spirit? It is Jesus. He is the first Recipient of the Spirit. So totally possessed does He become that at the end of His earthly life, His glorified Body constitutes the unquenchable source of the Spirit for the Apostles, for the Church, for the world. It is – *O magnum mysterium!* – in the Eucharist, therefore, that we, the disciples, the brethren, become membered to the fully Spirit-possessing Body of Jesus Christ, the Son of God, and the communication of the

Spirit is actualised in us according to our differing capacities. Where there is the Spirit, there is Jesus; where there is Jesus, there is the Spirit. He who on earth lived, at the human level, according to His own spirit, became in the Resurrection "the Spirit". From that time onwards He is pulsating with the overflowing and life-giving power of the Divine Spirit, for "now the Lord is the Spirit" (*II Corinthians 3:17*). So totally is the glorified Christ filled with the reality of the Spirit that, according to Paul, we can say with equal justification "a man is in Christ" or "a man is in the Spirit". By this second coming of God, we, in Christ, are likewise totally possessed. Christ comes from "without" to "within" because He is now conjoined with the Spirit. The Church becomes the Temple of the Holy Spirit.

This vision, however meagrely expressed, is breath-taking. So let us look on Jesus, beginning with that historical fact of infinite simplicity – that Our Lord was conceived by the Holy Spirit and that Mary herself is the one who received the Holy Spirit in order to conceive Him. The human flesh of mother and son are sanctified in growth and in potential by the overshadowing – the Shekinah – of God the Spirit. Till his baptism by John, the son grows in the Spirit with his mother, but the baptism isolates him for his mission. "When he was at *prayer*, after he had been baptised, the Holy Spirit descended upon him" – and *then* the Father reveals His son to the world. "You are my beloved Son" (*Luke* 3:21), and Jesus is thus consecrated for his mission. In the next chapter (4:1), "filled with the Holy Spirit he … was led by the same Spirit through the wilderness" (the unregenerate world? *Mark*). The Sanctifier has now found a lodging of permanence and power – it is He, in Jesus, who already governs, inspires, controls: so our Divine Saviour can declare in the synagogue of Nazareth: "the Spirit of the Lord has been given to me, for he has anointed me". From now on, in the power of the Spirit, he faces Jerusalem where God has ordained that He will re-make His creation in the person of the crucified but risen Lord.

Is there a conclusion for us to draw here that is pertinent to our overall theme? I have said earlier that the Holy Spirit is our environment. I would wish to go a step further and say that He is our *environer,* the one who creates and energizes the totality of our human environment, particularly by the effusion of His gifts within the Body of Christ. For now it is in Him, with Him, for Him that we, even as Jesus, have our being.

And so, almost abruptly, we turn to Mary – for from her conception to her consummation not only did she live in the environment of the Holy Spirit but He "environed" her breath and life so that she lived "in the Spirit" from whom she cannot be sundered.

2. The Progressive Sanctification of Mary by the Holy Spirit

Not a few people are surpised to learn that in John as well as in Luke we encounter a theology of Mary. It is not, however, my purpose to develop this at this particular moment (even were I competent), but I wish to indicate that, without neglecting the data of Matthew, it is from these two sources that there emerges, in outline, the result we are seeking – the relationship between Mary and the Holy Spirit.

It is perhaps best to begin with certain affirmations that will control the theme in its development. The first is that the moment of Mary's conception marks the beginning of her growth in holiness, not the end. Whether one speaks of her santification at birth or, in the less happy Latin expression, her immaculate conception, it is the same reality which Tradition affirms. This sanctification finds its consummation at Pentecost when she is utterly possessed by the Holy Spirit. The history intervening between these two events is a history at one with ours, for Mary, though the highest honour of our race, treads the same human path as the brethren of her Son, even though her steps are sinless.

But if we are to seize what is unique in Mary, then we must reflect on the spiritual force which structured her life interruptedly from the *fiat* of the Annunciation to the second *fiat* at the foot of the Cross. The strength of Mary is nothing other than the enduring power of virginal love, a love which gives her what the Greek Tradition has called her "parresia", her audacity of spirit. It is in the light of this affirmation that I now turn to a Gospel survey which discloses the intimate relationship of God the Holy Spirit to this privileged daughter of Sion who, alongside her crucified Son, becomes the first member of the new community of God which came to birth as our Redeemer died.

The Annunciation signals the meeting of God with His people in a completely new and unimagined encounter. The virginal conception is not only fact but symbolic of the uniqueness of God's action in the incarnation of His Son, Our Lord Jesus Christ, through the overshadowing of Mary by the Holy Spirit. The message given is a message of peace, the communication of new life, the breath of the Holy Spirit. "Behold, I make all things new" – hence Mary is indeed *kecharitomene*, the highly favoured one by reason of the grace given her, a grace utterly unique, a matter for overwhelming joy.

Mary's sanctification from the womb had not only created the space for this action of the Holy Spirit but given her the unique faith which could invoke a response of a kind no creature had yet made to God. Her *fiat* is no humble submission to God's will – or, rather, it is so much more than that. It is a reaching-out in unconditional acceptance to the vocation and summons by God: "O that this may be done to me." At last, in her, the expectation is fulfilled. "My being" she sings, "proclaims the greatness of the Lord, because my body contains the greatness of the Lord, and my spirit finds joy in God my Saviour".

The conception of Christ in her virginal womb is the second moment of Mary's sanctification by the Holy Spirit. Elizabeth, in her turn, is unable to contain her joy and, by the releasing power of the Spirit, welcomes her cousin as the Mother of her Lord. Simeon, prompted by the same Holy Spirit, prophesies not only the joy but the pain of her vocation. And, all the time, Mary grows in faith and fidelity, beginning to understand.

But a strange feature characterises the Gospel record once we leave the infancy narrative. Mary becomes elusive, going just out of focus as we begin to contemplate her. But deeper reflection yields an awareness of her growth in the Holy Spirit, sometimes in a sudden acceleration of interior knowledge. The story of the loss of Jesus, for example, in his Father's "house" in Jerusalem reveals a perplexed and sorrowing parent who, over a period of twelve years, has brought up in the fear of the Lord an exceptional son – but in a very normal scene and background. In a way Mary seems unprepared for the new knowledge that her son's response to her anxious chiding brings to her – she is left pondering in her heart. Who is this child of hers who now declares God to be His Father? From now on, it is right to think, there is a subtle reversal of roles, as over the next eighteen years or so Jesus learns to be a man, the man Jesus who will save his people from their sins. For from adolescent he must become full-grown man, like us in all things but sin. And the harsh lesson his mother is learning is that there will be a moment when she must let him go, not grudgingly but with pure and selfless generosity. If her son is sensitive as no other man has ever been sensitive, then he learnt that sensitivity from his mother. For, clearly, she "sends" him on his way and supports him from the shadows, undemanding, perhaps at times uncomprehending.

And now another scene. Cana in Galilee. Clearly, because of the language he uses, John wishes us to relate this scene to the culminating scene on the hill of Calvary. On every other occasion the evangelist speaks of "the mother of Jesus" – but here, as on Calvary, her Son is made to address her as "Woman". In John's theology this is an unequivocal statement that the role of Mary is greater than the limitations of flesh and blood, that she is within the world of the Spirit of the Incarnation, the Holy Spirit, and that she has meaning and relevance in this new creation over and above the limited *fiat* of the Annunciation. "The hour" of Christ's suffering and death has not yet come when the wonderful works of God will be manifest. Yet at the instance of his mother Jesus works the first of his signs – at Cana in Galilee. A point for us, in our turn, to ponder over.

Calvary is now within the perspective of Jesus as he pursues his mission of preaching and healing. But before that eventful "hour", there is the record of an incident that discloses yet more profoundly the interlocking of the unique mission of the son and the vocation of the mother. "Blessed is the womb that bore you, and the breasts that you sucked", cries that lovely anonymous woman of the crowd. And the response of Jesus? Not a disavowal, surely, but an affirmation of the deeper blessedness of Mary who, in the words of Tradition, first conceived in her heart before she conceived in her body. "Yes", says Our

Lord, "yes, she is blessed more than you think: she is blessed because she believes". All those who learn to believe will be with her now and for ever. For – to move quickly to the culmination – "Woman, here is your son." The wonder is that Mary does not then take John to herself. It is John who takes Mary to himself. Jesus looked on Mary, his mother, but his gaze rests on John, his brother. The new family of God is constituted on Calvary.

What began with the great response of faith at the Annunciation comes now to its climactic point as Mary gives her second *fiat* to the Divine will, accepting that her Son should die for us and so form for his Father a new people. Her suffering here is in sharp contrast to her joy at Bethlehem but both are held together in unity by that audacity of spirit whereby she embraces, even in the moment of her greatest agony, the will of the Father. Unlike Peter, she made no boasts. She is not reported as saying that, whatever happened, she would never desert her Son: she just *is* there – on Calvary – so that she can always be with those who hear the word of God and keep it. Not only with the successful but with the failures who crowded in fear into the Upper Room until the Holy Spirit, in fire and wind, transformed the infant Church into true disciples of their living and risen Lord – and Mary is in their midst. God has come a second time – and Mary is there even as she was at Nazareth for his first coming. The finale opens on the drama of God and man as Jesus and the Spirit, ineffably distinct but ineffably united, make their home, in the words of God, in every heart. The Church is born and the sinless Mother of Jesus is there at its birth. She will be here, in the Church, waiting with us for that other Second Coming when her Son will present his kingdom to the Father and God will be all in all.

. . . .

The *personae* have made their appearance. The work of the Holy Spirit in Mary has revealed a God of surprises whose categories of action are in so many respects totally dissimilar to ours. He works in the lowly, the poor, the sick. What does become patent and lucid to even our fumbling perception is that all five *personae* are interlocked within the drama of God and man: God, Christ, the Holy Spirit, Mary, the Church. The Christian thinker cancels the "performance" of any one part at the peril of ruining the understanding of the whole. This is so very important to grasp, for not only did Christ found the Church but, in the Holy Spirit, He continues to found it – and this divine action "explains", if that is the right word, the persistence of the movement towards Christian unity which suffers shock and check but continues its uneven path towards the merciful gift of God, demonstrating its vitality by the communion "not of this world" that is daily given us in joy and in pain.

In an attempt to bring together the multiple threads of the theme of this paper, I would like to return to St Augustine. The year is almost certainly 411, and the date may well be the 18th March. It is Holy Week when the ceremony of the *redditio*, the giving back of the Creed to the Master, is taking place. The catechumens have been called to repeat their lines to prove their knowledge of the faith into which they are to be baptised. Then the great African bishop speaks to them:

> "We believe in Jesus Christ our Lord, born through the Holy Spirit of the Virgin Mary. Yes, she is blessed, this Mary who engendered in faith, who conceived in faith. As a Son had been promised to her, she asked how this could be since she did not know man. She knew of only one way of knowing man and conceiving new life, not from experience but as it had been explained to her by other women with whom she conversed. She understood that a child needs both man and woman in order to be born. And in her perplexity she receives this answer from the Angel: 'The Holy Spirit will come upon you and the power of the Most High will cover you with his shadow. That is why he who will be born of you will be called Son of God'. To this word of the angel Mary brought full faith, responding in her spirit before conceiving in her womb; 'Behold the handmaid of the Lord.' 'Let it be done', she says, 'this conception without the seed of man in me, the virgin.' Mary conceived, and what she believed came to pass in her. Let us believe in order that what was done may be a reality for us also."

From God's point of view there is only one scene, the coming of the Son to man in the power of the Holy Spirit, but because of our human limitations and our insertion in human history we need to consider its different moments: the scene of Cana, the scene of the woman crying out from the crowd, the great mystery of Calvary, of Pentecost and the more hidden mystery of the Assumption of Mary, Mother of God. But these separate scenes find their unity in Christ, the Lord who is risen, operating in the Spirit to the glory of his Father and to the eternal happiness of the brethren – continuing to gather together those whom this infinitely loving Father has given him. There are no limits to the gifts he will give them, gifts of the Spirit. In a true sense it is the Spirit who administers this divine generosity, but Tradition affirms unambiguously that within that operation the Mother of Jesus, the one who prays, has her particular part to play.

The mystery of the Spirit's operation in the world is the externalising of the mission of the Spirit within the being of God. It is the follow-through to men of that divine operation, constitutive of His own Person, whereby He unites in love the Father and the Son. At our own level of earth and sky He, the Spirit, unites to the Word and brings us into the ambit of the Trinity. Within that great movement there is the first-born of the Church: Mary.

It is at this point that we need to proceed with great humility lest in expressing this mystery we misrepresent what is a vision of faith. Mary is not the centre of Christian living and dying but she is *found* at the centre and leads us *to* the centre. It is the Holy Spirit who transforms us into the body of Christ, but she is integral to that Body. We need to recall our re-birth, to remember ruefully that our natural origins are "dated" and out of fashion. "You are not in the flesh," says Paul, "you are in the spirit (with a small 's') since the Spirit (with a capital 'S') is within you, if anyone does not have the Spirit of Christ, He does not belong to Christ".

This belonging, this membering to Christ is the transforming action of the Spirit, and who most membered to Christ but Mary? That is why she is found at the centre and points to the centre. And, in turn, it is Christ who is most membered to Mary. Yet he, as we have seen, forsook the physical tie that bound him to his Mother in order to be united to her at the profounder richer level of faith and fidelity to the Word received from the Father. We, too, are called to shake off our material attachments in order to rise to that area of re-birth in which the Spirit, who broods over the universe, dynamically fashions and moulds us into the image – of Christ – in which we were created, for which we were predestined.

We stand, then, within the dynamic, creative action of the Spirit. We know His presence, we act in His power. In this we are only pursuing the path of Mary for whom lowliness was her prized possession. To say more is a way to confusion and misunderstanding, and it is from St Ildefonsus of Toledo (†667), that great lover of Mary, that one turns for help in order to bring to its conclusion and reduce to some order these lowly thoughts on Mary, Mother of God and Mother of the brethren of the Lord:

> I beg you, oh, I beg you holy Virgin,
> that I may have Jesus from that Spirit
> through whom you bore Jesus.
> Through that Spirit may my soul receive Jesus
> through whom your flesh conceived the very same Jesus.
> By that Spirit let me know Jesus
> whereby you yourself were given to know,
> to have in your care,
> and to give birth to Jesus.
> In that Spirit let me in my lowliness
> speak wonderful things of Jesus,
> for in that Spirit you confessed yourself
> to be the handmaid of the Lord,
> desiring it should be done to you
> according to the words of the angel.
> In that Spirit may I love Jesus
> whom you, from now on,
> adore as Lord but gaze on as Son.

May Mary unite us in our fumbling search – for in understanding her, we will understand ourselves. And knowing and loving one another, through her unremitting care, we will be "confident for unity". The significance of today's festival and particularly of our shared meditation and prayer is not just that it is happening but that our coming together to think on her who is "full of grace" was a necessity. The love of the Church begets a love of Mary which is always new. She stands in her loveliness among those "strange blessings never in Paradise" of which Edwin Muir speaks. I make my own the beautiful words of Field-Marshall Lord Wavell:

"Your red-gold hair, your slowly smiling face,
Your pride in your dear son, your King of Kings,
Fruits of the kindly earth, and truth and grace,
Colour and light, and all warm lovely things –
For all that loveliness, that warmth, that light,
Blessed Madonna, I go back to fight."

(The Madonna of the Cherries)

IV
DOCTRINAL

This section deals with the great doctrines concerning the Blessed Virgin; that she is Theotokos/Deipara/God-Bearer; that she was conceived without sin by the foreordination of her Son's redeeming work; that she was assumed into heaven before all other redeemed creatures, in view of her sinlessness, so that she has become Queen of Heaven.

The first address was given to the Society on 9 January 1968, by the Professor of Historical Theology in the University of London (King's College). He was at the time Dean of the Faculty of Theology. He was contributing editor of *The Mother of God* (1949), and *The Blessed Virgin Mary* (1963).

The second paper was delivered to the Society at a one-day conference at the Convent of the Handmaids of the Sacred Heart, Regent's Park, London, on 7 October 1978, by the Lady Margaret Professor of Divinity in the University of Oxford. He had shortly before written *Christian Unity and Christian Diversity* (1975).

The third paper was given to the Society at a one-day conference at the Convent of the Handmaids of the Sacred Heart, Regent's Park, London, on 6 October 1976, by the then Chaplain of Lincoln College, Oxford.

The fourth address to the Society was originally given as a sermon preached in the University Church of St Mary the Virgin, Oxford, and was subsequently printed in the Jesuit journal, *The Month*, July 1971. The author has been first Senior Tutor and then Master of Campion Hall, and has since been chairman of the examining board of the theology faculty at Oxford. He is Associate General Secretary of the Society.

The Mother of God

REV. DR. ERIC L. MASCALL, D.D., F.B.A.

One of the things which I am sure we are agreed upon in this Society is the importance of devotion to our Lady being based upon sound theology. It is because the title 'Mother of God' is the most theological of our Lady's titles, that when I was asked to address the Society I asked if I might take that as the title of my address. The term 'Mother of God' is a translation of the Greek word 'Theotokos', which began to be applied to the Blessed Virgin round about the middle of the third century and was adopted officially, and made the object of the dogmatic statement, by the Council of Ephesus, the third Ecumenical Council, in the year 431. We shall come back to the Council of Ephesus a little later on. This word 'Theotokos' is a compound of two Greek words: the noun *Theos*, which means 'God', and the verb *tikto*, meaning 'to give birth' or to bear'—in one of the senses of the word 'bear' ('Bear' of course is rather ambiguous, meaning either 'to give birth' or 'to carry', and that in fact is one of the things which makes it difficult to find a really Biblical translation of the word 'theotokos'.) The word 'Theotokos' was applied to the Blessed Virgin because it was she who gave birth—gave human birth—to God himself, to God the Son, to him who is God from God, true God from true God, as the Creed says.

The word 'Theotokos' is the common word for the Blessed Virgin among Greeks, and the corresponding words in different languages are the ordinary words for her in other parts of the Eastern Church. The Slavonic word *Bogoroditsa*, for example, is the precise equivalent of 'Theotokos'. When one tries to translate it into Latin, one can do it by the word 'Deipara'—again a literal translation—and one does find this word used. But usually in Latin the words used are 'Mater Dei', which is 'Mother of God', or 'Genitrix Dei', the giver-of-birth of God. Sometimes people make an unnecessary fuss about this, and they try to find some peculiar theological point in the fact that whereas the Eastern Church talk about 'Theotokos', the Latin Church normally talks about 'Mater Dei'; this has sometimes been made use of in an attempt to disparage the attitude to our Lady of the Western Church, But, as a matter of fact, this is entirely pointless. You will find the exact equivalent of 'Mater Dei' in Greek in the Words *Meter Theou*, Mother of God—the same words as 'Mater Dei'—and in fact if you look at any Greek icon, any Russian icon also, of our Lady, you will find that there are on either side of her head the initials, on one side, *MR* and, on the other side, *THU*—'Mother of God.' So there is certainly no significant difference between East and West on this particular point.

When one tries to find an English equivalent of the word 'Theotokos', it becomes a little difficult. We think of all the various possibilities: 'God-bearer' would seem to be possible, but, as I said, the word 'bear' has an ambiguous character in English; it can mean either 'to give birth' or 'to carry', and one certainly wants to say something more about the Blessed Virgin in relation to her Son than simply that she carried him. One could try, perhaps, at a more exact rendering if one could use the word 'God-mother', but of course the word 'godmother' in English has an entirely different sense: 'godmother' does not mean 'Mother of God.' Then if one tries to invent some phrase like 'the birth-giver of God' this is really very unnatural and awkward; we do not talk about 'birth-givers'; if you introduced somebody to your mother you do not say "May I introduce you to my birth-giver". The English word is 'mother', and in fact the quite obvious translation of 'Theotokos' is 'Mother of God'. It has been made absolutely plain by everybody who has used the term that it does *not* mean that the Blessed Virgin is the source of our Lord's Godhead. It means that she is the one who by the ordinary process of motherhood, while remaining a virgin, gave a complete human nature, body and soul, to him who before this happened was God, and, who, of course, remains God. He took human nature from her, therefore she is his mother, and because he who took human nature is God, she is the Mother of God. When one finds in the early dogmatic statements the word 'Theotokos', there is a really unnecessary but perhaps useful caveat put in, that this does not mean that she was the source of his Godhead, but simply that he to whom she gave birth was and remains for ever God.

All that is just about the word and its equivalents in different languages. I think it was well to say that at the beginning, to clear out of the way possible misunderstandings. As I said, the word first appeared round about the middle of the third century, but it was given a precise and dogmatic force by the Council of Ephesus in 431, the third Ecumenical Council. This was in connnection with the need for ruling out a certain heretical view about our Lord himself, the view which is called Nestorianism because it was believed to be held by a certain bishop called Nestorius. In the case of nearly all the ancient heresies, people have tried to show that the person the heresy was named after did not hold the heresy that was named after him, and a good many people in recent years have tried to prove that Nestorius was not in fact a Nestorian. This, of course, is of great importance to Nestorius, but is not of very great importance to us. What is important is not whether Nestorius himself held this view, but the fact that the Church condemned the view as a false and inadequate view about our Lord himself. The essence of this Nestorian doctrine was that it really made our Lord into two people, a human one and a divine one, although they were in very close association: "Two minds with but a single thought; two hearts that beat as one", is an excellent description of what Nestorianism meant. It was the doctrine that our Lord was simply a man in whom the second Person of the Blessed Trinity, God the Son, came and dwelt, and with whom God the Son formed an extremely close union, so close that in fact whatever was willed by the one was also willed by the other. But such a view really only makes our Lord different in degree, not in kind, from any very holy person, any person who in fact is living close to God and in whose life the grace of God is very fully operative. In fact one might say, that the Nestorian doctrine was not true about our Lord, but in fact it would have been true, or very nearly true, about his Mother. It was the doctrine that Jesus was a human being, a man, with whom the Person of God the Son had formed a very close union, but that it was not God the Son himself who was living the human life which we see described in the Gospels. In order to rule out this view, in order to make it plain that when we ask "Who is this that we read about in the Gospels?" the answer is that it is God living a human life and not just a man with whom God is very closely associated, The Church found that the word 'Theotokos', applied to our Lord's Mother, was just the word that was needed. She did not merely give birth to a man, not even a very holy man, not even a unique man, but she gave birth to God himself. God took of her a complete human nature and therefore she was and is the Mother of God, Theotokos. And so the Council of Ephesus decreed that 'if anyone should not confess that Emmanuel is truly God, and that as a consequence the holy Virgin is the Mother of God, for she brought forth in the flesh the Word of God made flesh, let him be anathema.' Now this, you see, was a definition about our Lord; it was only indirectly a definition about his mother. But it did in fact bring very much more clearly into view the precise function which she herself had, and exercised. If he had been only a very holy person with whom God formed a very close association, then presumably Mary would have been related to him in the same way that any other mother is related to her son and nothing more. There would have been nothing particularly unique about this. The important thing, the coming of God to dwell in Jesus, would have happened *after* she had fulfilled her function. But when it was fully realized and claimed that the Son of God, God the Son, took his human nature from *her*, then it was seen that she had an absolutely unique function above all other mothers and above all other human beings. There is not, never has been and never will be anybody else from whom God has taken human nature in order to live in it himself. There is only one Incarnation, and therefore there is only one Mother of the Incarnate.

Although the immediate purpose of the Council of Ephesus was to declare the truth about our Lord Jesus Christ, it indirectly emphasized the unique place in the whole work of redemption which was held by his Mother, and so it did in fact give a stimulus to a great development of Marian devotion, and not only devotion, but also theology. Now it is absolutely essential that the development of Mariology shall take place from the basic theological fact that she is the Mother of God. One must not develop Mariology by simply saying about Mary more and more elaborate, more and more emphatic, more and more exuberant things—there has of course been a tendency sometimes to do this. It is not necessarily wrong to do it, but what one must ensure is that the development comes out of, and is expressing, the truth contained in the fact that Mary is the Mother of God. For that is her theological function, that is her status in the work of redemption, that is what makes her unique in the whole human race.

When it is seen that that is her function, then one can see that the whole history of the Jewish people, and indeed the whole history of the human race, is focused on her, because it was the purpose of God that he should take human flesh and become a member of the human race in order to redeem it. Because of that, the whole of human history is concentrated on this moment. Of course, to the ordinary secular historian, it may not look exactly like that. There are certain things that have happened in human history that do not seem to have any connection with this. But when one is asking what the meaning of human history is, when one asks *why* it was that God chose the Jewish race to be his people, and *why* he did the things with it which he did, the answer is that it was in order to produce a woman who could be the mother of God, one from whom God could take human flesh. The Incarnation is not like a flash of lightning suddenly coming out of a completely blue sky; it is not something for which there were no apparent causes or antecedents. God did not work that way. No doubt he might have done so, but he did not. In fact he prepared the setting for the Incarnation: it was *in the fulness of time*, as the Apostle tells us, that God sent forth his Son born of a woman, born under the Law, to redeem those who were born under the Law. And therefore the whole purpose in the mind of God, from the moment in which he called Israel to be his people, was that in Israel there should be a woman from whom God the Son could take human nature and who could become his mother. One is not being fantastic if one suggests that Mary is, in a particular way, the type of the people of God.

If one asks what was God's purpose when he formed Israel, the answer is that it was the production of the Mother of God. He himself became man as a Jew, he became man as the son of a Jewish mother. So Mary is, as it were, the concrete embodiment of the Virgin daughter of Israel. The type of the Virgin daughter of Israel which we find in the Old Testament is fulfilled in Mary; and it is an interesting point that when Max Thurian, the Protestant member of the community at Taizé, wrote his book about Mary, he took this as a starting-point; this is what he saw Mary as really being. The whole of human history is concentrated upon her, and one might say, rather on the lines of what I was saying earlier, that in this respect a good deal that some people have said wrongly about our Lord is in fact true about Mary. In the last century there was a great deal of liberal evolutionary Christology (not *only* in the last century—there has been a certain amount in this century too), which represented our Lord as the climax to which the human race was brought by God's working from within, and nothing more. Now that is not true about our Lord; but it is true about his Mother; she is the greatest thing that the human race could produce through the grace of God working within. But when she had been produced, then the working of God from within was met by the act of God from without. The divine Word himself comes upon Mary and in her womb takes human nature: there the working of God from within is met by the act of God from without. *That* was the preparation for *this*.

Mary was produced by God's working within the history of Israel. Not only was there the preparation of Israel, but there was the preparation of Mary as well; and it is at this point, of course, that the problems arise about the Immaculate Conception. The Immaculate Conception has been a most contentious matter, not only between East and West, not only between Catholics and Protestants, but also, in fact, for a very long time within the Western Church, the Latin Church itself. But I think the whole matter has been very much clarified in recent years, and I myself hope that it will turn out not to be the kind of obstacle that people at one time thought. For example, Father Meyendorff, the Russian Orthodox theologian, in his book on St. Gregory Palomas, points out that if Gregory Palomas had looked on original sin in the same way as the Western Church looked upon it, then he would certainly have said that Mary was free from it. And in fact before 1854, when the dogma of the Immaculate Conception was promulgated by the Pope, there were a good many Eastern Orthodox theologians who did believe in it—that Mary from the first moment of her existence was in fact free from original sin. I think that as thought about the doctrine of original sin becomes further developed, and as original sin is seen more in the context of the human race as a whole, and less as a kind of infection passed on from parent to child, one will find that the Immaculate Conception will not be the kind of obstacle that it has been hitherto.

I want to go now to say something about this question: what does the fact that Mary is the Mother of God imply about her relation to us? Her relation to us is compounded of two relations: one is her relation to our Lord and the other is his relation to us. (This is what professional logicians call a relative product of two relations.) Her relation to us depends upon two things: first, that she is the mother of Christ, in the sense in which we have been thinking about this; secondly, that we are members of Christ, that we are incorporated into him. The Church is his body; he is the head, we are the members. The total Christ is Jesus and his members. And because Mary is his Mother, and we are his members, therefore she is our mother too. And motherhood, of course, is a permanent relationship. A mother does not cease to be a mother when she is not able to have any more children or when her children grow up. Mary is *now* the mother of Jesus, because motherhood is a permanent relationship, and we are *now* his members. Therefore she is *now* our mother too, for we are sons by adoption into him who is Son by nature. So Mary is our mother, and Mary is the Church's mother—the Mother of the Church, as Pope Paul declared her to be during the Second Vatican Council. But, of course, the Church also is our mother, and so there is a peculiar kind of typological identity and interchange between Mary and the Church. In this sort of question it is easy to get rather airborne, to be carried away into speculation which cannot have very much foundation. But this is something quite clear, and it has been recognized, perhaps implicitly, from the beginning. The great Biblical scholar, Sir Edwyn Hoskyns, an Anglican, who flourished at Cambridge after the First World War, had an extremely interesting passage in one of his articles about that mysterious figure of the woman in the twelfth chapter of the Apocalypse—the woman who is clothed with the sun, standing on the moon and crowned with stars, and who brings forth a child. Now, when you look at the details, that figure clearly cannot simply describe Mary in her relation to Jesus; the details do not fit like that. But it does seem to be a figure which combines Mary's relation to Jesus and her relation to us. And Hoskyns, who was not an extreme person in his theology at all, suggested that right from the beginning that figure was seen to be Mary and the Church, and that the child is both Jesus and us. I think it is worth while pointing out that such a very sober and balanced scholar as Hoskyns did in fact hold this point of view.

To conclude, I would like to bring our thoughts back to the word 'Theotokos', Mother of God, and to remind you of the tremendous importance of the last chapter—the eighth chapter—of the decree *Lumen Gentium*, the decree of the Vatican Council on the Church. Its title is: 'On the Blessed Virgin Mary, Mother of God (*De Beata Virgine Maria Deipara*) in the mystery of Christ and the Church (*in mysterio Christi et Ecclesiae*)'—a tremendously comprehensive phrase. It is because she is seen in relation to the Church that that chapter appears in the Constitution on the Church. Of course, there is a history behind this: There was a great desire on the part of some of the members of the Vatican Council that there should be a separate Constitution about the Blessed Virgin, but it was decided in the end to bring her into the decree on the Church so that it should be seen that the theology about our Lady is not an isolated thing, not something shut off in a particular enclosure to develop on its own. It is tied up with the whole mystery of the Church and of human salvation.

In this chapter she is referred to as the Mother of God, *Deipara*, and later on as *Mater Dei*. I remember saying once to Bishop Butler that I thought it had been rather a pity that the Council, in talking about our Lady, did not take as its starting-point the title 'Mother of God', which seemed to me to be theologically the basic fact about her. He pointed out to me (and I ought to have realized this without its being pointed out) that the Council was not in fact producing any decree about the Incarnation: if it had been, then Mary would have come into that. But because the central decree of the Council was about the Church, therefore Mary was seen in relation to the Church. However, it is not just the Church alone; it is 'in the mystery of Christ *and* the Church.' After the opening section of the chapter, the next section is headed with the words: 'On the function of the Blessed Virgin in the work of salvation' (*De munere Beatae Mariae Virginis in oeconomia salutis*). It is her place in the work of salvation which is taken to be the basic thing, even when she is considered in connection with the doctrine of the Church. And then the following section is explicitly headed 'Concerning the Blessed Virgin Mary and the Church' (*De Beata Maria Virgine et Ecclesia*). So the Constitution brings together Mary's relation to her Son and her relation to the Church, the whole body of her Son's members.

One of the important things about the chapter is that it is almost entirely scriptural. It does not start off from any kind of purely theoretical standpoint about Mary; it starts off by looking at Scripture and seeing there what was the function that she actually performed as God chose her for it and conferred it upon her. This is important, among other reasons, because it leaves the initiative with God, who is in control, in command of the whole work. Theologians have had a tendency (which I know only too well, being one of them) to try to lay down in advance what God was bound to do in a particular circumstance; as if you could say exactly what God was going to do, even if you did not know what he *had* done. But the greatest theologians (it is certainly true about St. Thomas Aquinas), have recognized that very often there were half-a-dozen things God could have done, and that it rested with him to decide on the precise way. I think this is very true about our Lady. If we want to have the proper kind of devotion to her, we have not just to theorize about what we think God ought to have done or might have done, or what we would have done if we had been God (I am afraid we sometimes think like that), but what in fact God himself decided to do. And one looks at Scripture to see what this was. It is therefore an extremely good thing that the Decree on the Church is so scriptural. Of course, the position of Mary as it came out in that chapter in the Decree is as exalted as it could possibly be, but it is one in which she is organically connected with Christ and with the Church of which we are part; she is not treated as somebody who can be dealt with simply on her own.

Immaculate Conception

REV. PROFESSOR JOHN MACQUARRIE, D.D., D.Litt.

Both before and since it was raised to the status of a formal dogma by Pius IX in 1854, the doctrine of Mary's Immaculate Conception has been the subject of much controversy. In the centuries before the dogma was promulgated, many theologians had opposed belief in the Immaculate Conception. Among them was St Thomas Aquinas himself. However, when we consider what he says on the subject,[1] we see that he did not deny the sanctification of Mary before her birth and that his difficulty lay to some extent in his theories about the beginnings of a human person, and in particular with his view that animation is subsequent to conception. He rightly held that it is unintelligible that either sin or grace can be attributed to anything but a rational creature, and so Mary could be sanctified only after her animation. We still argue over the question of when a human person comes into being—is it at conception, understood as the union of the spermatozoon and ovum from which the child will develop, or is it only after the implanting of the conceptus in the wall of the womb, or is it at some other time? I mention this to show that the alleged objections of St Thomas and others to the doctrine turned largely on technical points, and were not intended as a denial of Mary's sanctification at or near the beginning of her life as a human person.

In the decades following the promulgation of the dogma, objections have come from Orthodox, Anglican and Protestant theologians. Vladimir Lossky claims that 'the dogma of the Immaculate Conception is foreign to Eastern tradition, which does not wish to separate the Holy Virgin from the sons of Adam'.[2] But once again this objection is less formidable than it sounds, for he goes on to claim that sin did in fact find no place in the Virgin, but this was due not to some special privilege in the mode of her conception but to a purifying grace which did not impair her liberty. Many Anglicans who have objected to the dogma of the Immaculate Conception have done so not because they reject its essential teaching but because they think it should not have been proposed as dogma. Thus, in the Anglican/Roman Catholic Agreed Statement 'Authority in the Church', we read: 'Special difficulties are created by the recent Marian dogmas, because Anglicans doubt the appropriateness, or even the possibility, of defining them as essential to the faith of believers'.[3] Nothing is said about the content of the dogmas, and the objection is to their dogmatic form. Still, it cannot be denied that the objections of some Anglicans would go further than

98

this. Protestant theologians go further still. Karl Barth, though he has many affirmative things to say about Mary, objects to the modern mariological dogmas partly on the grounds that they represent an arbitrary innovation, partly on the grounds that they contradict the principle *sola gratia* by allowing some part to the creature in the work of redemption.[4] Whether these charges can be sustained must be judged in the light of what follows.

It has become customary nowadays to distinguish between doctrines which constitute the core of Christian faith and those which are more peripheral, or, as it is also expressed, to recognize a hierarchy of truth. This is not perhaps as helpful as it is sometimes supposed to be, for Christian truth is really one, though we express it in a number of doctrines; and because it is really one, all of these doctrines are mutually implicative or coinherent. Nevertheless, we can acknowledge that the doctrine of creation, let us say, is clearly attested in scripture, and that the doctrine of the triunity of God, though not explicitly taught in scripture, belongs to the universal Christian tradition and is implicit in scripture, so that we can say that both of these doctrines would have strong claims to be considered as belonging to the core of Christian truth or as standing high in the hierarchy of truths.

By contrast, the dogma of the Immaculate Conception of Mary would seem to be much less securely founded. According to Ludwig Ott's manual of Catholic dogma, 'The doctrine of the Immaculate Conception of Mary is not explicitly revealed in scripture'.[5] He goes on to say that 'according to many theologians' it is implicit in a few scripture passages, beginning with the so-called *protoevangelium* of Genesis. But it can hardly be denied that the exegesis of these passages is somewhat strained. They could hardly be used as a support for the dogma, and it is only in the light of the dogma itself that retrospectively we might see them as having a measure of symbolic appropriateness. Ott then goes on to say that 'neither the Greek nor the Latin fathers explicitly teach the Immaculate Conception of Mary', but he claims that it is implicit in their teaching about the holiness and purity of Mary and the contrast which they develop between Mary and Eve. It is only in the much later tradition that the doctrine takes definite shape, and here one should perhaps notice that the influence of Christian art has had its effect. This is entirely proper, since dogma is a matter not only of concepts but of images. Velasquez's great picture, 'The Immaculate Conception', surely tells us more about the meaning of the doctrine than many a treatise, for the idealized but entirely human figure of the Virgin, standing on the moon as it passes over the sleeping earth, clothed with the stars and illuminated with a mystic light, teaches a high metaphysical understanding of conception, to which we shall return presently. Still another argument adduced by Ott is based on reason. He expresses it in the formula: *Potuit, decuit, ergo fecit*, which might be translated, 'It was possible, it was fitting, therefore it was done'. This, however, is said to yield no certainty, but only probability.

It might be thought that the case for the dogma, as stated here, is decidedly weak. I think, however, that the appeal to scripture, tradition, development and reason, while appropriate in the case of the major Christian doctrines, is not appropriate in the case of those which stand lower in the hierarchy. The test for such doctrines is to consider whether they form part of the one truth of Christianity, and this in practice means considering whether they are implicates of those doctrines which can be founded on scripture and which have been acknowledged in the universal tradition of the Church. This procedure will show whether these secondary doctrines are, as Barth maintained, innovations and falsifications, or whether they are part of the fulness of Christian truth, when we try to bring it to maximal expression. Incidentally, while I have referred to mariological doctrine as 'lower in the hierarchy' and as 'secondary', I have deliberately avoided the expression 'peripheral'. Mariology seems rather to be the meeting point for a great many fundamental Christian doctrines, almost like a railway junction where many lines converge and where connections are established. Anthropology, christology, ecclesiology, hamartiology, soteriology—these are among the doctrines which all touch upon mariology. If the dogma of the Immaculate Conception can be established, this will be accomplished by showing that it is an implicate of these other Christian truths. But the mariological doctrine will, in turn, throw new light on the truths from which it has been derived and will also show new connections among them and so will strengthen the coherence of Christian theology. This is one reason for believing that mariology is worthy of study.

The historical and methodological remarks made so far are of a preliminary character, and it is now time to confront the dogma directly, as it was expressed in the words of the constitution *Ineffabilis Deus: Declaramus ... beatıssimam Virginem Mariam in primo instanti suae conceptionis fuisse singulari omnipotentis Dei gratia et privilegio, intuitu meritorum Christi Jesus Salvatoris humani generis, ab omni originalis culpae labe praeservatam immunem.*[6] 'We declare ... that the most blessed Virgin Mary in the first moment of her conception was, by the unique grace and privilege of God, in view of the merits of Jesus Christ the Saviour of the human race, preserved intact from all stain of original sin.'

The language of the constitution is that of mid-nineteenth century Catholic dogmatic theology, but we must pay attention not so much to the actual formulation as to what Bishop Butler once described as the 'governing intention',[7] the essential meaning which the words seek to convey but which today we might express differently. The main difference would, I think, be this, that our theology today prefers personal to impersonal categories. If we can open up more clearly the personal meanings involved in the idea of an immaculate conception, then the doctrine will come alive for our minds and in this way too its close connection with some of the most fundamental doctrines of the Christian faith will become apparent.

Let us begin with the idea of conception itself. We have already noted that some of the earlier controversies and confusions turned on questions about the moment of conception and the moment of animation, and that even today, in discussions about abortion, for example, there are different opinions about the beginnings of a human life. What is important for the doctrine of Immaculate Conception is that we move away from any merely biological understanding of conception. Clearly, of course, Mary was conceived in a biological sense and in the normal way—there was never any suggestion of a virginal conception. But when we consider the theological question, we are not concerned with the biology of conception or with the many different ways in which conception has been understood, in ancient, medieval and modern times. The doctrine of Immaculate Conception is not tied to any theory about how conception takes place, and it was the recognition of this that led to the overcoming of some of the early difficulties with the doctrine.

So I want to define 'conception' for the purposes of this discussion as *the absolute origination of a person*. This is not a biological but a philosophical definition, and it speaks not of the fusion of cells or anything of the sort but of the mystery of the coming into being of a person. The conception of Mary, in this philosophical sense can be considered on three levels: her conception in the mind of God, her conception in the people of Israel, and her conception in the family of Joachim and Anna.

Let us begin then with her conception in the mind of God. Here we come back to that profound metaphysical understanding of Immaculate Conception expressed in the painting of Velasquez. It is expressed too in the portion of scripture that used to be read for the epistle on the feast of the Immaculate Conception: 'The Lord possessed me in the beginning of his ways, before he made anything, from the beginning. I was set up from eternity, and of old, before the earth was made. The depths were not as yet, and I was already conceived' (Prov. 8, 22ff). That last sentence is translated in the Vulgate as *ego jam concepta eram*. The passage referred originally, of course, to wisdom, but it was felt to be fitting to apply it to the Blessed Virgin, just as many other passages in the Old Testament that originally had nothing to do with the Messiah came to be applied to Jesus in Christian interpretation.

'The depths were not as yet, and I was already conceived.' This is the ultimate conception of Mary, her conception from eternity in the salvific purposes of God. Not only Mary originates in this ultimate conception. What we are thinking of here is the mystery of election and predestination as it affects the whole human race. In the beginning or even before the beginning, God conceived humanity as his child and his partner. He purposed to bring the human race into loving communion with himself, and he purposed to do this by himself assuming humanity and tabernacling with this people. He must then also have purposed to bring the human race to the moment when it had been so cleared of sin and filled with grace that it would be ready to receive the gift of himself. That moment in the history of humanity was Mary. Even if we did not know Mary's name and knew nothing at all about her history and background, nevertheless if we believed in the doctrines of creation and incarnation, we would have to posit this moment in humanity. There is a sense in which Mary's significance lies not in herself as an individual but as that moment in the spiritual history of mankind. Yet on the other hand we must not allow her individuality to be entirely swallowed up in her universal significance. History is compounded of the universal and the particular together, and its concreteness depends on the particular. When we speak of God's election and predestination, we are thinking not only of the general purposes of his providence but of his infinite care in choosing and calling particular individuals, usually weak and obscure individuals, to be the agents of his purpose. Among the highest of these was Mary, and we are not wrong in believing that long before she was physically conceived in the womb of Anna, she was ontologically conceived and sanctified in the divine purpose, so that we could also apply to her the word of the Lord that came to Jeremiah: 'Before I formed you in the womb, I knew you, and before you were born, I consecrated you' (Jer. 1, 5).

No individual exists in a vacuum, but always in a stream of history and in a culture. It is out of this historical and cultural background that the individual is formed. For Mary, this background was Israel, and we now go on to think of her as conceived in the history of Israel. We call Israel the chosen people, because this whole nation was elected by God to a peculiar destiny. God created the human race in his own image and gave to them an original disposition toward righteousness. Sin marred that image, and the original righteousness was perverted through the massive distortions of human life that persist from generation to generation and that have earned the name of original sin. But the human race did not fall into a total depravity, as some theologians have mistakenly taught. Something of the original capacity for righteousness survived and something of the divine grace continued to operate. God was still seeking to bring human beings into that relation with himself that he had purposed, and, according to the Bible, his way of achieving his purpose was typical of him. He chose or elected or predestined a weak and obscure people. He bound that people to himself through successive convenants, he spoke his word to them through a long line of prophets and teachers. He kindled in them the thirst for righteousness, and encountered them in grace and judgment. It is rather as if the capacity for righteousness which survived in a sinful

102

world and the divine grace by which that righteousness was elicited and sustained became concentrated in this nation of Israel. Its election was not a privilege, but a call to servanthood. God was preparing a people for the moment when it would be ready to receive, not for itself alone but for the whole race, what Newman called 'a higher gift than grace— God's presence and his very self'. Mary was conceived and brought forth by Israel as the culmination of its long history of education in the ways of God. We could say that the sparks of righteousness and grace that had been kindled and nursed in the story of Israel were now ready to burst into flame.

If the ultimate origin of a person is in God and the secondary origin in a history and culture, the proximate origin is in a human family. Conceived in the mind of God, conceived in the history of Israel, Mary was also conceived in the womb of Anna. This is indeed how we most naturally understand conception. But even on this level it is important not to think of conception in merely biological terms. The conception of an animal can be so understood, but not the conception of a human being, for a human being has his proximate origin in the personal relation of the parents, and this is never merely biological. At this point we must turn to the apocryphal *Book of James* or *Protoevangelium of James* as it has also been called, a writing perhaps as old as the second century. Even if it is purely legend from the point of view of strict history, it presents an interesting account of the conception of Mary. It is a common story in the literature of Israel—that of a couple who have no children and are now almost past the age for parenthood. The husband Joachim went into the wilderness to fast, and prayed for a child. Meanwhile his wife Anna was making a similar prayer at home. Each of them was visited by an angel who gave assurance that the prayer had been heard. As Joachim returned from the fields, Anna went down and met him at the gate of the city. Now we come to the interesting point, and again it is Christian art that has interpreted the story. Artists have seized on the meeting of Joachim and Anna at the gate as the moment of the Immaculate Conception. A flash of light passes between their eyes, and that symbolizes the beginning of the new life in the womb of Anna. Now these artists were not implying that Mary was conceived without intercourse between her parents—they were not teaching a virginal birth or conception. But they rightly saw that the conception of a child is not primarily a physiological happening, but the loving personal commitment of the parents. Children, unfortunately, are sometimes conceived in drunkenness, sometimes in lust, sometimes by accident, and such children, alas, from the very moment of conception are being warped by the distortions of human sin. If we could imagine a child conceived out of pure love before God, would not such a child be from the very moment of conception— I mean, conceived in the loving desire of the parents for the child, even before they come together in sexual union—would not such a child be from the beginning the recipient of grace? It is no mere sentimentality but simply the recognition that human beings are persons, not animals, that sees the creative moment of conception, whether for good or bad, in the personal relation subsisting between the parents rather than in the biological phenomenon of the union of cells. Even before birth, a child is growing into relation with its mother, and from the beginning of life is becoming one kind of person or another through the relation with other persons.

To sum up these remarks, then, when we talk about the conception of Mary and understand by this her origin as a person and not just her physical beginnings, we understand this first as her origin in the mind of God in eternity, next in the history of Israel as it moved towards spiritual maturity, and lastly in the loving devotion of her parents, represented in the tradition as faithful to the claims of Jewish piety. So when we read in the constitution of 1854 the words *in primo instanti suae conceptionis* ('in the first moment of her conception'), we do not understand this as the moment in which some physiological event occurred, but as an extended moment which goes back even into the eternity of God.

Having discussed the noun 'conception', I turn next to the adjective 'immaculate'. This introduces the subject of sin, and we must be determined to think of sin also in a personal way. This brings into question the notion of sin as 'stain', which appears in the formulation of the dogma. It is true, of course, that the image of a stain has been used since ancient times for sin, but it is an image which suggests too physical an understanding of sin. One might even say that it is somewhat Manichaean in tendency, as if sin were somehow a substance, or something existing in its own right, rather than essentially a lack or distortion, that is to say, something negative. Incidentally, the objection I am making here would strictly speaking apply also to the use of the adjective 'immaculate', which literally means free from spot or stain. But I think this adjective has been so long associated with Mary's conception that one would not wish to challenge it, and in any case its specific etymological sense is no longer obtrusive. With the rejection of the notion of sin as stain goes also the rejection of any understanding of original sin that would think of it as a kind of hereditary taint, passed along in the genes, as it were. It is, however, astonishing to find Hans Küng saying that the doctrine of the Immaculate Conception is made 'pointless' because we have turned away from the 'view of the transmission of "original sin" by the act of procreation'.[8] This is a very superficial judgment, for the doctrine of Mary's Immaculate Conception is far more than just a safeguard against the infection of a hereditary stain.

What then would be a more definitely personal way of understanding sin? I think this is to be found in the concept of alienation. Sin is alienation from God, and this carries with it alienation from one's fellow human beings and even from one's own true nature. Alienation, moreover, has social as well as individual dimensions, and these social dimensions which pervade all human society, persist from generation to generation and weigh upon individuals, constitute original sin. Alienation is nothing in itself. It is rather a lack, the lack of a right relation to God. Thus, when it is claimed that Mary was free of original sin, what is meant is that she did not lack a right relation to God. We must notice, however, that the expression I have used, 'she did not lack', is a double negative and therefore something affirmative in the highest degree. The traditional formulation, using as it did the image of sin as stain, represented Immaculate Conception as itself something negative, and so we get the statement that Mary was 'preserved intact from all stain of original sin'. This is far too negative and passive a way of expressing what is intended. The Immaculate Conception of Mary, like the sinlessness of Jesus Christ, is not a negative idea but a thoroughly positive one. Instead of putting the matter in the negative way of saying that Mary was preserved from stain of sin, we may put it in an affirmative way and say she was preserved in a right relation to God or that she was never without grace. Rather, she was surrounded with grace from her original conception in the mind of God to her actual historical conception in the love of her parents. This interpretation receives support from what Ludwig Ott says about the nature of original sin. 'Original sin', he declares, 'is the deprivation of grace'.[9] It is, according to the Council of Trent, the 'death of the soul', and the death of the soul is the absence of supernatural life, that is, of sanctifying grace. Mary, by contrast, was the recipient of grace from the beginning, in the traditional phrase, she was 'full of grace'. To be filled with grace is to be in the opposite condition from that of original sin. Alienation has been overcome, the channels from God are open, the moment is ripe for incarnation. It is of this moment that Paul spoke: 'When the time had fully come, God sent forth his Son born of a woman ...' (Gal. 4,4).

These remarks bring us now to consider Mary's place in the central doctrines of incarnation and atonement, and so of her relation to Jesus Christ. At this point a difficulty may arise. If one develops a high mariological doctrine, especially one that includes a doctrine of Immaculate Conception, then is there not a danger of making Christ Himself superfluous? If the human race could be brought in the person of Mary to the point at which original sin had lost its power, was there need of anything or anyone further? Have we not exalted Mary into the place that belongs to Jesus Christ alone, as indeed critics of what is called 'Mariolatry' have consistently claimed?

There are at least four responses that can be made to such a charge.

1. We may first of all ask the counter-question whether anything *less* could be claimed for Mary. She was, after all, the Mother of the Lord, and like all the other matters we have considered, motherhood is to be understood in its full

personal sense. It cannot be understood as simply the biological relation of motherhood. The mother is, in her personal relation to her child, the principal formative influence in the formation of his mind and character. If Jesus Christ was to develop in a perfect filial relation to the Father, was it not necessary that his Mother's relation to the heavenly Father should be one of constant grace, certainly not of alienation?

2. Further, the dogma of the Immaculate Conception states explicitly that Mary's 'unique grace and privilege' in this matter (which we may equate with her election and vocation) were granted 'in view of the merits of Jesus Christ, the Saviour of the human race'. Mary does not have her significance in herself, but in her relation to Christ. The latter's saving work, again, reaches backward in time as well as forward. So Mary is subordinate to her Son. She is the God-bearer, fully human. He is the God-man, fully human and fully divine.

3. I think this distinction becomes clearer when we consider the different kinds of righteousness that we see in Mary and Jesus. Mary's righteousness is faithful obedience to God, summed up in the famous words, 'Be it unto me according to thy word' (Lk. 1, 38). This perfected the old righteousness of obedience, and reversed that history of disobedience which is also the history of sin. Jesus too was faithful in his obedience to the Father, but he brought to light a creative innovating righteousness that opened up new spiritual horizons. The difference between the two has been very well brought out by John de Satgé. Recalling how the gospels depict Jesus as walking out in front of the disciples, he writes: 'We cannot fully identify with Jesus. He remains the one who strides out ahead of his disciples ··· But it is not so with Mary'.[10]

4. The last point I want to make concerns the charge made by Barth and others that the mariological dogmas infringe the principle of *sola gratia*. Perhaps it should first of all be said that this principle must not be understood in any way that would reduce the human being to a mere puppet, and this has been a constant danger in the Augustinian-Calvinist tradition. Men and women cannot be saved from sin without their consent, and there is this much truth in a doctrine of synergism. It is the human consent and cooperation with God in the work of salvation that finds expression in the application to Mary of the title *Co-redemptrix*. I think myself that this title suggests too much and obscures the fact that the human role is always no more than response to the divine initiative. But then is it not precisely the doctrine of Immaculate Conception that prevents such an exaggeration in the case of Mary, for that doctrine teaches that divine grace was there from the very first (prevenient) and that Mary's place is due not to anything of her own but to the gracious election that looks toward the incarnation of the Son?

No doubt it is possible to be a good Christian without making any explicit affirmation of the Immaculate Conception. For many centuries, indeed, there was no such explicit affirmation. No doubt too there are misleading ways of formulating the doctrine, and these call for critical scrutiny. But I think that its essential truth, its 'governing intention', is a clear implicate of basic Christian doctrines which we all accept. Immaculate Conception therefore is neither innovative, perverse or pointless, as some of its opponents have claimed, but is yet another precious insight into the one fundamental truth of God in Christ.

NOTES

1 St Thomas, *Summa Theologiae*, 3a, q. 27.
2 V. Lossky, *The Mystical Theology of the Eastern Church*, p. 140.
3 'Authority in the Church, I', p. 20.
4 Karl Barth, *Church Dogmatics*, 1/2, p. 138 ff.
5 Ludwig Ott, *Fundamentals of Catholic Dogmas*, p. 200.
6 H. Denzinger, *Enchiridion Symbolorum*, No. 1641.
7 B.C. Butler, *The Tablet*, 5 July 1975, p. 624.
8 Hans Küng, *On Being a Christian*, p. 454.
9 Ott, op. cit., p. 110.
10 J. de Satgé, *Mary and the Christian Gospel*, p. 51.

The Assumption

REV. JOHN SAWARD, M.A.

On 1 November 1950 Pope Pius XII issued the Apostolic Constitution *Munificentissimus Deus* (MD), which declared as a matter of divinely revealed dogma that 'the Immaculate Mother of God the Ever-Virgin Mary, having completed her earthly course, was in body and soul assumed into heavenly glory'.[1] At the time the Definition was regarded by some non-Catholics as tactless and triumphalistic; indeed, the Archbishop of Canterbury wrote to the Pope expressing his anxiety that the new dogma might further deepen the divisions of Christendom. In the scholarly pages of the *Journal of Theological Studies* the Assumption went unmentioned – except on the last page of an article by a young Cambridge don. At the end of a very influential study of 'The Eucharist and Christology in the Nestorian Controversy' Henry Chadwick wrote that 'there seems little need for surprise that such a story as the Assumption became current in Monophysite circles' during the fifth and sixth centuries. The Monophysites, with their one-nature Christology, had lost all sense of Christ's solidarity with mankind, and so, Chadwick argued, it was imperative for their piety to clutch on to someone who was beyond question an ordinary human being. That ordinary human being was Mary. The resurrection of Christ, for the Monophysite, was the resurrection of a God and therefore just did not count so far as mere mortals were concerned. But the resurrection of Mary provided the human reality that was otherwise absent.[2]

Dr. Chadwick's challenge to the Assumption of Our Lady is a serious one. It implies that the doctrine is co-ordinated to a low or even negative view of the humanity of Our Lord. On his view, Mary's Assumption simply services the needs of an heretical piety and is presumably therefore an alien intruder in primitive Catholic tradition. That is perhaps to overstate Chadwick's case, but it is not untypical of the misgivings expressed over the years by Anglican students of Christian antiquity. Thus John Cosin, the seventeenth-century Bishop of Durham, explains that the Assumption was omitted from the Kalendar of the Prayer Book because it 'is grounded only upon uncertain fables, first devised by men that gave their minds to vanity and superstition'.[3] And only in the last few weeks the suggestion that a feast of the Blessed Virgin Mary be celebrated officially by Anglicans on 15 August provoked a letter to the *Church Times* from a leading Evangelical, who described the Assumption as a 'Gnostic heresy'. 'Monophysite', 'superstitious', 'Gnostic' – that would seem still to be the attitude of many Anglicans to the Assumption. And even where it is accepted, there is very often the guilty feeling that it has no theological respect-ability.

What I would like to do today is to answer some of these misgivings expressed by non-Catholics about the Assumption. Using as my primary sources the first theological exposition of the doctrine in the Byzantine homilies of the sixth, seventh and eighth centuries, I shall try to show that the Assumption of Our Lady must be seen, like all Mariology, in the context of the doctrines of Christ, salvation and the Church and that seen thus its dogmatic status appears in a new light. I speak as an Anglican Catholic who is painfully aware that the Assumption of Our Lady is not yet accepted or celebrated by the majority of the members of my own communion. I offer these reflections now in an ecumenical and eirenical spirit with the hope that this great and glorious part of the tradition of Catholic Christianity, both western and eastern, be finally reappropriated by my fellow Churchmen.

The Apocryphal Narratives

Let me begin by posing and answering the question: what is the source of the Assumption? I believe that the ultimate source of the belief is Mary herself; that we know that she is alive and glorified because of our fellowship with her in Christ through the working of the Holy Spirit. That, it seems to me, is the axiom upon which the Assumption as a dogma rests. It cannot be over-emphasized that it does not depend for its truth on the historical reliability of the various apocryphal accounts of the death, burial and assumption of Our Lady. This is the fear of many non-Catholics, and we can allay it at once; the Fathers themselves are emphatic on this point as well and make guarded and sparing use of the apocryphal material. Nevertheless, we must not go too far in the opposite direction and deny the apocrypha any theological or historical value at all. What we must do is to remind ourselves of their exact status: they are not in competition with Holy Scripture but are rather to be seen as inspired visionary literature with all the strengths and weaknesses of such literature. Their literary structure and history are notoriously complex, and I do not wish to discuss such issues now. This much, however, can be said. First, it cannot any longer be seriously maintained that these early stories are simply fictions concocted by heretics. It is true that an heretical *Transitus Mariae* was included in the so-called *Decretum Gelasianum*, a list of heretical books condemned in the south of Gaul in the sixth century.[4] But the stories are far too wide-spread to be simply the work of one group or to have originated in one particular theological milieu. Of course, the story attracted fringe groups, but the fact of predisposition cannot in any way prejudice the truth-claim of the doctrine. It may be true that an heretical group is predisposed towards a certain doctrine (that is the 'choosing' (*haeresis*) characteristic of heresy), but such predisposition cannot be taken as a sign of the falsity or even impropriety of the doctrine concerned, which must be assessed by other criteria. To take an example from later Church History, the licentious 'Familists' of sixteenth-century Europe were predisposed towards Christ's teaching on love to the neglect of the rigours of the moral law. That in no way invalidates Our Lord's new commandment; it is the neglect, not the predisposition, that is culpable. Secondly, the claim that the Assumption is the work of radical Monophysites will just not stand up to close examination. If we consider versions of the *Transitus* without doubt associated with Monophysites, such as the Discourse attributed to Patriarch Theodosius of Alexandra (533-567), we find its Christology would be better described as 'non-Chalcedonian' in the non-pejorative sense of that word as used of the Oriental Orthodox Churches today.[5] Theodosius' Discourse reflects the views of the disciples of Severus of Antioch in Alexandria and is almost indistinguishable from Catholic Orthodoxy. It is in fact fervently anti-Docetic and several passages are directed against the followers of Julian of Halicarnassus, the truly extreme Monophysite who taught the heresy of the incorruptibility and immortality of the body of Christ. Finally, it must be said, again contrary to much non-Catholic opinion, the stories do not teach the deathless immortality of Mary. They are all different ways of understanding her real human death, her falling asleep, and her resurrection, the glorification of her body and soul. There *is* a tradition of Mary's immortality – Epiphanius refers to it in the fourth century – but that is not the teaching of the vast majority of the versions of the story of Mary's Passing, nor is it the belief of Catholic Christendom. The doctrine common to both Catholics and Orthodox is that of the resurrection of Mary, body and soul. The point is perhaps made most clearly by the Copts, who celebrate two feasts – one of the Virgin's death and one of her resurrection separated by several months.

This, then, I hope, makes clear the status of the narrative of the Assumption. I would now like to proceed to the main purpose of my paper: to show, following the first Catholic preachers of the doctrine, how Our Lady's Assumption relates to the central dogmas of Christology, soteriology and ecclesiology.

In the first homilies on the Assumption the foundation of the doctrine is stated to be orthodox belief about the person of Jesus Christ. St. John Damascene (c.675-749), whom MD rightly describes as 'the expositor of this tradition *par excellence*', begins his first homily on the Dormition with a lively presentation of orthodox Christology, the dogma of the Council of Chalcedon. He addresses Christ thus:

'You have come from her, you the one Christ, the one Lord, the only Son, at the same time God and man, at once perfect God and perfect man, entirely God, and entirely man, composed of two perfect natures, divinity and humanity.'[6]

But then in his second homily he goes further. He argues that just as the title *Theotokos,* God-bearer, is primarily Christological in reference and protects right belief in the Incarnation, so the implications of the same title constitute the foundation of belief in the Assumption; the Assumption too has an essential Christological reference, teaches us something about the person of Christ.

'And he was made flesh, being born of the sacred Virgin without human union, himself remaining wholly God with his flesh, and fully man with his infinite divinity. *It is thus in recognizing this Virgin as Mother of God that we celebrate her Dormition*'.[7]

Damascene then goes on to explain why. According to him and the other Doctors of the Dormition, it is the relationship of Virgin Mother and divine Son that is primordial for belief in the Assumption. They stress constantly the *proximity* of Mother and Son in Incarnation, the beginning of redemption, and thus also in resurrection, its consummation; indeed, Damascene applies to Mary a text from the Canticle/'she who is near to me', *proxima mea*; Mary is the one who is close to the God-Man.[8] There is no melodrama of the dealings of a remote God with an all-too-human woman (as Chadwick would seem to suggest) but constant emphasis on Christ's solidarity in his humanity with Mary, who thus becomes the representative of the whole human race. St. Germanus, Patriarch of Constantinople (c.634-733), puts these words into the mouth of Christ as he tells his Mother of her impending Assumption:

'It is time ... to take you to be with me, you, my mother. Just as you filled the earth and its peoples with joy, so now you shall bring joy to the heavens, bring happiness to the mansions of my Father ... Where I am there is light eternal, joy without compare, a palace without equal, a city safe from ruin. *And so where I am, you shall be also, Mother inseparable in her inseparable Son.*'[9]

And again:

'Just as a child seeks and desires the presence of his mother and as a mother likes to live close to her son, so it is fitting that you, whose motherly love for your Son and God was never in doubt, should return to him.'[10]

The Incarnation took place through the faith and in the flesh of Mary; as Nicolas Cabasilas says daringly, it was as much the work of *her* will as that of the Father. It is from Mary that the Son takes his humanity; through her the Word incarnate is related to mankind and made part of human history. Now what the homilies on the Assumption suggest is that there is something indestructible about this relationship; in living and dying they will have us see Mother and Son together. Moreover, they seem to suggest that this relationship, in living and dying, of both Mother and Son, is essential to a full Chalcedonian faith in Christ.

What sense can we make of this? One of the besetting sins of our culture is individualism, the belief that persons are separated atoms or units loosely, accidentally, tied together; we fail to see, in Professor John Macmurray's term, 'persons in relation', persons necessarily and not contingently in relationship. To be human is to be in a network of relations, biological and social, with other members of the human race. Now pernicious individualism, the failure to see the solidarity of mankind, can affect our appropriation of Christology. There is a Docetic tendency in a certain kind of fashionable liberal Christology which, by its very Christocentrism, dehumanizes Christ. At the heart of the new creation is not some unrelated Gnostic Redeemer, some isolated individual demigod, but two persons in relationship, a man born of a woman. Almost like an incantation, the Fathers of the Assumption stress this relationship of Jesus and Mary in both Incarnation and Resurrection, for I believe they saw in their own time, as much as we in ours, sinful man's tendency to divide, isolate and alienate person from person. Of course, stress on the 'proximity' of Jesus and Mary does not in itself give us the full doctrine of the Assumption, but this at least is its base, as I hope we can now see: orthodox, Catholic belief about the One Lord Jesus Christ.

The Assumption and the Resurrection

We must now examine the relation of the doctrine of the Assumption to that of salvation, and in particular to what Scripture and Tradition have to say about the Resurrection. I shall try to show that there was a preparation for the doctrine of the Assumption in the early Christian understanding of the corporate nature of resurrection. Whether or not it was believed universally from earliest times that Mary was risen, this much at least was believed by the majority of the Fathers before the fourth century: namely, that Jesus Christ was not raised from the dead alone.

I would like to begin by speaking of how Scripture intertwines the ideas of body and community. It is a commonplace of Biblical commentaries that the body, for the Jew, is a social concept. The body binds a man in the bundle of the living. The body of one person, on the Hebrew view, only has meaning in a world of other bodies, bodies that function independently but are related biologically and socially; the body, indeed, is the very medium and source of all our communication and relationship. Nevertheless, as the NT makes clear, the body awaits its redemption; the body of the flesh has only a limited capacity for communion; sin and death threaten its social destiny; the community of the flesh is but a type of deeper, perfect bodily community – the bodily community of the redeemed. The concepts of body and world are interdependent. The fleshly body exists only as part of a social world; the body of glory, the risen spiritual body, is the world of the future, the world of the Kingdom. In the Pauline literature we see the development of the imagery of the Body of Christ from mere simile in Romans (the Church is *like* a human body) to the richer conception of

112

Colossians and Ephesians, where the eschatological vision is of a perfectly interrelated body, one complete man, in which Christ, the Head of the Body, is seen as in some sense himself the future world in which men will enjoy the fulness that he has received from the Father.

What is important from our point of view is that this one-body solidarity is a fruit of the resurrection. Resurrection creates what one might call 'concorporality', a 'co-body' (*sussoma*), a word actually used in Ephesians to speak of the reconciliation of Jews and Gentiles in the one body of Christ. The word has no parallels in secular Greek and yet is frequently used by the Fathers to speak of the solidarity of Christ and the Church, and of the union of Christ and Mary in glory. St. Gregory of Nyssa, commenting on 1 Cor 15.28, speaks thus of the resurrection:

'When ... like our first fruit we have put off from ourselves all evil, then the whole of our nature will be absorbed in him who is our first fruit, and we shall become one continuous undivided body with him?'[11] St. Paul tells us that our resurrection will be 'like' Christ's; our lowly bodies will be changed to be like his glorious body. What is now true of Christ will then be true of us, so that just as his glorified body is now open to all, since his so-to-speak 'availability' transcends the limits of time and space, so our bodies too will be given the same openness and potentiality for communion. And because each individual body will be open to all, there will be, as St. Gregory says, one undivided body, the perfect Man, 'the measure of the stature of the fulness of Christ'. Resurrection is, then, essentially communal, inclusive, social.[12]

And indeed the NT regards the resurrection of Our Lord not as an isolated event with only indirect repercussions for mankind, but as the beginning of the universal resurrection of the dead. St. Paul, in his discussion of resurrection, in 1 Cor 15, makes the following remarkable statement: 'If there is no resurrection of the dead, Christ himself cannot have been raised' (v. 13); and again, 'If the dead are not raised, Christ has not been raised' (v. 16). To be possible at all, resurrection must be shared: by this man, he says, has come the general resurrection. The resurrection of Christ, for Paul, is not some random miracle, affecting only one individual; Christ's resurrection and ours represent, as it were, two 'moments' within the resurrection of the dead. They are inseparable, held together in the more inclusive concept. Of course, it is also essential to our faith, as 2 Timothy reminds us, that we do not delude ourselves into thinking that our resurrection is past already; the End is not yet; death still awaits its final destruction. Nevertheless, in one sense we are already raised with Christ; our inner nature is being renewed every day; eschatology is inaugurated; the possibility of transfiguration is real; we are being changed from glory into glory. The power of the resurrection has already seized this present age: we are caught up in the wake of Christ's glory. Resurrection, we must say again, is communal.

Now there was one Biblical text that led the Fathers of the first three centuries to explore this mystery of the communal nature of resurrection at great depth; that text was Mt 27.52ff, where it is said that after Christ's death the tombs were opened, 'and many bodies of the saints who had fallen asleep were raised, and coming out of the tombs after his resurrection they went into the holy city and appeared to many'. In the first centuries of the Church this mysterious event was almost unanimously understood eschatologically; it was taken as a self-evident truth that it concerned a full resurrection in the power of Christ's death and as a share in his glory; thus 'holy city' was taken to denote the *heavenly* Jerusalem; only later was it maintained that those who awoke would die again later. The earlier writers regard the incident of the saints' resurrection as a sign that death and the powers of hell have been conquered by Jesus. Among the Fathers who follow this interpretation are St. Irenaeus and St. Ephrem Syrus.[13] St. Cyril of Jerusalem in the fourth century states firmly that Christ 'descended into hell alone, but ascended thence with a great company; for he went down to death, and many bodies of the saints who slept arose through him'.[14]

For the Fathers of the first four centuries the resurrection of the saints as described at Mt 27.52ff. is but the visible and external effect of Christ's descent into hell, which for them was quite central to the doctrine of redemption, and to the resurrection in particular. The traditional Byzantine icon of Easter makes the dogmatic point very well. Here the resurrection of the Lord is shown as the resurrection of humanity, the raising of Adam and Eve from the depths of hell. Christ stands not as a solitary figure above the tomb, as in late medieval and Renaissance images, but clasping the hands of Adam and Eve, in perfect solidarity, in what one might call 'resurrection-relatedness' with him. The words of the great Holy Saturday homily ascribed to St. Epiphanius might almost be a verbal description of the icon. Christ descends into hell and speak thus to Adam.

'I am your God, and through you I have become your Son. Arise, sleeper, for I have not created you to be fettered in Hades. Arise from the dead; I am the life of the dead. Arise, my creature, my form, made in my image and likeness. *Come and let us go hence, for you are in me and I in you, and both of us together are one single and inseparable person.*'[15]

It would be difficult to find a more eloquent summary of the grasp of Scripture and early tradition of Our Lord's solidarity with mankind not only in the days of the flesh but also now, even more intensely, in the glory of the resurrection. As I hope this over-long section has shown, for both Scripture and Tradition, the heart of the doctrine of the resurrection is this sense of the communal, inclusive body of glory. Now I believe that it is precisely this sense of 'resurrection-relatedness' that is the foundation of the doctrine of the Assumption of Our Blessed

Lady. As we can now see from what the Fathers say about the resurrection of Jesus, we can affirm that, while the victory over death that has taken place in Mary may not be general, there is an important sense in which it can be said to be thoroughly 'normal', a direct upshot and fruit of Christ's own victory over sin and death. None of the texts we have cited from Fathers of the first four centuries can be adduced as proof that these same Fathers explicitly believed in the Assumption, but they do certainly place arguments for the fittingness of the doctrine of the Assumption in a new light; the Assumption is 'fitting', not in the sense of 'it would be nice if it were true', but because it can be seen to maintain the coherence of the divine economy and to be integrally related to those central dogmas of Christ and salvation so long fought over during the first four hundred years of the Church's existence.[16]

It must be admitted that these early patristic commentators on Mt 27.52 do not extend the principle to Mary. Nevertheless, the almost unanimous witness of the first four centuries remains impressive in its declaration that there is an inclusiveness, a generosity, about the resurrection of Christ, in the context of which the Assumption can no longer be seriously seen as an heretical intrusion into orthodox soteriology.

The Typology of the Assumption

However, we must now go on to consider the extent to which the first Catholic preachers of the Assumption (almost all eastern) remain faithful in their exposition to this earlier, more general conception of the corporate nature of Christ's resurrection. Theoteknos, sixth-century bishop of Livias in Palestine and author of our earliest homily on the Assumption, begins his *encomium* by setting Mary's Assumption firmly within the context of Easter, the resurrection of the Lord.

'In the resurrection of the Lord, our God and Saviour Jesus Christ, we all rejoice with happiness in spiritual songs, praising without ceasing him who has made ready all things for our salvation.'[17]

According to Theoteknos, in being taken into heaven Mary is not given some, as it were, élitist privilege, but shares fully now in the resurrection that is the hope of all men. Indeed, it is precisely the typological role of the Assumption, its prefiguring of the general resurrection, which we find most consistently stressed in our earliest witnesses. Despite the many differences in detail in the versions of the *Transitus*, it is significant that most include the story of the reassembly of the Church, the coming together of all the apostles from their various fields of mission, round the death-bed of Mary. The resurrection of Jesus leads, we are told in St. John's gospel, to the 'gathering into one of the scattered children of God' (11.52); Mary's resurrection is a type, an anticipation, of that ingathering. The resurrection of Jesus is not simply typological but effective, it has a causal and not simply iconic relation to the general resurrection. It does not simply prefigure the reassembly of all men but actually sets it in motion. Now Our Lady *receives* resurrection as we all shall through the power of God; the difference in her case being only its anticipation, its role as sign and type.

The theme of reassembly is pivotal for St. John Damascene. The cloud which brings the apostles to Zion for the Dormition is the fulfilment of the cloud which the OT prophet said would announce the coming of all peoples to Jerusalem at the end (Isaiah 60.8).[18] He makes a similar application of the gospel text 'wherever the body is, there the eagles will be gathered together' (Mt. 24.28).[19] The apostolic 'eagles' fly from the four corners of the earth for the laying to rest of the precious body of the Theotokos. In a word, the events surrounding the Dormition prefigure those of the end of time – the general resurrection and the ingathering of the nations in Jerusalem – which accompany the second coming of the Messiah. In this interpretation of the Assumption we see already the notion of Our Lady as the type of the Church, of the redeemed humanity. Damascene sees Mary as the figure of the Church triumphant, the heavenly Jerusalem, the definitive city of God. Thus he finds it most significant that Mary has lived and died in blessed Zion.[20]

The New Roman Missal, in its Preface of the Assumption, recapitulates well this teaching of the Fathers when it says: 'today the virgin Mother of God was taken up into heaven to be the beginning and the pattern of the Church in its perfection'. And, of course, this typological and ecclesiological dimension of Mariology in general and of the Assumption in particular is right to the fore in the treatment of Our Lady's role in salvation in both *Lumen Gentium* and the more recent *Marialis Cultus*. As I hope is now clear, all these contemporary documents are profoundly true to the spirit of the early Fathers of the Assumption.

The Assumption is typological in another sense. Not only does it look forward as a type to the general resurrection, it is also the antitype of an event in the past – the Lord's descent into hell. In one of the Syriac MSS on Mount Sinai, c.500, Mary's death-bed is the scene for the reassembly of the saints of the old covenant – Adam and Eve Seth, Shem and Noah, Abraham, Isaac and Jacob, and Anna, the Grandmother of the Lord.[21] Those figures traditionally believed to have been raised by the Lord when he descended into hell here come together as his Mother descends into death and is taken into heaven. There are, in fact, many structural resemblances between the early stories of the descent and the apocrypha of the Dormition, resemblances of great theological importance when we recall that the descent crystallizes what we have called resurrection-relatedness. It would seem very probable that from the time of the emergence of the *Transitus* an analogy was seen between Jesus' descent into hell and Mary's ascent into heaven: both are the upshot of Christ's solidarity with mankind.

116

Let us compare, for example, the words of Pseudo-Epiphanius already quoted from his homily on the descent with a passage from St. Germanus in which he recounts the incident of Our Lord telling his Mother that she is soon to be glorified. First, Christ to Adam in Pseudo-Epiphanius:

'I am your God, and through you I have become your Son.... Come and let us go hence, for you are in me and I in you, and both of us together are one single person.'

And Christ to Mary in Germanus:

'It is time to take you to be with me, you, my mother.... Where I am, you shall be also, Mother inseparable in her inseparable Son.'

Common to both the narrative of the descent and those of the Dormition is the stress on the union of Christ and his saints – he is inseparable from his Mother, and with Adam he is one inseparable person. Because of Our Lord's union with humanity his risen power, as it were, flows over to those who are one with him – to the saints of the old covenant and to his blessed Mother. As we have said now several times, what holds this bundle of descent, Assumption and general resurrection together is the Biblical-patristic idea of corporate resurrection. Christ has not been raised alone. Thus the word we took as the hall-mark of this theme, *sussoma* ('co-body'), re-emerges in the homilies of the Assumption. In that of Pseudo-Modestus, we find the following passage:

'Because Mary was the Mother of the Giver of Life and Immortality, Christ our God and Saviour, Mary was made alive by him so that she might be *concorporate* with him in incorruptibility for eternity. It is he who has raised her from the tomb and placed her beside him in a manner known only to him.'[22]

Similarly, in the fourth homily of Cosmas Vestitor, a Byzantine author of the mid-eighth century, we are told that for Christ and Mary

'... there was the same burial and the same translation to immortality since the flesh of the Mother and of the Son is one and the same flesh.'[23]

All the preachers return to this, perhaps the most fundamental theme: Mary gave flesh and life to him who is the life and the resurrection; therefore she now receives from him the gift of risen life. They recapitulate the teaching of the Lazarus story: resurrection involves a believing, bodily relation to Jesus: 'whoever lives and believes in me will never die.' Our Lady has the closest bodily, indeed 'concorporal,' relation to Jesus her Son, and her faith at the Annunciation reversed the disloyalty of Eve. Therefore she is now raised from the dead, and her relics are not here but in glory in heaven. Her virginity, perpetual in both conception and birth of the Saviour, was already, as St. Gregory of Nyssa said, like a rock upon which death may be dashed.[24] For in being Virgin Mother she demonstrates that with God all things are possible and that human nature, in all of its physical and spiritual aspects, is not a machine governed by deterministic laws and doomed to death but rather capable of transfiguration by the Spirit of God. All this the Fathers saw crystallized in the events of Mary's God-bearing, and now the possibility of transfiguration and of death's destruction becomes actual. She passes into life.

After this over-long discussion, it should now be clear that the basis of belief in the Assumption is not, as some have claimed, a minimal estimation of Christ's humanity but rather a vigorous affirmation of his solidarity with us in his living, dying and rising again. It is the Christological dogmas, not Docetism or Monophysitism, which are the heart of the Marian dogma. The Assumption preserves a sense of the humanity of Christ against all Docetism and of the corporate nature of salvation against the heresy of pernicious individualism.

Ecumenical Implications

Having concluded the major part of my paper, I would like to go on to consider the ecumenical implications of what I have said, and first of all, with regard to the Holy Orthodox Churches of the East. It is occasionally maintained that the term 'assumption' (in the West) and 'dormition' (in the East) reveal a disagreement over the nature of Mary's end, that 'dormition' implies something less precise than 'assumption', perhaps not even a bodily passage at all. This, of course, is nonsense: while it is true that the Orthodox have preserved the older name Dormition, they celebrate that day precisely as the day of Our Lady's *bodily* glorification. As MD itself points out, the great Fathers of the bodily Assumption are all eastern – Damascene, Germanus, Andrew of Crete, and the others we have mentioned. Not only did the *Transitus* originate in the East, but these first theological expositors of the bodily ascension of Mary were all in the Byzantine theological tradition. If anything, the eastern liturgies are far more explicit in teaching the bodily assumption than the western. Consider, for example, from the Liturgy of the Feast of the Dormition this contakion:

'The tomb and death have not been able to hold the Mother of God, who is constant in supplications, in intercession and unfailing hope; for the Mother of Life is come into the presence of the Life, who took up his abode in her ever-virgin womb.'

In fact, both East and West are united in their belief in, and celebration, of the Assumption, that is, the resurrection and glorification of Our Lady in body and soul; united too in their devotion to her as Queen of Heaven and as advocate of the human race in and through her Son. No, what remains at issue is the status of the belief. While for the West the Assumption is defined as a dogma, for the East the Assumption remains without precise definition. It would be wrong, however, to exaggerate these differences. For the Orthodox, there can be no question of the 'optional' nature of the Assumption of the Mother of God. Because of the doxological and liturgical orientation of their theology the enormous importance attached to the Dormition as a liturgical celebration is sufficient guarantee of its theological place. And many modern Orthodox theologians, among them Bulgakov, Losskii and Evdokimov, have written theologically about the Assumption. Moreover, it would be wrong to see MD as a prosaic Curial document, rationalistically laying down the law about Mary's departure from this world, although I am afraid that this is how many non-Catholics would want to see it – a product of what Austin Farrer called the papal 'fact-factory' going full blast. Objective reading of the document, however, creates a different impression. To begin with, its language is strikingly austere, drawn primarily not from philosophical or Scholastic sources but from Scripture and the Fathers. In many ways MD has characteristics in common with the older and more central Christological definitions: it strives, like them, to protect a mystery from one-sided rationalization. It can be seriously argued that MD has the same intentions as one of its sternest critics, the late Vladimir Lossky, who while being a most passionate believer in the bodily Assumption, opposed its formal definition, since he regarded the mystery of Mary as 'not so much an object of faith as a foundation of our hope, a fruit of faith, ripened in Tradition'. 'Let us', he said, 'keep silence, and let us not try to dogmatize about the supreme glory of the Mother of God.'[25] I believe that it was precisely to preserve this authentic contemplative silence with regard to Mary and to prevent dogmatization in the pejorative sense, dogmatization by the various schools of Mariological thought, that the Apostolic Constitution was promulgated. MD is both an end and a beginning: the end of perhaps several generations of Mariological *speculation* and the beginning of that movement of renewal and *ressourcement* that was to bear fruit at the Council ten years later. Seen in its historical context, the Dogmatic Definition is neither tactless nor triumphalistic, but a decisively prophetic act. It anticipated *Lumen Gentium* and *Marialis Cultus* by situating the Assumption firmly within Christology and soteriology. Above all, close reading of MD demonstrates, I believe, that the dogmatic status of the Assumption does not place it in competition with the great Christological and Trinitarian dogmas, but rather brings before the mind of the Church its essential links with those dogmas, which are the very foundation of the faith. Those non-Catholics who in the past have protested, 'But only the doctrines of God and Christ may be dogmatized', have expressed perhaps unwittingly, a little of the *raison d'etre* of MD, which intended to defend a full doctrine of Christ as much as that of Our Lady.

I have tried to show how the Assumption depends on a very strong sense of Christ's solidarity with mankind. I believe that it was this Christological idea, with its moral and social implications, that constituted at least one of the major intentions in the mind of the Church at the time of the Definition. In an address given two days before the

Definition, Pope Pius XII, speaking in Italian, had this to say about the historical predicament of modern man to which he believed the dogma offered healing and constructive help:

'The world is without peace, is tormented on every side by hostility, division, opposition and hatred, because faith has grown weak, and almost all sense of love and brotherhood in Christ has been lost, while we pray in all ardour that she who has been assumed may be a sign of the return to human hearts of the warmth of human affection and life. We do not tire in reminding this world that nothing can ever prevail over the fact and the knowledge that we are all children of one and the same Mother, Mary, who is alive in heaven and is a bond of union for the Mystical Body of Christ, as new Eve, and new Mother of the Living, who wishes to lead all men to the truth and the grace of her divine Son.'[26]

Pope Pius saw that the Assumption struck a prophetic blow against the institutionalized individualism of the modern world, its competitive and alienated spirit, demonstrated in a global way in the Second World War, which had ended only five years before, and daily seen in men's lives. A dogma that is based on an indestructible relationship of Mother and Son, and of the Son with humanity, has much to offer the world. Indeed, one may go further and say that devotion to Mary is always a challenge to our capacity for love and brotherhood and solidarity. Pope Pius XII perceived a connection, not sufficiently proclaimed today, between love of Mary and love of neighbour. Those who find love of Mary inconceivable or impossible because it conflicts with love of Christ have failed to see that the love of Christ precisely sets us free from the narrow, calculating, individualistic heart and mind, which would set limits on love. True love of Jesus is proved not by the incantation of the limits of that love but by allowing that love to overflow – to our neighbour, to the sick and poor and hungry, in whom Christ dwells, to our enemies, yes, even to the unloved and unlovable. Above all, our love of Jesus shows itself in our love of his Blessed Mother and his saints who share his glory and who indeed are living icons of Christ. If there is a scandal about our love of Mary and the saints, then there is a scandal about our love of neighbour and enemy. And indeed there is such a scandal for the kind of world described by Pope Pius. Such a world cannot comprehend love so amazing, so divine, so inclusive, so generous. And yet that love alone can give meaning to human life.

Upon lines such as these I would urge the non-Catholic world to begin the appropriation of the profound theology and spirituality of the Assumption of the Blessed Virgin Mary. It is an appropriation that must begin with orthodox Christology and soteriology and must continue by exploring the social implications of the dogmatic foundations of the faith. Our Lady of the Assumption is protectress, *pace* Dr. Chadwick of Christ's solidarity with mankind and of the social teaching that flows from it. She is, after all, also Our Lady of the Magnificat, the poor virgin heralding the exaltation of God's poor. In her Assumption we see the fulfilment of the Magnificat. For Christ, who preaches good news to the poor and oppressed, has raised up his Mother in her poverty and made her a sign to the wretched of the earth that their final liberation is promised and certain.

The Source of the Doctrine

Finally, if I may presume on your patience for a few moments more, let me keep *my* promise and return to a question I mentioned at the very beginning: what is the source of the doctrine of the Assumption? Given that neither the *Transitus* nor the first homilies have the same relation to the Assumption as the gospel texts have to the resurrection, what sense can we make of the late appearance of the doctrine? For the subject of Mary's death is not even brought up, let alone satisfactorily dealt with, until the late fourth century – in an enigmatic passage of St. Ambrose's commentary on St. Luke and in St. Epiphanius, who discusses the various possibilities of Mary's departure from this world. There can be no satisfactory answer to all this except in terms of the Church's Tradition, especially when we recall that, among other things, Tradition is an organically growing *language*, indeed a participation through the Spirit in the language of God himself, the Word made flesh. I believe that the resurrection-relatedness, which we have seen to be so significant for our doctrines of the Church and the Assumption, is the key also to the idea of Tradition. The Church can only claim to speak and know the truth because of her believing, bodily inherence in Christ, the Word incarnate, and because of the Spirit's indwelling of her. We know the Assumption to be true not on the basis of interior speculation but through the communal experience and wisdom of the Body of Christ, the Catholic Church. We can now see an even deeper sense in which the Assumption is 'fitting': the 'co-body' that made it possible is also the means by which *we know it*. We know it only through, with and in the risen Christ. The 'source' of the doctrine of the Assumption is ultimately the interpretation within the Church, precipitated by, but not simply a function of, the growing Christological sense of Mary's role, that Our Lady is risen with Christ, reigns with him in heaven, and intercedes for us, and that her relics are there, not here. As I hope is now clear, that vision of heavenly reality was fired by the doctrines of Christ, salvation and the Church. It is a vision that Catholic Christendom must never lose or compromise and that the Anglican Church must at all costs regain.

NOTES

[1] AAS, ser. 2, V.17, n.15 (4 November 1950), 761.

[2] Henry Chadwick, 'Eucharist and Christology in the Nestorian Controversy', *JTS*, N.S., ii (1951), 163f.

Dr. Chadwick points out that in his article quoted by Father Saward he made two points: (1) that the apocryphal stories of the Assumption were connected with Monophysitism; (2) that some Roman Catholic writers had held that the resurrection of Christ was incomprehensible, and that we could only comprehend a resurrection of a solely human person, namely Mary. Dr. Chadwick, in writing the article, expected Roman Catholic writers to reject this view.

[3] Cited by H. S. Box, 'The Assumption', in *The Blessed Virgin Mary*. Essays by Anglican Writers, edited by E.L. Mascall and H.S. Box (London, 1963), p. 89.

[4] Text in Migne, PL 59,157-161; ed. E. von Dobschutz T.U., xxxviii, hft.4 (1912).

[5] 'The Falling Asleep of Mary', *Coptic Apocryphal Gospels,* transl. Forbes Robinson, *T.S.* 4,2 (Cantab., 1896), pp. 106ff. See also the text of M. Chaine, *Rev. de l'Or. Chret.* ix (xxix) (1933-34), 290f.

[6] *Hom. 1 in dorm.* 3; PG. 704Af; ed. P. Voulet (Paris, 1961), p. 86f.

[7] *Hom. 2 in dorm.* 15; 744B; p. 162.

[8] Cf. *Hom. 2 in dorm.* 10; 736D; p. 148.

[9] *Hom 2 in dorm.*; PG 98.361A. Migne's division into two homilies is mistaken. The two are, in fact, sections of the same homily. See M. Jugie, *Echos D'Or.* xvi (1915), 219ff.

[10] ibid., 348A.

[11] *Hom. 10 in 1 Cor. 15.28.*; PG 44.1316 AB.

[12] Cf. K. Rahner, 'Zum Sinn des Assumpta-Dogmas', *Aschriften zur Theologie,* vol. 1. (Einsiedeln., 1960), p. 244; *ET* (London, 1961), p. 219.

[13] For references, see H. Zeller, 'Corpora Sanctorum. Eine Studie zu Mt. 27.52-53', *ZKT,* lxxi (1949), *passim.*

[14] *Catech.* 14,18; PG 33.843C.

[15] *Hom. 2*; PG 43.461BC.

[16] Cf. Zeller, op. cit., p. 464f.

[17] Text in A. Wenger A A., *L'Assomption de la t.s. Vierge dans la tradition Byzantine du Vle-au Xe siecle.* (Paris, 1955), p. 272.

[18] *Hom. 3. in dorm.* 4; 757D; p. 188.

[19] *Hom. 2 in dorm.* 6; 732A; p. 138f.

[20] *Hom. 1 in dorm.* 12; *3 dorm.* 2.

[21] In the 'Sinai dossier', Syriac manuscripts of the 6th century professing to be translation of Greek books brought together at the monastery of St. Catherine on Sinai in 500 AD. Other early texts include some in Greek, attributed to St. John the Evangelist; there is also a fragmentary Syriac MS of the fifth century. The Syriac texts were published with *ET* by Wright in *JSL* vii (1865), pp. 129ff. The Greek is in *Apocalypses apocryphae,* ed. C. Tischendorff (Leipzig, 1866), pp. 95ff.

[22] *Hom. in dorm.* 14; PG86. 3212B.

[23] Wenger,p. 330.

[24] *De virg.* 13; PG 46.377CD; ed. J.P. Cavarnos (Leiden, 1952), p. 305f.

[25] '*Panagua*', *The Mother of God.* ed. E.L. Mascall (London, 1949), p. 35.

[26] *AAS,* ser 2, V. 17, n. 15 (4 November 1950), 781.

Many valuable points were made in the discussion which followed Fr. Saward's paper. We have space to print extracts from only two contributions.

Archdeacon G.B. Timms:

I listened with a profound appreciation of the paper this morning, but I fear that at the end of the paper I was as sceptical of the truth as I was at the beginning. I speak, I hope, as a Catholic-Anglican, and I have no difficulty whatsoever in giving a wholehearted assent to the words of Bishop Ken, in his hymn on Our Lady: 'Transcendent joys her entrance grace'.

Next to his throne her Son his mother placed! I can accept that *ex animo*, believing that Our Lady enjoys the beatific vision and is clothed in that body which is from heaven and of which St. Paul speaks in his second Letter to the people of Corinth. My difficulty arises in what I believe to be the basis of belief in the Assumption, namely that the body of the Mother of Jesus saw no corruption. May I get this straight at the beginning, because if I have got it wrong I don't wish to say any more? This is where my difficulty comes in, because, in spite of his learned and most attractive paper, Father Saward failed to deal with what to me is the absolutely fundamental problem of the total lack of any historic evidence whatsoever for this event. Now if we look at the Resurrection and the Ascension of Our Lord, we do have, in the New Testament writings, the record and the testimony of witnesses who declare that they experienced these events in some historic sense. One might argue about certain discrepancies, but the witness to the reality of the events is strong, and hence these documents concerning Our Lord's Resurrection and Ascension have been believed by the Christian community from the beginning, and have found their place in the Catholic creeds of Christendom. But the Assumption of Our Lady is very different case. There are not contemporary, or near contemporary, witnesses. For four hundred years or more, the Christian world is silent. I take the point that silence does not necessarily mean disbelief but I find a difficulty in this case. If this amazing event of the bodily Assumption took place, it must have done so during the period of some at least of the New Testament writings. Now here is an amazing event comparable to the Resurrection and Ascension of the Lord, yet no New Testament author, nor indeed any of the early Christian Fathers, shows any knowledge of it whatsoever. And then suddenly it begins to be adumbrated in those strange apocryphal writings which we heard of today. I don't depreciate the importance of Christian tradition. I feel very tied by loyalty, in a sense, to a tradition which seems to have existed in both East and West for a long, long time. This is the nub of my difficulty.

Bishop B.C. Butler:

Archdeacon Timms said that if it were only a question of believing that Our Lady is with Our Lord in the beatific vision, and clothed with that spiritual body of which St. Paul speaks, with that doctrine he would not have very much positive quarrel. Did I get you right on that? (Archdeacon Timms: I affirm in *ex animo*.) I must confess the thought went through my mind that this is precisely what I mean when I assent to the Roman Catholic doctrine of the Assumption. (Archdeacon Timms: Glory be!) Archdeacon Timms then went on – and he looked round to the Roman Catholic members of the panel here for confirmation – to say that there is a further affirmation about the incorruptibility of Our Lady's body. And I was rather dismayed to find that everybody agreed that there was that further thing. Now this is the precise question that I would like to ask here. I think we have to do a lot of really deep demythologisations of this particular problem. First of all, if I study what Pius XII actually defined, I find no reference to the incorruption of Our Lady's body as it was known on earth. I find no reference to an alleged empty tomb. I am not talking about all the sort of paraphernalia that the pope wove around this definition; I am talking about the actual definition to which he requires assent of his fellow Roman Catholics. I am not at all convinced in my own mind, and I am speaking now as a theologian not as bishop, that if we could conduct the right excavations we would not find the skeleton of Our Lady somewhere. It would be difficult to identify it, but theoretically it might be a discoverable thing. What I believe is affirmed is that Our Lady enjoys, in virtue of her close union with her Son, that fullness of bliss which we all hope to enjoy after the final Resurrection; in a sense you have a case of anticipated eschatology. Now if that is the case what about all these apocryphal traditions? And what about the way in which this has been talked about and depicted in Christian tradition? I don't think I have very much difficulty at this particular point. I suspect, that, after the first Council of Ephesus, the intuition which Archdeacon Timms shares with his Laudian spiritual ancestors that Our Lady is already in heaven in the fullness of possession of what goes with the beatific vision, seized the Church. How did the Church express it in those days when they had not made that marvellous division that we have made between mythology and truth, and so forth? They had to clothe it mythologically to express it. Hence you get the apocryphal traditions, and the implication that the tomb was empty and that Our Lady's earthly body was uncorrupt and so forth. A Christian must hold, it seems to me, that when St. Paul says that the body in which we shall be clothed at the Resurrection shall be a spiritual body, he was not intending to affirm a failure of identity between that spiritual body in heaven and the earthly one. The material constituents may have changed, but the identity of a body, as I understand it, is constituted by its being the body of one identical soul; and therefore to ascend body and soul into heaven could be taken as affirming precisely what Archdeacon Timms believes and need not be taken as affirming anything more. I don't want any one to be misled into thinking that I suppose that a Catholic need not believe that Our Lady is assumed bodily into heaven. That is defined and for me that settles the matter. The question is the undertanding of that phrase.

124

The Immaculate Conception, the Assumption and Reunion

REV. EDWARD YARNOLD, S.J.

It is fashionable nowadays among Roman Catholic theologians to talk about theological pluralism. This is something new with us. Our Anglican friends of course have always made a point of this. They call it comprehensiveness and we used to poke mild fun at them for it – as, I more than suspect, they sometimes do at themselves. But it is quite clear that Roman Catholics now practise the same art, though without such confidence and with less balance and nimbleness of footwork – as you would expect from beginners at the game. Indeed, as discreet a theologian as Karl Rahner, advocates a high degree of pluralism of belief within a united Christian Church.

Bishop B.C. Butler has criticised this view in the *Tablet*, and I must say I share many of his misgivings. Even though *lex orandi statuat legem credendi,* there is an enormous difference between pluralism of devotion and pluralism of belief. Devotion is so closely connected with cultures and temperaments that the church would be intolerably impoverished if its private prayer and public worship were forced to conform to a single pattern. But it seems to me that it is quite different with beliefs. Christians cannot simply tolerate, or even welcome, differences of belief as a sign of a healthy vitality and catholicity. We cannot be content with the knowledge that all Christians share the supernatural gift of faith at a level which is prior to any formulation in words; each tradition needs to satisfy other traditions that its credal formulas truly articulate this non-conceptual faith, and each will itself wish to be satisfied that the formulae of other traditions are similarly valid. As the Apostle John recognized, when he ran unwashed out of the baths at the sight of the heretic Cerinthus, there are limits to theological pluralism. Once the Church gives up the concept of doctrinal orthodoxy, it would do best to shut up shop.

The Dean of York in discussion stated that belief in the Assumption seemed to him not unreasonable, but that he could not see how this could be an article of faith, as it is not taught explicitly in scripture. This is a commonly stated Anglican position which I take very seriously. My aim is to seek some contact between this view and the Roman Catholic's belief that the two recently-defined Marian dogmas, the Immaculate Conception and the Assumption, are essential parts of the Christian faith.

Some Roman Catholics have recourse to a simple appeal to the concept of a hierarchy of doctrines that has become current since

Vatican II. These two dogmas, it is said, rank low in the hierarchy, and therefore assent to them need not be imposed on any other Church that seeks union with Rome.

This line of argument, however, though promising, is not a short cut to a solution. Not only on the Roman Catholic side but also on the other, serious difficulties remain. The Catholic needs to satisfy himself that these dogmas, which he accepts as part of revelation, are nevertheless not so essential that reunion is possible only with those who are prepared to accept them. The Christian of another tradition, on the other hand, will need to consider whether he can trust himself to a united Church of which perhaps the greater part claims the power to define doctrines to which he cannot give the assent of faith.

Evidently greater precision needs to be given to the concept of a hierarchy of doctrines. The phrase is a new coinage and in the documents of Vatican II occurs only in a sentence which was a late addition to the Decree on Ecumenism, where it interrupts the logic of the paragraph on ecumenical dialogue into which it was inserted:

> When comparing doctrines, they should remember that in Catholic teaching there exists an order or 'hierarchy' of truths, since they vary in their relationship to the foundation of the Christian faith (n.11)

No further explanation is given. (Cf. Commentary on the Documents of Vatican II, ed. H. Vorgrimler, Burns and Oates/Herder and Herder, Vol. 2, pp. 118–121.]

It seems quite unacceptable as an explanation to suggest that some doctrines of the faith are not of the first rank because they are about inessential areas of Christian belief. All articles of the faith are essential, because they must all be about Christ, about the way he saves, the way he reveals the Father and sends the Spirit to his Church. They can be Christian dogmas only in so far as they do this. In this respect there is no hierarchy of doctrines. But where there is a hierarchy is in the immediacy of the connection of the saving work of Christ with a particular verbal formulation of doctrine. Some doctrines can be couched in such a form that they make no explicit mention of Christ at all. In this sense they could be regarded as of secondary rank; but ultimately they must be about Christ, and in this all doctrines are equal.

The two recently-defined Marian doctrines, therefore, impose upon the Roman Catholic ecumenist a double task. First, he has to show that they do cast light upon 'the foundation of the Christian faith', because otherwise they cannot form part of revelation. Secondly, he has to show that these dogmas are nevertheless of secondary rank, so that the 'one faith' (Eph. 4.5) would not be fragmented by those who do not believe they are among the revealed truths of the Gospel.

126

In 1854 Pius IX with all solemnity declared that it was an article of faith that 'the most blessed Virgin Mary, by a unique grace and privilege bestowed by almighty God, by virtue of the merits of Jesus Christ the Saviour of the human race, was at the first moment of her conception preserved from all stain of original sin.'

The Church had taken its time in making up its mind: indeed, several of the greatest medieval theologians had completely rejected the suggestion that Mary was free from original sin. The reason for this hesitation was crucial: if Mary had never been affected by Adam's sin, she was not one of the fallen human race, and therefore she was saved without being redeemed by her son. It was Duns Scotus who explained why Mary's immaculate conception did not in fact imply that she was not redeemed; her exemption from original sin, he said, was precisely a redemption, an anticipation of the salvation brought by her Son; this is the meaning of the words 'by virtue of the merits of Jesus Christ' in Pius' definition. Far from being unredeemed, she is, in Karl Rahner's phrase, the most perfectly redeemed: she had never been outside the body of the redeemed, and there was no part of her personality that resisted redemption.

Many theologians have spoken of the Immaculate Conception as Jesus' gift to his Mother, and have thus attempted to 'prove' it: it was fitting that he should honour her in this way; he was able so to do; therefore he must have done it – *decuit, potuit, ergo fecit*. Pius' decree spoke of Mary's 'unique privilege'. But this cannot be the heart of the matter, if we have been right in insisting that a doctrine of the faith must be about Christ. Any doctrine about Mary has to be fundamentally a doctrine about her Son and his universal saving mission. Freedom from original sin is not so much Mary's privilege as a qualification for her role in the history of salvation.

This is true in at least two ways. First, Mary had the unique duty of educating the Saviour of the World in his most formative years. It would be a derogation from her son's humanity to maintain that he came into the world with miraculously innate ideas, or that his human mind participated freely in the infinite divine knowledge. No, he had to learn, as any child had to learn, not only, not chiefly, facts; but attitudes, responses, moral values. In the hypersensitive first weeks, months and years of infancy the child's character is decisively moulded by its parents, especially its mother. Impatience, selfishness, self-distrust in her are assimilated with frightening readiness by an infant's absorbent mind. Mary needed to be holy for the sake of her influence on the character of her Son, and her Immaculate Conception provided the starting-point of her growth in holiness.

Secondly, Mary was preserved from original sin so that she might be able to speak her Fiat at the Annunciation. Luke emphasises the importance of her assent to God's plan, and contrasts it with Zechariah's disbelief in a similar situation. 'Blessed is she who believed that there would be a fulfilment of what was spoken to her from the Lord' (Lk. 1.45). The reward of her belief in the fulfilment of God's word seems to be precisely its fulfilment: the Incarnation is consequent upon her Fiat, though not caused or merited by it. St. Luke interweaves strand upon strand of symbolism into his narrative of the Infancy to show that Mary stands for Israel, God's Chosen People. In the words of a contemporary Anglican theologian, Derek Allen, 'Mary, at the end of Israel's history, the final personification of Israel, made the final act of faith, and so she realises the promise made to Abraham and brings forth his seed, or offspring, the Messiah' (*Mary in the Bible*, pp. 3–4).

We must not, however, place a false value upon her *fiat*. It is not the redeeming Yes to God's will that the author of Hebrews puts in the mouth of Christ as he 'came into the world': 'Lo, I have come to do thy will, O God' (Heb. 10.5–7). Mary is redeemed not Redeemer. Nevertheless the doctrine of the Communion of Saints implies that we each benefit by the charisms, the gifts of the Spirit, given to other members of Christ's Body. Salvation does not come to us without human assent and cooperation. Just as God cannot save me without my consent, he does not save me except through others. As St Augustine said, 'qui creavit te sine te, non redimit te sine te.'

Karl Rahner expresses the point in another way. Christ saves us through his Church: the Church is a means or sacrament of holiness. Because men are sinners, holiness is always transmitted through unworthy human instruments. But the gift of holiness with which Christ endowed his Church implies that some members of the Church will be outstandingly holy, and that this will be especially true at certain key-moments of the Church's history. The Annunciation was such a moment, was in fact the turning-point of history. The Church at this moment when the last remnant of the old Israel received the new, exhibited its holiness in both old and new, mother and Son. The Fiat needed to be spoken by one who was pre-eminently holy, with all the freedom of one whose choices were unclouded by original and personal sin.

The Assumption

In 1950 Pius XII 'for the glory of Almighty God ... and to increase the glory of his venerable Mother' declared that it was a revealed dogma that 'the immaculate, ever-Virgin Mary, the Mother of God, was taken up, body and soul into heavenly glory when her life on earth had run its course.' But the Assumption, like the Immaculate Conception, insofar as it is an article of faith, cannot be simply about the glory of Mary: it must be about Christ and the redemption.

Karl Rahner has put the Assumption firmly within this context. It is simply the completion of her redemption. She was the perfectly re-deemed on earth; there was nothing to prevent her from enjoying the glory of heaven as soon as she departed from this life. She is already in glory, body and soul; redemption is a glorification of the whole personality. Heaven is indeed a transformation: 'we are God's children now; it does not yet appear what we shall be' (1 Jn. 3.2). But, though transformed, we shall still be ourselves. What we have allowed grace to make of us in this life, that we shall be in heaven – purified, glorified, but still the same selves. 'Not that we would be unclothed, but that we would be further clothed, so that what is mortal may be swallowed up in life' (2 Cor. 5.4). Salvation is not liberation from the body, as En-cratites, Gnostics, Manichees and Cathars have taught at various periods of the Church's history, salvation is the fulfilment of the self of which the body is one dimension.

A Suggestion

These are ways, then, in which these Marian doctrines can be expressed in terms which make them capable of being articles of faith. However, I have no illusions: I have not answered the Dean of York. The greatest assent I can hope to have won from someone who is not already committed to them is the judgment that they are not unreasonable, that they may well be true; but articles of faith – that is another matter. Though the reason for the doctrines is Christological, all the same they are in content expressions of faith about Mary, and as such are not contained in Scripture or early tradition. They are, it will be felt, at best reasonable theories, to which respect and even adherence may be given, but not the assent of supernatural faith.

When one section of Christianity holds beliefs which seem unacceptable to other Christians, the onus is on the former to try to commend their beliefs to the rest. If they do not succeed in this urgent task, the only alternatives are doctrinal indifferentism or the continuance of our divisions. It seems to me that theologians of my Church have not done enough to meet the difficulties of others. I wish therefore briefly and tentatively to suggest a possible solution.

Many, perhaps all, doctrines have two levels, which for convenience can be called the symbolic and the theological. I am aware that I am raising difficult and important questions, such as that of the meaning-fulness of distinguishing between an unchanging belief and its changing formulations. I do not wish to discuss whether a doctrine can be stated theologically without symbols. What I mean is that some doctrines which are formulated in historical or quasi-historical terms can have a further meaning which is expressed by these terms in a non-literal way, but could be expressed without them. The historical or quasi-historical formulation I call the symbolic meaning; the ulterior meaning the theological. The theological meaning is directly concerned with Christ

129

and the Redemption; the symbolic meaning need not be. Although it is not easy to formulate clear criteria for distinguishing between the symbolic and the theological, in some cases, at least, the distinction can be clearly drawn. Take as an obvious example the article of the Apostles' Creed: 'he descended into hell' The symbolic content of this doctrine is its literal meaning, that Jesus spent the time between his death and resurrection with the dead in hell (or limbo). The theological meaning is that those who died before Christ were saved only through him, that they had to wait for him in the sense that they owed their salvation to him.

I wish to suggest the following four theses concerning doctrines which have these two levels of interpretation:

(1) It sometimes happens that some Christians accept the literal truth of the symbolic form of a doctrine, while others do not, though without ceasing to affirm the doctrine.

(2) In these cases it sometimes happens that Christians, while not agreed whether the symbolic content should be accepted literally, agree about the theological meaning. This seems to be the situation with regard to such doctrines as the Virgin Birth or the Ascension.

(3) By contrast, there can be disagreement about the theological interpretation among those who accept the traditional verbal form of a doctrine, such as the doctrine of hell.

(4) – and most important for our present purpose – If there is agreement over the theological meaning, but disagreement over the interpretation or even the validity of the symbolic form in which it is expressed, there is no need for the one side to give way and agree to accept the symbol, nor for the other side to renounce it or cease to believe in its literal truth.

It is, I would suggest, this fourth type of agreement that we may hope can be reached over the doctrines of the Immaculate Conception and the Assumption. Roman Catholics may believe as of faith that Mary was preserved from original sin and assumed into heaven; other Christians may be unable to accept that these doctrines, so expressed, can be part of the Gospel. Both convictions could co-exist in a fully united Church, provided there was agreement about the theological level of the doctrines, which seems to me to be this: The Immaculate Conception means that it is of faith that God's grace requires human co-operation, provides the conditions which make the response possible and fruitful, and results in sanctification, so that the holiness of the Church will be verifiable in the lives of its members, and will overflow from member to member; the Assumption means that all that is truly of value in human existence continues after death, when it is transformed in heaven.

V
THE PROTESTANT TRADITION

Her can be found the eye of the sotrm in Marian ecumenical dialogue. In caricature, Protestants accuse Catholics of attributing to Mary, Mother of the Christ, what rightly belongs to her Son alone, as Son of God and Saviour of mankind. Catholics accuse Protestants of failing to include the Marian and sometimes even feminine dimensions in their doctrine and thought. Neither, of course, are quite fair in those accusations.

The first paper was given at a meeting of the Society in Washington DC on 3 November 1979 by the Professor of Church History and Director of the Institute for Luther Studies, Lutheran Theological Seminary, Gettysburg, Pa.

The second paper was given at a meeting of the Society in Washington on 30 April 1977 by the Professor of Theology at Union Theological Seminary, Richmond, Virginia. He is also President of the United States Chapter of the Society.

The third paper was read to the Ecumenical Society of the Blessed Virgin Mary in January 1968 by the Principal of Queen's College, Birmingham. He is also Executive Co-Chairman of the Society.

The fourth paper was given to the Oxford Branch of the Society on 23 October 1979 by the Rector of St Ebbe's Church, Oxford. The paper and concomitant discussion proved valuable not least in showing that many Evangelical misgivings about Marian doctrine may be directed against beliefs which are, now at least, not held by Catholics. Regrettably a report of the discussion cannot find space here, though it appeared in the Society's pamphlet.

Embodiment of Unmerited Grace

The Virgin Mary according to
Martin Luther and Lutheranism

REV. ERIC W. GRITSCH, Ph.D.

I. PREFACE

Although Luther research has unearthed sufficient evidence to suggest that the Wittenberg reformer was more "ecumenical" than "schismatic," his critical relationship to the Western liturgical-sacramental tradition, especially the role of Mary in that tradition, deserves renewed attention.[1] Luther, to be sure, rejected a Mariology which proclaimed in doctrine and cult the "mother of God" as mediator of all grace (*mediatrix omnium gratiarum*).[2] In the face of a massive medieval sacramental materialism grounded in the sacrament of penance, Luther took a minimalist position in order to communicate as clearly as possible the need for the reform of the church catholic: the center of the church is "Christ alone (*solus Christus*)." As he put it in a "table talk" on "How to Preach on the Annunciation of Mary" in 1933

> The incarnation ... should be held high. *Mary can't be sufficiently praised as a creature, but that the Creator himself comes to us and becomes our ransom – this is the reason for our rejoicing.*[3]

Luther, therefore, did not do away with the veneration of Mary. He preached ca. 60 sermons on Mary, usually at the festivals of Mary's epiphany (February 2) and annunciation (March 25). He never removed images of Mary and criticized those who did. Consistent with his emphasis upon God's incarnation in Christ as the center of Christian thought and life, he rejected only two festivals: Mary's resurrection (August 15) and the immaculate conception (December 8).[4] Mary was the "mother of God (*theotokos*)" precisely because Jesus was the "son of God"; but the "son" gives her the honour she deserves. That was to Luther the unanimous testimony of the apostles and the post-apostolic creeds.[5]

This paper presents Luther's view of Mary in the context just described – a christocentric theology which Luther saw affirmed in apostolic and patristic thought, but no longer in the normative scholastic tradition of the medieval Western church. To accomplish this basic objective; I shall 1) sketch Luther's exposition of the *Magnificat* (Luke 1:46–55) as the centerpiece of his view of Mary; 2) relate his exposition of the *Magnificat* to his basic theological and liturgical stance; and 3) show briefly how paradigmatic Luther's view of Mary is for Lutheranism.

II. THE EXPOSITION OF THE MAGNIFICAT
(LUKE 1:46–55)

Luther wrote his commentary on the *Magnificat* between December 1520 and September 1521, the stormiest period of his career:[6] he had published his reform proposals in well-known treatises during the summer of 1520; he had been condemned by papal bull and imperial edict during the first half of 1521; and he was an "exile" at the Wartburg when he put the finishing touches on the manuscript of the commentary in June 1521. He dedicated the *Magnificat* to the young Elector John Frederick of Saxony who, unlike his Uncle Frederick "the Wise," openly supported Luther and his cause. It was characteristic of Luther to turn to Holy Scripture in times of crisis and to ponder the relationship between the Word and God and the constellation of history in 1521, especially the role of political government. This seemed quite appropriate because Luke contrasted the humility of Mary with the arrogance of political power. Thus the theme of the canticle in the reversal of roles by God as the father of Jesus Christ.

> Even now and to the end of the world, all his [God's] works are such that out of that which is nothing, worthless, despised, wretched, and dead, He makes that which is something precious, honorable, blessed, and living. On the other hand, whatever is something precious, honorable, blessed, wretched and dying. In this manner, no creature can work; no creature can produce anything out of nothing.[7]

In a verse-by-verse exegesis ending in a systematic description of "God's works of mercy," Luther elaborated his view of Mary as the embodiment of God's unmerited grace. Here are the main features of this view:

1. Mary is the prototype of how God is to be "magnified." He is not to be "magnified" or praised for his distant, unchangeable majesty, but for his unconditional, graceful and ever-loving pursuit of his creatures. Thus Mary magnifies God for what *He* does rather than *magnifying herself* for what was done to her. "She finds herself the Mother of God, exalted above all mortals, and still remains so simple and so calm that she does not think of any poor serving maiden as beneath her."[8] This is truly "humility (*humilitas*),", "lowliness (*Niedrigkeit*)," indeed "nothingness (*Nichtigkeit*)."

> How lowly was the estate of this tender virgin and how unexpectedly this honor came to her, that God should regard her in such abundant grace. Hence she does not glory in her worthiness nor yet in her unworthiness, but solely in the divine regard, which is so exceedingly good and gracious that He deigned to look upon such a lowly maiden, and to look upon her

in so glorious and honorable fashion. They, therefore, do her an injustice who hold that she gloried, not indeed in her virginity, but in her humility. She gloried neither in the one nor in the other, but only in the gracious regard of God.[9]

2. "Being regarded by God" is the truly blessed state of Mary. She is the embodiment of God's grace by which others can see what kind of God the father of Jesus Christ is. This is Luther's interpretation of verse 48b, "All generations will call me blessed."

> Note that she does not say that men will speak all manner of good of her, praise her virtues, exalt her virginity or her humility, or sing of what she has done. But for this one thing alone, that God regarded her, men will call her blessed. That is to give all the glory to God as completely as it can be done.... Not *she* is praised thereby, but God's *grace* toward her.[10]

3. Mary is a model for theologians who need to properly distinguish between human and divine works. "She divides all the world into two parts and assigns to each side three works and three classes of men, so that either side has its exact counterpart to the other."[11] Like Jeremiah (9:23,24), Mary sees wisdom, might and riches on one side and kindness, justice and righteousness on the other. The former reflect human works, the latter the works of God. God uses his works to put down the works of men who are always tempted to deify themselves. God's works are "mercy" (v.50), "breaking spiritual pride" (v. 51), "putting down the mighty" (v.52), "exalting the lowly" (v.53), "filling the hungry with good things" and "sending the rich away empty" (v.53).

4. Ultimately, Mary points to the incarnation of God, Jesus, the "seed of Abraham" (v.55).

> She found the promise fulfilled in herself: hence she says: "It is now fulfilled; He has brought help and kept His word, solely in remembrance of his mercy." Hence we have the foundation of the Gospel and see why all its teaching and preaching drove men to faith in Christ and into Abraham's bosom. For where there is not this faith, no other way can be devised and no help given to lay hold of this blessed Seed. And indeed, the whole Bible depends on this oath of God, for in the Bible everything has to do with Christ.[12]

To sum up: To Luther, Mary is the "mother of God" who experienced his unmerited grace. Her personal experience of this grace is an example for all mankind that the mighty God cares for the lowly just as he cares for the exalted. That is God's work in history. Mary has no special qualifications for becoming the "mother of God"; she was chosen because she was a woman – just like the wood that was used for the cross of Christ.[13] Thus the contrast is not between Mary and other women, or between her and those who came after her, but between Mary and God. "She should be, and herself gladly would be, the foremost example of the grace of God."[14]

III. RELATION TO LUTHER'S THEOLOGY AND
LITURGICAL REFORM

The contrast between the "lowly virgin" and the "mighty princes" in the *Magnificat* reflects Luther's basic view of the contrariness of God who is both "hidden" and "revealed" in his creation and redemption. God works his "alien work" through creation, especially through political government. When one prince defeats another in battle, God discloses that he uses one against the other in order to make his judgment in history. History is the battleground God's "carnival" (as Luther likes to say). When God does his "proper" work, he uses his power directly, the power of the Holy Spirit mediated through the "audible" and "visible word" (St. Augustine's terms for word and sacrament). Only faith "knows" this work. Mary is the embodiment of God's "proper" work and an example of faith. Luther commends her *Magnificat* to Prince John Frederick of Saxony so that he may understand God's work in the "law" and the "gospel." The *Christian* prince, according to Luther, should understand both his duty to use the law of the sword as well as his responsibility to provide space for the gospel of God's unmerited grace. Mary is the example that God is in control of human history; he can choose the lowliest of the lowly and put down the mightiest of the mighty. Thus the *Magnificat* is the swansong, as it were, for those who think they have absolute power in the world. Only God has such power; he can remove tyrants and replace them with "good men".

Mary as the "mother of God" also discloses the peculiar dialectic of God's actions in history. By reversing her situation from "nothingness" to "exaltation," God discloses his unconditional love which is truly embodied in Jesus of Israel. Mary points to the saving reversal of the situation between God and his creatures. Instead of condemning them for their sin of disobedience, he accepts them through His Son. Luther like to call this reversal the "cheerful exchange (*fröhlicher Wechsel*)" between sin and grace, analogous to the relationship between a bride and bridegroom. As he put it in his famous treatise, "The Freedom of the Christian":

> Faith united the soul with Christ as a bride is united with her bridegroom. By this mystery, as the Apostle teaches, Christ and the soul become one flesh [Eph. 5:31–32]. And if they are one flesh and there is between them a true marriage – indeed the most perfect of marriages, since human marriages are but poor examples of this true marriage – it follows that everything they have they hold in common, the good as well as the evil. Accordingly, the believing soul can boast of and glory in whatever Christ has as though it were his own, and whatever the soul has Christ claims as his own.[15]

Although such faith is always personal, "for me (*pro me*)," the focus of attention is to be on God who grants it rather than on the believer himself/herself. "Mary, therefore, calls God her Saviour or her Salvation, *even though she neither saw nor felt that this was so, but trusted in sure confidence that He was her Saviour and her Salvation.*"[16] Luther was always concerned to distinguished between divine and human righteousness. Divine righteousness is "active" and human righteousness is "passive"; God gives and the believer receives. Faith is never earned but graciously granted. God "recreates" the way he "created": out of nothing. Thus Mary's canticle is a praise of God the creator and redeemer.

Luther's theological view of Mary also informed his liturgical reforms. He retained the use of the *Magnificat* in the Vespers with the *tonus peregrinus* (Pilgrim Tone) as the most frequently used congregational setting. The Lutheran hymnal of Joseph Klug, used in the Wittenberg order of 1533, states Luther's rationale in the preface to the canticle:

> First, she [Mary] sings with a joyous heart of the grace and blessing which the merciful God has shown to her, praising and thanking him for it.
>
> Second, she sings of the blessing and great and wonderful work which God continually does for all men in all the world; namely, that he takes mercy on the miserable and meek, that he raises the lowly and enriches the poor. Again, that he puts to nought the wisdom of the proud ⋯
>
> Third, she sings of the proper and highest; namely, that God has visited and redeemed Israel through his only Son Jesus Christ.[17]

The Wittenberg Order of 1533 also stated that before a particular feast and after the sermon, the German *Magnificat* is to be sung.[18] During and after the Reformation, Lutheran composers created elaborate choir settings for the canticle.[19]

To sum up: the *Magnificat* is a testimony to God's work of salvation which is directed to those who are most lowly and despised. Mary embodies both grace and faith in a world filled with suffering, struggle and conflict. God chooses suffering (*Anfechtung*) to disclose his will for mankind in the Jesus of Israel. Mary, like Jesus, is despised. She and Joseph become refugees: Jesus is born in a stable. And yet, Mary already knows of her future with God by her firm faith that He will deliver her from sin, death and devil. She always points to God and Christ. "I am to accept the child and his birth and forget the mother," Luther told his congregation in a Christmas sermon in 1530,

> as far as this is possible, although her part cannot be forgotten, for where there is a birth, there must also be a mother. Nevertheless, we dare not put our faith in the mother but only in the fact that the child was born.[20]

IV. LUTHER'S VIEW IN LUTHERANISM

Normative Lutheran theology, grounded in the Lutheran Confessions (*Book of Concord*, 1580), affirms Mary as "mother of God" echoing the classic Christian position. Since the eucharistic controversies between Lutherans and other "Protestants," especially Zwinglians and Calvinists, touched upon Christology and Mariology, the Lutheran "Formula of Concord" offered the normative formulation in 1577:

> On account of this personal union and communion of the natures [of Christ – *communicatio idiomatum*], Mary the most blessed virgin, did not conceive a mere, ordinary human being, but a human being who is truly the Son of the most high God, as the angel testifies. He demonstrated his divine majesty even in his mother's womb in that he was born of a virgin without violating her virginity. Therefore she is truly the mother of God and yet remained a virgin.[21]

Philip Melanchthon, the author of the Augsburg Confession of 1530, clearly distinguished between the proper veneration of Mary as the mother of Christ who died for the sins of mankind and any other "merit". In the "Apology" of Article 21 of the Augsburg Confession on the "invocation of saints," Melanchthon rejected Gabriel Biel's interpretation of the canon of the Mass which stated, "It is a divinely instituted order that we should take refuge in the help of the saints, so that we may be saved by their merits and vows."[22] He found that a form of absolution was used which appealed to the merits of Mary in addition to the passion of Christ for the forgiveness of sins.[23] Since the invocation of saints was understood to be a practice which threatened the article of justification about God's unmerited grace in Christ, Melanchthon used strong words and examples in his rejection of merit besides the merit of Christ:

> Granted that the blessed Mary prays for the church, does she receive souls in death, does she overcome death, does she give life? What does Christ do if blessed Mary does all this? Even though she is worthy of the highest honors, she does not want to be put on the same level as Christ but to have her example considered and followed. The fact of the matter is that in popular estimation the blessed Virgin has completely replaced Christ. Men have invoked her, trusted in mercy, sought strength through her to appease Christ, as though he were not a propitiator but only a terrible judge and avenger. We maintain that we dare not trust in the transfer of the saints' merits to us.... We obtain the forgiveness of sin only by Christ's merits when we believe in him.[24]

Melanchthon regarded the preoccupation with saints and their special spheres of influence as an unhealthy return to the Roman pagan tradition which assigned various gods to various works of merit for the redemption of Roman people. Once one gets started with special merits, he argued, the door opens to liturgical abuses and theological errors. "In one monastery we saw a statue of the blessed Virgin," he reported, "which was manipulated like a puppet so that it seemed to nod Yes or No to the petitioners.[25] Recent research into the late medieval practices has disclosed a casuistic preoccupation with the sacrament of penance could easily lead to abuses such as indicated by

Melanchthon.[26] But be that as it may, the Lutheran reform movement made it quite clear that Luther's christocentric stance seemed more ecumenical than late medieval practice and theology.[27]

A survey of traditional Lutheran theology since the 16th century reveals the same basic stance: the *solus Christus* is to be the center of any doctrine of grace, and any other "merit" by any saint or the Virgin Mary can only be seen as a humble testimony to the work of Christ. Thus Mary is at best a "serving background figure (*dienende Nebenfigur*)", as one of the less liberal but very influential Lutheran theologians, Adolf Schlatter, called her at the turn of the century.[28] Karl Barth, though not a Lutheran but certainly speaking for many Lutherans, may have summarized both the convergence and the divergence between Lutheran views of Mary and Roman Catholic Mariology: Mary is, in the non-Pelagian sense of the word, a "creature" who embodied the grace of God in Christ without, however, germinating any merit independent of the merits of Christ. That is the way Lutherans and Protestants would like to read in Thomas of Aquinas that "the mother of God is a pure creature (*mater Dei est pura creatura*)."[29] But this is not the way Thomas interpreted "pure (*pura*)!" Thus the divergence is once again evidenced in the christocentric Lutheran stance.

V. CONCLUSION

Karl Barth has reminded Protestants that their traditional rejection of Roman Catholic Mariology as a semi-Pelagian "cancer (*Wucherung*)" on the body of the ancient christological dogma may not be wholly justified in the face of Protestant interpretations of *solus Christus* and *sola fide*. For there have been various compromises in the Lutheran and Protestant history of doctrine between the doctrines of sin and grace.[30] The burden of certain Christian anthropologies, stressing the stance of the believer in a kind of proud fideism, has frequently weighed down the Reformation understanding of justification by faith in God's unmerited grace. The history of Lutheranism cannot really be written without the caveat, "Lutheran theologian, heal yourself!" As one of the very few Lutheran Mariologists put it in his efforts to renew Lutheran-Roman Catholic relations after World War II:

> As long as the veneration, which we direct to the Lord Jesus Christ, remains without the echo of the blessing granted by God to the mother of Jesus Christ, we may have to live with the suspicion of being not serious in our attention to the one mediator, Jesus Christ. He may have become a timeless idea which we call "Jesus".[31]

Although official Lutheran-Roman Catholic doctrinal dialogs have not directly dealt with Mariology, discussions of the different understanding of "teaching authority (*magisterium*)" between the two communions will indirectly influence mariological stances.[32] Moreover, significant convergences between Lutheran (and other Protestant) and Roman Catholic biblical scholars will also have their effect on Mariology in the future.[33] When Luther understood the vocation of the theologian to be the comprehension of God seen through suffering and the cross, he confessed the cruciformity of all theological formulations.[34] Thus even the best and brightest Mariology will remain within the context of a "theology of the Cross," which drives believers to praise God rather than to argue the difference between divine grace and human merit.[35] The proper function of the creature is to worship the creator whose truth will be revealed in fullness only when we meet God face to face in the name of Christ through whom we come to the majesty of the everlasting God.

REFERENCES

[1] For a general treatment see Vilmos Vajta, *Luther on Worship* (tr. U.S. Leupold, Philadelphia: Muhlenburg Press, 1958). Vajta, however, does not analyze Luther's views on Mary. See especially Hans Düffel, Luthers Stellung zur Marienverehrung (Göttingen: Vandenhoeck & Ruprecht, 1968); Horst-Dietrich Preuss, "Luthers Hauptgedanken über Maria, die Mutter Gottes", Luther XX (1955), 20–26; and Walter Tappolet, *Das Marienlob der Reformatoren* (Tübingen: Karzmann, 1962). For a recent reappraisal of Luther's liturgical views see "Luther, Worship and Liturgical Renewal" (The Martin Luther Colloquium 1975, Institute for Luther Studies, Lutheran Theological Seminary, Gettysburg, Pa.) *Bulletin* LVI (February 1976).

[2] An essential definition undergirded by the dogma of Mary's assumption promulgated November 1, 1950. For a Lutheran response to the dogma see Gerhard Ebeling, "Zur Frage nach dem Sinn des mariologischen Dogmas", *Zeitschrift für Theologie und Kirche* LXVII (1950), 383–391.

[3] Vol. 54 of *Luther's Works* (American Edition, ed. & tr. Theodore G. Tappert, Philadelphia: Fortress Press and St. Louis: Concordia Publishing House, 1967), "Table Talk" No. 494, p. 85. The 55-volume edition of *Luther's Works* (eds. Jaroslav Pelikan and Helmut T. Lehmann, Philadelphia and St. Louis, 1955–) is hereafter cited LW. Italics mine.

[4] Walter Delius, "Luther und die Marianverebrung", *Theologische Literaturzeitung* LXXIX, 7/8 (1954), 414.

[5] Luther analyzed the christological and mariological controversies associated with Nestorius and the Council of Ephesus in 431 in a lengthy treatise "On the Councils and the Church", 1539, LW 41, pp. 94–106. For Luther's christology see Ian D. Kingston Siggins, *Martin Luther's Doctrine of Christ* (London and New Haven: Yale University Press, 1970).

[6] For the historical context see Jaroslav Pelikan, IW 21, pp. xvii-xix. The original German text is found in vol. VII of the Weimar Edition of Luther's Works (*D. Martin Luthers Werke,* Weimar 1833–), pp. 538–604. English translation by A.T.W. Steinhaeuser in LW 21, pp. 297–358. For a detailed study of Luther's "Magnificat" see William O. Avery, "Martin Luther's *Magnificat*" (unpublished S.T.M. Thesis, Lutheran Theological Seminary, Gettysburg, Pa., 1973, Thesis Volume 722a).

[7] LW21, p. 299.

[8] *Ibid.*, p. 308.

[9] *Ibid.*, p. 314.

[10] *Ibid.*, p. 321.

[11] *Ibid.*, p. 331.

[12] *Ibid.*, pp. 353–354.

[13] *Ibid.*, p. 327.

[14] *Ibid.*, p. 323.
[15] LW31, p. 351.
[16] LW21, p. 309. Italics mine.
[17] LW53, pp. 176–77.
[18] See Luther D. Reed, *The Lutheran Liturgy*, (Philadelphia: Fortress Press, 1947), pp. 439–440.
[19] For example, the choral motets by Albert Dietrich, Karl Hassler, Melchior Vulpius, Johann Crüger; or the elaborate five-part setting by Johann Sebastian Bach. Reed, p. 440.
[20] "Sermon on the Afternoon of Christmas Day, December 25, 1530 on Luke 2:1–14." LW 51, p. 213.
[21] See Theodore G. Tappert (ed. & tr.), *The Book of Concord* (Philadelphia: Fortress Press, 1959), "Formula of Concord", "Solid Declaration" VIII, 24, p. 595. Original German and Latin editions in *Die Bekenntnisschriften der evangelisch-lutherischen Kirche* (Göttingen: Vandenhoeck & Ruprecht, 1956), p. 1024. Luther defended the doctrine of the perpetual virginity of Mary in the treatise "That Jesus Christ was Born a Jew", 1523. LW 45, pp. 210–213.
[22] "Apology" 21, 23. Tappert, p. 232. Latin text in Gabriel Biel, *Sacri canonis missae expositio*, 1488, Lect. 30. Quoted in *Die Bekenntnisschriften, op. cit.*, p. 321, n. 2.
[23] "Apology" 21, 25. Tappert, p. 232: "The passion of our Lord Jesus Christ and the merits of the most blessed virgin Mary and of all the saints be to thee for the forgiveness of sins". Similar formulae were used in Paris until 1682. See *Die Bekenntnisschriften, op. cit.*, p. 321, n. 4.
[24] "Apology" 21, 27–28. Tappert, *op. cit.*, pp. 232–233.
[25] *Ibid.*, 21, 34. Tappert, op. cit., p. 234.
[26] For a general description of the situation see Thomas W. Tentler, *Sin and Confession on the Eve of the Reformation* (Princeton, N.J.: Princeton University Press, 1977).
[27] See, for example, Ernst Wolf, "Luther und due 'Reformation' der Kirche" in: *Die Reformation, ihr geschichtlicher Ablauf und ihre Bedeutung für die Gegenwart* (Halle: Martin-Luther-Universität Halle-Wittenberg, 1969, pp. 22–33. Luther always sided with Chalcedonian christology in his struggles against Zwinglian and other Swiss "reformed" arguments on Christ's eucharistic presence. For a sample of Luther's argumentation see his treatise "Admonition Concerning the Sacrament of the Body and the Blood of our Lord", 1530. LW 38, pp. 97–137. That Luther and his movement wanted to be ecumenical is argued in Eric W. Gritsch and Robert W. Jenson, *Lutheranism. The Theological Movement and Its Confessional Writings* (Philadelphia: Fortress Press, 1976).
[28] Quoted in Karl Barth, *Church Dogmatics* 1/2 (Tr. G.T. Thomson and Harold Knight, New York: Charles Scribner's Sons, 1956), p. 139.
[29] *Summa theologica* III, qu. 25, art. 5, *sed contra.* Quoted in Barth, *op. cit.*, p. 143.
[30] *Ibid.*, p. 146. Barth's summary of mariology is found *ibid.*, pp. 139–149.
[31] Hans Asmussen, *Maria die Mutter Gottes* (Stuttgart: Evangelisches Verlagswerk, 1951), p. 61.
[32] See the findings of the Lutheran-Roman Catholic Dialog in North America, especially round VII on "Teaching Authority and Infallibility in the Church", "Common Statement", *Theological Studies* XXXIX, No. 1 (March 1979), pp. 113–166.
[33] See the first ecumenical study by Raymond E. Brown et al. (eds.), *Mary in the New Testament* (Philadelphia: Fortress Press and New York: Paulist Press, 1978).
[34] See Walter von Loewenich, *Luther's Theology of the Cross* (tr. Herbert J.A. Bouman, Minneapolis: Augsburg Publishing House, 1976).
[35] To make the move from the scholastic "sin-grace-theology" to doxology as the most appropriate response of believers to God's incarnation in Christ would be very helpful in avoiding future deadlocks between Lutheranism and Roman Catholicism. The veneration of Mary could then become a significant point of convergence for both traditions.

From Dysfunction to Disbelief

The Virgin Mary in Reformed Theology

REV. DONALD G. DAWE, Th.D.

I. The Ambiguity About Mary

Religious traditions in their historical development are dense with complexities. The difficulties of identifying the essence of a religion are manifold. As the critical historians remind us, often we do not so much discover the essence of a religion as create it. This is a particular danger in ecumenical dialogue as we seek to find those elements that we confess together in Christian faith. In ecumenical thinking on the Virgin Mary, it is usually the custom to discover within a tradition, in this case the Reformed tradition, the central and vital place of Mary in the scheme of salvation. Indeed, for the Reformed, there is to be found in the dogmaticians of the sixteenth and seventeenth centuries clear and pervasive testimony to the importance of Mary. While questions arose in the late eighteenth century about the place and importance of the virgin birth, there was a determined defence of its historicity by Reformed theologians in the nineteenth and early twentieth centuries. And Charles Augustus Briggs, the father of modern biblical studies and ecumenical theology in the United States, held to the doctrine of the Immaculate Conception.[1] In the twentieth century, Karl Barth and the Reformed Community at Taizé have given eloquent testimony to the theology and liturgical importance of Mary.[2] In face of all this evidence, it would be all too easy in the goodwill of ecumenical conversation to announce that this is, in fact, the essence of the Reformed tradition on Mary. But such a move would be only the premature creation of an essence on Reformed theology rather than its discovery. For as the critics of ecumenical theology are quick to point out, the Taizé Community is an anomaly in the Reformed tradition and that Briggs finished his ministry as a priest in the Episcopal Church.[3]

There had been an abundance of polemics against Mariolatry on every level of teaching of the Reformed churches. Even in Karl Barth, who is the major Reformed interpreter of Mary in this century, there are polemics against many forms of Marian devotion and doctrine. The modern Marian definitions, given by the Papacy, of the Immaculate Conception and the Bodily Assumption of the Blessed Virgin have been viewed negatively by Reformed theologians, as not only unwarranted in Scripture, but as being antithetical to the teachings of Scripture. The use of the term "Co-Mediatrix" as a title for Mary has been strongly rejected as compromising the sole mediatorship of Christ. Even amongst Reformed theologians themselves, there has been little dialogue on Mary. Both the conservatives, who hold to the historicity of the virgin birth, and the modernists, who reject it, agree that it is an issue that calls for little attention. So before reaching any premature, although comfortable conclusions, it is necessary to face the negative side of Reformed theology in its approach to Mary. If I may use the language of modern systems analysis, we must face "the worst case scenario" before concluding what options are open to use for the future. Hence, the rather dolorous sounding title of my essay "From Dysfunction to Disbelief." Out of examining the difficulties and ambiguities of the teachings on Mary in Reformed tradition, the way may be opened for a fresh restatement of our common faith.

II. Piety and Theology

My purpose in this essay is not simply to recite a history of doctrine but to explore the forces that shape and create the development of thinking about Mary among Reformed theologians. My contention is that you do not really understand how theologies function if you only study the succession of one theologian or group of theologians by another as if their predecessor were the causal agent that give rise to the followers. And further, theologians are not adequately understood simply as "teachers of the Church." We must also realize that the Church is the teacher of the theologians. What I am rejecting is the Platonic mythology of the theologian as "philosopher-king" who receives the clear and unbroken light of truth which he then tries to impose, with only indifferent success, upon a recalcitrant and often ungrateful Church. Rather, theology arises out of a complex dialectic between the religion of a confessing community and its relationship to the revelational sources of its faith. The piety, the cultus, the moral response, the institutional forms and liturgical life of a community of faith create the context of life through which the community receives and interprets the revelational sources of its unique faith. Those events which a community accepts as disclosures of ultimate meaning and takes a decisive for its existence are its revelational sources. For Christians this is the self-disclosure of God in Jesus Christ. A clear part of this revelational event, as witnessed to by Scripture, is the function of Mary in the entrance of the savior onto the plane of history.

The Christian religion, in its myriad forms, is the context within which the Christian community receives and interprets its revelational sources. While the revelational events form a source of the religion, the religious life of the community also creates the possibility and the limits of interpreting revelation. What a particular Christian community can confess in its theology about Mary and her function in salvation is shaped decisively by the place Mary is given in its piety and worship.

The ambiguities of modern Reformed theology on Mary are a function of the deep ambiguities in its piety and liturgy. The disbelief in the Virgin Mary found in much modern Reformed theology is a function of the loss of a vital place for Mary in the religious life of the Reformed churches. It is this shift in religiosity, far more than the advent of modern rationalistic and scientific arguments against the virgin birth, that created the present situation in Reformed theology. It was dysfunction that created disbelief and not vice versa.

III. The Place of Mary in the Ordo Salutis

The historicity of the virgin birth was universally accepted by both Catholic and Reformed theologians in the sixteenth and seventeenth centuries, even the heretic Michael Servetus accepted it, as did the Socinians and Anabaptists. This was not the issue. Calvin spoke of how Christ "chose for himself the virgin's womb as a temple in which to dwell." (*Institutes*, II, xiv, 1). The language of the seventeenth century Dutch theologian Henrici a Diest is detailed in the exposition of how the union of the human nature with the person of the Logos is achieved in the conception of Christ. "It is the conception of Christ, by which without male action and with the sole blood of the Virgin Mary, his human nature was formed, sanctified by the operation of the Holy Spirit, assumed by the Son of God and united personally to himself."[4] The *Seiden Synopsis* could speak of Mary as *theotokos* and *deipara* as well as the biblically sanctioned *mater Domini* (XXV, 25).

It has only been in the twentieth century in which a theologian aligned with a Reformed Church and its confessions could reach the conclusions of Emil Brunner that the Virgin birth obscures the meaning of the Incarnation and represents the introduction of a docetic trait that undercuts the biblical doctrine of creation.[5] Brunner goes on to argue, in an anomalous fashion, that even if the historicity of the virgin birth narratives could be established, they would not remove the theological objections to the doctrine. But the polemics of the earlier Reformed theologians against Marian devotion know nothing of Brunner's argument. Rather early Reformed polemics derived from a basic reconception of the *ordo salutis* – the ways by which the saving benefits of Christ are applied to the believer. The Reformed held to the historicity of the virgin birth and the importance of Mary in effecting the *unio personalis* that is the basis of the Incarnation. But this was a matter completed in the past. What they rejected was the ongoing function of Mary as a channel through whom the grace of Christ could enter the believer.

In medieval Catholic piety, Mary had emerged as the pre-eminent saint. The powers that were partially present in the host of saints were supremely present in Mary. As the polemic of the Reformers against the veneration and invocation of saints as a means of receiving salvation proceeded, it inevitably included a polemic against Marian devotion. Yet it is interesting to note that the vituperation frequently shown against other saints was seldom visited on Mary herself because of the high dignity she had for her role in the Incarnation. There is a real sense of horror in Calvin as he contemplates the impiety of men calling upon saints, who are simply human themselves, to provide a salvation which can come from God alone. "There are very many who do not refrain from the horrid sacrilege of calling upon the saints now not as helpers but as determiners of their salvation." Citing conciliar authority he goes on, "It was forbidden in the ancient Council of Cathage to direct prayers at the altar to saints'..." This included even prayers of people to "the holy virgin to bid her Son do what they request?" (*Institutes, II, xx, 22*).

This polemic against the saints and against Marian devotion was not simply a protest against late medieval abuses but was a part of a larger reordering of the theology of redemption. The aim of this reordering was to eliminate all human claims to having contributed anything to salvation. Every opportunity for the entry of what the Reformed theologians called "the conceit of works" must be eliminated. Faith itself is not a human act of will predisposing the mind to accept the truth of what the Church teaches. Rather, faith is the gift of God given only by the Holy Spirit which enables the believer to accept the truth of the Gospel as found in Scripture. But in Reformed theology this acceptance of the Gospel by faith is not simply receiving a truth about God which may subsequently become the basis of the conversion of life and sanctification that leads to salvation. Instead, faith is "saving faith", that is, it is the grounds for the forgiveness of the believer because as a person "in Christ" the believer has had imputed to him or her the righteousness of Christ. The benefits of the atoning death of Christ are applied directly to the believer by the Holy Spirit without the aid of the intercession of the saints or of the Blessed Virgin herself (*Second Helvetic Confession*, 5). The merits of the saints are of no avail because all of the necessary or possible merits needed for salvation come from Christ alone.

In the *ordo salutis* in Reformed theology the work of applying grace and enabling good works is done by the Holy Spirit directly. The *Westminster Confession* sets forth the steps of the *ordo salutis* with care: Effectual calling leads to adoption, sanctification, the granting of saving faith and repentance unto life which, in turn, produces good works, perseverance of the saints and the assurance of grace and salvation (X-XVIII). Each one of these steps is accomplished by the direct action of the Holy Spirit. The preaching of the Word and administering of Baptism and the Lord's Supper are the means ordinarily appointed for effectual calling of the believer. But even these external offices are not effective *ex opere operato* because they avail nothing for those who are not elect. (X, 4). Christian piety, the example of Mary and the saints, the Christian cultus, including the sacraments, are not so much means of grace as expressions of grace. The sole means of grace is the Holy Spirit working invisibly and inwardly on the heart of the elect. Mary and the saints have lost their function and have been consigned to the category of "dead men." Calvin speaks in a strange reversal of his position on immortality of the soul, of "the devilish insolence" of those who "do not hesitate to transfer to the dead (i.e., the saints) what properly belonged to God and Christ" (*Institutes*, III, xx, 22). In the classical teachers of Reformed theology, Mary's function was historically complete in the virginal conception and bearing of the Saviour. She had no ongoing function in the *ordo salutis* which is the work of the Holy Spirit alone. The nature of piety had been changed from that of a chain of meditation in which Mary was a vital link to that of direct divine intervention, inwardly and invisibly effective, on the heart of the believer. To channel this intervention through any human means, even that of Christian piety to the Blessed Virgin, would compromise the sovereignty of God and ground salvation in human powers.

IV. The Virgin Birth and the Authority of Scripture

With the disappearance of Marian devotion came also the disappearance of any but the most scattered and peripheral mention of Mary in formal theology until the end of the nineteenth and beginning of the twentieth centuries. At that time, concern for the virgin birth took on importance in Reformed theology as the crucial test case in the struggle over the authority of Scripture posed by the rise of modern, critical, historical analysis and theology.[6] A.M. Fairbairn, James Orr, Louis M. Sweet and J. Gresham Machen undertook a defense of the historicity of the virgin birth as part of the defense of the authority of Scripture against the modern biblical scholars.

The Bible-centered piety of the Reformed churches was intimately involved with the reliability of the Scriptural witness to the events in the history of salvation. This piety had been resistant to the rationalistic criticism that argued that the virgin birth was biologically impossible because it believed that the Bible gave an accurate report of a unique, miraculous event. But now new critical arguments were being advanced which maintained that the Scriptural accounts of the virgin birth were themselves contradictory, mythological and historically inaccurate. Conservative Reformed teachers rushed to the defense of the historical veracity of the biblical reports of the virgin birth. There was here no concern for Marian devotion but rather devotion to the Bible. There was an inseparable connection, these theologians argue, between the virgin birth and other Christian doctrines. As Machen put it, "If Christ really rose from the dead, if He really was at all the kind of person that He is represented in the New Testament as being, then there is every reason to think that He was conceived by the Holy Ghost and born of the Virgin Mary."[7]

What conservative Reformed teachers were rejecting was the accommodation modernists were making to scientific world views and historical criticism. Ever since the treatment of the virgin birth by Frederich Schleiermacher, modernists had affirmed their belief in the Incarnation, but separated this from acceptance of the virgin birth. It was, they argued, only a picture language used by the ancients to point to the real miracle of the relationship of God and man in Christ.[8] In face of such arguments, the virgin birth became a test case for orthodoxy because unlike the other miracles it could not be reinterpreted experientially. Modernists could treat the healings of Jesus psychosomatically, his atoning death could be viewed as the inspiration of others to deeds of heroic virtue, and his resurrection could be interpreted as his continuing influence over his followers in all ages. This allowed the liberals to affirm their belief in the major Christian doctrines by means of reinterpretation, while still keeping alive their claim to being truly modern. But when it came to the virgin birth such experiential reinterpretations were not a possibility. Here was an irreducible problem over which a "yes" or "no" decision was necessary. And as Machen concluded, "...if the Bible is regarded as being wrong in what it says about the birth of Christ, then obviously the authority of the Bible, in any high sense, is gone."[9]

Mary had come back into theology if not into piety. For piety she still remained the briefly seen figure in the Christmas pageant given in the Sunday School. Theology has claimed not so much Mary as a person as the isolated fact of the virginal conception. In a strange reversal of Catholic piety, for Reformed conservatism, it was not Mary, Mother of Christians, but Mary, Hammer of Heretics. The intellectual and spiritual anomaly of this position has left it the preserve of a small, and often shrill minority.

The confusion over Mary has continued in the Reformed tradition. Most theologians and pastors treat the question with silence. Their silence is seldom challenged since a liturgy and piety that give no function to Mary never raise the question of her meaning. Most Reformed theologians follow the lead of Schleiermacher. They separate faith in the Incarnation from belief in the virgin birth. They accept the findings of biblical scholars in the *Formgeschichte* and *Traditionsgeschichte* schools that the virgin birth does not belong to the basic *kerygma* but represents a derivative expression of early Christian liturgy of teaching. The question of the virgin birth and of the place of Mary is thus cut free from the authority of Scripture to be investigated historically and theologically as an expression of early church piety. And in this investigation many have concluded with Brunner that belief in a virgin birth is not only unnecessary but may well be inimitable to faith in the Incarnation.

It has only been since the emerging ecumenical dialogue with Catholicism, both eastern and western, that the question of Mary has become an inescapable one for the Reformed churches. How is it possible to affirm our oneness with other Christians for whom a Marian piety and theology are so important, if our own position remains one of either confusion or indifference? I believe a reconceptualization is not only needed but possible. It takes its point of departure in the theology of Karl Barth whose reflection on Mary stands as a great witness to her place in Christian faith and life. I should like to advance a thesis on Mary Eternal Bearer of Christ.

V. Mary in the Theology of Barth

The context for any consideration of Mary in contemporary theology must not be simply the history of dogmatics but the spiritual situation of the Church today in its relationship to the world. The fundamental reordering of theology from its revelational basis which Karl Barth claimed was necessary, was a response to his perceptions of the Christian religion. With the rise of modernity in the west, through the Renaissance and Enlightenment, a new religion became the spiritual basis of Christendom. It was a religion that saw in Incarnation not the miraculous disclosure of a mystery but the spiritual and religious confirmation of a fact intimated, if not completely revealed, in philosophy, poetry, ethics and social reform: God and man are ultimately one. History is but the actualization of the underlying unity. Faith in such a religion and its "natural theology," Barth argued, renders revelation unnecessary, and ultimately impossible. Conversely, Christian faith is the abolition of this religion.

Two aspects of the Gospel story, according to Barth, serve in a unique way as indicators of the presence or absence of this religion of modernity: beliefs concerning the virgin birth and the empty tomb. Where these are rejected as miracles, the mystery of Incarnation is rejected also, despite disclaimers to the contrary. Barth rejects all modernist attempts to split off the virgin birth, as picture language or myth, from faith to Incarnation. The virgin birth is not simply a restating of the *vere Deus vere homo* in picture language, it presents the mystery of Incarnation itself.[10]

The mystery of *vere Deus vere homo*, for Barth, encompasses two assertions. First, this event is God's event at every point. Faith in the virgin birth is the basis of a spiritual understanding of the Incarnation "in which God's own work is seen in God's own light."[11] The virgin birth is the necessary tie between the divine initiative that makes salvation possible and its concrete historical embodiment that makes salvation accessible. Second, the mystery of *vere Deus vere homo* is grounded on the human side in a receptivity that itself is the work of God. The virgin birth is the revelation of this receptivity because in it human powers have been rendered irrelevant. Even the humble reception by Mary is itself grounded in the work of the Holy Spirit. The virgin birth is the negation of the last possible claim that humankind has reached out in some way to claim God. It is the act of pure receptivity. And, as such, it is the final rejection of the humanistic, secular religion of modernity.

Ultimately, these two assertions about the virgin birth are but different sides of the same coin. The virgin birth is the disclosure that salvation in Christ is all of God. Even our response to salvation is in a humility granted only by God the Holy Spirit. Mary is not simply the One who once bore the Christ, so that the event of *vere Deus vere homo* could be a fact in our history. She is still the One, who in the miracle of her virginity, protects the mystery of the Christ from the alien religion that replaces him with another Christ created by human powers and made accessible by human reason.

VI. Mary Eternal Bearer of Christ

In many respects, Barth still speaks as our contemporary, and in another way, he speaks out of struggles that have faded in the ever changing kaleidoscope of modern life. The struggle over the revelational basis of theology and piety, however, still stands as the prime questions for the Church today. How can we authentically confess in theology and celebrate in a liturgy Jesus Christ? The temptation to misbelief is still strong. On the one hand, we are being tempted to an ebionite Christ by the claim of secular ideologies that know only of a salvation accomplished by the process of history. On the other hand, we are being urged toward a docetic Christ by a misleading charismatic spirituality and a falsely supernaturalistic piety.

In the joyful celebration of the Virgin Mary, we hear the needed word of truth. God has taken the initiative for human salvation. It is not our doing but his gift. Yet it is a gift that has entered our time and place. Mary the virgin is the continuing witness to the divine initiative. Mary the mother, as the bearer of Jesus, makes of this divine initiative a flesh and blood fact in our lives. The receptivity of Mary is God's "No" to the secular religion of human apotheosis. She is receiving by the Holy Spirit the gift of the salvation that no human power could create. She is the living expression of *sola gratia*. As such, she is the prototype of every believer. Her, "Yes" to God's call is the opening of the way to salvation. So we join in saying, "Blessed are you among women, and blessed is the fruit of your womb!" But this is not a fact sealed off in the first century. She still stands before us, through the witness of Scripture, as the Mother who bears and protects her Son. Just as in her womb and in her home she bore and protected her Son from the forces of a despising society and a murderous king, she now bears and protects the mystery of his being in our midst. Without her the redemptive mystery of her Son is lost. With her it is received with joy.

NOTES

[1] Briggs, Charles Augustus, *The Incarnation of the Lord* (New York: Scribners, 1902), pp. 215–235. "Criticism and Dogma," *North American Review*, Vol. 182, June, 1906, pp. 861–874.

[2] For an example of such theological reflection and liturgy on Mary see Thurian, Max, *Mary Mother of All Christians* (New York: Herder and Herder, 1964). This book was first published in French by the Taize Community.

[3] Briggs was deposed from the ministry by the Presbyterian Church, U.S.A., for his supposedly heretical views on the authority of Scripture not for his views on Mary. His Marian writings come from a period in his life in which he had hopes for a closer rapport with Roman Catholicism. This hope sprang from his conviction that the biblical scholars and theologians of the Catholic Church of his time were opening new possibilities for ecumenical understanding. When subsequently many of these scholars were silenced by the antimodernist campaign Briggs was painfully disappointed.

[4] a Diest, Henrici, *Theologia Biblica* (Deventer, 1643), p. 178. The translation is from Heinrich Heppe, *Reformed Dogmatics* (London: George Allen & Unwin, 1950), p. 421. It should be noted that in the Reformed dogmaticians there was no separate section of Marian teaching. All treatment of Mary came in the section on the Incarnation.

[5] Brunner, Emil, *The Mediator* (Philadelphia: Westminister Press, 1947), pp. 325–7 and *The Christian Doctrine of Creation and Redemption* (Philadelphia: Westminster Press, 1952), pp. 352–6.

[6] The point of departure for the supernaturalistic, conservative defense of the virgin birth was the appearing of D.F. Strauss's *das Leben Jesu* in 1835–5. The historical research behind Strauss's position was greatly enlarged by the end of the nineteenth century by Keim, Lobstein, and Harnack. For an account of this period see Boslooper Thomas, *The Virgin Birth* Philadelphia: Westminster Press, 1962), pp. 113–32

[7] Machen, J. Gresham, *The Virgin Birth of Christ* (New York: Harper & Brothers, 1932), p. 268.

[8] Schleiermacher, Friedrich, *The Christian Faith* (Edinburgh: T & T Clark, 1956), par. 97, p. 405. This first appeared in German in 1821–2.

[9] Machen, *op. cit.,* p. 383.

[10] Barth, Karl, *Church Dogmatics,* 1/2 (New York: Charles Scribner's Sons, 1956), pp. 179–84.

[11] *Ibid.,* p. 177.

The Virgin Mary in Methodism

REV. GORDON S. WAKEFIELD, B.Litt.

In considering the place of the Blessed Virgin Mary in the Methodist tradition, I am reminded of the celebrated claim of Dr Johnson that he 'could repeat a complete chapter of *The Natural History of Iceland* from the Danish of Horrebow, the whole of which was exactly thus: "Chapter LXXII. *Concerning Snakes*". There are no snakes to be met with throughout the whole island.' At first sight there is no devotion to Mary and little teaching about her among Methodists. Lady Day has never been kept and at Christmas and on Mothering Sunday, Mary is honoured as the Mother of Jesus but more as a witness to his true humanity than for her part in redemption. The present Methodist hymn book, compiled in 1933, includes a translation of the thirteenth century *Stabat Mater*, but it is, in my experience, rarely sung. The same book corrected the amended version of Henry Hart Milman's funeral hymn which the 1904 collection had printed:

> When our heads are bowed with woe
> When our bitter tears o'erflow
> When we mourn the lost, the dear,
> Jesus, Song of *David,* hear.

(Not, as Milman wrote, *Son of Mary*.)

This shows a welcome reaction from the more pathological bigotry of the earlier book, but, again, the hymn is not sung. Otherwise the only references in the hymns, which are, of course, more significant for Methodist devotion than for that of most Churches, are in the incarnational affirmations of Charles Wesley and in such other hymns as these:

> Mary and Joseph in stable bare
> Watch o'er the Child beloved and fair.

> Mary was that Mother mild
> Jesus Christ her little child.

> That he who wore the thorny crown,
> And tasted death's despair,
> Had a kind mother like my own,
> And knew her love and care.

There are, among Methodists, those who have a very high regard for Mary and, had they been born into other communions, they would doubtless have found devotion to her congenial. I remember a sermon preached at my home church in, I think, 1939, in which the minister, a resolute Protestant, had temperately and kindly set true faith in Christ

151

over against undue veneration of Mary and had concluded, rather inconsistently, if you think about it, with the refrain of the *Adeste Fideles*, 'O come let us adore him, Christ the Lord'. Some members of the congregation found this mild and reasoned polemic little to their taste and one gentleman protested that he had always had a particular veneration for the Virgin Mary and disliked any attempt to demote her.

If we go back to the teaching of the Wesleys and the foundation documents of Methodism, we shall find, in effect, the same type of devotion as was characteristic of the great seventeenth century Anglicans and puritans with its patristic loyalties and roots.

In Wesley's many published Prayers and Offices, derived largely from Catholic and non-juring sources, there is no specific Marian devotion. In his eirenical *Letter to a Roman Catholic* Wesley affirms: 'I believe that he (the Son of God) was made man, joining the human nature with the divine in one person, being conceived by the singular operation of the Holy Ghost and born of the Blessed Virgin Mary, who, as well after as when she brought him forth, continued a pure and unspotted virgin.'

In the *Notes on the New Testament*, which are based on the work of the German scholar J. G. Bengel, and are part of the Methodist doctrinal standards, there is this comment on Matthew 1:25: '*He knew her not till after she had brought forth*). It cannot be inferred from hence that he knew her afterward; no more than it can be inferred from that expression (2 Sam. 6:23), "Michal had no child till the day of her death", that she had children afterward. Nor do the words that follow, "the firstborn" son, alter the case. For there are abundance of places wherein the term "firstborn" is used, though there were no subsequent children.'

The 'brethren' of Jesus (Matthew 12:46 and parallels etc.) are 'his kinsmen. They were the sons of Mary, the wife of Cleophas or Alphaeus, his mother's sister'. Revelation 12:1, however, 'a woman clothed with the sun, and the moon under her feet, is 'the emblem of the Church of Christ'. On Mark 3:35 *Behold my mother and my brethren!* Wesley writes: 'In this preference of his true disciples, even to the Virgin Mary, considered merely as his mother after the flesh, he not only shows his high and tender affection for them, but seems designedly to guard against those excessive and idolatrous honours which he foresaw would in after ages be paid to her.'

In his tract *A Word to a Protestant,* Wesley further voices Protestant opposition to Mariolatry: 'To the Virgin Mary, they pray in these words "O Mother of God, Queen of Heaven, command thy Son to have mercy upon us!" ' This, coupled with genuflection before images, he castigates as 'gross, palpable, idolatry such as neither can be denied nor excused; and tends directly to destroy the love of God, which is indeed the first and great commandment'. But these unequivocal condemnations are written simply to hoist the Protestant with his own petard: 'Are you clear of idolatry any more than the Papists are? It may be, indeed, yours is in a different way. But how little does that signify! They set up their idols in their churches; you set up yours in your heart. Their idols are only covered with gold or silver; but yours is solid gold. They worship the picture of the Queen of Heaven; you, the picture of the Queen or King of England.'

Modern Methodism, as much as any other Church, has been assailed by all the searching and questioning of biblical criticism. It is poignantly appropriate that I should be preparing this paper in the very week of the death of Dr C.J. Wright, about whom in 1952 there was one of those familiar storms which follow the press reports of the Modern Churchmen's Conference. C. J. Wright was the most notable liberal theologian in Methodism in the 1930s, who, to the surprise of his friends, joined the Church of England in 1944, out of the conviction that the future of English Christianity lay in one liberal, comprehensive English Church. His dream, if it were such, was not fulfilled but, after the controversy which followed his paper to the Modern Churchmen, he seemed to become increasingly certain that to accept the Virgin Birth was what he called a 'bastard supernaturalism' and a betrayal of true and enlightened Christian faith. This dogma seemed to him to enshrine the corruption of Christianity, but in this few Methodists would follow him.

Dr Leslie Weatherhead in *The Christian Agnostic* (1965) speaks for many in the liberal tradition when he says: 'I do not ask the reader to accept the Virgin Birth if it offends his intellect. I do not ask him to reject it as impossible, but to hold it *sub judice,* awaiting further light, to be a Christian agnostic about it'. For some readers he then proceeds to spoil this judicious suspension of judgement by introducing a fanciful theory that Jesus was the fruit 'of a sacred marriage' between Zacharias (John the Baptist's father) and Mary.

Two notable Methodist scholars have had occasion to deal with Mary and the Virgin Birth in the course of their researches. John Lawson received a Cambridge B.D. for *The Biblical Theology of Saint Irenaeus* (1948). He endorses the verdict of Vernet that 'St Irenaeus was the first theologian of the Virgin Mary' but shows with meticulous care that Irenaeus is dominated by the idea of *Anakephalaiosis*, and just as Christ is the second Adam, so, for him, Mary is the second Eve whose virginal obedience loosens the knot of virginal disobedience and performs 'a subsidiary recapitulating action'. Hers is 'that pure womb which regenerates men unto God'.

Pusey limited this to Mary's giving birth to the redeemer. Newman interpreted Irenaeus to mean that the Virgin is not merely a physical instrument but a co-operator in redemption. Lawson admits that on the face of it the language used inclines one to Newman's view but goes on: 'It should be noted, however, that the motive of these statements of

153

Irenaeus is not to elevate the Blessed Virgin to a place of honour, but to trace out further details in the "analogy". He hereby gives recognition to the fact that Christ did not save the world automatically, but was dependent to a certain extent upon the moral goodness of the men and women who lived about him. Our Lord lived as part of human society, not as an alien thrust in. There is thus a distinct value in the place given by Irenaeus to the Virgin in the scheme of salvation, nor need the honour be limited to her. There is, however, no evidence in *Adversus Haereses* to support Vernet's claim that it is reasonable to see in Mary as the advocata of Eve the power of the Virgin to intercede in heaven.'

In his great Commentary on St John's Gospel, C. K. Barrett sees in John 1:13, 'born not of blood, nor of the will of the flesh, nor of the will of man, but of God', a Johannine allusion to the Virgin Birth and clear evidence that the Evangelist knew of the tradition. It is in his earlier work, *The Holy Spirit and the Gospel Tradition* (1948), that Dr Barrett has a most important study of 'the conception of Jesus by the Holy Spirit'. Here he establishes that: 'there is nothing truly akin to the Gospel narratives in the pagan stories of divine births, in the Old Testament, or in Philo ... All parallels break down (if nowhere else) at the point with which we are most concerned, that is, the part played by the Spirit of God'. The birth of Jesus was a new act of God comparable to the creation of the world. In the stories there is a reconciliation of Old Testament background with Hellenistic notions of divine begetting and uniquely Christian claims. But the central actor in the stories is not the Virgin Mary, but the Holy Spirit and he, be it noted, is not a male principle or demigod, since the word *Ruah* in Hebrew is feminine. Mary is subordinate to the Holy Spirit and in no sense divine, she is the human agent, obedient and receptive to the new creative act of God.

Having thus put together these fragments of Methodist opinion and scholarship, let me try to lay down some lines of construction for a Methodist doctrine of the Mother of our Lord in this present century.

First we must note that Wesley was a truly ecumenical or, as he would have said, *catholic* person, though I think, in spite of his undoubted Puritanism and the importance of German pietism in his experience, that the formative influences in his life were Anglican. And in this doctrine he was neither more nor less than Anglican. There was much of the latitudinarian in him. He was governed by reason though within the bounds of an intense biblical and patristic orthodoxy. He hated sentimentality, what he called the 'namby-pambical'. Yet he was not a man of a naturally sceptical or questioning mind. He was not a David Hume. He would not have found it easy to make common cause with those in our day who question everything, and yet still call themselves Christians. He was evangelical in that he believed in a Gospel given by God which could change men's hearts and lives and make them holy as God was holy, that is, perfect in love. He admired some of

154

the Roman Catholics he met and read about because of their holiness. Deep spoke to deep. He could not despise a creed in which Christ was known by his fruits. He also had links with the Byzantine tradition through Macarius the Egyptian, who was not Egyptian but Syrian, a monk of the school of the Cappadocian Fathers. Wesley's doctrine of holiness was near to that of the Orthodox. It was 'the life of God in the soul of man', revealed in the encounters and conflicts of life, rather than the infusion of grace. Wesley would never question the Virgin Birth and his attitude to Mary would be to fit everything that Scripture says about her into a Gospel harmony, to agree with patristic developments and to ask: did devotion to her hinder or help devotion to Christ in men's hearts? He would revere Mary as a pattern of obedience and holiness. Those who believe that Mary was the perfect woman are naturally interested as to whether or not Wesley would have welcomed this development of doctrine since it might accord with his conviction that it is possible for the Christian to be perfect in this life. Certainly, there is nothing in this claim which would conflict with Wesley's idea of Christian perfection. The modern Methodist would be inclined to say: 'Where is the evidence, other than a tradition received by some Christians?' The whole problem for Protestants is the extent to which the cherished devotions of large numbers of Christians, unsupported by the unequivocal testimony of Scripture, should be given dogmatic status. Admittedly, there are many facts about the life of Jesus himself which we simply do not know and a great deal of our faith is directed towards a Christ symbol who may sometimes be more our ideal of perfect manhood than the actual Jesus of history. But Holy Scripture claims to give us a good deal more information about Jesus than ever it does about his mother. He is its central figure, and traditional Protestantism feels that on the whole it is better to keep silent about all matters to which Scripture does not give prominence. Otherwise it is not easy to distinguish fact from fancy, truth from legend, or to safeguard the distinctively Christian world view from that of the varied and differing cultures and philosophies amid which Christianity must live.

Today we are perhaps more aware of the need for both sceptics and sentimentalists to find a home in the Church than Wesley was. And we are also aware that our divisions are much more in minds and temperaments than between our denominations. The former Dean of St Paul's, Dr W. R. Matthews, has told me how in the faculty meetings of King's College, London, he always felt that there was a closer affinity between the Congregationalist A. E. Garvie and the Anglo-Catholic Charles Gore than there was between Gore and his fellow Anglo-Catholic, H. M. Relton. As I illustrated earlier, there are undoubtedly Methodists who, reared in a different tradition, might have felt strongly drawn to Marian devotion and I have heard of Methodist ministers with nervous breakdowns invoking the Blessed Virgin. In our time too, the image of the Mother is much more powerful than that of the Father.

But the ultimate question is not what image or model is pastorally or psychologically helpful but what is the truth. And here we may apply Leonard Hodgson's celebrated question alike to the Bible and to our varied Church traditions: 'What must the truth be and have been if it appeared like that to men who thought and wrote as they did?'

With regard to Mary this sends us back to the Gospel narratives to undertake the kind of investigation of which C. K. Barrett's work is so notable an instance. Before we ask 'Is the Virgin Birth true?' We must ask 'Why did the narratives arise?' Barrett himself suggests an answer and we may also find a parallel Hebraistic way of thinking in Paul's account of God's dealings with him in Galatians and the call of Jeremiah in the Old Testament. In both instances, the divine initiative begins in the womb of the mother. And the Virgin Birth stories are the assertion that the way of Christ was prepared in the life of his mother and, indeed, throughout the whole history of God's people, Israel.

In these ecumenical days, it is essential that we ask as well: 'Why has devotion to Mary occupied such a dominant position in the life of worship of the majority of Christians throughout the ages?' Here we must nor forget that even in its excesses Mariology has been a branch of Christology and emphasis on the Virgin has been very closely connected with a very human and tender love of Christ—witness St Bernard of Clairvaux. Some, of course, would argue that this is effete and dangerous pietism and that too great a concentration on Jesus borders on heresy. The Gospel is first and foremost about God and must be Theo-centric.

We must admit that it seems as though sometimes devotion to Mary arose from a deficient doctrine of God and a wrong attitude to sex. I have long been impressed by Emil Brunner who, unlike Karl Barth, disbelieved in the Virgin Birth because he said it was an attempt to try and explain the inexplicable, a piece of human ratiocination where faith only is possible. We cannot know *how*—only that God *was* made man. Certainly, the other alternative that Christ's birth was illegitimate shocks our sense of morality, and makes us feel, as did Hugh Montefiore's inference about Christ's possible homosexuality, that he is less than perfect man. But is this necessarily so? Dare we limit God to our standards of respectability? May not this be one more instance of the weak things of the world confounding the morally mighty? After all, the letter to the Hebrews includes Rahab, the harlot, among the women of faith.

What does seem certain is, as Harry Williams wrote in his essay in *Soundings* (1962), that the influence of a man's mother is often decisive. However little we know about her, whatever the precise relations between her and Jesus may have been, however much we may feel unhappy about excessive Marian piety—humanly speaking we owe Jesus principally to his Mother, and the more the humanity of Jesus is recognized in its fullness, the more prominent his Mother may become— witness the Methodist minister Geoffrey Ainger's carol about Mary's child. This in our time is perhaps less likely to degenerate into maudlin sentimentalism, since for us the enigmatic figure of Christ is much more represented by Sutherland or Epstein's *Pantocrator* than by a counter-reformation, or Victorian gentle Jesus.

But some of the foregoing is vain speculation, if not near blasphemy. Perhaps there are two ways in which Mary may help our understanding of the Gospel and of life.

1. She may be a sign of God's independence of ordinary human processes, and of our proud masculinity. Sex is important and not to be ignored or despised. It is one of the tremendous creative forces of the universe. But sex includes far more than the act of physical intercourse, and it is not to be worshipped any more than Mary is. God chose a woman and so did not act in the world's redemption without sex—in any case, the Word made flesh was a man. But the Virgin Birth stories do imply that God managed without male desire and that proud and complaisant power which subdues and possesses. He did not use the will of man or of the flesh. We need to recover the understanding that there is a great deal in life besides sex and that woman is to be honoured not simply for the appeal of flesh, but for the distinctly feminine capacities for purity and love.

2. Mary is ever woman. The New Testament does not record her as divine. She stands with sinners beneath the cross as the representative not of the kingdom of God but of the Church on earth. The words of Christ in the Johannine passion, 'Woman behold thy son', legitimately allow us to think of Mary as the Mother of the Christian family, the Church—the Church which is left on earth to be the community of the Holy Spirit and a home for all men. If we want to draw theologically precise distinctions, we must leave her there. Yet, like all creatures and more than most, she should point us to God. And for too long God has been thought of as a man. If the influence of our mothers, their self-denying love, their bearing with us and yearning over us is so great, how much more must God guard us and care for us and give himself to guide, sustain, protect, and save us?

If Mary be so wonderful,
What must her Maker be?

Mary: An Evangelical Viewpoint

REV. KEITH WESTON, M.A.

The picture I have of the Virgin Mary is one of great attraction and wonderful example, as also of high privilege and heavy responsibility: all of which are focussed for me whenever we sing her beautiful song "Magnificat". The human grace, humility and spirituality which shine there have always made a great impression upon me. What lovelier name could there be by which to call a daughter at her baptism?

Now you have invited my contribution as an Evangelical, and I must keep to my brief. But in doing so I have to confess that much of what I will say may grate in the hearts of some present. If I do (as I will have to) say things in opposition to what may be the viewpoint cherished among you, I do so with humble conviction and with desire to heal, not to hurt. But I am bound to say at the outset that much that belongs to Mariology appears to speak to me of a Mary far removed from the lady I find in the pages of my Bible. And I have to go further: much of the doctrine that has come to be associated with her appears to me explicitly to detract from the utter uniqueness of the person and saving work of the Saviour; and if the first I find strange and even grotesque, the second I have to confess I find wholly abhorrent and totally unacceptable.

Perhaps the best way to get at my viewpoint would be to divide the material into two halves:

1. The theological considerations.
   Mary's part in the Incarnation and her part (if any) in our doctrine of salvation, and considerations concerning concepts of *grace* and any idea of human contribution in God's work of Grace.

and

2. The Evidential Considerations.
   Where do we look for authority in these matters? How does Scripture (which clearly speaks with one voice on these matters) fit with tradition (which clearly speaks with another voice)?

I am aware that I am likely to cover ground you will have no doubt covered many times before – and that my covering of it will be only scratching the surface at best. But as an Evangelical, I feel that these two headings are the real nub of the problem: the evidence in Scripture and our approach to its final authority, and (what to me are) disturbing theological consequences if the teaching of Scripture is departed from or added to.

I start with theological difficulties.

158

1. Theology

I want to start with my whole-hearted agreement with my Catholic friends as we acknowledge together the truth of the Virgin Birth of our Saviour, and of the Saviour's unique personhood as fully God and fully man. I join in the current R.C. repudiation of the liberal position which tells me that the virgin birth is not strictly true from a historical standpoint but simply the Early Church's attempt to state an important religious truth. I confess with a true heart in the words of the Apostles' creed that Christ was "born of the Virgin Mary", an event of total uniqueness when Mary bore a Child, conceived not by means of a human father, but by the operation of the Holy Spirit.

But I begin to part company with Catholic teaching in certain areas when we progress from the Credal Statement. Let me refer to three areas of differing importance.

a. *Perpetual Virginity.* I put this at the bottom of the ladder of importance. As an Evangelical, I read my Bible and seek to conform to the statements I find there.

I have no doubt that I am taught first that Mary was a virgin at the time of the birth of Jesus (Matthew 1, 18–25; Luke 1, 26–38). The careful, sensitive way in which this awkward truth is handled is to me totally convincing. It is impossible to read the scriptures without imagining something of the cruel slanders which must have surrounded the pregnancy.

> The innocent sounding "Son of Mary" in Mk. 6.3 must have carried the meaning – he's son of Mary, and Mary alone, and not of Joseph (for Son of Joseph would be the more usual form).
> Is not John 8.41 barbed with innuendo "*We* were not born of fornication".

That this accusation of immorality persisted is evident in Jewish tradition. A Jewish genealogical table for the period before A.D.70 refers to Jesus as "the bastard of a wedded wife". Later rabbis call Jesus the son of an adulteress, the son of a prostitute etc., etc. But these references only serve to underline the accuracy of the birth narratives, and to highlight the burden Mary (and Joseph too) carried all the days of Jesus' upbringing – as they taught him bit by bit the truth about himself, and the wonder of Gabriel's description in Luke 1. 32–35.

But Scripture seems to me, in its plainest sense, to indicate that Mary was not ever-virgin after the birth of Jesus. To me it is in no way offensive, but rather to the great enhancement of the teaching concerning her, to accept that

> Matthew 1.24. She became after the birth, the true wife of Joseph in every respect

and that

> Matthew 1.25, Luke 2.7. She gave birth to other sons (implied there).

159

References to Jesus' brothers (Matthew 13.55) and sisters (13.56) do not have to be got around by making them cousins. The word *could* mean cousins. But why should Mark use the normal Greek word for brother when there was a perfectly good Greek word for cousin? (Mark 6.3).

I am aware of the ideas of Jerome, and Epiphanius (respectively that these were children of his mother's sister, and children of Joseph by a former wife). But I prefer Henry Latham's comments in "The Risen Master" (p. 305)

> "What weighs most with me is the repeated mention of the brethren as being in company with their Mother. We find them clinging to her in a way which we should not expect to find in 4 stepsons, the youngest of whom must have been well over 30 years of age; and their doing so is still more improbable if we suppose them to be nephews."

For me the natural meaning of the Scripture references takes nothing *from* the beauty of the character of Mary, but rather adds much *to* her attractiveness as a mother who in the grace of God bore all the burdens of motherhood, from real sexuality to real responsibility of a family fraught with problems.

I move secondly to a more important issue.

b. *Sinlessness*. My understanding of the straight study of scripture is that the adjective "sinless" can only be applied to the life and character of Christ. To attribute sinlessness to any other person among the human race not only detracts from the perfection of the Saviourhood of Christ, but is in my opinion to squeeze into scripture an unwarranted intrusion of idea.

Ludwig Ott, in his book "Fundamentals of Catholic Dogma" frankly admits that the doctrine of the Immaculate Conception is not explicitly revealed in Scripture. But is it *implicit* either? The arguments will be familiar to you all.

I understand Romans 3.23 to mean "All have sinned and fall short of the Glory of God – save one, Jesus the Son of God". Or *are* we to understand it to mean "Save two, Jesus the Son of God and Mary his mother"? We know that comparing scripture with scripture Jesus *is* excepted. (2 Cor. 5.21; Hebrews 4.15; John 8.46). But the mother of our Lord is never so excepted. Rather, we should understand (with Rom. 5.12) that "death spread to all, because all sinned" and that part of the wonder and the mystery of the incarnation was precisely this, that he "did not abhor the Virgin's womb". Indeed, I find Mary quite explicit on this. She describes God as "my Saviour" (Luke 1.47). The title Saviour speaks clearly of a salvation needed. She is confessing that she is simply one of those for whom the Saviour came "to save his people from their sins". Why otherwise did she present herself to fulfill the mosaic law of purification – to offer what is clearly described (Lev. 12:6ff.) as a sin offering which made atonement for her? As others have written "It was not as one Immaculate that Mary worshipped that day, but as a humble woman of God, acknowledging her need of a Saviour, and her indebtedness to the grace of God".

I find the rest of the Gospels consistent with this view.

> Luke 2.48 Is this anxious questioning typical of one with perfect trust in God, or simply the reaction of a harrassed mother?
> John 2.5 (at Cana) Is this not the gentlest of rebukes to a mother who has failed to understand? As at –
>
> Mark 3.32 where she must surely be included among those in verse 21 who doubted Jesus.

The doctrine of Immaculate Conception of the Blessed Virgin does not appear to me to be either implicit, and certainly not explicit, in the NT. Indeed my view of the Saviour is enhanced, as the totally unique One; and my grasp of the doctrines of Grace enhanced also, when I take Scripture to mean what it appears to mean.

> It is needless to add that this view is the view of the 1st Centuries A.D., and that the doctrine of the Immaculate Conception is much later – possibly in the first more explicit exposition, as late as the 12th century.

c. *The Doctrine of the Assumption.* This is of course the most recent of the dogma concerning the Blessed Virgin Mary, having been promulgated by Pope Pius XII in 1950. As defined then it states that "Mary the immaculate perpetually Virgin Mother of God, after the completion of her earthly life, was assumed body and soul into heaven".

Part of my difficulty here is to know what exactly is meant by "assumed". I suppose the meaning used is similar to the "assumption" of a title when a son takes over from his deceased father who was in the House of Lords. As such I am told the word in the dogma may simply mean the reception of the Blessed Virgin Mary body and soul into heaven. That it should mean that she did not die, is contrary to Roman teaching as late as the 7th century when the feast of "the sleeping of Mary" was observed in recognition of her death. If "reception" was all that was meant by the "assumption" of Mary, then I would happily go along with what I could understand is covered by the term: the glorious hope of the Christian Gospel is that believers will be received into heaven, and by the wonder of the resurrection of the dead, will receive glorified, raised bodies "like unto His glorious body" which even now is in heaven, the marks of his passion still upon his brow, hands feet and side. "A man stands in heaven" (as it has been put), the first fruits of the resurrection, and the great divine forerunner and trail blazer. As he is, so shall we ever be who have faith in Him. This Gospel truth is one on which I never tire of preaching. Concepts of time and eternity are difficult, and I can quite see that the language used of dying in the N.T. is overlapping – On the one hand the dead are raised when he appears (1 Corinthians 15 and 1 Thess. 4) and yet at the same time, to the penitent thief the Saviour says "Today shalt thou be with me in paradise". This is not the place to discuss interpretations of these passages (and others) which will be familiar ground for us all. I am simply saying that there is no difficulty for me if asked to affirm that, in accordance with the Gospel, I shall one day see Mary "*received* body and soul in heaven". That is the truth revealed for all believers, and in it I rejoice. But of course, the dogma of the assumption goes further than this. It is argued upon the basis of teaching concerning her freedom from sin and her perpetual virginity, that her relationship to her son demands that in body and soul she should be made like him. Indeed, if she shares in redemption's work, it is only appropriate that she should already share in redemption's fruit. But if I challenge the bases, I must also challenge the conclusion concerning her death or otherwise. There is of course no evidence in Scripture to support the doctrine. Indeed it would seem extraordinary to me that neither the New Testament nor the infant Church knows anything of such an amazing and striking event as the ascension of Mary into heaven without death.

And I have to pull back further still when Mary's role in heaven is spoken of. Here, enthroned as Queen, in Catholic devotion, she intercedes for her children, and is thought of as "Mediatrix with God of all graces". To quote from Pope Leo XIII in his Rosary Encyclical of 1891:

> "From that great treasure of all graces which the Lord has brought nothing according to the will of God comes to us except through Mary, so that, as nobody can approach the Supreme Father except through the Son, similarly nobody can approach Christ except through the Mother."

1903–1914. Pope Pius X speaks similarly of Mary as "the dispenser of all gifts which Jesus has acquired for us by his death and his blood". My Evangelical mind however leaps to 1 Timothy 2:5 "There is one God and there is one mediator between God and men, the man Christ Jesus".

> As has been said, I trust not provocatively, "if I am invited to dine with the Sovereign of this realm, I am not content to dine with the Prime Minister, far less with a lady in waiting".

Jesus said (John 14.6) I am the Way, the truth and the life: no one comes to the Father but by me. He calls men *directly* to himself "Come to me, all who labour and one heavy laden" – not to other mediators or intermediaries. He is, says the Apostle John, "the advocate with the Father".

The development of the concept of the role of Mary in our salvation has of course been the main spring of the development of veneration of her. I fail to see this in any other way than according to Mary a kind of worship which is indistinguishable from that offered to God himself. I am of course aware that the Catholic theologian is careful to distinguish between Latria (adoration) which is due to God alone. Dulia, which is veneration offered to saints, and Hyperdulia, special veneration offered to Mary. But I do not on the one hand find any hint of this in scripture, nor do I believe that the normal worshipper can sustain the distinction, when he invokes, e.g. the aid of Jesus (latria) Mary (hyperdulia) and Joseph (dulia). I fail to distinguish any difference of laud between a prayer offered to God, and a prayer such as is found in the Litany of the Blessed Virgin.

> "We fly to thy patronage O holy Mother of God. Despise not our prayers in our necessities, but deliver us from all dangers, O Ever glorious and blessed Virgin".

I must be honest, and tell you that my Evangelical heart is deeply hurt when I come across, or hear, such praying. As I am grieved to find titles which only and scripturally belong to the Saviour, being applied to Mary. (Advocate, Mediator, King of Angels etc.) (made of course feminine).

Now may I add at this point my own Evangelical conviction concerning the meaning of Elizabeth's words "Blessed are you among women, and blessed is the fruit of your womb" (Luke 1.42); and of the woman in the crowd (Luke 11.27) "Blessed is the womb that bore you (the Lord) and the breasts which you sucked". It is commonly thought that this "blessedness" marks Mary out as more than "Highly favoured", and gives her a kind of glory which is uniquely hers.

But wherein does her blessedness consist? It does not seem that it marked her out for any special mention or leadership role in the Early Church. In fact the absence of prominence given to Mary in the N.T. is quite remarkable. In spite of her supreme privilege she appears as altogether Self-effacing. Scripture seems determined not to draw the conclusions which our frail human logic could so easily draw concerning her who bore the Incarnate Son.

In fact Jesus himself points to a higher glory than the glory of being Theotokos. When the woman in the crowd referred to the blessedness of Jesus' mother, he said "Blessed rather are those who hear the Word of God and keep it". Again, he asked "Who is my mother, and who are my brothers?" And stretching out his hand towards his disciples he said "Here are my mother and my brothers. For whosoever does the will of my Father in heaven is my brother and sister and mother". (Matt. 12.48–50; Mark 3.33f. and Luke 8.21).

That Mary should be called highly favoured is without doubt most applicable. But do we not infer that her blessedness consisted in her obedience expressed in her words "Let it be to me according to your word" (Lk. 1.30) rather than in her conception of our Lord? Her glory is that she did the will of God, and that glory is one which any humble but obedient Christian may, by the Grace of God, share. Surely the Lord would be expected to endorse the eulogy of his Mother expressed by the woman in the crowd. Instead he rejects it, but in doing so emphasises the essential thing about Mary – her obedience.

2. Conclusion

Now let me try to draw together some theological reservations which one can summarise from what I have said.

First, I see in Scripture a view of the Mother of our Lord which safeguards and glorifies the utter uniqueness of the Saviour. Her unspoken testimony, lying behind every verse of Magnificat, is the testimony of John the Baptist. "He must increase: I must decrease". To me this is one of the most sacred truths of scripture: that Our Lord is incomparable, unique in his holy, sinless perfection and in his resplendent, majestic godhead. He is in character and person wholly "other", just as in status he is exalted "high above rule and authority and power and dominion and above every name that is named, not only in this age but in that which is to come. God has put all things under His feet and has made Him head over all things for the Church" (Eph. 1.21f.). I feel very strongly that Scripture would adjure me not to raise any person whatever to anything approaching a like character or status, that Christ may be *all* in *all*. I humbly believe that the beauty of the humility of the Virgin Mary would cause her to say fervently "Amen" and to be deeply grieved at what tradition has sought to achieve concerning her.

Secondly, I see in Scripture a view of the Son of God which sets him totally apart in his Saviourhood, one God, and one mediator. Any suggestion that the Mother of Jesus has any saving role in heaven which would detract from the unique Saviourhood of Christ, grieves me deeply. Her part, Scripture tells me, was to be the human instrument or channel by which the mystery of the Incarnation took place. That done, Mary takes her place alongside all others who delight to call Jesus "God my Saviour". You can see, I'm sure, how such as I react to the kind of doctrine involved in Pope John's words to Vatican II, when he placed the Council under Mary's protection as "the Immaculate Queen of the Church and Mother of Unity", and (on 15 February '59) went on to state "It is through Mary that we come to Jesus, to love Christ means to love Mary *his* Mother and in the light of redemption *our* universal Mother."

Thirdly, I detect a fault in a doctrine of grace which, it seems to me, lies behind much Catholic teaching about Mary. This teaching, I suggest, becomes the supreme illustration of a particular view of man – the possibility and even necessity of human merit. Thus Mary cooperates in the work of redemption, and so epitomises the view that human ability enables man to have some part in his own salvation. Yves Congar in his book *Christ, Our Lady and the Church* says that in Mary we see supremely the element of cooperation in the work of redemption which we see now in the Church. "In Christ heaven and earth are united, but in setting up this union of heaven and earth accomplished in person by Jesus Christ a share is also to be attributed to our Lady through her cooperation in the mystery of the incarnation ... Each, (Our Lady and the Church) represents the part that human instrumentality is given in the work of Salvation."

But this is not the view of Grace which I find in Scripture, which seems better represented in such familiar words as

> Nothing in my hand I bring
> Simply to thy cross I cling.

Man's totality of inability to save himself, or to contribute anything whatever to his salvation (for he is dead in his trespasses and sins Eph. 2:1) is met by the *total* ability of God *totally* to meet that need through the *finished* work of Christ on the Cross (Ephesians 2.8–10).

Now these views are well known, and have been at the nub of the controversy for centuries. Nor are they particularly Evangelical views. This is well represented in various comments in the report on the current state of play in the Anglican/Roman Catholic Dialogue published in 1974. Matters included as tricky to resolve invariably have Mariology in the list, and there is reference to Anglicans being "motivated by the fear that man's part in the work of salvation will be exaggerated and God's part minimized" (48). The Anglican Commission (page 49) is said to have been "concerned to safeguard the fundamental truth that God alone is man's redeemer and that no mere man is able to save himself let alone anyone else. It is this concern that has made Anglicans critical of any Mariological thesis or of any aspect of the cult of Mary and the Saints which might seem to compromise the Gospel of Redemption. For example, the description of Mary as mediatrix even when it is duly qualified (as in Lumen Gentium No. 60) creates serious difficulties for Anglicans." Similarly, on page 56, the report states that it is "the fear that Mary will be regarded as a source rather than a recipient and instrument of grace, that has led to prolonged distrust and controversy. More precisely it is the tendency to assimilate Mary to Christ in a way which seems to isolate her from the Church's other members – e.g. in the development of a doctrine of co-redemption – that arouses deep fears."

I quote these passages from the report to show that Evangelicals like me share with many non-Catholics concern over implications about the NT doctrines of grace, of the utter uniqueness of the Saviour, and of the complete saviourhood of Christ, which modern development of Mariology suggests.

I would dearly like to continue to discuss the more basic questions about authority in matters of the faith – referred to by me at the beginning as Evidential Considerations. These are obviously at the root of our disagreement as Christians. Mariology belongs to tradition, not to scripture. It is never argued that development of Mariology is

165

explicit in Scripture, but it is claimed to be implicit there. If any idea of development of doctrine means that the *explicit* teaching of scripture appears to be endangered, then I would hold that tradition must be brought into line with Scripture and not otherwise. Development of doctrine for me *must* be development of our *understanding of doctrine* explicit in Scripture, and as an Anglican, I have no reservations about Article 6 which states that nothing must be taught or required as necessary to salvation which cannot be clearly proved from scripture.

In a word, that is where my hangups concerning the development of Marian dogma begin and stick fast.

VI
Other Traditions:
Christian and Non-Christian

It is salutary to know of the high esteem accorded to Mary, the Mother of God, in the Near Eastern religious, Russian, Serbian and Greek Orthodox; Syriac Orthodox; and the Monophysite and Nestorian Churches (with their Uniate counterparts). It is no less salutary to see how well Mary has emerged in the Jewish and Muslim religions which pervade the world.

The first paper was read to the Glastonbury Branch of the Society on 17 February 1969 by the Spalding Lecturer in Eastern Orthodox Studies at the University of Oxford.

The second lecture was delivered to the International Conference of the Society at Newman College, Birmingham, in Easter Week 1973, by the Lecturer in Aramaic and Syriac Studies at the University of Oxford. The paper was revised and published many years later as one of the Society's current pamphlets.

The third paper was read to the Cambridge Branch of the Society in 1978, by a Lecturer in Rabbinics at the University of Cambridge.

The fourth lecture was delivered to the London Branch of the Society at the Francis Holland School, London SW1, on 17 June 1971. In its pamphlet form, Fr McCarthy provided a three-page appendix listing the principal texts of Mary in the Koran, also printed here.

The Mother of God in Orthodox Theology and Devotion

ARCHIMANDRITE KALLISTOS WARE, M.A., D.Phil.

I. Then and now

Some forty years ago, during the Faith and Order Conference at Lausanne in 1927, one of the Russian Orthodox delegates, Archpriest Sergius Bulgakov, caused a great uproar by mounting the rostrum and beginning a speech about the Blessed Virgin Mary. It was a subject which had not been included on the agenda, and so the chairman interrupted the speaker and told him to sit down. Fr. Sergius flatly refused. He continued to address the meeting about the place of the Mother of God in Christian theology and devotion; and he insisted that this was a theme which inter-Church assemblies such as that at Lausanne could on no account afford to ignore.

The attitude of the chairman at the Lausanne Conference is understandable. At any ecumenical gathering forty years ago, the subject of the Blessed Virgin Mary would have been theological dynamite; it was a topic of such delicacy that it could not safely be raised at a public meeting. Today, happily, the situation is very different. The very existence of our Ecumenical Society of the Blessed Virgin, and the kind of conference that we are having here at Glastonbury, are sufficient indication of how far we have travelled since 1927. Friendly and open discussion about the Holy Virgin, such as was psychologically impossible between the divided Christians at Lausanne, has now become not only a possibility but a reality.

II. Mary's place in the scheme of Christian doctrine: the two aspects

When thinking about the Blessed Virgin Mary, the Orthodox tradition tries always to see her in relation to her Son, never isolated and by herself. For this reason, Orthodox usually avoid such a term as 'Mariology'—a word which is Greek in outward form, but which is never used by the Greek Fathers and is not to be found in the Oxford *Patristic Lexicon*. It is a word which can too easily be interpreted to mean that there is a special branch, a separate and enclosed compartment, of dogmatic theology concerned exclusively with the Virgin Mary. Orthodox Christians feel deeply uneasy about any such 'departmentalism'. When we speak of Mary, we must speak of her relationship with Jesus: we must keep in view her rôle at His Incarnation and her place as a member within His Mystical Body. There can be no 'Mariology' as such: 'Mariology' is a facet of Christology or of ecclesiology.

These, then, are the two primary ways of approaching the life and work of the Blessed Virgin: as a part of the mystery of the Incarnation, and as a part of the mystery of the Church. From the first point of view, she is regarded above all as Mother, or more exactly as Mother and Virgin. She is the Mother of the Saviour, from whom God the Word took His humanity. But since her Son was different from all other sons—not only man but God—the Holy Trinity ordained that the manner of His birth should be different from all other births: and so, in her divine Motherhood, her Virginity was preserved unimpaired. From the second point of view, she is regarded above all as a model and paradigm of what each Christian hopes to be. In her is exemplified, not as an abstract ideal but as specific reality, the full meaning of membership in the Church. In her is seen a human person, entirely 'deified' by divine grace, living in complete unity with God. The first of these two aspects makes clear the uniqueness of Mary, the difference between her and us: there could only be one Incarnation, and so there could only be one Mother of God. The second aspect emphasizes what Mary has in common with other members of the Body of Christ: she is the most perfect member of the redeemed community, but in that same perfection we are all of us called to share.

III. Mary and the Mystery of the Incarnation

The first or Christological aspect is summed up in the title *Theotokos,* usually translated 'God-Bearer' or (more elegantly if less literally) 'Mother of God'. This one word provides the key to the whole Orthodox understanding of Mary. Immediately it makes evident the close link between devotion to Mary and the doctrine of the Incarnation. When we venerate the Virgin, we do not honour her by herself and apart from her Son, but precisely because she is the Mother of Emmanuel. Honour shown to Mary, if offered in a truly Catholic and Orthodox spirit, is necessarily honour shown to her Son; it is impossible that such honour should in any way detract from the worship due to Jesus Christ, for it is specifically on account of the Son that we honour the Mother. When the Fathers of the Council of Ephesus (431) insisted on calling Mary *Theotokos*, it was not from any desire to glorify her on her own, but because only so could they safeguard the correct doctrine of the Incarnation. They were concerned, not with some optional title of devotion, but with a dogma that lies at the very heart of the Christian faith: the essential unity of Christ's person. As St Cyril of Alexandria realized, if we are to confess that 'Emmanuel is truly God', we must also confess that 'the Holy Virgin is *Theotokos*, for she bore, according

170

to the flesh, the Word of God made flesh' (*Third Epistle to Nestorius*, anathema 1). What Mary bore was not just a man more or less closely linked to God, but a single and indivisible person who is God and man at once. 'The Word was made flesh' (John 1:14): that is why Mary must be termed *Theotokos*, and that is why she is of such high importance for Orthodox theology and worship.

It is significant that not only the appellation *Theotokos* but most of the other titles and symbolic descriptions applied to Mary in Orthodox devotion refer directly or indirectly to the Incarnation. The Burning Bush (Exodus 3:2), the Mountain overshadowed by the forest (Habakkuk 3:3), the East Gate through which none may pass save the Great Prince (Ezekiel 44:1–3), the Fleece of Gideon (Judges 6:36–38; Psalm 71[72]:6), 'Chariot of fire', 'Bridal Chamber of the Light', 'Book of the Word of Life', 'living heaven', 'holy throne', 'mystical Paradise'—all these and countless other such designations are emphatically Christological, underlining Mary's rôle as God's Mother, her place in the Incarnation.

Here, then, is the basis of all true 'Mariology'—in the fact that the Word was made flesh. But there is a further and vitally important point concerning Mary and the Incarnation. Mary did not become God's Mother against her will. When God made man after His own image and likeness, He endowed His creature with the gift of free will; and despite the distortion of man's nature at the fall, this divine gift of freedom has never been withdrawn. The relationship between man and God is one of love; and it is therefore essentially a free relationship, for where there is no freedom there is no love. We are, in St Paul's phrase, 'fellow workers (*synergoi*) with God' (1 Corinthians 3:9); as St Augustine put it, without God we can do nothing, but without us God will do nothing. To quote the Homilies of St Macarius, a book much loved by John Wesley: 'The will of man is an essential precondition, for without it God does not do anything' (xxxvii. 10).

This cardinal principle of liberty applies at the Incarnation as at all other times. In St Luke's account of the Annunciation, Mary is revealed as the supreme example of *synergeia* or voluntary co-operation. Had God become man without His Mother's consent, this would have constituted an infringement of man's free will, a denial of the divine image in man. And so the archangel waited first for her response, 'Be it unto me according to thy word' (Luke 1:38). Mary could have refused, although God in His foreknowledge knew that she would not in fact do so—just as He also foreknew that Judas would betray Him, even though Judas acted in entire freedom. Thus, even though Mary was 'preordained from generations of old as Mother and Virgin and Receiver of God' (hymn at Great Vespers for the Nativity of the Theotokos), this 'preordaining' in no way deprived her of personal autonomy.

We honour Mary, then, not only because God chose her as His Mother, but also because she herself chose aright; not only because

171

the archangel addressed her as 'highly favoured', but because she answered, 'Behold the handmaid of the Lord'. She was not merely a passive and external 'instrument' but the positive and indispensable 'condition' of the Incarnation. In the words of Nicolas Cabasilas, a lay theologian of 14th century Byzantium (*On the Annunciation*, 4–5 [*Patrologia Orientalis*, xix, p. 488]; quoted by Vladimir Lossky, 'Panagia', in *The Mother of God: A Symposium by Members of the Fellowship of St Alban and St Sergius*, ed. E. L. Mascall, London, 1949, p. 30):

> The Incarnation was not only the work of the Father, of His Power and His Spirit ... but it was also the work of the will and the faith of the Virgin. Without the consent of the All-Pure Virgin and the co-operation of her faith, this design would have been as impossible of realization as it would have been without the intervention of the three Divine Persons themselves. Only after teaching and persuading her does God take her for His Mother and receive from her the flesh which she wills to offer to Him. Just as He became incarnate voluntarily, so He willed that His Mother should bear Him freely and with her full consent.

It is in this context that the idea of Mary as the second Eve acquires its full significance: Eve chose freely when she fell, and in the same way Mary chose freely when she obeyed.

This insistence upon the freedom of Mary's response is clearly evident in the selection of the Gospel reading at feasts in her honour (8 September, 1 and 22 October, 21 November, 8 July, 15 August, Saturday of the Akathist). The story of the woman in the crowd is read: 'A certain woman in the company lifted up her voice, and said unto Him, Blessed is the womb that bare Thee, and the breasts which Thou hast sucked. But He said, Yea rather, blessed are they that hear the word of God and keep it' (Luke 11:27–28). At first sight these must appear strange words to choose for a festival of the Blessed Virgin, since seemingly they imply that no special veneration is due to her as Christ's Mother. But our Lord, so far from slighting her in His answer, is in reality indicating where the true glory of her divine Motherhood is to be found. The woman in the crowd referred to the physical fact: Christ directed attention to the spiritual attitude which underlay that physical fact, and without which the physical fact would not have been possible. 'Blessed are they that hear the word of God and keep it': Mary is blessed because she heard the word of God and kept it when the archangel spoke to her at the Annunciation, for if she had not first heard the word and been obedient to it, she would never have borne the Saviour in her womb or nursed Him at her breast.

But her response to Gabriel, 'Be it unto me according to thy word', if it is the chief instance of Mary's obedience, is not the only occasion on which she heard the word of God and kept it. The same acceptance of God's word was manifested throughout her life. At the end of the Nativity story St Luke writes, 'Mary kept all these things, and pondered them in her heart' (2:19); and again, after the account of Jesus at twelve years old in the temple, 'But His Mother kept all these sayings in her heart' (2:51). Mary displays the same obedience to God's word, the same humble acceptance of what she does not yet fully understand, at Cana in Galilee when she says to the servants, 'Whatsoever He saith unto you, do it' (John 2:5). This is her last utterance recorded in the Gospels: and it is instructive that it should be an expression of submission to God's word.

IV. Mary and the Mystery of the Church

Mary is thus throughout her life the supreme example of those who 'hear the word of God and keep it', who make the divine will their own, and who are therefore truly 'blessed'. This brings us to the second or ecclesiological aspect of the Virgin's life. To a member of Christ's Church, there can be nothing higher and more glorious than this: that he or she should willingly and joyfully accept God's plan and answer Him as Mary did, 'Be it unto me according to Thy word'. As a pattern of obedient union with the will of God, the Mother of God shows us what a human being can and should be. She is, in Wordworth's phrase, 'our tainted nature's solitary boast'. She is the gift which a fallen—and, for that matter, a redeemed—humanity can most fittingly bring as an offering to Christ. In the words of an Orthodox hymn at Christmas Vespers:

What shall we offer Thee, O Christ,
Who for our sakes hast appeared on earth as man?
Every creature made by Thee offers Thee thanks:
    The angels offer Thee a hymn;
    The heavens, a star;
    The magi, gifts;
    The shepherds, their wonder;
    The earth, its cave;
    The wilderness, a manger;
And we offer Thee—a Virgin Mother.

As members of the Body of Christ, it is our vocation to become 'partakers of the divine nature' (2 Peter 1:4), and to share in the glory which the Father has given to Christ (John 17:22). To use the language of the Greek Fathers, we are to become 'deified' or 'divinized': not that we become God by nature—for only the persons of the Blessed Trinity are that—but we become god by grace and by status. The fullest example of this 'deification' (*theosis*) by grace is the Mother of God; and in this sense she is justly termed by St Gregory Palamas 'the boundary between the created and the uncreated' (*Homily* 37: Migne, *Patrologia graeca* 151. 472B).

At this point two notes of warning are advisable. First, in speaking thus of Mary, we Orthodox do not intend to set her upon a remote pedestal, cutting her off from any involvement in the ordinary cares and anxieties of life. On the contrary, we fully recognize that as Mother of the Incarnate God she was at the same time mother within an earthly family. In providing a home for her Son and for His foster father St Joseph, Mary was confronted by the same difficulties and problems as other mothers. It is in virtue of this very closeness that she is so precious to us, because she experienced all our tensions and sorrows, and yet succeeded in transfiguring them with divine grace and glory. The path of 'deification' need not imply a way of life that is outwardly remarkable: often the indwelling splendour of God is only evident to those who have eyes to see, and this was doubtless the case with the holy family at Nazareth.

In the second place, when we say with St Gregory Palamas that she is 'the boundary between the created and the uncreated' and the like, we do not for one moment intend to ascribe to Mary the honour that is due to God alone. In Greek the distinction between God and man is very clearly marked by the use of two different words: *latreia*, indicating the adoration ascribed only to the Deity; and *douleia*, indicating the qualified veneration that may be rendered to the Mother of God and the saints. Unfortunately in Latin—as St Augustine pointed out (*Against Faustus*, xx. 21: Migne, *Patrologia latina*, 42. 385)—and in other western languages there is no convenient way of reproducing this distinction: the English terms 'worship' and 'adoration' are ambiguous in a way that the Greek terms *latreia* and *douleia* are not.

V. Why ask Mary to pray for us?

What has been said about the ecclesiological aspect of the life of the Holy Virgin, about Mary as the most perfect member of Christ's Mystical Body, will help to explain why she is so often invoked by Orthodox in prayer. The *Theotokos* is a true mirror and a living icon of what it means to belong to the Church. And how is the Church to be understood? The Church is a single family, including both the living and the dead. It is an all-embracing unity in Christ, a unity expressed and realized above all through prayer. Here on earth it is our custom to pray for each other and to ask for one another's prayers: and this mutual intercession is an essential characteristic of our Church membership. To the Christian believer death is no final barrier, and so the bond of mutual intercession extends beyond the grave. We pray, therefore, for the faithful departed as well as for the living, and we ask the faithful departed in their turn to pray for us—not knowing exactly how such prayers prove effective, yet confident that in the sight of God's mercy no prayer offered in faith can ever be wasted. And among all the faithful departed for whose prayers we ask, to whom should we turn more frequently and more fervently than to the Holy Virgin? If she is a model of what it means to belong to the Church, then she must be, among other things, a model of intercessory prayer.

174

That we should so turn to her in prayer seems to an Orthodox Christian something altogether natural and inevitable. For him there is nothing exotic or polemical about such prayer, but it forms an integral and unquestioned part of his life in Christ. He does not think of such prayer in legalistic categories, attempting to measure divine grace or employing the concept of 'merit'; nor does he think of it in a sentimental fashion, as if Mary were more 'lenient' and 'indulgent' than her Son. For Orthodoxy, this prayer springs quite simply from the sense of 'belonging together', from the feeling that we and she are members of the same fellowship, that she is Mother within the great Christian family of which we are also part. We and she belong to one Church, and the unity of that Church is a unity in prayer—that, in a word, is why we ask her to pray for us.

It is misleading to speak, in this context, of praying 'to' Mary. We pray only to God, whereas we 'invoke' or 'call upon' His Mother: we do not pray *to* her, but we ask her *for* her prayers—an important distinction. And we are firmly convinced that these requests for her intercession, so far from diminishing our devotion to Christ, serve rather to enrich it. While asking her to pray for us, we do not pray on her behalf because we believe that she has already entered fully into glory.

The meaning, to an Orthodox Christian, of the Virgin's intercession for the needs of mankind is most beautifully expressed by the title 'joy of all who sorrow', applied to her in eastern devotion:

> Thou art the joy of all who sorrow,
> The champion of all who suffer wrong.
> Food to the hungry,
> Comfort to strangers,
> A staff for the blind,
> Visitor of the sick,
> Protection and aid to all in trouble,
> And the helper of orphans.

In the words of another Orthodox hymn, the Mother of God is 'ever watchful in her prayers and in her intercession lies unfailing hope'.

VI. Mary and the sanctity of the Old Testament

If, for the Orthodox tradition, the Blessed Virgin Mary is the fullest example of man's deification and a model of union with the will of God, what then does the Orthodox Church believe concerning her sinlessness and her final glorification? What, to put the matter more specifically, is the attitude of Orthodoxy towards the Roman Catholic dogmas of the Immaculate Conception (1854) and the Assumption (1950)?

In Orthodox devotion Mary is constantly termed *panagia*, 'all-holy', *panamomitos*, 'without blemish', and *achrantos*, 'without spot' or 'immaculate'; and in the liturgical texts for her feasts it is easy to find such statements as this, 'Before thy conception, O pure Virgin, thou wast consecrated to God' (Entry of the Mother of God into the Temple, kathisma at Matins). Does such language imply that Orthodoxy accepts the doctrine of the Immaculate Conception, as formulated by Pope Pius IX in 1854? There have in fact been a number of Orthodox theologians who adopted the full Latin teaching, or something virtually indistinguishable from it: this occurred above all during the seventeenth and eighteenth centuries, when Latin influence on Orthodox theology was at its height. Among the Greeks, the most celebrated example of those who accepted the doctrine is probably Elias Miniati (1669–1714), Bishop of Kernitsa and Kalavryta; among the Russians, St Dimitri of Rostov (1651–1709). The doctrine is taught in *The Sceptre of Government* by Symeon of Polotsk, a work praised and recommended by the great Council of Moscow in 1666–7.

But Elias Miniati, St Dimitri, and Symeon are not here typical of the Orthodox tradition as a whole. Today the normal Orthodox view is that Mary was subject to the consequences of *original* sin, even though she was free from all *actual* sin. I know of no Orthodox writer since the proclamation of 1854 who has explicitly followed the Latin teaching. An Orthodox is still free to believe the Latin doctrine as a private opinion, and he could not rightly be branded a heretic for so doing; but he would be going against the clear *consensus* of modern Orthodox theologians.

Why is the Orthodox Church so reserved towards the doctrine of the Immaculate Conception? Two main considerations are involved: first, Mary's rôle as a link between the Old Covenant and the New; and secondly, the doctrine of original sin.

(i) Orthodox feel that the Latin doctrine of the Immaculate Conception separates Mary from the rest of the descendants of Adam, putting her in a different class from all the other righteous men and women of the Old Testament, and in this way destroying the continuity of sacred history. Before the coming of the Messiah at the Incarnation there was a long and careful preparation extending over many generations. God did not intervene abruptly as a *deus ex machina*, but through a series of 'elections' He made the world ready for His advent. Mary is the culmination of this process, the summit and recapitulation of all the sanctity that existed under the Old Covenant; and when she said 'Behold the handmaid of the Lord', she spoke not only in her own name but in the name of all the Old Testament saints who went before her.

This sense of the continuity of sacred history is plainly expressed in the liturgical texts for the two Sundays immediately preceding Christmas. The first of these is dedicated to the 'Forefathers' of Christ, to His ancestors after the flesh, and the second to all the righteous men and women from Adam down to Joseph the betrothed of Mary. Before celebrating the Incarnation, the Church celebrates the memory of all those who providentially prepared the way for the long-expected Messiah.

The Latin theory of the Immaculate Conception, so it seems to Orthodoxy, weakens this precious link between the Virgin and the remainder of humanity before Christ. Mary no longer shares in the destiny of fallen mankind: she is removed from the Old Dispensation, and from her conception she is placed proleptically and by a special privilege under the New. This is to obscure her true place in the scheme of redemption and to misunderstand the real significance of her response to the archangel.

(ii) Orthodox feel, in the second place, that the 1854 definition implies an understanding of original sin which they do not share. From the time of St Augustine the West has tended to envisage original sin as a fault committed by all mankind 'in Adam', involving each new-born child in hereditary guilt, so that he or she is in some measure an object of God's wrath, deserving punishment. The Christian East, whether during Patristic or more modern times, in its doctrine of original sin has placed far less emphasis on the idea of inherited guilt. The fall is seen primarily as an enslavement to the devil, involving liability to sickness and physical pain, also bodily death, and perhaps in addition a certain moral weakening of the will (yet not such as to abolish man's basic freedom to choose good rather than evil).

It is easy to appreciate why, on the Augustinian understanding of original sin, the doctrine of the Immaculate Conception seemed appropriate and even necessary to many western theologians. How, it was asked, could Mary be at once God's chosen vessel and a guilty object of His just anger? But on the less sombre and less guilt-ridden eastern view of the fall no such difficulty arises; the doctrine of the Immaculate Conception is rendered unnecessary. The Blessed Virgin, although sinless, was still subject to physical pain and bodily death; and therefore, on the eastern understanding of original sin, while holy and pure from her mother's womb, she was not exempt from the consequences of the fall. She participates organically in descent from Adam, but by the grace of God and through her own unremitting struggle against sin she was guarded from all personal impurity. 'The purity and holiness of the Mother of God', observes Fr Sergius Bulgakov, 'belong not to her nature but to her state—to her attitude towards sin and her personal victory over it' (quoted in A. S. Merslukine, *Le dogme romain de la Conception de la Vierge Marie et le point de vue orthodoxe*, Paris, 1961, p. 35). In the words of Vladimir Lossky, 'For the Virgin, as for John the Baptist, this holiness consists, not in an abstract privilege of exemption from guilt, but in a real transformation of human nature, progressively purified and raised up by grace during previous generations' (*Le dogme de l'Immacule Conception*, Paris, 1953, p. 6).

What is here in question, however, is a difference, not in the Roman

177

Catholic and Orthodox attitudes towards Mary, but in our respective doctrines of original sin.

Some words may be added in parenthesis about the Orthodox attitude towards Lourdes. There are Russians and Greeks who count it a privilege to go there on pilgrimage, and who are happy to pray to the Mother of God in the place where (so they firmly believe) she appeared to her servant Bernadette, and where so many miracles of divine grace have been manifested. But they interpret the events of Lourdes in a sense somewhat different from that accepted officially in the Roman Catholic Church. Why, they ask, did the Virgin say 'I am the Immaculate Conception', and not 'I am the fruit of the Immaculate Conception' or 'I am she who was immaculately conceived'? It is as if our Lord were to say 'I am the Virgin Birth'. It is surely significant that the Mother of God spoke these words to Bernadette, not on 8 December, the feast of her conception by her mother St Anne, but on 25 March, the feast of the Annunciation, when she conceived our Lord. May it perhaps be that she was referring, not to her conception by St Anne, but to the virginal and immaculate conception of Jesus Christ within her own womb?

VII. 'I look for the resurrection of the dead': Mary as an eschatological figure

If the Orthodox tradition is distinctly reserved towards the doctrine of the Immaculate Conception, in regard to the Bodily Assumption of the Mother of God the situation is very different. In the Orthodox liturgical texts for 15 August it is plainly stated that Mary, after her death, was received into heaven with her body as well as with her soul. She underwent, as her Son had done, the experience of physical death: but just as He rose from the dead and ascended into heaven, so she was likewise raised up by His divine power and entered with her material substance into His glory, while her grave was found to be empty.

This belief in the Assumption of the Mother of God is best understood in eschatological terms. When it is stated that Mary was taken up with her body into heaven, this is neither more nor less than a way of affirming that she had passed beyond death and judgment, and that she dwells already in the life of the age to come. Man, so the Bible teaches, is not a soul imprisoned in a body, but a unity of body and soul; the body is to be redeemed along with the soul, and is to be made a 'spiritual' instead of a 'carnal' body (heaven is not a geographical area, and so the statement that Mary's body has been 'assumed into heaven' is simply another way of saying that her body has now become in the fullest possible sense a 'spiritual body'). As Christians we believe not just in the immortality of the soul but in the resurrection of the body: the 'deification' to which man is called is something that will embrace his entire being, body as well as soul. But this full 'deification' of the body, in the case of other human beings, occurs only at the last day. What has happened in the Holy Virgin's case is simply that the resurrection of her body has been anticipated and is already an accomplished fact.

The Assumption of the Mother of God, therefore, does not set an impassable gulf between her and the rest of humanity. In the same bodily glory which she enjoys even now, we also hope eventually to participate. She is, along with her risen Son, the first fruits of the eschatological harvest; but that great harvest will eventually embrace all the faithful who have lived and died in Christ. By God's grace we shall all be what she is now: wholly 'spiritual', wholly transfigured in body and in soul, wholly transparent with the uncreated energies of God.

But Orthodox, while firmly believing in the Bodily Assumption of the Mother of God, have no wish to see it proclaimed as a dogma. It is something that belongs to the inner tradition of the Church, to the life of prayer and worship, and not to the public preaching where formal definitions are appropriate and necessary. There are many Christian truths not included in this public preaching which the believer learns through sharing in the corporate life of the redeemed community, in its liturgical and sacramental experience. When the Mother of God appears in the public preaching of the Church, it is primarily in the context of the Incarnation: '... and was incarnate by the Holy Ghost and the Virgin Mary'. For the rest, her rôle within the Body of Christ is not a subject of public proclamation but constitutes part of the inner tradition, preserved through worship. The point has been excellently expressed by Vladimir Lossky ('Panagia', p. 35):

> It is hard to speak and not less hard to think about the mysteries which the Church keeps in the hidden depths of her inner consciousnes. ... The Mother of God was never a theme of the public preaching of the Apostles; while Christ was preached on the housetops, and proclaimed for all to know in an initiatory teaching addressed to the whole world, the mystery of His Mother was revealed only to those who were within the Church. ... It is not so much an object of faith as a foundation of our hope, a fruit of faith, ripened in tradition. Let us therefore keep silent, and let us not try to formulate dogmas concerning the supreme glory of the Mother of God.

The mystery of the blessed Virgin's final glorification is not to be regarded as a further truth added to the truths already found in Scripture. Rather, it is the fruit of the assimilation of those Scriptural truths under the inspiration of the Holy Spirit; and as such it is accessible only to 'those who are within'.

VIII. The liturgical approach to Orthodoxy

This reference to an 'inner tradition', experienced liturgically, brings us to a final point, of crucial importance for any correct appreciation of Mary's place in the Orthodox tradition. Our belief as Orthodox concerning the Mother of God is expressed above all through the medium of prayer and worship. *Lex orandi lex credendi*: our faith is disclosed through, and conditioned by, the way in which we pray. In the words of Archpriest George Florovsky, Christianity is first of all a worshipping community. Worship comes first, doctrine and discipline second.' If this is true of Orthodox theology in general, it is true in a special sense of the Orthodox approach to the *Theotokos*. The mystery of the Mother of God is *par excellence* a liturgical mystery.

In 1950, when Pope Pius XII was about to proclaim the dogma of the Assumption, members of the Roman Catholic hierarchy in France approached Metropolitan Vladimir, head of the Russian Archdiocese, and they enquired what the belief of the Orthodox Church might be in this matter. In reply the Metropolitan recommended them to read the service for 15 August in the Orthodox liturgical books; and he said that he had nothing to add to what was written there. Such is precisely the Orthodox approach. He who would know what Orthodoxy thinks concerning the Mother of Jesus must not look only at the formal dogmatic pronouncements, of which in fact there is no more than one—the definition of Ephesus: and that is primarily a definition about the Incarnation, not the Virgin. He must also look at the prayer of the Eastern Church: at the use made of Holy Scripture in the lectionary for Mary's feasts, and at the liturgical texts in the office books.

IX. Two icons

In addition he should look at the Holy Icons, which are part of the Church's tradition, expressing the faith not through words but through line and colour. And he should look in particular at two icons, which sum up vividly the two aspects of the Blessed Virgin, the Christological and the ecclesiological. Better than any verbal explanation, these two icons will help him to understand the place of the Mother of God in the scheme of redemption. The first is the large icon which stands on the iconostasis of every Orthodox Church, immediately to the left of the royal doors, depicting Christ as a child in the arms of His Mother. In this, as in the great majority of icons, the Virgin does not appear alone but together with her Son: it is an icon, not of Mary, but of the Incarnation. Here, then, is the Christological aspect—Mary as *Theotokos*. The second or ecclesiological aspect is expressed symbolically by the icon of the *Deisis*, which appears frequently, though not invariably, on the upper part of the iconostasis: it shows Christ enthroned, while to His right hand and to His left stand Mary and John the Baptist, with their heads bowed and their hands raised in intercession. Here the Mother of God is seen as a member of the Church, ranged with another member, the Forerunner and Friend of the Bridegroom. 'More honoured than the cherubim and incomparably more glorious than the seraphim', she stands at the King's right hand, interceding with confidence on behalf of all the world. But she stands with her head bowed before Him who is not only her Son but her Creator and her God.

Mary in Syriac Tradition

SEBASTIAN BROCK, M.A., D.Phil., F.B.A.

Since Syriac literature will be somewhat *terra incognita* to many, it may be helpful to begin by charting out very briefly something of the territory. Syriac is a dialect of Aramaic, the language spoken by Jesus; it is related to Hebrew and Arabic, and it became the literary language of Christians living in the most easterly part of the Roman Empire, as well as those living further east still, in the Persian, or Sassanid, Empire (roughly modern Iraq and Iran). It thus from the first became the liturgical and literary language for the churches in this area, and it still survives today in its role as a liturgical language in the Maronite Church in the Lebanon, and in the Syrian Orthodox Church and the Church of the East (or, to use the sobriquets for the latter two that are more familiar in the west, the Jacobite or Monophysite, and the Nestorian, Churches), together with their Uniate counterparts.

Because it was transmitted in ecclesiastical circles, almost all Syriac literature that survives is Christian, and the earliest literary texts go back perhaps to the second century AD, but it is not until the fourth century that the sources become at all extensive. The golden age of Syriac literature may be said to extend from the fourth to the sixth century; at any rate this is the period of the best and most creative examples of that literary genre in which Syriac writers excelled, namely liturgical poetry. This does not mean to say that the literature came to an end with the Arab conquests in the seventh century—in fact a great deal has continued to be written in Syriac right up to the present day.

Here I shall make use only of texts from the golden age of Syriac literature, employing in particular the writings of two of the greatest of all Syriac poets, St Ephrem who died in 373, and Jacob of Serugh, a Syrian Orthodox writer who flourished around the turn of the fifth/sixth century. Most of the themes I shall deal with could equally well be illustrated from the liturgical texts of both the Syrian Orthodox and the East Syrian (Nestorian and Chaldean) traditions, which in fact often draw extensively on Ephrem and Jacob; and here attention may be drawn to what at first may seem a surprising fact: Nestorius is well known to all as having rejected the title of *Theotokos*, 'bearer of God', for Mary, and in view of this one might have expected the East Syrian liturgical texts to be less concerned than their Syrian Orthodox counterparts with the role of Mary, but this is in fact far from the case: the general tone of both traditions is very similar, and on a number of occasions I have even come across the term objected to by Nestorius 'Mother of God', in East Syrian liturgical texts. In actual fact, the

Christological differences that separate the Syrian Orthodox, Greek Orthodox (Chalcedonian) Churches and the Church of the East do not appear to have had much effect on their attitudes to Mary, at least outside technical theological discussions. Thus those who are familiar with the Byzantine tradition will find much of what Syriac writers say on the subject of Mary not unfamiliar.

My choice of poetic, rather than prose, texts is deliberate. There is a large corpus of pseudepigraphical literature about Mary in prose in Syriac, as well as a small amount of specifically theological writing, but it is the poetic texts which provide by far the most sympathetic treatment, and their approach, essentially suggestive, avoiding cut and dried dogmatic statements, is one that seems to me to have a real validity.

There remains one final introductory point: the language that Syriac writers use of Mary is very largely biblical, or inspired by the Bible. The Syriac-speaking churches possess their own Bible, of very great antiquity, the standard text being known as the Peshitta, the Old Testament translated directly from the Hebrew, the New from the Greek. This means that there are a number of differences between the Syriac, Greek and Latin Bibles, and these of course, to a certain extent, have influenced the interpretation of individual passages. For the New Testament there was actually another, earlier, translation available, but of this only the Gospels survive; this, rather than the Peshitta New Testament, was the text known to Ephrem, along with a second-century harmony of the four Gospels, known as the Diatessaron: this earliest New Testament translation was considerably freer than the Peshitta, and the Diatessaron in particular introduced into the Gospel text certain apocryphal elements, such as the bright light accompanying the Baptism of Christ in the Jordan. Finally, an important fact to remember is that the Apocalypse did not form part of the original Syriac New Testament canon, and it was not translated into Syriac until the early sixth century.

To introduce the main part of this paper I take a rather surprising text — a Syriac Orthodox calendar copied in North Iraq in 1689. Commenting on the feasts of March, the compiler states: "As for the Feast of the Annunciation, the church celebrates it on whichever day of the week the 25th falls: even if it falls on Good Friday, we still celebrate the Liturgy, since the Annunciation is the beginning and source of all other feasts". This text excellently exemplifies the emphasis one finds, throughout Syriac literature, that the Annunciation, and Mary's role there, is the crucial starting point for the events of the Incarnation: in other words, the view is taken that, without Mary, the Incarnation would not have taken place.

The vital role played by Mary at the Annunciation is a theme developed at some length by Jacob of Serugh in a famous series of metrical homilies on the Virgin. In the first place Mary is chosen as being

183

worthy of Gabriel's visitation because she is the most perfect mortal ever to have lived:

> Because God saw her, and how pure and clear her soul,
> He wished to dwell in her who had been purified from every wickedness,
> for no woman had ever appeared like her. (p. 622).

And a little further on Jacob bluntly states:

> Had any other woman pleased Him more than Mary, He would have chosen her instead.

Mary is, however, by no means a mere tool of divine providence in Jacob's eyes; in a dramatic dialogue between her and Gabriel Mary cross-questions the angel, for she recalls how Eve had fallen through unquestioningly accepting the serpent's suggestion. Jacob comments:

> Through Eve's silence came defeat and disrepute,
> through Mary's words, Life, Light and victory. (p. 631).

Everything depends on Mary's answer to the angel. Jacob firmly rejects the view, apparently current, that the word entered Mary's womb *before* the angel had spoken, thus implying that her answer was a foregone conclusion; rather, in his view,

> The moment she replied in the affirmative, she conceived (lit. received the fruit) in her womb. (p. 739).

Before leaving the Annunciation three rather individual features of Syriac tradition in connection with it should be mentioned. Firstly, the Logos, or Word, is regarded as having entered Mary quite literally through her ear:

> Through her ear the Word entered
> and dwelt secretly in the womb. (Ephrem, *H. Nativ.* XI, 6)

Ephrem's words here represent a commonplace among Syriac writers. As we shall see, this — to us somewhat bizarre — ideas was popular for typological reasons, Mary's obedience being contrasted with Eve's disobedience.

The second feature is an exegesis of Luke 1:35, "the Holy Spirit shall come upon you, and the Power of the Most High shall overshadow you", which is developed notably by Jacob of Serugh, but which is by no means confined to him. On a number of occasions Jacob is careful to differentiate between the 'Spirit' and the 'Power', the 'Spirit' being the Holy Spirit who first sanctifies Mary's womb, and the 'Power' being the Word, who then enters and dwells there. The basic reason for this exegesis is evidently a grammatical consideration: in Syriac *ruha*, 'spirit', is feminine and in early Syriac literature the Holy Spirit, *ruha d-qudsha*, is mostly construed grammatically as a feminine, although later on, under Greek influence, it was treated as a masculine (Syriac having no neuter). The word for 'Power' on the other hand is masculine (whereas *dunamis* of the Greek is feminine). One might have thought that this grammatical feature, the Spirit being feminine, would have played an important role in the way the Syriac-speaking church thought of the Holy Spirit, but with a few notable exceptions, among which the exegesis of Luke 1:35 is one, this has apparently not been the case — at least in the texts which survive.

The third feature is of rather a different order, and concerns the calendar. In the East Syrian tradition the period known as Advent in the west is called the 'Annunciation', thus laying stress once more or the intimate relationship between Mary's initial acceptance and the consequence of the Incarnation and Nativity.

I shall in fact pass very quickly over the theme of the Nativity, since I wish to dwell at rather more length on the subject of Mary and the Old Testament. Syriac writers regularly stress Mary's perpetual virginity, but regard it as a mystery which should not be pried into. According to Jacob of Serugh, some people posed the dilemma: "If the Incarnation is a reality, then virginity *in partu* is impossible: but if Mary remained a virgin *in partu*, then the incarnation was not real". Jacob rejects this as a false dilemma, since it takes no account of the 'miracle' of the Incarnation itself: such a miraculous event takes place in a miraculous way, breaking the physiological laws of nature. This sort of attitude is very much in line with that of the Greek Fathers, and, as we shall shortly see, it was given a typological basis.

Let us turn now to the subject of Mary and the Old Testament. Early Syriac exegesis of the Bible was essentially typological, that is to say connections between persons, objects and events were sought out and brought together, either as complementing, or as contrasting, each other. This typological exegesis can take on two main forms: on the one hand it can be purely historical, confined to the framework of the biblical revelation: Paul's Adam-Christ typology belongs to this category, and we shall shortly be concerned in particular with the Eve-Mary typology, first found in Justin Martyr, in the second century. On the other hand, the typological relationships can also be between this world and the heavenly world, and this variety can best be described as symbolic typology. Very often both kinds of typology, historical and symbolic, are used simultaneously, and frequently in a very elaborate way.

To Ephrem's fertile mind these types or symbols (in Syriac they are usually called 'mysteries') are to be found everywhere, and on one occasion he self-mockingly complains:

> This Jesus has made so many symbols that I have fallen into the sea of them.

Ephrem's highly allusive poetry, shifting almost relentlessly from one set of symbols to another, makes considerable demands on the reader who, above all, if he is to appreciate Ephrem to the full, must know his Bible as well as Ephrem did. Much of this typological exegesis will appear to modern readers as forced, or it may even be described as 'wrong', but I think it is misleading to speak of this kind of exegesis in absolute terms of 'correct' and 'incorrect'. The very fact that quite often one finds side by side two pieces of typological exegesis which are logically incompatible when taken together, seems to be an indication that what is being offered was never meant to be 'the correct exegesis', such as modern biblical scholarship likes to impose, but possible models which are held up, and whose purpose is to make meaningful, and give insight into, some aspects of a mystery that cannot be fully explained.

One might perhaps view Ephrem and his fellow poet-exegetes as offering to their readers a garden full of every kind of flower; their readers are the bees, which, as they go around collecting honey, enjoy the fragrance of all the flowers as a whole, but each individual bee will alight only on those particular flowers which take its fancy.

This method of exegesis is in fact essentially meant as an aid to devotional contemplation, and as such seems to me to be eminently successful. That it is definitely mythopoietic in character should not be considered as detracting from its value, for mythology, in the proper sense of the word, is precisely what mankind has always used to help explain what is beyond the bounds of full human comprehension: it simply provides possible analogies and models — precisely what the Syriac poets are doing.

Furthermore, what these poets are offering are not only spiritual delights, but also aesthetic ones, for typological exegesis has also been developed into something of an art-form, where the external symmetry of the, often intricate, typological pattern is also meant to please, quite apart from its inner spiritual content.

Syriac writers saw an abundance of types and symbols of Mary when they read their Bibles, and in passing it is worth noting that the vast majority of these types (e.g. 'ark', 'temple', 'cruse', 'chariot') are objects that *contain* something holy, in other words they are essentially Christocentric in character. Here I shall confine myself to one particular area that is of basic importance, the Eve-Mary typology.

At the outset it will be helpful to note various distinctions in the way this parallelism is applied. Paul's First Adam - Second Adam typology would demand as a logical extension the equation of Mary, not with Eve, but with the Earth from which the First Adam sprang. This pattern is indeed found in Syriac writers; as Ephrem puts it:

> The virgin earth of old gave birth to the Adam who is lord of the earth,
> but today another virgin has given birth to the Adam who is Lord of heaven. (*H. Nativ.* I, 16).

Here the aspect emphasized is the relationship mother-child, given in simple, contrasted form. Ephrem actually provides in this poem a more subtle and intricate piece of typology, for he combines this with the parallelism between Adam, the begetter of Eve, and Mary the bearer of Christ; once again the interest is in the genetic relationship, and in particular in its miraculous nature:

> Adam brought forth travail upon the woman who sprang from him,
> but today she (Mary), who bore him a Saviour, has redeemed that travail.
> A man (Adam) who himself knew no birth, bore Eve the mother:
> how much more should Eve's daughter (Mary) be believed to have given birth without the aid of a man!
>
> (*H. Nativ.* 1,14–15).

The same idea is found in Jacob:

> As our father (Adam) begot our mother without intercourse,
> so did Mary give birth, just as Adam did before he had sinned.
> The Holy Spirit blew on Adam's face,
> and he gave birth to Eve: this Spirit did Mary too receive, and she gave birth to a Son.
> Adam gave birth to the 'mother of all living things' without intercourse,
> thus depicting the birth of our Lord, who is the fountain of all life. (p. 634).

Here the pattern Adam:Eve::Mary:Christ is a twofold one, for Ephrem and Jacob quite certainly see this as a chiastic arrangement as well: Mary corresponds to Adam in her miraculous childbearing, but at the same time she *also* corresponds to Eve, and Christ to Adam, following the customary typology.

The prime concern of the long-established Eve-Mary typology, to which we now turn, is of course the contrast between Fall and Restoration, and not with relationships, as in the previous examples. There appear to be two rather different ways of looking at this contrast between Eve and Mary. On the one hand, one can take a cyclical view of salvation-history, and regard Mary as reversing what Eve brought about, in which case Mary starts off, as it were, in the position into which Eve had reduced the human race, but through the Incarnation Mary is able to bring mankind back into Paradise, the pre-Fall state. I shall call this the 'dynamic' view. On the other hand, one can regard Mary's position as having been *throughout* her life that of Eve *before* the Fall. This I shall call the 'static' view. Now the dynamic view is quite certainly the earlier, and as far as I can see, the normal view of the Fathers, of whatever language; it is certainly the view of Ephrem and Jacob, the two Syriac poets who have the most to say on the subject of Mary.

Since, however, most writers were interested in describing Mary only in the light of the Incarnation, they naturally refer to her in terms of Eve before the Fall, and so an undiscerning reader might assume that what is predicted, in paradisiacal terms, of Mary *after* the Incarnation, equally applied to all her life before: it is at this stage that one arrives at what I am calling the 'static' viewpoint. It is this static view that essentially underlies the various apocryphal lives of Mary; it also seems to me to be the basis for some of the less fortunate trends in Western Marian devotion.

Linked with this static view is a tendency, frequently to be observed in the history of religions, to take as literal truth what was originally intended to be the language of symbol, poetry, metaphor midrash, myth (in the good sense of the word), or whatever one may like to call it. This is basically a fundamentalist approach, and one that fossilizes typology, using it as a basis for creating fixed dogmas, whereas the typological approach to the Bible as found in the Syriac (and of course other) Fathers is essentially a fluid one, refusing to be contained by dogmatic statements on the one hand, or considerations of modern biblical scholarship and its findings on the other. Indeed, one wonders whether this approach does not offer the openings of a *via tertia* for twentieth-century western Christianity in its dilemma when faced with the liberal critical approach to the Bible that to many seems purely destructive, on the one side, and a distastefully fundamentalist approach on the other. It must of course be realised that typological exegesis can never, by its very nature, lay any claims to scientific objectivity, seeing that it belongs to a completely different mode of thought.

The parallels and contrasts between Eve and Mary are drawn in great detail by the Syriac poets, and the love of symmetry has resulted in the appearance of a number of purely 'mythological' elements, such as the quaint idea of Mary conceiving through her ear, mentioned earlier, the object being to provide a contrast with Eve's disobedience through listening to the serpent, sin being pictured as entering through her ear, like poison, as the serpent spoke.

Another recurrent piece of imagery, and one of some importance is that of the 'robe of glory'. According to widespread Syriac tradition (probably of Jewish origin), Adam and Eve were stripped of their original 'robes of glory' when they were expelled from the Garden of Eden. With the coming of Christ, however, the 'robe of glory' is restored for mankind, in the sacrament of Baptism. Mary's essential role in this is once again stressed by Jacob:

> The second Eve gave birth to Life, among mortals;
> she wiped clean the bill of debt incurred by Eve her mother.
> The child (Mary) gave her hand to help her aged mother (Eve), who lay prostrate;
> she raised her up from the Fall that the serpent had effected.
> It was the daughter (Mary) who wove the robe of glory and gave it to her father (Adam),
> who then covered his body that had been naked ever since the affair of the tree. (p.616).

As we shall see later on in another connection, this robe of glory is essentially a symbol of Baptism; Adam, according to legend, was buried on Golgotha, and there he was baptized in the water and blood that flowed from the side of Christ (John 19:34).

Although not directly relevant to our theme, it might be added that the imagery of the debt (taken from Colossians 2:14) in the passage quoted above was also extremely popular, and in turn gave rise to all kinds of what can best be described as 'documentary' imagery. Thus, for example, to contrast with the document of debt given by Satan to Eve, Gabriel is commonly depicted as bearing a 'royal missive', containing the message of the Annunciation. It was not for nothing that Aramaic had been the chancery language of the Achaemenid empire.

Woven into this basic Eve/Mary typology one finds numerous logical extensions of the initial contrasted equation between Eve and Mary. I shall dwell here momentarily on one of these. Once Adam and Eve had been expelled, the entrance to Paradise was guarded, according to the biblical account (Genesis 3:24), by a cherub with a revolving sword. It is Mary who, by giving birth to Christ, removes this obstacle. In Jacob's words:

> Through Mary the path to Eden, that had been shut, was trod again;
> the serpent fled, and men could pass over to God.
> Through Mary the cherub turned aside his sword, to guard no more
> the Tree of Life (i.e. Christ), which had now given itself over to be eaten.
> (p. 637).

Now this sword of Genesis 3:24 was very frequently connected typologically by Syriac writers with the lance that pierced Christ's side in John 19:34 (a single Syriac word is often employed for both weapons), and the water and blood which issued from the pierced side were regularly interpreted in a sacramental sense – Baptism and Eucharist; – in other words, just another aspect of the return to Paradise. Mary and the Sacraments are thus pictured in virtually identical roles, and the same 'equation', if one can call it such, will be found if one considers the typological relationship (equally commonly found) between Adam's rib and Christ's side, where Adam's rib giving birth to Eve is contrasted with Christ's side 'giving birth' to the Sacraments. We have already seen how Jacob also contrasts the first half (i.e. Adam: Eve) with Mary's giving birth to Christ, and so this accordingly becomes the theoretical equivalent to Christ's side giving birth to the Sacraments. Such a typological pattern is never, of course, given explicitly by Jacob, but its implicit presence is characteristic of the great flexibility in the '*communicatio typorum*', if I may so call it, that one finds in these Syriac poets. We shall see very much the same sort of thing in connection with the last topic I want to deal with, Mary and baptism.

To Ephrem, Christ's birth from Mary as well as from the Father was an indication that man too requires a second birth, that is, at baptism, and once again the chiastic structure of this piece of typology gives the artistic symmetry that the Syriac poets loved so much. A number of factors suggested these links. In the first place one must remember that in Ephrem's day Christ's nativity and baptism were still celebrated on the same day (our Epiphany), and that, at least in some localities, baptisms were held at this time, rather than at Easter. The links were further suggested by the characteristically Syriac imagery of the baptismal waters as a womb and the fact that Christ's presence in the Jordan was widely regarded in the early Syriac-speaking church as having potentially sanctified all baptismal water. The parallelism thus created between Christ in his mother's womb and in the 'womb' of the Jordan water leads Ephrem to regard Christ's very presence in Mary's womb as the equivalent of *her* baptism:

> The Light settled on Mary, as on an eye;
> it purified her mind, it cleansed her understanding,
> it washed her thought, it made her virginity shine.
> The river in which Christ was baptized conceived him again symbolically,
> the damp womb of the water conceived him in purity,
> and bore him in holiness, made him rise up in glory.
> In the pure womb of the river you should recognize the daughter of man,
> who conceived without the aid of man, and gave birth as a virgin,
> and who brought up, through a gift, the Lord of that gift. (*H. Eccles.* XXXVI, 2-4).

It will be noticed here that, to Ephrem, the whole of Christ's incarnate life, from the nativity to the ascension, is gathered up in his baptism, thus explaining the apparent reversal of time in Mary's baptism. Elsewhere Ephrem makes the point more explicitly:

> O Christ, you have given birth to your own mother
> in the second birth that comes from water.

> (*H. Nativ.* XVI, 9).

And a little later on he says the same thing in terms of the imagery of the 'robe of glory', touched on above: (Mary speaks)

> The Son of the Most High came and dwelt in me,
> and I became his mother. As I gave birth to him,
> – his second birth – so too he gave birth to me
> a second time. He put on his mother's robe
> –his body; I put on his glory. (*H. Nativ.* XVI, 11).

Further connections between Mary and Baptism are provided by the imagery of Christ as fire, particularly common in Ephrem:

> Fire and Spirit are in the womb of her who bore you,
> Fire and Spirit are in the river in which you were baptized,
> Fire and Spirit are in our baptism,
> and in the Bread and Cup is Fire and the Holy Spirit.

> (*H. Fid.* X, 17).

Ephrem's picture of Mary's baptism is extended by Jacob of Serugh in a curious passage, where he regards the baptism of John the Baptist as having taken place in his mother Elizabeth's womb, on the occasion of Mary's visit:

> Mary's greeting fulfilled the priest's role there:
> Elizabeth's was like a womb of baptism;
> the Son of God sent the Spirit from his own essence,
> and the child John was baptized by the Holy Spirit while still in his mother's womb. (pp. 646-7).

With this somewhat bizzare picture we may draw to an end. The important thing to remember, however, when faced with passages such as this, is that the Syriac poets provide this wealth of phantasmogoric imagery and this kaleidoscope of 'mythological' pictures as contemplative aids towards a deeper appreciation and understanding of the mysteries that surround the incarnation. To take them at their face value would be to misunderstand them completely and totally.

If one were to try to summarize the attitudes towards Mary as exemplified in early Syriac literature, I think it would be true to say that she is always regarded in relationship to the Incarnation, and never *in vacuo*. In Orthodox icons the virgin is normally depicted with the incarnate Christ in her arms, symbolic of her role of cooperation with the divine economy; although the Syriac-speaking churches in fact do not make great use of icons, this iconographical tradition admirably exemplifies their Christocentric approach. And Mary's relationship to the Holy Spirit is always clear cut: the Holy Spirit is essentially the Sanctifier, while Mary is the sanctified, *par excellence*. This relationship of cooperation receives its perfect expression in the words of the Nicene creed, in their eastern form: "... born of the Holy Spirit *and* Mary the Virgin".

BIBLIOGRAPHICAL NOTE

Ephrem's poems are quoted from the recent edition (with German translation) by Dom E. Beck, in the Louvain Corpus of oriental Christian writers, while Jacob of Serugh's Marian homilies are quoted from P. Bedjan's edition, at the end of his *S. Martyrii qui et Sahdona quae supersunt omnia* (1902; Italian translation by C. Vona, Rome 1953).

For some further aspects of Marian typology reference may be made to R. Murray, S.J., "Mary the Second Eve in the early Syriac Fathers", in *Eastern Churches Review* 3 (1971), pp. 372-84; and "The lance which re-opened Paradise, mysterious reading in the early Syriac Fathers", in *Orientalia Christiana Periodica* 39 (1973), pp. 224-34, 491. English translations of some relevant hymns of Ephrem will be found in the following: R. Murray, "A hymn of St Ephrem to Christ on the Incarnation, the Holy Spirit and the Sacraments", *Eastern Churches Review* 3 (1970), pp. 142-50; *Symbols of Church and Kingdom* (Cambridge, 1975). S.P. Brock, "St. Ephrem on Christ as Light in Mary and in the Jordan", *Eastern Churches Review* 7 (1976), pp. 137-44; and *The Harp of the Spirit: Twelve Poems of Saint Ephrem* (Studies Supplementary to Sobornost, 4, 1975).

A Woman in Israel

RABBI NICHOLAS DE LANGE

If you want to understand Judaism and Jews, one of the best ways is to visit a Jewish family for the Friday evening meal, when the Sabbath, 'the Bride, the Queen', is welcomed into the Jewish home. The Jewish home has been called 'the other Sanctuary', and the Sabbath table has been compared to an altar. On a spotless white tablecloth stand a pair of candles in silver candlesticks, a silver goblet of wine, a loaf of bread baked in the traditional plaited shape. The mother lights the candles and says a Hebrew blessing, and this act is the formal inauguration of the Sabbath. The father lays his hands on his children's heads and pronounces the ancient priestly blessing (*Num* 6. 24-6). Then after a song welcoming the angelic visitors who are supposed to enter the home on the Sabbath, he turns to his wife and recites the Hebrew poem which ends the Book of Proverbs:

Oh to find a worthy wife,
　　more priceless far than pearls.
Her husband's heart trusts her,
　　he feels no lack.
She repays him with good, not evil,
　　all her life long.
She brings home wool and flax
　　and willingly works them with her hands.
She is like the merchants' ships:
　　she fetches food from afar.
She rises while it is still dark
　　to give food to her family
　　and orders to her servants.
If she sets her sights on a field she will have it;
　　she plants a vineyard from the fruit of her hands.
She girds her loins with power
　　and strengthens her arms.
She knows that her trade goes well;
　　her lamp never goes out at night.
She puts her hand to the distaff,
　　her hands grasp the spindle.
She opens her palm to the poor,
　　and holds out her hand to the needy.
She has no fear for her family when it snows:
　　they are all clothed in scarlet cloaks.
She makes her own bedspreads,
　　she dresses in fine linen and purple.
Her husband is known in the gateways
　　where he sits among the elders of the land.

She makes and sells linen,
  she sells sashes to the trader.
Power and honour are her clothing,
  she is cheerful to her last day.
She opens her mouth with wisdom,
  the teaching of love is on her tongue.
She is watchful for the ways of her family,
  she eats no idle bread.
Her children rise up to bless her,
  her husband, too, to praise her:
"Many women are worthy
  but you excel them all.
Charm is a cheat, beauty is a breath,
  but a God-fearing woman is truly to be praised.
Give her credit for her achievements
  and let her deeds bring her praise in the gateways".

This biblical poem, and its honoured place in the Sabbath ritual, highlights at once the great respect traditionally accorded to the Jewish wife and mother, and also her distinct role in society. She maintains her family by her labours, and they 'rise up to bless her'; but while she works her fingers to the bone her husband sits among the elders at the gate of the city. She is both housewife and breadwinner, working to keep up her husband's leisured and honoured status. This can be seen as a division of labour, but other biblical passages make it plain that behind the lavish praise there lies the presumption of the wife's subordination to her husband. 'Your longing shall be for your husband, and he shall be your master' (*Gen* 3.16).

The subordination of women to men has, of course, been taken for granted almost everywhere until recent times. In the time of the Gospel, in the early years of Roman rule in Judaea, although women were in some ways relatively free, their lives, and the possibilities open to them, were strictly circumscribed. The position of the Jewish woman was in some respects better than that of her non-Jewish counterpart, but it cannot be compared with that of a woman in modern Western society. Nor can we expect it to be.

Legal Status

In biblical law women had very little independence. An unmarried woman was under the control of her father, and on marriage she passed directly under the control of her husband. From the earliest times, however, there are signs of improvement; a notable example is the rule, arising out of the claim of the daughters of Zelophehad, that if a man dies without sons his property can pass to his daughters or other female relations (*Num* 27.7-11). By Gospel times the position had changed considerably: Once a girl reached her majority (*i.e.* from the age of twelve and a half) she was virtually free from parental control.

Her income and incidental earnings were her own, and she could choose her own husband. True, she lost many of her privileges on marriage, but the position of a married woman was by now relatively secure. As a father was obliged by law to house and provide for his daughters while they were minors, so a husband was obliged by law to maintain his wife in a decent manner, and a minimum acceptable standard was laid down.

In primitive society a man might purchase his wife from her father or the father might pay over a dowry to the husband. The different systems were eventually merged, so that the bride-price was returned to the husband at the wedding, and it became a jointure payable to the woman on the death of her husband or in the case of divorce, like the dowry. In either case, therefore, the woman was protected against frivolous divorce and provision was made for her if she was widowed or divorced. These provisions were stated explicitly in a document, called the *ketubah*, which was drawn up at the time of marriage. The husband, on the other hand, was entitled to all his wife's earnings and to the usufruct of her property, and became her sole heir if she died first.

In theory a man could have more than one wife, although a woman could only have one husband. In practice, however, monogamy seems to have been the rule at this time, although lawyers continued to legislate for a very long time on the basis of polygyny.

A man could divorce his wife, even against her will, but a wife could not divorce her husband. Divorce by mutual consent was an easy affair, and did not even require an appearance in court. All that was necessary was the presence of two witnesses. 'Thus if Joseph of Nazareth and his betrothed bride had mutually consented to a divorce, there is no reason in Jewish law why he should not have "put her away privily" (*Mt* 1.19)' (Israel Abrahams, *Studies in Pharisaism and the Gospels*, 1917, p. 70). If, on the other hand, one of the parties contested the divorce, the case would probably be heard in a court of law, and satisfactory grounds would have to be given. There was some disagreement as to what constituted grounds. The School of Shammai only permitted a husband to divorce his wife if she had been unfaithful to him (*cf. Mt* 5.32); the School of Hillel allowed him to divorce her for any cause, even for 'spoiling his dinner'. The debate, which centred on the correct interpretation of the law in *Deut* (24.1) 'When a man has married a wife, but she does not meet with his favour because he finds something shameful in her ...', was waged with vigour. There is a trace of it in the Gospel (*Mt* 19.3), when the Pharisees ask Jesus, 'Is it lawful for a man to divorce his wife on any and every ground?" Jesus's reply conforms to the Shammaite rule, in that he regards unfaithfulness as the only ground for divorce (see Abrahams, *op. cit.*, p. 71).

To digress for a moment, an understanding of the Jewish law can help us to understand the statement in the Gospel (*Mt* 1.19) that

'Joseph, being a righteous man, and being unwilling to expose her to shame, decided to divorce her privately'. Betrothal, in Jewish law, is as solemnly binding as marriage; the principal difference is that the couple do not live together. Joseph, suspecting his bride of unfaithfulness to him, was entitled, and indeed as a righteous man obliged, to divorce her, even according to the stricter Shammaite interpretation of the law in *Deuteronomy*. The choice facing him was whether to take the case before a court of law, in which case the grounds must be publicly stated, or to secure her consent and divorce her privately. He had decided on the latter course, when his fears were allayed (*Ibid.*, pp. 72f.)

Ritual Law

Biblical law recognises certain states of ritual uncleanness, which arise from particular conditions or from contact with unclean persons or objects. Women are particularly liable to ritual uncleanness since, in addition to the causes which can affect either sex, they are unclean during menstruation (*Lev* 15.19-24) and for a period after childbirth (*Lev* 12.2-8).

A person in a state of uncleanness is forbidden to enter the precincts of the Temple or to partake of sacred foods, but in the particular cases of female uncleanness marital contact is also forbidden. Thus, whereas for most men ritual uncleanness was a remote possibility and was generally easy to avoid, for all women it was frequent and unavoidable, as well as carrying more severe consequences.

The principal remedy for uncleanness was ritual immersion or baptism, although it is clear that in Gospel times baptism was practised for other reasons than strict ritual uncleanness. (It was practised regularly by certain pietist sects, and was required as part of the admission of converts to Judaism.) In the two particular cases I have mentioned, however, there was also a period of waiting. In the case of menstruation this was seven days; in the case of childbirth the law lays down, if the child is a boy, that the mother is unclean for seven days as for menstruation; the boy is circumcised on the eighth day, but the mother continues unclean for thirty-three days. For a female child these periods are doubled. At the end of the period the mother brings two sacrifices, a ram for a whole-offering and a young pigeon or turtledove for a sin-offering; if she cannot afford a ram she brings two pigeons or turtledoves, one for the whole-offering and one for the sin-offering.

Divorce in itself bore no moral stigma, and it carried the advantage that the divorced woman was free to remarry, with two exceptions: she could not remarry her ex-husband if she had been married to another man since the divorce (although where there was no such bar the divorced couple were encouraged to remarry) (*Deut* 24.1-4), and she could not marry a member of the hereditary priesthood. This advantage can be appreciated if we compare it with the plight of the woman whose husband has deserted her or whose whereabouts are unknown. Even if he is believed dead, she may not remarry, and this law has caused a great deal of misery and suffering right up to the present day, since it is still in force in Orthodox Jewish law. The Rabbis did everything they could to relieve this hardship, even setting aside the strict rules of evidence if there were any witness to the husband's death. Although they frowned on gladiatorial combats and similar spectacles, they granted that a man might legitimately attend them so as to be able to testify to a man's death and so release his widow. Men, of course, did not suffer under this law, since they were technically free to take second wife even if the first wife were still alive.

A woman could not be a judge or a witness in a court of law. On the other hand, women could appear in court in person, without the intercession of a male counsel. There is an amusing story about the awkward predicament of a judge faced with the prospect of the appearance of the wife of one of his colleagues in a lawsuit. He felt bound to stand up when she came in, out of respect to her husband, but he was afraid that this might embarrass the other party. He solved the dilemma by arranging for a duck to be set free in court when she arrived. In the ensuing commotion he was able to stand up unobtrusively.

Luke describes (*Luke* 2.21-4) how these rituals are carried out after the birth of Jesus. He was circumcised on the eighth day and, like Jewish boys to this day, he received his name at the time of circumcision. Later, 'after the purification had been completed in accordance with the Law of Moses', his parents took him to Jerusalem to offer the sacrifices, in this case, since they were not wealthy, 'a pair of turtle doves or two young pigeons'.

'The Burden of the Commandments'

Besides the rules of uncleanness, Judaism knows a good deal more ritual law, and it is considered the mark of a good Jew 'to accept willingly the burden of the commandments'. It is traditionally calculated that there are 613 commandments, of which 365 are given in the form of prohibitions and 248 in the form of positive commands. The study of these commandments has always been a most important part of Jewish religious education, and Jews take an almost unhealthy interest in the minute details of their operation. There is a vast literature concerned with them, going right back to the Five Books of Moses; two books in particular, the Mishnah and the Tosefta, give a detailed account of the working of the law as it operated in the time of the Gospel.

The position of women with regard to the commandments was somewhere between the position of men, who had to obey all the commandments which could possibly apply to them, and the position of children and slaves, who had hardly any commandments to obey. The rule is laid down in the Mishnah:

'The observance of all positive commands which are restricted to a certain time is obligatory for men but not for women, but the observance of all positive commands which have no time specified is obligatory for men and women alike. All prohibitions, whether there is a time specified or not, are binding on men and women alike, except for three: 'You shall not round off your hair' and 'You shall not shave the edges of your beard' (*Lev* 19.27), and 'You shall not become unclean because of the dead' (*Lev* 21.1).' (Mishnah *Kiddushin* i. 7).

The Mishnah goes on to add that the rituals connected with making offerings in the Temple were also restricted to men for the most part, although women could make offerings, and might under certain circumstances be permitted to take part in the ritual.

'Positive commands which are restricted to a certain time' include those connected with the annual festivals. Women were not bound to their observance, no doubt, because of the high probability that ritual uncleanness would make it impossible for them to observe them. They were thus freed from the obligation, although they could certainly participate in the celebration if they wished. Sadly, a provision which was clearly intended to bestow a measure of freedom on women came in time to contribute to their enslavement. The fact that women were not obliged to perform certain rituals came to be regarded by men as a sign of their inferior status. A blessing was introduced into the daily service in which men thanked God 'for not making me a woman', while women humbly substituted the words 'for making me according to your will'. The commentators explain that a man thanks God daily for not making him a woman because as a man he has a greater share in the performance of God's will in the form of the commandments; the fact remains that throughout the generations the blessing has encouraged an attitude of superiority on the part of males.

If there are some commandments which women are not obliged to observe, there are others which devolve especially upon them. Those concerning female uncleanness, of course, are purely the preserve of the woman, but there are other commandments, such as setting aside the dough-offering when baking bread, and lighting the sabbath lamp, which, while strictly being the responsibility of the householder, fall to the woman's lot as mistress of the home. The rabbis, who piously believed that every illness has its origin in human failings, set these apart as commands especially binding on women, and declared that their neglect is the cause of women dying in childbirth. (Mishnah *Shabbat* ii. 6).

Women in Temple and Synagogue

In the public life of Judaism, in the Temple and Synagogue, women played an enthusiastic part, and their righteousness and piety were admired even by men who have little good to say of women in other respects.

The Bible tells (*Ex* 38.8, cf. 1 *Sam* 2.22) of the women who ministered at the entrance to the Tent of Meeting, who donated their bronze mirrors for the making of the lavers. Philo, who was a contemporary of Mary, expresses his admiration for this action. 'They brought them,' he says, 'with great enthusiasm and zeal, rivalling the men in piety, resolved to compete in this noble contest and eager to do all in their power not to be outstripped by the men in holiness; they gave the mirrors which they used in titivating and beautifying themselves, not under orders but of their own enthusiastic accord, as a most appropriate firstfruit offering of their modesty and marital purity and what must be surely described as spiritual beauty.' (Philo *Life of Moses* ii. 136-7. Cf. *Migration of Abraham* 98.)

Philo firmly believed tha a woman's place was in the home, and that she should not 'show herself off in the streets like a vagrant in the sight of men', but he adds, as a clear concession of the religiosity of women, 'except when she has to go to the temple (or synagogue), and even then she should take pains to go, not when the marketplace is crowded, but when most people have gone home; then she can offer her sacrifices and her prayers to avert evil and bring good in solitude like a free-born lady and a true citizen.' (Philo *Special Laws* III. 169-171.)

The Rabbis, too, who like Philo insist on modest and becoming conduct in women, mention their piety and keen attendance at religious ceremonies. It was even taught that it was as a reward for the righteousness of the women of the time that the Israelites were rescued from Egypt. (Babylonian Talmud, *Sotah* 11b.)

Despite their religious zeal, women were not given a full part to play in the public worship.This was particularly true in the great public ceremonial of the Temple. As I have said, although women could, and on certain occasions were obliged to, offer sacrifices in the Temple, they were not bound to perform all the details of the offering, as men were. They were never admitted to the Sanctuary itself, but were restricted to a special area called the Court of the Women. This court was lower than the Court of the Israelites, where the sacrificial altar stood and where the sacrifices were usually offered. Fifteen steps led down from this main court to the Court of the Women. The Levites stood on this staircase to sing, and underneath the Court of the Israelites there were chambers opening into the Court of the Women in which the musicians played. (Mishnah *Middoth* ii. 5-6). If a woman wished to participate in the ritual of sacrifice, although it was not necessary, the victim could be taken out into the Court of the Women. (Babylonian Talmud *Hagigah* 16b). Originally the sexes were not segregated in the Court of the Women, but at a later date a gallery was constructed around the court for their exclusive use. (Mishnah *Middoth* ii. 5). On the great festivals the Women's Court was the scene of part of the celebrations. On the Feast of Tabernacles, for example, which was the culmination of the great autumn festival-period, enormous lamps were lit there, which lit up the whole of Jerusalem, enormous numbers of musicians played, and pious men sang and danced with burning torches. (Mishnah *Sukkah* v. 2-4.)

The Temple, of course, was only used by women who lived in Jerusalem, or who made the pilgrimage or came up to offer sacrifices on special occasions. For most Jewish women public worship meant the synagogue. It was here that people met regularly to pray and to hear the Bible read and expounded. The Gospel (*Luke* 4.16ff.) gives us a graphic picture of the public reading and exposition in the synagogue in Nazareth. There is ample evidence of women attending synagogue services, not only on Sabbaths and Festivals, but on weekdays too. Although women could not be counted in the quorum for public worship, which was ten adult males, they were permitted to read the lesson. (Tosefta *Megilla* iv (iii). 11, Babylonian Talmud, *Megilla* 23a) There is an anecdote which tells of a woman who was more interested in the sermons than her husband, who stayed at home on Friday evening. She stayed so long at the synagogue that the lamps at home went out. Her husband grew so irritated at waiting for her in the dark that he made her offend the preacher, to make sure that she would not dare go to listen to him again.

Although women came to be segregated from men in the Temple, and later in the synagogue too, there is no evidence that the sexes were separated in synagogues in Gospel times. We read in Acts (1.14) how Mary and a group of women joined the apostles in prayer in their lodging-house in Jerusalem, and there are many references in Acts to women being present in synagogues in the Diaspora. If there was segregation, it cannot have been very rigorous, since a Roman poet describes Roman gentlemen going to synagogues on the Sabbath in quest of amatory adventures. (Ovid, *Ars Armatoria* I. 75.)

In addition to the formal prayer, women sometimes uttered extempore prayers which they composed themselves. The Bible records the beautiful prayer of Hannah after the birth of Samuel (1 *Sam* 2.1-10), which is closely paralled in the New Testament in the Magnificat (*Luke* 1.46-55). The rabbinic literature provides a rather later example. A rabbi tells how he saw a young girl fall on her face and pray: 'Lord of the world, You created paradise and You created hell; You created the wicked and You created the righteous. May it be Your will that I may not serve as a stumbling block to them.'

The rabbinic literature also preserves snatches of laments composed by women and sung at funerals. This activity, which seems to have been, as in other societies, a characteristically feminine one, has a long history, going back perhaps to the daughters of Israel who annually lamented the fate of Jephthah's daughter (*Judges* 11.40). There may have been women who made a speciality of the lament, and were much

199

in demand at funerals. The vivid image of the mourning mother is used, both in the Bible and by the rabbis, in connection with national calamity.

One more aspect of the piety of women which is frequently mentioned in the sources is their charity. Almsgiving was one of the highest obligations under the religious law, and in fact the Hebrew for almsgiving is the same as the word for righteousness. There are many references to the generosity of women, and they seem to have outdone the men in this regard. The designation 'mother of the synagogue', which is found on some inscriptions, is probably a tribute to outstanding generosity, and some rabbis were embarrassed by the suspicion than women were illegally giving away their husbands' riches. On a more reduced scale, Jesus drew attention to the great generosity of the poor widow, who gave away all that she had to live on (*Luke* 21.1-4).

Education

Judaism has always placed a high premium on education, and especially on the study of the Bible. Women, as we have seen, attended the synagogue and heard the Bible being read and expounded. Unfortunately, the biblical commandment to teach children Torah (*Deut* 6.7) was interpreted narrowly by some authorities so as to apply to sons but not to daughters. According to one rabbi, 'to teach a daughter Torah is tantamount to teaching her lechery' (Mishnah *Sotah* iii. 4). Fortunately there were other rabbis who disagreed with this opinion, and gave their daughters the same education as their sons. There are even recorded cases of women scholars, whose opinions were listened to with respect by men. Such cases, however, are rare, and are outnumbered by the instances of women who worked, like the 'worthy wife' of Proverbs, so that their husbands would have the leisure to study.

Wife and Mother

The ideal role of a woman was to be a good wife to her husband and a good mother to her children. At the very beginning of the Bible God says that 'it is not good for man to be alone' (*Gen* 2.18), and the first commandment is to be fruitful and multiply (*Gen* 1.28). The rabbis commented: A man who has no wife lives without good, without help, without joy, without blessing, without protection, without peace and without life. Of a widower they say that it is as if the Temple had been destroyed in his lifetime. Celibacy was frowned on, and barrenness was a reproach (cf. *Luke* 1.25).

Even though many of the rabbis were themselves unfortunate in their choice of wives, they persisted in believing that marriages were made in heaven, and they never tired of insisting on a man's obligations to his wife. 'A man should always eat and drink less than his means allow, clothe himself in accordance with his means, and honour his wife and children more than his means allow, for they are dependent on him as he is dependent on Him at Whose word the world came into being.' 'One must always observe the honour due to one's wife, because blessings rest on a man's house only on account of his wife.' 'A man should always take care to avoid hurting his wife, for her tears come easily and her grief is near to God.' 'Our Rabbis taught: If a man loves his wife as himself, honours her more than himself, guides his sons and daughters in the right path and arranges for them to be married as soon as they are of age, it is of him that scripture says 'You will know that your tent is in peace' (*Job* 5.24).'

The rabbis also emphasised that Scripture is at pains to demand that one should honour one's mother equally with one's father, and in fact they put greater emphasis on honouring one's mother. Many stories are told of the great lengths to which they went in obedience to this command. One rabbi, whenever his mother wished to climb into bed, would crouch down and let her step up on his back. Another, on hearing his mother's footsteps, said, 'I shall arise before the approach of the divine Presence.'

This may seem an almost blasphemous exaggeration, but in the later literature God's love of Israel is frequently likened to a mother's love for her children, just as the biblical prophets compare it to a man's love for his wife.

However circumscribed a woman's position might be outside the home, then, within the family she was supreme. She was their life and the light of their eyes, as the rabbis put it, and they applied to her the verse (*Psalm* 45.14) 'The king's daughter is all glorious within'.

Mary in Islam

REV. R.J. McCARTHY, S.J.

The relatively important position of Mary in Islam goes back to the first half of the seventh century of the Christian era. According to Islamic tradition, it was in the year 612 that the 40 year old Muhammad ibn Abdullah received from the Angel Gabriel the first of a series of revelations which were ultimately enshrined in the Koran. This unique scripture of Islam contains many references to Mary, the Mother of Jesus. It may even be said, in the phrase of Father Abd-El-Jalil, to adumbrate a particular Marian psychology. The allusions to Mary in the Koran and in the collections of traditions confronted Muslim exegetes, historians, theologians and sufis (mystics) with certain problems which they tried to resolve in a manner consonant with the sacred text and the "tradition" of Islam. Some of them, transcending the level of problems, seem to have had some insight into the Marian mystery. Indeed, it seems that Muhammad himself was to some degree aware of this mystery, as Louis Massignon suggested in his perceptive remarks on "*le signe marial*" with reference to Islam.

The Second Vatican Council, in its extraordinary words concerning Islam, mentions the veneration which Muslims have for the Mother of Jesus. It is one of the factors supporting the Council's appeal for a dialogue which can be fruitful in charity and justice [*Nostra Aetate*, 3]. In 1969 the "Secretariatus pro nonchristianis," as part of its efforts to implement the Council's suggestion and appeal, issued a handbook entitled *Guidelines for a Dialogue between Muslims and Christians*. This little book can be read with profit by all concerned Christians. One of the chief obstacles to such dialogue has been the rather appalling ignorance shared by both parties. The average Christian's knowledge of Islam is still woefully weak. In many cases it is grotesquely distorted because of age-old prejudices and misconceptions. Emotions, too, have played their divisive role, emotions excited and exacerbated by factors which have been political and "economic" rather than religious. This is true, not only of average Christians, but also of many highly educated Christians, and even of many Christians who hold responsible positions in their Churches.

Whatever we may think of the past, this situation is deplorable and inexcusable today. Since the Second World War much has been written about Islam and the Muslims. I am thinking particularly of the noteworthy books of Kenneth Cragg, W. M. Watt, Sir Hamilton Gibb, Louis Massignon, Louis Gardet, George Anawati, Fazlur Rahman, 'Abd-al-Rahman Abbas, and many others, Christians and Muslims, who have provided intelligent and interested readers with excellent surveys and informative studies designed to help them to acquire a sympathetic understanding of the creed and culture and history and thought of our nearly 500,000,000 fellow men who at this moment follow the religion of Islam.

If time permitted, I am sure it would be useful, even for such a select audience as this, to say something about Islam before embarking on a discussion of Mary in Islam. In this context, however, I shall have to limit myself to such general remarks as may be occasioned by what I shall be able to say about our particular subject. Later questions, and their possible answers, may lead to further enlightenment.

In 1950 Father Jean-Marie Abd-El-Jalil published a small book of 90 pages entitled *Marie et L'Islam*. The author, a Moroccan and Franciscan, was himself a convert from Islam, and therefore very well qualified to write on the subject with sympathy, insight and delicacy. I may also mention his book called *Aspects intérieurs de l'Islam* (1949), and his shorter *L'Islam et nous* (1947). Unfortunately, all these books are now out of print, though they are all worth reading. The book on Mary and Islam contains a useful bibliography to which the last twenty years have contributed little of special significance.

In this brief talk I shall confine myself almost entirely to the "Mariology" of the Koran. I shall also offer some remarks on certain problems connected with our subject. And finally we shall inquire briefly into the relevance of our subject to ecumenism, intra-Christian, and between Muslims and Christians.

* * *

It is impossible to exaggerate the central importance of the Koran in Islam. For Muslims it is the literal word of God revealed to their Apostle and Prophet Muhammad on various occasions spanning the last twenty years of his life, ten years in Mecca, and the ten years he lived in Medina after his *hijra* (emigration) from Mecca. So if Mary has a place in Islam, our first question must be: Does the Koran say anything about Mary?

It does indeed, and what it says is the primordial reason for the relatively important place of Mary in Islam. We must recall that the Koran was the compelling reason for the development of the specifically Islamic disciplines of *tafsir* (exegesis), *hadith* (traditions, i.e. the dicta and gesta Muhammad as reported by his contemporaries and handed down by chains of transmitters), *fiqh* (jurisprudence), *kalam* (theology, defensive apologetic), *ta'rikh* (history), and even, it seems, of *tasawwuf* (sufism, mysticism). The assiduous commentators on the Sacred Book could not fail to be interested in an explanation of every reference and allusion contained in the divine text. They certainly had this interest to a high degree in the many references to Jesus and his

203

Mother, references which sometimes presented problems because of the striking, and often unique, epithets applied to Mary and the Son of Mary. Here, however, I must regretfully pass over most of the Christology of the Koran and limit myself to some observations on its Mariology.

> [A note on the Koran: It contains 114 suras, or chapters, each referred to by a traditional title. These are not arranged in chronological order. From Sura 2 they are classed, roughly, in descending order of length and ascending order of interest. The most satisfactory way to read the Koran is to follow the four chronological periods of revelation. It is truly untranslatable in any fashion which will convey an idea of the effect which it has, when recited or chanted, on Muslims, especially Arabic-speaking Muslims.]

What seems to be the most ancient text referring to Mary is that listed first in the Appendix: Sura of Mary (XIX), vv. 16—34/33. I propose to make some comments on certain features of the text. These are not my own comments, but those of Muslim commentators, except for a few recognizable asides. The first fifteen verses are an account of the annunciation to Zachary of the birth of John the Baptist.

> vv. 16-17: allusion to the Presentation of Mary in the Temple and to her youth among the servants of the Temple. Cf. Protoevangelium of James and Pseudo-Matthew. These last two, along with other apocrypha, seem to have been the source of certain details in this and in other texts. I cannot dwell on them here. And of course, for the Muslim, there is no question of any "source", since the Koran is God's word.
> "Our Spirit"—*ruh* has several meanings in the Koran. Later (at Medina) identified with Gabriel, and the commentators identify this "Spirit" with Gabriel.
> v. 18: modest reaction of Mary (cf. Lk. 1.29).
> v. 19: the breath of the Spirit (God or angel) in the garment of Mary will cause her to conceive and bear a child without sin.
> v. 22: Mary takes refuge in the desert because she is ashamed to be seen pregnant while unmarried.
> v. 24: "below her"—rather, "at her feet". It is Jesus who speaks.
> v. 25: This is one of the two facts reported by the Koran [the other is Sura 3.32/37] in which Father Abd-El-Jalil sees a kind of "Imitatio Mariae". The most widespread opinion is that the palm-trunk was dried up and God miraculously made it produce dates immediately. Popular piety dwells on the aspect of the cooperation demanded by God: "Shake ⋯ the palm trunk". Many ordinary Muslims cite this in the sense of "God helps those who help themselves".
> v. 27/26: This fast of silence has been meditated on by the Muslim mystics (sufis). They find in Mary an example of a twofold silence: silence, to think only of God; and silence when one is unjustly accused, to allow God to defend one.
> v. 29/28: "Sister of Aaron"—an apparent confusion with the sister of Moses and Aaron. The commentators offer various explanations: Mary descends from a brother of Aaron, or from Aaron himself, or there is question of

another Aaron. Christian polemic in the past probably exaggerated this apparent confusion.

The following pericope (vv. 35/34—41/40) is probably an addition of later date, when Muhammad undertook the struggle against the Christian doctrine of Jesus, Son of God. "That is Jesus, son of Mary ..." (35/34), a phrase with a double meaning: positive, in the sense that Jesus has no human father and his mother is a virgin; negative, in the sense that Jesus is the son of Mary, and not the son of God.

Before leaving this text, it may be of interest to give an example of sufi (mystical) commentary. *Al-Baqli* (d.1209), in his *Tafsir*, II, 7, comments thus on 19. 16:

> "The real indication here is that the substance of Mary is the very substance of original sanctity. Brought up by the Real in the light of intimacy, she is in each of her respirations 'magnetically drawn' by the signs of nearness and intimacy towards the source of the divine lights. She was on the lookout at every instant for the rise of the sun of Power in the east of the Kingdom. She withdrew far from all created beings by her lofty aspiration penetrated with light of the hidden mystery. She turned herself towards the horizon whence flash the gleams of [God's] Essence and Attributes, 'breathing in' the breezes of union blowing from the world of eternity. To her came one of the breezes of the eternal encounter, and upon her rose the sun of the contemplation of holiness. When she had contemplated the manifestation of the orient bursting forth from the eternal, its lights invaded her and its secrets reached the inmost depths of her soul. Her soul conceived by the breath of the hidden mystery. She became the bearer of the Word most high and of the light of the Spirit most lofty. When her state became grandiose by the reflection in it of the beauty manifesting the eternal, she hid herself far from creatures, putting her joy in the nuptials of the Reality."

Let us now turn to the fourth text, from the Medinan Sura 3 (The House of Imran).

v. 31/35: The commentators know the name of the wife of Imran: Hanna, daughter of Faqudha. St. Anne vows the infant she bears in her womb to the service of the Temple, for she hopes it will be a boy. The "vow of St. Anne" is the oriental form of belief in the Immaculate Conception—cf. Protoevangelium of James, Ch. 3-4.

v. 31/36: Mary's mother is disappointed at having borne a daughter, who will not be able to be dedicated to the service of the Temple. She names her Mary—according to the commentators "servant-adorer" (*'abida*). She places her and her son under God's protection so that the Demon may not attain them. In this connection we have the celebrated tradition from Muhammad: "Every newborn child of Adam is touched by Satan, except the son of Mary and his Mother; at this contact the child utters its first cry." Another *hadith* says: "Mary and Jesus did not sin as all other men sin." Islam believes that only Mary and Jesus did not sin from their very birth. Islam believes in the *fact* of the Immaculate Conception, but not in the *dogma* of the Immaculate Conception, since the latter presupposes belief in the dogma of Original Sin; which the Koran and Islam deny—men are born without sin and as already believing Muslims (the fitra, or natural religion, is Islam).

v. 32/37: Mary is presented in the Temple as a child. The priests ask who will take charge of her; lots are drawn (cf. v. 39/44) and her Uncle Zachary is chosen. The Muslim mystics have meditated on the life of Mary, enclosed in the Temple, praying and receiving her nourishment, material and spiritual, from God. [Perhaps it was in connection with this that the famous woman mystic, Rabi'a was called "a second Mary" by 'Attar.]

In this verse we have the second fact in which Father Abd-El-Jalil sees a kind of "Imitatio Mariae." The prodigies manifesting the special providence of God in favour of Mary during her stay in the Temple are connected with Zachary's prayer for a son, despite his advanced age and his wife's sterility. His faith is said to have become more confident as a result of what he observed in Mary. Often, even in daily life, Muslims cite this verse to stimulate faith and prayer.

This verse is used as the principal inscription above the mihrab (niche indicating the *qibla*, or direction of Mecca) in many mosques, e.g. in the great Aya Sofya (Hagia Sophia) of Istanbul. The occurrence of the word "mihrab" in the verse may have determined the choice, though it is also found in another verse (3.33/39), which is used less often. At any rate, the fact is there, and the text speaks for itself. It is also one of the texts of calligraphy placed by many Muslims in their homes and shops.

The commentators relate a story about Fatima (the daughter of Muhammad). She once benefited from a multiplication of food in a time of need. Her father asked her about the provenance of the food, and Fatima made the same answer as Mary: "From God. Truly God provisions whomsoever He will without reckoning." And the Prophet said: "Praise be to God, Who has bestowed on you this likeness to the Princess of the women of Israel!" [Zamakhshari, II, 409]

vv. 33/38—36/41: annunciation of the birth of John to Zachary.

v. 37/42: Mary chosen by God, like the prophets. The commentators in general regard her as a prophetess (*nabiyya*), since God spoke to her. But she is not an envoy, or apostle (*rasula*), since she was not sent to a people. She was the object of a double election: once when God received her in the Temple, and then when He chose her to be the virginal mother of Jesus.

This verse confronted Muslim scholars with the problem of the hierarchy of holy women in Islam. Some traditions seem to give Mary the absolute primacy over all women. Others reflect the hesitations of the Muslim conscience divided by the desire to remain faithful to the apparently unconditional affirmation of the Koran and the preoccupation of trying to reconcile this desire with the clearly manifested preference of Muhammad for Khadija (his first wife), Ayesha (his favourite wife), and Fatima. In Sura 33.32 it is said that the wives of the Prophet are not as other women. They are also referred to in tradition as the "Mothers of the Faithful."

Mary's most serious rivals are Fatima and Ayesha. The average preference of orthodox (Sunnite) Muslims is for Fatima over Ayesha. Of Mary and Fatima they say that each is superior to the other from different points of view: Fatima because she resembles her father and is, as it were, "a piece of him"; Mary because she conceived and gave birth miraculously. If pressed as to which is absolutely superior, they usually resort to *al-tawaqquf* (abstention from pronouncing), not as a simple subterfuge, but as an attitude of profound respect vis-a-vis the texts of Koran and Sunna—"*Allahu a'lam!*" (God knows best!).

The Shiites are of two tendencies. The moderate majority often seem to "condense" Mary and Fatima, but without any real confusion. In some Iranian families the education of daughters is a kind of imitation of Mary: one will say to a little girl 'Do not do that, because Hazrat Maryam (Lady Mary) would not have done it'. Iranian women like to have statues of Mary, who seems to them a pure being, ideal, ethereal, almost incorporeal. The extremists, especially the Nusayris, applying a cyclic conception of history, declare that Fatima is, in the cycle of Muhammad, the incarnation of Mary's spirit, holding the same position as Mary in the cycle of Jesus.

v. 40/45: "Word" and "Messiah". Cf. Abd-El-Jalil, *Marie et L'Islam*, pp. 58-59.

Here I would like to say a few words about the second, third and sixth texts of the Appendix. In the second and third texts Mary and her Son are designated by God as one of His "signs". The sixth text is in an eschatological context, and it belongs to the Medinan period of the revelations to Muhammad. The notion of sign and the eschatological context are strikingly combined in the remarks of the late Louis Massignon on what he calls "*le signe marial*". Let me try to epitomize what he says. Muhammad in Medina, i.e. in exile in an Israelite biblical milieu, affirms that Jesus will return triumphant at the Hour of the Judgment, and that the world, if it is obstinate like unbelieving Israel, will be judged and condemned by this sign of the Immaculate Conception of Mary, pure vessel of the virginal birth of Jesus, Ark of salvation of the predestined. There is no suggestion, of course, that Muhammad believed in the divinity of Jesus. But the Koran declares that it is only at the Last Judgment that God will pose this sign as the supreme question, not only for men, but for the prophets, by demanding of their spokesman Jesus if he ever proposed for the adoration of men the only two pure creatures, his mother and himself, as "two Gods" (5.116). The Koranic prophecy of the end of time stops there, having mysteriously recalled in the preceding verse (5.115) the damnation which on that day will await those who have denied the holy Table to which Jesus invited the Apostles.

Massignon does not claim that this "sign of the two" adumbrated in the Koran is much clearer for the Muslim reader than the "sign of the three" before Abraham at Mamre [Gen. 18] is for the rabbinic reader of the Bible. But it cannot be doubted that Muhammad offered himself as Witness to it before the Jews of Medina in order to give this proof of the rigorous transcendence of God which destroys their hope of a Messiah who, through his forebears, would be descended from David. It is not a question of making them divine the eternal generation of the Word, but of suggesting to them that the Immaculate Conception permitting the virginal birth of the Messiah is the sole safeguard of pure monotheism. In the phrase of Massignon: "it predecarnalizes the Incarnation". All Muslim protest against the Incarnation is against a carnal paternity; and all Muslim witness to the Immaculate Conception is to a virginal maternity, this supreme parable [Kor 16.62/69] of God in the Woman who conceives the "fiat" (*kun*), cited eight times in Koran, always for Jesus, son of Mary, and the Judgment.

Massignon concludes: "I can only admire the mission of Muhammad at Medina as witness to this marian Sign, which no tactical or self-interested reason could have made this Chief of State invent. ..." Whatever we may think of Massignon's interpretation, there is surely evidence here of what I previously called "the Marian mystery" as perceived, however obscurely, by Islam.

Before concluding, let me attempt a brief synthesis of the data concerning Mary in the Koran and Islamic Tradition and Islamic devotional life.

1. The Koran

(a) *Life of Mary*: God chooses her among all women and purifies her. He loads her with divine favors. She is born miraculously of the wife of Imran and is consecrated to God from her mother's womb and is preserved from the touch of the demon. She is presented in the Temple and welcomed by God, Who makes her grow, confides her to the charge of Zachary and miraculously provides her with sustenance. An angel appears to her and announces to her the miraculous birth of a child, the Word of God and the Messiah. She accepts, conceives Jesus and gives birth to him near a palm tree. She is nourished (miraculously?), returns to her people, is unjustly accused, then defended by the infant Jesus. There is a possible allusion to the flight into Egypt 25.52/50 (Text 2).

(b) *Privileges and Virtues of Mary*: Chosen and purified by God, she is the best (?) of all women. She is the virgin par excellence who guarded her womb (Texts 3 and 5). God breathed into her and cast into her His Word. Calumniously accused by the Jews, she is defended by the Koran—"[We cursed them] for their unbelief, and their uttering against Mary a mighty calumny" (4.155/156). Very believing, she has faith in the words of the annunciation—"His mother was a just woman" (5.79/75—and cf. Text 5). Most devout and prayerful, she is a sign to the world. She is above all the mother of Jesus, who is almost always called "the son of Mary", and who owes filial piety to her. The two of them are a single sign. But she is a simple mortal and not a goddess.

2. Islamic Tradition

There is not very much about her in the actual hadith collections. The commentators and historians draw on Christian reports, authentic or apocryphal, to enrich her life so simply set forth in the Koran. She is made the fiancée of Joseph, her cousin and a carpenter, who becomes her quasi-spouse (*shibh zawj*), notices that she is pregnant, and delicately questions her. They recount the flight into Egypt, the coming of the Magi, the massacre of the innocents, the miracle of Cana, the utterance of the woman (Happy the womb that carried you and the breasts that suckled you!—Luke 11.27), the appearance of Jesus to Mary after his 'elevation to heaven', and finally her death six or eight years later at the age of 51.

I cannot refrain from citing a beautiful and delicate page which occurs in the great Commentary on the Qur'an by al-Tabari (d. 923 A.D.) [XVI, 43]:

When Mary conceived, there was with her a close relative named Joseph the carpenter. They were on their way to the Temple, which is near Mount Sion. At that time this was one of their greatest temples. Joseph and Mary served therein. (The service of this Temple was very highly regarded, and it was an honour to serve therein.) Joseph and Mary were devoted to it. They used to sweep it, clean it; and do all the necessary tasks. And, in their time, no one equalled them in zeal and piety.

The first one to be startled by seeing Mary's condition (pregnancy) was her companion Joseph. When he saw her state, he was shocked, scandalized and saddened. He did not know how to explain it. Whenever he tended to suspect Mary, he would recall her virtue and her innocence and the fact that she had never left him for an instant. But whenever he rejected her guilt, he would be led back to it by what was before his eyes. When it became too heavy a thing to bear any longer, he spoke to her.

J—I have had a thought about you. Though I have done my utmost to suppress it, it has overcome me. To speak of it would assuage my heart.

M—Speak, and utter none but gracious words.

J—I would utter no others. Can wheat grow without seed?

M—Yes.

J—Can trees grow without rain?

M—Yes.

J—Can there be a son without a father?

M—Yes. Do you not know that God, Blessed and Exalted, made wheat to grow, when He created it, without need for seed? Today's seed simply comes from the wheat which God first made to grow without seed? And do you know that God, Blessed and Exalted, by His omnipotence made trees grow without the aid of rain? It is by this same omnipotence that He has made rain capable of vivifying trees. Or would you say that God, Blessed and Exalted, was unable to make trees grow without the help of rain, the lack of which would make it impossible for Him to make them grow?

J—No, I do not say that. For I know that God, Blessed and Exalted, can do whatever He wills. He says to a thing "Be!", and it is.

M—Do you not know that God, Blessed and Exalted, created Adam and his wife without the assistance of a father and a mother?

J—Yes.

When she had said that, Joseph knew intuitively that her state was the realization of a volition of God, Blessed and Exalted, and that he could not question her about it because of the secret she was keeping (the mystery she was guarding). Thereupon he alone took over the service of the Temple and himself undertook all the work that Mary had been doing. ...

Vatican II mentioned the devotion which Muslims have to Mary: "Matremque eius virginalem honorant Mariam et aliquando eam devote etiam invocant" [Nostra Aetate, 3: They also honour Mary, His virgin mother: at times they call on her, too, with devotion.] I have already mentioned some Iranian practices. Her name is frequently given to Muslim girls. And Muslims, especially women, come to pray to her in Christian churches and sanctuaries, e.g. Ephesus, Algiers (Notre Dame d'Afrique), Baghdad, etc. I have preferred, however, to concentrate my limited remarks on Mary in Islamic scripture and tradition, leaving aside what might smack of superstition.

From the little I have said (and the much more I had to leave unsaid) it is clear that Mary has an assured and relatively important place in Islam. Is this simply an historical footnote, of more or less interest, to be added to the not inconsiderable literature on Mary? Certainly it makes no great contribution to Mariology in any significant theological or spiritual sense. The place of Mary in Christian thought and life is not much enhanced by the witness of Islam, since this witness is due in any case to Christian sources and influences.

We may also ask a final question: Has the place of Mary in Islam any relevance to ecumenism in any or all of its three senses which interest us? I mean: ecumenism in the very broad sense of dialogue between Muslims and Christians; ecumenism in the narrower sense of inter-Christian dialogue; and ecumenism in the particular sense which presumably is the aim of this Ecumenical Society of the Blessed Virgin Mary.

In the case of this Islamo-Christian dialogue it seems that the position of Mary in Islam and the veneration which many Muslims have for her are elements which can contribute to what we may term a friendly climate. They may even be good talking-points, though perhaps in a somewhat marginal sense. But it is only fair to add that I, along with many better informed persons, feel that the Islamo-Christian dialogue is as yet almost nonexistent. Thus far almost all the good-will and practically all of the effort at sympathetic comprehension have been on one side—the Christian side. Of course we must not confound religious dialogue with a mere verbal and intellectual exchange of observations and ideas. Even more important, dialogue is not to be identified with evangelization or islamicization. Does this mean that we must despair of ever initiating a true dialogue with our Muslim brothers? Not at all. There have been a few hopeful signs recently. But the realization of a fruitful dialogue will take time and much patience and most of all great and sincere love. In this Mary, though she may not be a touchstone, may well be a stepping-stone. Certainly she will not be a stumbling block.

The place of Mary in Islam may seem to have no very direct bearing on ecumenism in the sense of the inter-Christian dialogue. But perhaps the witness of Islam to Mary is itself an incentive to Christians to realize and appreciate all that they hold in common and to return again and again, and ever more deeply, to their own Scripture and Tradition in the sure hope of finding, under the guidance of the Spirit, the matter and form of a solid and fruitful reconciliation, in Him who is our reconciliation and our principle of unity: Jesus, Son of Mary and Son of God.

Finally, it seems to me that the subject of Mary in Islam does have some bearing on the ecumenism fostered by this particular Society. Negatively it suggests that we refocus our attention not so much on Mary in Islam as on Mary in Christian traditions and cultures. Positively it offers some points which may be helpful. Muslim veneration for Mary shows that such veneration need not be a form of Mariolatry. More than that, Mary's position in Islam rests on the very firm and factual footing of her relation to Christ Jesus her Son. Some may find it not quite correct, and others will find it more than merely correct, to speak of the Marian sign as Louis Massignon did. But even in his case the sign was not Mary alone. The sign was, and is affirmed by the Koran itself, Mary *and* her Son, Jesus *and* His Mother. See texts (2) and (3).

The Koran does not separate those whom God joined in a union most profound and fruitful, virginal and immaculate. Nor can they be separated by a vibrant Christian faith and hope and love. In Islam, as in Christian history and theology and spirituality, Mary is clearly and distinctly inferior to her Son in holiness and mission. But she is *there* in a sense far more profound than Everest's being *there* or even our being *here*. She is *there*—in the Incarnation, in the Visitation, in the Nativity, at Cana and at the foot of the Cross, a witness to the Resurrection and a recipient, surely more than others, of the pleroma of grace and the Spirit of Pentecost. She is *there*, eternally with her Son, and she is *here*, with her Son, tirelessly and urgently repeating her word about God's Word: "Do whatever he tells you!". Here indeed is a catchword and a watchword, a first word and a last word.

*NOTE

The texts are cited according to the excellent translation of A. J. ARBERRY: **The Koran Interpreted** (George Allen and Unwin, Ltd., London, 1955). We thank the publishers for graciously granting permission to cite these passages.

APPENDIX

Mary in the Koran: Principal Texts

(1) Sura XIX (Mary)* 16—34/33.

16　And mention in the Book Mary when she withdrew from her people to an eastern place,

17　and she took a veil apart from them; then We sent unto her Our Spirit that presented himself to her a man without fault.

18　She said, 'I take refuge in the All-merciful from thee! If thou fearest God ...

19　He said, 'I am but a messenger come from my Lord, to give thee a boy most pure.'

20　She said, 'How shall I have a son whom no mortal has touched, neither have I been unchaste?'

21　He said, 'Even so thy Lord has said: "Easy is that for Me; and that We may appoint him a sign unto men and a mercy from Us; it is a thing decreed".'

22　So he conceived him, and withdrew with him to a distant place.

23　And the birthpangs surprised her by the trunk of the palm-tree. She said. 'Would I had died ere this, and become a thing forgotten!'

24　But the one that was below her called to her, 'Nay, do not sorrow; see, thy Lord has set below thee a rivulet.

25　Shake also to thee the palm-trunk, and there shall come tumbling upon thee dates fresh and ripe.

26　Eat therefore, and drink, and be comforted; and if thou shouldst see any mortal, say,

27/26　"I have vowed to the All-merciful a fast, and today I will not speak to any man".

28/27　Then she brought the child to her folk carrying him; and they said, 'Mary, thou has surely committed a monstrous thing!

29/28　Sister Aaron, thy father was not a wicked man, nor was thy mother a woman unchaste.

30/29　Mary pointed to the child then; but they said, 'How shall we speak to one who is still in the cradle, a little child?'

31/30　He said, 'Lo, I am God's servant; God has given me the Book, and made me a prophet.

32/31　Blessed He has made me, wherever I may be; and He has enjoined me to pray, and to give the alms, so long as I live,

33/32　and likewise to cherish my mother; He has not made me arrogant, unprosperous.

34/33　Peace be upon me, the day I was born, and the day I die, and the day I am raised up alive!'

(2) Sura XXIII (The Believers) 52/50: And We made Mary's son and his mother, to be a sign, and gave them refuge upon a height, where was a hollow and a spring.

(3) Sura XXI (The Prophets) 91: And she who guarded her virginity, so We breathed into her of Our spirit and appointed her and her son to be a sign unto all beings.

(4) Sura III (The House of Imran)

31/35　When the wife of Imran said, 'Lord, I have vowed to Thee, in dedication, what is within my womb. Receive Thou this from me; Thou hearest and knowest.'

31/36　And when she gave birth to her she said, 'Lord, I have given birth to her, a female'. (And God knew very well what she had given birth to; the male is not as the female.) 'And I have named her Mary, and commend her to Thee with her seed, to protect them from the accursed Satan.'

32/37　Her Lord received the child with gracious favour, and by His goodness she grew up comely, Zachariah taking charge of her. Whenever Zachariah went in to her in the Sanctuary, he found her provisioned, 'Mary,' he said, 'how comes this to thee!' 'From God,' she said. 'Truly God provisions whomsoever He will without reckoning.'

37/42 And when the angels said, 'Mary, God has chosen thee, and purified thee; He has chosen thee above all women.

38/43 Mary, be obedient to thy Lord, prostrating and bowing before Him.'

39/44 (That is of the tidings of the Unseen, that We reveal to thee; for thou wast not with them, when they were casting quills which of them should have charge of Mary; thou wast not with them, when they were disputing.)

40/45 When the angels said, 'Mary, God gives thee good tidings of a Word from Him whose name is Messiah, Jesus, son of Mary; high honoured shall he be in this world and the next, near stationed to God.

41/46 'He shall speak to men, in the cradle, and of age, and righteous he shall be.'

42/47 'Lord', said Mary, 'how shall I have a son seeing no mortal has touched me?' 'Even so,' God said, 'God creates what He will. When He decrees a thing He does but say to it "Be," and it is.'

43/48 'And He will teach him the Book, the Wisdom, the Torah, the Gospel.'

(5) Sura LXVI (The Forbidding) 12: (God has struck a similitude for the believers) Mary, Imran's daughter, who guarded her virginity, so We breathed into her of Our Spirit, and she confirmed the Words of her Lord and His Books, and became one of the obedient.

(6) Sura V (The Table) 116: And then God said, 'O Jesus son of Mary, didst thou say unto men, "Take me and my mother as gods, apart from God"?' He said, 'To Thee be glory! It is not mine to say what I have no right to. If I indeed said it, Thou knowest it, knowing what is within my soul, and I know not what is within Thy soul; Thou knowest the things unseen,'

VII
HISTORICAL

The historical view is opposite to the theological, being not God's complete plan but man's record of his discovery of it. This is better seen nowhere else in religious study, except perhaps in regard to the Church which stands so close to Mariology, than in our constant and recent advances in understanding the role of the Blessed Virgin in the economy of grace. Christology yields its essentials logically before Mariology, which in turn has yielded more of its own logically before Ecclesiology. As there is a hierarchy of truth, so there is a hierarchy of religious discovery and doctrinal establishment. Thus truths may take two millennia to reach definition.

The first paper was given on 3 November 1977 to the Canterbury branch of the Society, the Anselm Society and the Society of St Alban and St Sergius, at the Deanery by the Church History tutor of Ampleforth Abbey and Editor of the *Ampleforth Journal*. It was then given to the Society's Oxford branch.

The second paper was given at the Francis Holland School, London SW1, on 18 May 1971, by the biographer and editor of the works of John Henry Cardinal Newman, a father of the same Oratory at Birmingham.

The third lecture was delivered on the occasion of the Annual General Meeting of the Society in Central Hall, Westminster, on 4 March 1969, by the then Apostolic Delegate to Great Britain. Charmingly he ended by quoting from Martin Gillett's book on *Walsingham*.

The English Tradition
of the Doctrine of the
Immaculate Conception

DOM ALBERIC STACPOOLE, O.S.B.

It is a long journey from the impoverished Mariology of the early Church to the moment when, in 1854 on the feast day, Pope Pio Nono judged it ripe – pious belief then being integral with the Catholic faith – that the doctrine should be defined as revealed by God and so firmly and constantly to be believed by the faithful, that 'the most Blessed Virgin Mary was preserved from all stain of original sin in the first instant of her conception, by a singular grace and privilege of Almighty God' in view of the foreseen abundant merits of her only-born son, our Saviour Jesus Christ. As if to confirm the Holy Father's pronouncement, a fourteen year old girl in the Pyrenees, at her sixteenth vision of *Aquero* ('she'), was told on the feast of the Annunciation in 1858 at her fourth time of asking that day: *Que soy era Immaculata Counception.* Thus St Bernadette at Lourdes, before the Blessed Virgin.

Of her, several of the early Fathers took it for granted that, though Mother of Christ Jesus, she was guilty of faults like any other human being: in their homilies on the gospels they even used her as a type of sinful humanity over against the holiness of Christ. Tertullian claimed that Christ had denounced Mary's lack of faith, when he asked 'Who is my mother?' Origen, often finding fault with her, suggested that her faith had been shaken by the Cross. Others took her to task for questioning the angel Gabriel, for calling her Son to account in the Temple, for the inopportuneness of her Cana request, for interrupting his preaching. St John Chrysostom, in his gospel homilies, proved one of her severest critics.

But by degrees the inclination to put a bad construction upon the actions of the Blessed Virgin receded, at last disappearing altogether, driven out by profounder reasons favouring Mary's holiness. She emerged as the model of both faith and obedience, as the virgin soil of our redemption. Her holiness was realised to be not only without fault, but immense and unique: St Augustine, master of the theology of sin and grace, formulated for the first time the idea of her perfection: 'All men have sinned ... except for the holy virgin Mary, whom I do not wish to be brought into the question when sin is discussed; for whence do we know what greater grace of complete triumph over sin may have been given to her who merited to conceive and bear him who was certainly without sin?' The great doctor stood at the threshold of the doctrine, sensible of its possibility.

Gradually it came to be understood that the fundamental reason for Mary's profound holiness was the fact of her being *Theotokos, Deipara, Dei Genitrix*, the God-bearer or Mother of God; and the very early hymn in Greek and Latin, *Sub tuum praesidium Sancta Dei Genitrix* (Rylands fragment, late 3rd century), attests to the emerging understanding of all this long before its definition at the Councils of Ephesus (431) and Chalcedon (451). Mary's holiness was glorified rather than defined, indeed in words such as this: 'Though her praises are heaped up without end, they do not attain the measure of the truth, or even draw remotely near to it; for her beauty infinitely transcends all speech and thought' (St Germanus of Constantinople). She was described in poetic terms – as dough from which the Bread of life was made, as the living book in which the Spirit wrote the Word of God, as the earthly palace of the heavenly king; as the Ark, the Temple, the Sanctuary. Eastern theologians such as St Germanus and St John of Damascus came close to asking the questions that would evoke the doctrine, when they spoke of Mary as designed by God for her sublime office, made suitable for it by his agency, 'virginal in soul and body', free from all stain in body, soul and spirit'.

In the Latin West, St Augustine was not taken up; and it took a long time for theologians to emulate the East in their supreme eulogy of Mary's holiness. Paul the Deacon, Alcuin, St Paschasius Radbert and a few others stand beside the East; but where the East exhausted itself in eulogy of Mary's eminent holiness (calling her 'unstained', 'integral', 'utterly blameless', 'the only pure one', 'perfect reproduction of the original beauty', and so forth), the West became more conscious of the law of sin – largely through the preoccupations of St Augustine – and so of the possibility of original sinlessness. An 8th century treatise on the Assumption of Our Lady, attributed to Alcuin of York (Charlemagne's mentor) had this to say: 'From Mary God took his nature, not his origin, the Holy Spirit himself sanctifying her womb, purifying and cleansing it in readiness for the conception of the Son, ⋯ a most holy body which he, the spotless one, had preserved from all stain.' A stronger voice came from St Paschasius of Corbie in his *de Partu Virginis* (c. 850): 'She did not contract original sin, being sanctified in the womb of her mother.' How influential such treatises were it is hard to say; but it is clear they did not change the face of western devotion or theology. These were intimations, to be taken up a long way in the future.

The next stage of development was liturgical and devotional, not theological. It seems that a feast of Mary's conception was being kept in the East, at a nine-month interval from the 8th September feast of her Birth. In the 9th century Constantinople Synaxary (a kind of eastern menology or liturgical account of saints of the day) a set of Marian connected feasts occur, including the Conception, which found their way into 11th century English monastic liturgical books. One of the reasons for the emergence of such a feast was that a similar one for the Forerunner, St John the Baptist, had been kept; and his place in the economy of grace was a lesser one. So from the early 8th century the Marian equivalent feast of the Conception began to be celebrated on 9th December. It spread to the Greek monasteries of southern Italy – at Naples, Grottaferrata and Monte Gargano – and on up to the one in Rome. These monasteries gave inspiration to the Italian monastic revival of 1000, and being in turn revived from the East, took up the eastern feasts of the 'three conceptions' (St John on 24th June, the Virgin Mary on 8th December and Christ the Saviour on 25th December – two of them in fact Nativities). Various strands of liturgical evidence show a distinctive eastern tradition developing.

That tradition came to the West, as we have it, by a single leap in the mid-11th century into the world of southern English monasticism. I am following Edmund Bishop, Fr Herbert Thurston, Fr S.J.P. van Dijk, Mgr Francis Davis and Hilda Graef in plotting this, and I shall take their conclusions as perhaps rather more confirmed than they would grant, after complex and careful argument. The first evidence comes from Old Minster, Winchester and then New Minster; that is, from the old priory of St Ethelwold and the adjacent new monastery. It appears in two kalendars dated about 1060. From there it seems certain that Bishop Leofric (1046-73) took it westwards to his cathedral in Exeter, where there are two liturgical manuscripts still extant, a sacramentary and a pontifical-benedictional showing that the feast of the Conception (not that of the Presentation) was being kept in his time. The sacramentary, known as the Leofric Missal (Bodl 579), contains in one of its last leaves a Mass for the Conception.

The feast of the Conception is attested in only six pre-Conquest manuscripts in three places in the West – Winchester, Exeter and Canterbury. At Canterbury both monasteries contain evidence of the feast: from the cathedral priory of Christ Church comes a pontifical-benedictional (BM Harley 2892) dated about 1070; and from St Augustine's comes a martyrology (BM Cotton Vit.C xii) of the same time. There are special entries for the Presentation and the Conception, the latter written in such a way that it appears to date from a former book written before the Conquest. How did this feast come from Winchester to Canterbury, assuming that it did? Canterbury had, during the reforms of the 10th century, adopted the monastic reform of Bishop Ethelwold, which had gone out especially to the cathedrals of Canterbury, Sherborne and Worcester (all of whose liturgical books contain feasts culled from the East). However, there is a more direct explanation that involves a monk called Aethelsige or Elsin or Aelsi, and his part in one of the so-called *Miracles of the Virgin* (*Marienlegenden*).

Aethelsige or Aelsi was a monk of St Swithun's cathedral priory or Old Minster, Winchester, who during 1061-67 was Abbot of St Augustine's, Canterbury. It seems that in 1067 or 1070 he ceased to be abbot, and in that time was sent as William the Conqueror's agent to Denmark to placate the Danes, who were displeased at the Conquest. The ambassadorial mission completed, Aelsi set off for England, but was caught, Jonah-like, in a storm so fierce that all on board took to prayer. Aelsi invoked the help of Our Lady, imploring her to save the ship's company from what looked like certain death. There then appeared to him a figure in pontifical robes, who promised him that all would be saved if he pledged himself to introduce the feast of the Conception to his monastery and celebrate it annually on 8th December, the Office to be used being that of the Nativity of Our Lady with the word 'Conception' substituted for 'Nativity'. Aelsi pledged himself, and the storm abated. Aelsi, by that time (what time was it? How long had the mission lasted?) was no longer an abbot, but in about 1077 he was given the abbacy of Ramsey, remaining there till his death in 1087; and there he duly fulfilled his vow by introducing the feast of the Conception. If this story is true, it would account for the link Winchester-Canterbury-Ramsey. There is a good deal to corroborate it. The St Augustine's Canterbury copy of the Anglo-Saxon Chronicle records that when Abbot Wulfric II died in 1061 the news was brought to King Edward, holding a session of the witan at Winchester. Edward chose Aelsi from Old Minster, who followed Archbishop Stigand to the royal seat of Windsor, where the primate of Canterbury administered the abbatical blessing on St Augustine's day. Two years later the Abbot was granted by the pope the privilege of mitre and sandals, putting him practically on a par with a bishop. In his last year the Confessor seems to have entrusted Abbot Aelsi with a charge over Ramsey Abbey (of which he was eventually to be Abbot before 1080) without surrendering his charge over Canterbury. Clearly Aelsi was a monk of considerable political substance, and it is no surprise that the Conqueror used him as an ambassador. However it seems that in 1070 Aelsi incurred his wrath, fled (again?) to Denmark, and was replaced at Canterbury by a monk of Mont St Michel who ruled till both Abbots and the king died in 1087. Forgiven in due course, Aelsi went on to rule Ramsey, and from there the feast that he inaugurated spread further. Incidentally the Canterbury-Ramsey connection in matters liturgical is not difficult to establish: an early Ramsey martyrology has a St Augustine's exemplar, and also a benedictional – and so forth.

From Ramsey the feast would inevitably have been translated to Worcester cathedral, for that connection had been strong from the days when St Oswald was abbot of the first and bishop of the second. It was sustained when the relics of St Ethelred and St Ethelbriht were translated from Ramsey to Worcester. And, of course, Worcester had its own connections with Winchester. Moreover there were surely other strands to reinforce the pattern, of whom the most interesting is, maybe, king Canute's second wife Aelfgifu. She claimed Winchester as her 'morning gift' or dowry, had extensive rights at Exeter, shared a friendship with

Archbishop Stigand and the ideas of Aelsi. For many years she lived at Winchester, and among the many treasures which she presented to the New Minster was a 'Greek shrine'. To Christ Church, Canterbury she presented a relic she had been given by the Archbishop of Benevento. She was buried next to her husband in the cathedral abbey she had so much enriched, Old Minster. There, then, seems a channel for the transmission of the tradition of the feast of the Conception.

The next stage gathers theological interest, beyond the merely devotional. Robert Losinga was Abbot of New Minster during the 1090s till his death in 1098. His son Herbert, a monk of Fécamp in Normandy, succeeded Aelsi as Abbot of Ramsey and in 1091 became Bishop of Thetford (later Norwich, a monastic cathedral priory). There are fourteen extant sermons of Herbert Losinga preached at liturgical feasts at Norwich; and, while they do include the Nativity of St John and both the Purification and Assumption of the Blessed Virgin, they do not include any feast for 8th December. Bishop Losinga appears to have preached two doctrines at two different times, and since these sermons are not easily datable we cannot thereby posit a development in his understanding. In his Christmas sermon he supports St Anselm, his Archbishop, in suggesting that Mary was made immaculate after her own conception and before the conception of her Son. These are his words: 'The Holy Spirit comes upon the Virgin and purges from sin, original and actual, her whom he was about to fill with grace. The angel cries to her, "Fear not, Mary ..."' This is no more than the doctrine put forth by St Gregory of Nazianzen in 350, that Christ 'became man in all things save sin, conceived of the Virgin who was previously purified by the Spirit in both soul and body.' The time of Mary's purgation, by this argument, was perhaps the time of her *fiat*.

In his twelfth sermon on the Assumption of the Blessed Virgin Mary, which can in fact be dated to about 1113, Bishop Losinga has much more to say, coming as he does to the very threshold of the doctrine of the Immaculate Conception. His words deserve respect as the first utterance in the western Church of a doctrine which was to find final form from the pen of the subtle doctor, Duns Scotus (the Scot John Duns, whose mentor had been the English Franciscan, William of Ware). This is what the Bishop wrote for his sermon on 15th August:

> *Of the lineage of Abraham, of the tribe of Judah, sprung from the root of Jesse, of the House of David, she was a noble child of noble parents. Not that any blemish attached to her from her parent stock. Both Joachim her father and Anna her mother were barren; but by the power of the Holy Spirit and at the annunciation of [the angel] Gabriel, they were made fruitful. From these chaste parents the chaste virgin is nurtured, and protected from all incentive to vice, preserved in the presence and guidance of the Holy Spirit alone. Hence in Hebrew she is called* olma, *'hidden'; that is to say, free from all knowledge of sin and so from all will to it.'*

Bishop Losinga, by these words, has surely claimed for the Mother of God at her conception all that is claimed for her own conception of her son. Mary's parents were barren, and their barrenness, reinforced by age (as with the parents of the Baptist), was overcome by the power of the Holy Spirit at the instance of Gabriel's first declaration – *per virtutem Sancti Spiritus et per annunciationem Gabrielis* – that means surely at the instant of conception: and that purity established at the moment of first existence continued to be guaranteed for Mary throughout her life by the same Spirit – as Bishop Losinga puts it, *ab omni vitiorum incentive abscondita, SOLIUS Spiritus Sancti presentia et municione conservabatur.* The Mother of God, in these words, was instructed and guarded not by Anna her mother nor Joachim her father, but solely by the Spirit. The Bishop's use of the word *oalma* applied to the Virgin carries the intensive sense: 'a virgin who has never been submitted to the gaze of men, but has been secluded with diligence by her parents'. Behind this generous wording of Herbert Losinga is a mass of oriental influences, fragments of apocryphal gospels and legends of Palestine and Egypt brought back from pilgrimages and crusades to the Holy Land and worked up into ballads, drama and fireside tales that caused new reflection upon Marian doctrine. Among these were legends of Joachim and Anna, and the assumption and coronation of their offspring; and with these a learned monk-bishop would be familiar in an age where learning rested principally with such men. Here at Norwich, in the first years of the 12th century, was realised a doctrine that would take centuries to be promulgated.

Before moving the action to Canterbury, it might be worthwhile to stress how much resistance the doctrine met in subsequent years. St Anselm, in dealing with the sinlessness of Christ in *Cur Deus Homo* II.16, found it a problem in that he could not accept that Christ's Mother had been born free of original sin. Peter of Poitiers in about 1170 held that it was the Incarnation that purified the Virgin Mother, though he spoke also of an earlier cleansing from original sin at an unspecified time. Neither St Bernard nor St Thomas Aquinas, for differing reasons, could accept the initial sinlessness of Mary: Aquinas wrote, 'Had she been conceived free of original sin, she would not have needed to be redeemed by Christ; and so he would not be the universal Redeemer of men' – which was of course right, except that Aquinas should have applied the principle of fore-ordination, prevision, retroactive effect of redeeming grace. (The *oratio* for 8th December includes the words, 'You let her share beforehand in the salvation Christ would bring by his death'). In 1570 St Pius V, in a curious bull, forbade either the opinion which affirmed the doctrine, or that which denied it, to be censured. In 1622, Pope Gregory XV gave the Dominicans a special licence to affirm that Mary was conceived in original sin, provided that they did not broadcast such a doctrine. In 1671, Pope Alexander VII prohibited the censuring of those who could not believe Mary's conception was immaculate. The doctrine took a long time to make its way in the universal Church.

In the years following the Conquest, Canterbury was at the centre of both the monastic and the theological world (and of course the ecclesiastical world of England). This was due to a concatenation of the Norman monastic tradition, whose finest flowers were Lanfranc (1005-1070-1089) and Anselm (1033-1093-1109): and the same Anglo-Saxon tradition, represented by Eadmer and Prior Elmer. The two traditions sat uneasily with one another, as Eadmer had cause to complain, loyal as he nevertheless was to his two Norman archbishops. When the Normans came in 1066, they found – as William of Malmesbury put it – that 'the zeal for letters and religion had grown cold'. So they set in train a reform that submerged, and in some instances obliterated, the Anglo-Saxon devotional customs. English abbots and bishops were soon replaced by Norman; Lanfranc drew up a new monastic constitution for common observance; new Norman abbeys were founded, notably Battle in the south and Selby in the north; and the liturgical custom, especially in regard to the specifically Anglo-Saxon kalendar, was revised (so that such names as St Ethelwold and St Edward lost their feasts). Among the devotional feasts dropped by the standardising Lanfranc reforms, worked out principally at Canterbury, were those two distinctively Anglo-Saxon ones, the Presentation and the Conception of the Virgin, which do not appear again in any liturgical document for almost half a century. When Christ Church priory obtained permission from their archbishop, Anselm, to celebrate the octave of the Nativity of Our Lady – a devotion Anselm was fond of, for he had first come to England on 8th September 1092 – the monks did not seek to re-establish the feasts of Presentation or Conception, though they did include other local feasts in the request, and with success. Worcester cathedral annals recorded under 1125 that 'the Conception of St Mary is celebrated *for the first time* in England', and in 1126 it was taken up at Winchcombe abbey. It seems then to have been taken up at St Peter's, Gloucester; and at St Albans and Bury St Edmunds. Under the year 1129 several chronicles record that the feast of the Conception was confirmed by apostolic authority at the Council of London in the presence of Henry I. Gradually the old tradition reasserted itself as Normans and Anglo-Saxons buried their differences; but it did so in face of a good deal of resistance, and that is why it claimed the attention of so many of the chroniclers.

The feast of the Conception of the Blessed Virgin cannot have been entirely submerged, for Eadmer made out a continuous and enthusiastic defence for it, and when it was brought back, some of the earlier prayers of the feast were brought back with it, notably the three prayers from the Leofric Missal. The evidence of Abbot Aelsi's bid to have the devotion retained and extended by way of a 'supernatural argument', the re-emergence of Anglo-Saxon prayers, the enthusiasm for the devotion in face of Norman disregard for it, all suggest that it went underground but not out of mind in England, remaining alive at least among the common people, who are slower to change or forget. If it was any one person who brought it to light again, that person was surely the monk Eadmer of Canterbury: and in so doing, he needed to express an insight of considerable consequence to overcome the prejudice of the Normans and their underlying misunderstanding. This Eadmer achieved in 1125 or more probably in the early 1130s; yet even so late as 1137, an erstwhile Prior of Westminster Abbey is still able to write with chagrin to the Dean of Worcester, 'let those infidels and heretics cease their idle talk about this sacred solemnity, let them learn that the children of the Mother of Grace make no celebration of a sinful act, but of the beginning of our salvation'. Those words highlight the significance of the Anglo-Saxon feast we have painstakingly traced from its inception. The Normans saw in it only a scandal; for by the act of generation, sinful in itself, is original sin transmitted, so they thought and said. They were not easily convinced that the feast marked the joyful honouring of Mary, child of a miracle which itself proclaimed the greatest miracle, man's redemption. Eadmer himself, introducing his *de Conceptione Sanctae Mariae*, made much the same point as Prior Osbert de Clare, when he wrote: 'In former days [the feast] was more frequently celebrated, particularly by those of pure simplicity of mind and humble devotion to God. But afterwards among those exalted by learning and research, there were some who were contemptuous of the simplicity of the poor of spirit and who did away with the celebration of the feast, banishing it as lacking reason. Men of wealth they were, of secular and ecclesiastical authority. But when I ruminate upon the simplicity of mind of earlier men as against the eminence of mind of such moderns, some words of Scripture come to me; and they are these, that the simple converse with God!' One can hear the loaded sarcasm of the old monk, who had had to live through cold winters watching rich custom scorned as meaningless by rich men able to misemploy Church authority. Old piety came under the dispassionate stare of more articulate churchmen, the mute instincts of Anglo-Saxon veneration having no champion, till Eadmer, to speak for their devotion.

The most articulate churchman of his age, and one who had an immense sympathy for all devotions to the Blessed Virgin Mary, was the great doctor of the Church of Canterbury, Eadmer's mentor and archbishop, St Anselm of Bec. He is traditionally aligned with those who opposed our doctrine, but that is far from the whole account; and indeed it was he who formulated the mode of theologising which brought Eadmer to his great judgment upon the Virgin's immaculate conception. Anselm's Marian theology is contained in three works, his famous *Cur Deus Homo*, his treatise *de conceptu Virginali et Originali Peccato*, and his *Orationes* or *Prayers & Meditations*. Only the first forecloses against our doctrine, and that only once in the interests of St Anselm's characteristically feudal soteriology. His words upon Our

224

Lady are these: 'The Virgin herself, from whom (God made man) was taken, was shaped in iniquity, and in sin did her mother conceive her. [An echo of Psalm 50]. She was borne in original sin, for she herself sinned in Adam, in whom all sinned. [An echo of the incorrect Vulgate rendering of Romans 5.12, "Death pervaded the whole human race, in as much as all men have sinned" being the correct quotation) ... The Virgin from whom the man we speak of was taken was one of those who, before his birth, had been purified by him from sins. And it was in her state of purity that he was taken from her. *Questioner:* But he ought to have purity from sin in virtue of himself; he seems in fact to have it from his mother, and thus to be pure not in virtue of himself but of her. *Anselm:* Not so. Since his mother's purity, through which he is pure, came only from him, he also was pure from himself and in virtue of himself.' (*CDH* II.16). That is most heartening: Anselm may not have been able to posit Mary's original sinlessness, but he has here posited her sinlessness before the Annunciation; indeed possibly before her own birth, so that she will have been free of all actual sin relating to her own acts. Anselm's reason is the one required for the doctrine of the Immaculate Conception, and it proved the stumbling block to later doctors of the Church such as Aquinas, namely the anticipated or retroactive effect of the redeeming grace of Christ Jesus her son on the Cross. Some important parts have been brought into place.

Anselm's earliest writings, dating from the period when he was Prior of Bec in Normandy, were his *Prayers & Meditations*, through which he first became more widely known in the monastic world. Among them are three that he sent to his friend Gundulf at Canterbury in 1072, who had gone there with Lanfranc from Bec. Gundulf was destined soon to become Bishop of Rochester after some seven years at Canterbury. In his lifetime Anselm's *Orationes* contained, as Sir Richard Southern described it, 'the fullest expression of that fervid and personal devotion, especially to the Virgin Mary, which was winning adherents everywhere in Europe. Anselm was not only among the first to express these sentiments, but he was the first to express them in a way which satisfied the needs of the educated laity, as well as the cloister.' He realised that the brevity of traditional prayers, above all those to the Virgin Mary, could no longer fulfil the ardour of the time. He introduced into old manners of liturgical writing a new note of personal passion, of poignant intellectual effusion, owing its power to a quite unique combination of intensity of feeling and clarity of both thought and expression. Consider this passage from the third of his Gundulph *Prayers* to Mary, the only one that satisfied him:

'*O Woman uniquely to be wondered at, to be wondered at for your uniqueness,*
by you the elements are renewed, hell is redeemed, demons are trampled down,
men are saved, and even the fallen angels are restored to their place.

225

O Woman, full and overflowing with grace,
plenty flows from you to make all creatures green again.'

This was the tenor of Anselm's reverence for the Blessed Virgin, richly uncritical, desirous to give her all that may be given.

That being so, we are not surprised to find in a work later than his 1098 *Cur Deus Homo* words which seem to reverse Anselm's foreclosure of the doctrine of the Immaculate Conception. In 1099-1100, as Eadmer tells us, almost immediately after that other work, St Anselm wrote his *de Conceptu Virginali*, in which he set out to prove that Christ could be without sin even if Mary was not, for original sin was transmitted by natural propagation, whereas Christ was born virginally. In that treatise lies a passage that exercised a decisive influence on the furtherance of the doctrine we are discussing, a passage quoted indeed in the 1854 Bull defining it. St Anselm wrote: 'It was fitting that this Virgin should shine with a degree of purity than which no greater can be imagined apart from God' (*Decebat ut ea puritate Virgo niteret qua maior sub Deo nequit intelligi:* Chapter 18). Anselm was clear enough about the principle, but he could not bring himself to its application and consequences – the Augustinian tradition of sin and redemption was too strong within him for him to make the theological leap that was needed. Further on in the same treatise (Chapter 27, *Quid sit originale peccatum*) he defines original sin as absence of original justice, due to Adam's disobedience; and, granted that the Virgin is purest of all creatures, not much more was needed than to posit the anticipation of the effects of Christ's passion to render the Immaculate Conception theologically acceptable.

Anselm, father of Scholasticism and a doctor of the universal Church, was unable to make the necessary theological leap, though he had prepared the ground for it. In his early *Prayers* he had written, 'Nothing is equal to Mary, nothing but God is greater than Mary.' He compares the motherhood of the Virgin with the fatherhood of God, the Father being beyond all greatness, the Mother beyond all save the Father: it is an extravagance which blurs the distinction between infinite and finite, as Anselm's so-called ontological proof blurs the distinction between mental conception and reality. This is what he wrote in his final Prayer: 'Every nature is created by God, and God is born from Mary. God has created everything, and Mary has given birth to God. God, who made all things, made himself from Mary; and in so doing, he has re-created all he had created ... God, then is Father of all created things; and Mary is Mother of all re-created things. God is Father of the constitution of things, Mary Mother of the restitution of things. For God generated him through whom all was made, and Mary gave birth to him through whom all was saved.' Such language, coming early in Anselm's monastic life (in 1072, a dozen years after he had joined Bec), was more exalted in fact than the doctrine from which he later hesitated.

The man who was able to make the vital leap had lived the greater part of his monastic life as Anselm's monk-secretary (and was to be the same for his successor, Ralph d'Escure, 1114-22). He was successively Anselm's public and personal biographer, and in theological processes his imitator. An Anglo-Saxon by birth, he was inordinately proud of the pre-Conquest tradition, including the old simple devotion to the Virgin. His considerable corpus of work includes two important treatises on Our Lady, the first being *de Excellentia Virginis Mariae*, bearing the marks of Anselm's strong influence interspersed with the old naivety of popular devotion. It is dated from before 1115, when Eadmer gathered up his first collection of his works; and we are drawn to ask how much he may have gathered from the monk-bishop, Herbert Losinga of Norwich, or he from Eadmer. There was a traffic between the two cathedral monasteries, for political reasons if no other in the turbulent age leading to the Council of London in 1107; and that may have brought the two scholar-monks together from time to time. In 1107 the Bishop of Norwich had assisted Archbishop Anselm in his episcopal consecrations after the Peace. We know that when in 1115 Archbishop Ralph inherited the Canterbury-York quarrel and decided to take his case to Rome the next summer, he took with him (so we are told by Hugh the Chantor) three companions for the journey – Bishop Losinga, Abbot Hugh of Chertsey and William of Corbeil (then a canon of Canterbury and one day to be its archbishop); and Eadmer tells us that he went too, giving an account of the collapse of the Bishop of Norwich en route. At such times preacher and writer upon the perfections of the Blessed Virgin must surely have entertained some conversation on their joint interest. By then Losinga had uttered his judgment (in 1113c) and Eadmer had completed the first of his two works, so they may well have discussed it as *au current*.

De Excellentia Virginis Mariae was a meditation undertaken in an effusive manner following the Anselmian mode – in both the devotional enthusiasm and the form of argument, which deduced the necessity of otherwise unknown historical events from reasons of theological propriety, as Anselm did with dogmatic truth. Its counter, written a decade later, perhaps in 1125 to justify the reintroduction of the old Conception feast at the abbey of Bury St Edmunds under a new abbot, St Anselm's nephew by his sister, was theologically far more important. *De Conceptione Sanctae Mariae** constituted a new level of thinking, at once theological and devotional, simpler than that of Eadmer's successors but undoubtedly more sophisticated than all that had gone before. The shift of thought in those ten years is very clear. In 1115, Eadmer had written: 'Her heart was made clean from all sin, whether original or actual if anything there were, by faith' – not before the Virgin's birth. In 1125, Eadmer wrote: 'If there was anything of

---

* As to its structure, see Appendix I

original sin in her procreation, it belonged to the parents and not to the progeny. Consider the chestnut,† prickly without but smooth and white as milk within. Could not God grant that, though conceived among the spikes of sin, she likewise could be altogether free from their sting? Clearly he could and would; and if he would, he did. *Potuit plane, et voluit; si igitur voluit, fecit.*' (PL 159. 305B). 'She who was created to be the palace of the Redeemer of sinners was therefore free from the servitude of all sin'; if Jeremiah and John the Baptist were sanctified in their mothers' womb, 'who dares to say that the unique *propitiatory* [i.e. the holy place where sins are forgiven] of the whole world and the resting place (*reclinatorium*) of the Son of the Almighty was deprived of the grace and illumination of the Holy Spirit from the very moment of her conception?' Eadmer went on to link Mary's freedom from original sin both with her dignity as Mother of our Saviour and as Queen of the whole of creation, including the angels, some of whom had been preserved from any sin. All this was characteristically Anselmian, and most especially the argument *Deo decuit, Deus potuit, ergo Deus fecit.* Propagated under the name of Anselm, as was the way of the Middle Ages when the works of small men swam in the shadow of greater men, this treatise swam into the world of the Schoolmen, till all the great universities had their consulted copies. By degrees it came to change the face of a Marian doctrine to what we know today. Anselmian in thought, it drove out Anselm's own main tenet.

The centre of the controversy eventually shifted back to Europe, perhaps most markedly in 1139 when the ever argumentative and usually conservative St Bernard berated the canons of Lyons for taking up Eadmer's doctrine. But before that there is still to record the return of the Feast of the Conception of the Blessed Virgin to liturgical use in England. Anselm, nephew of St Anselm, Abbot of the Greek monastery in Rome, St Saba, friend and legate of popes, spiritual counsellor of Henry I, brought the feast to Bury St Edmunds soon after he became its abbot in 1123; and it was to him that the former Prior of Westminster, Osbert de Clare, in 1129 addressed the first of his two letters that began: 'You have spread the feast', and ended: 'Complete what you began'. He told Dean Warin of Worcester in another such letter to remind any critics of the feast that they were celebrating not sin but 'their manifold joy concerning the first fruits of our redemption'. And so the doctrine and the feast spread together, reaching out into the realm. How far it travelled, we can see by recalling a sermon of St Aelred, from the so-called 'Desert of the North', the Rye valley. In mid-century, Abbot Aelred was speaking of the Blessed Virgin as taking precedence in dignity, holiness, purity, self-mortification: 'She was the first of all the human race to escape the curse of our first parents. She alone deserved to

† A long analogy. See Appendix II

hear from the angel, *Benedicta in mulieribus*, for while all women are under the curse, she alone among them is counted worthy of this blessing.' (Sermon xvii). So the tradition spread. Nicholas of St Albans at about this time wrote from his great abbey a sophisticated refutation of St Bernard, and went on to conduct a correspondence upon the issue with Peter of Celles, the argument being furthered into a new generation of thought upon the matter. Eadmer's argument went far afield and even to the heart of 12th century learning, Paris University. There the Chancellor himself in the 1160s, Peter Commestor, provided in his treatise on the Blessed Virgin new authorities from his learning upon the past, but using arguments essentially culled from Eadmer and echoing his very phrases. Such were his words: 'No reason can be found to overthrow the feast of (the Virgin's) Conception which would not equally avail to destroy the regard paid to her Nativity, . . . a feast which the Church has adopted. For what mysterious reason can be given why, if her Conception be at fault, her Nativity should be free from fault? If she be conceived in sin, in sin also was she born. Or again, if her sin be remitted in the womb, then it is not the day of her Nativity that ought to be solemnised; but the proper day to choose for honouring her is the day when she was first free . . . In the Conception of Mary, Mother of God, we pay honour not to the concupiscence of any carnal love.' (He had earlier argued, with Eadmer, that carnal love—with whatever fault of sin attaching—belonged to the active conceiver, the parents, not to the passive conceived, the child: *In conceptione matris carnis signatur luxuria, in conceptu prolis suscepta est hominis materia*). Thus our doctrine fared forward.

It found its way into the other great seat of medieval learning, Oxford. It is interesting that Oxford's bishop and former lector at the Franciscan house of studies there, Robert Grosseteste, Bishop of Lincoln, was one of a very few Schoolmen to ask whether Mary may not have been sanctified 'in the very infusion of her rational soul' —and he asked the question in 1230, while he was teaching at Oxford. In his time, all Oxford was Marian. Mass of Our Lady was said daily in the church of St Mary the Virgin; and it was so in six other churches, endowed chantries. In the church of St Ebbe there was a fraternity of St Mary to 'honour God, St Mary and the festival of the Assumption', a priest being retained to say Mass and the canonical hours at St Mary's altar on Sundays and festivals. On the feasts of the Conception and the Assumption, the University held no lectures: both feasts, incidentally, survived the Reformation in the English Book of Common Prayer. Around Oxford, churches were dedicated to Our Lady (particularly to her Assumption) in some profusion; and even inns, such as 'Salutation Inn'. Finally in the 14th century, following the example of Paris, Oxford and Cambridge Universities required those taking their degrees to swear an oath to defend the

Immaculate Conception. By then, our doctrine had come a long way in England. |See also Appendix III, p. 231 below.|

Nevertheless there was still a long way to go until it became a doctrine of the universal Church, as defined at Rome in 1854. What is so interesting in this long tale of theological development, a tale of some 1800 years and complex comprehension, is that the most vital devotional and intellectual bridge was built in monastic and scholastic England, built by Anglo-Saxons and Normans in strife and in concord together. There is good reason why this is an island dedicated to the Blessed Virgin.

We must end where we began – at the end. The end is so brilliant that it surely leaves us breathless, and on our knees. In 1858, when all was signed and sealed, when men and women had prayed and fought and thought and defined, the poorest girl-child in the poorest corner of France, far from such deliberations, asked *Aquero*, her Lady, a fourth time who she was: and she received this reply:

Que soy era Immaculata Counception.

Appendix I.
De Conceptione Sanctae Mariae:
Eadmer's Personal Manuscript

Corpus Christi College, Cambridge ms 371 is the main, and for several works the only, manuscript of Eadmer's writings. It was his own manuscript, containing virtually all his known works, and to it he made additions and amendments. In large measure it is written in his own hand. After returning from Scotland in 1121 (where he was unsuccessfully contending his call to become Bishop of St Andrews), he added a new series of works to the accumulating collection. They include four new quires added at the end, in a tremulous hand, ruled in pencil instead of with a hard point: they probably record works that belong to the last years of Eadmer's life. Of them, the *de Conceptione* is not earlier than 1125, and the whole group appear to cover the years 1124-30. All other manuscripts except the most telling one, CCCC 371, attribute the *de Conceptione* to Anselm. This manuscript also includes, in its earliest sections, Eadmer's *de Excellentia Gloriosissimae Virginis Matris Dei*.

The *de Conceptione* falls into three main divisions, and Fr Bonnar (*infra*) has argued that only the first is the original treatise. The divisions are these:

I. The feast of Our Lady's Conception should be celebrated because of her dignity as Mother of God (4 pages); because even in her conception she was free of original sin (17 pages).

II. If our first parents had not sinned, the Incarnation would not have taken place. So all Our Lady's dignity and glory comes from the fall: all of us, she included, have more glory than we would have had if our first parents had not sinned (9 pages).

III. Evils resulting from the sin of our first parents: remedy through Christ (5 pages). Help through Our Lady's intercession (8 pages); that help applied personally to the writer (4 pages); then an appeal to Christ for mercy through the intercession of Our Lady (1 page).

Clearly there are three related dissertations here, rather than a single whole. They have some affinity, which justifies their being grouped together. Only I. is given to the title subject. II. makes no mention of Our Lady's conception or its feast, or to her exemption from original sin as celebrated in that feast. It has a separate theme that occurs seven times, and only in this part, viz. *Si Deo inobediens non fuisset Adam, numquam filius Dei*

230

homo fieret. III. similarly makes no mention of Our Lady's privilege and its attendant feast. Passages of the last two treatises, from beginning to end (Cf. Num.21, 25, 31, 32, 34, 36) relate closely in their phrasing to *de Excellentia*, notably Ch.IX and XII, but not to *de Conceptione.*

Cf. Fr Alphonsus Bonnar O.F.M., Eadmer 'de Conceptione Sanctae Mariae', *Irish Ecclesiastical Record*, Dec 1958, pp. 378-91.

R.W. Southern, *Anselm & His Biographer*, Cambridge 1963, Appendix III, Eadmer's Personal Manuscript, pp. 367-74.

Appendix II.
Eadmer's 'Chestnut' Analogy as to the
Doctrine of the Immaculate Conception,
Chap. 10. Translation Fr Herbert Thurston, SJ, *The Month* CIV (1904), p.573.

Take an example from the chestnut. When it comes to birth on a tree of its kind, the husk shows rough and shaggy, bristling on every side with prickles. Inside, the nut itself takes shape (*concipitur* = is conceived), and at first it is like a milky juice. There is no roughness, no unevenness; it has nothing prickly in itself, nor is it lacerated by anything around it. There gently and slowly it grows and swells and is nourished, until when it has been built up into its proper form and habit, bursting its husks in the hour of full maturity, it escapes from its prison, absolutely free from all puncture or roughness of prickles. Mark me, then. If God so guards the chestnut that in the very midst of thorns it is conceived and nourished and shaped without injury of thorns, could he not bestow upon that human body which he prepared for himself as a temple to abide in, and out of which in the oneness of his person he was to assume that which would make him perfect man; could he not, I say, so preserve that same body that although it was conceived among the thorns of sin, it should itself be free from all puncture of thorns? Assuredly he could. If then he wished it, he also did it.

Appendix III.
An Exhibition of liturgical vestments, etc
belonging to St John's College, Oxford.
19 February 1982.

When recently the old Cistercian St Bernard's College (founded 1437, dissolved 1542), now refounded in 1555 by a City of London alderman as the College of St John the Baptist, put on display their remarkable collection of pre-Reformation ecclesiastical embroidery, what was particularly interesting was the extent to which the Blessed Virgin Mary is prominent in the motifs. Of the eleven exhibits, four relate directly to her. The first set, English and dating from c1440–60, includes a hood proclaiming the Annunciation: figures carry scrolls inscribed: *Ave gracia plena* and *Ecce ancilla domini*. The second is an English altar frontal which depicts at its centre the Virgin with angels. The third set, Flemish dating c1500, includes a cope 'of blewe velvett & cloth of goold with the Coronation of the Virgin upon the cape'. The sixth is a 'banner of Our Lady', bearing, *inter alia*, representations of the Trinity and the Assumption of the Virgin; and carrying the inscription: *ex dona Thome Campyon* i.e. colleague of the Founder and father of a Fellow of St John's, the martyr St Edmund Campion S.J. Thus prominent was the Blessed Virgin in England in the late middle ages.

Cardinal Newman's Teaching about the Blessed Virgin Mary

REV. CHARLES STEPHEN DESSAIN, Cong. Orat.

The only book which Newman wrote ex professo about our Lady had an ecumenical purpose, his *Letter to Pusey*, and he began it by remarking what joy it would give those who came in any way under the latter's influence, 'to be one with ourselves. I know how their hearts would spring up with a spontaneous transport at the very thought of union'. And so, Newman concluded, 'there just now seems a call on me, to avow plainly what I do and what I do not hold about the Blessed Virgin, that others may know, did they come to stand where I stand, what they would, and what they would not be bound to hold concerning her.'[1] Since that time, over a hundred years ago, many more people on all sides have come to share the longing for unity, and the Blessed Virgin does not appear, in the way that she then did, as a wall of separation between Roman Catholics and the other Christian Communions of Western Europe and America. The former try to give practical expression to Pope John's remark that we do not honour the Son by making exaggerated claims for His Mother. As to the latter, many more have come to accept in practice, now that certain fears have been removed, what some have always accepted, the full implications of the Motherhood of Mary.

Newman illustrates both Catholic moderation and Protestant fears. For years as an Anglican he found great difficulty in what he considered the deviations and exaggerations of Catholics about our Lady, while later, as a Catholic, he preached, against the extremists of his own communion, that moderate doctrine, which had been held and practised in England, whatever may have been the case in the Latin countries. He tells us in the *Apologia*, about passages concerning the Blessed Virgin he found in Italian authors: 'Such devotional manifestations in honour of our Lady had been my great *crux* as regards Catholicism; I say frankly, I do not fully enter into them now; I trust I do not love her the less, because I cannot enter into them. They may be fully explained and defended; but sentiment and taste do not run with logic: they are suitable for Italy, but they are not suitable for England.'[2] A year later he used much stronger language about exaggerated or erroneous statements by Catholics, in reply to Pusey's *Eirenicon*. For Pusey there took up his phrase and spoke of how 'That vast system as to the Blessed Virgin ... to all of us has been the special *crux* of the Roman system.' Newman outlined the principle on which he would base his reply: 'The Fathers made me a Catholic, and I am not going to kick down the ladder by which I ascended into the Church. ... Though I hold, as you know, a process of development in Apostolic truth as time goes on, such development does not supersede the Fathers, but explains and completes them. And, in particular, as regards our teaching concerning the Blessed Virgin, with the Fathers I am content. ... I do not wish to say more than they suggest to me, and will not say less.'[3]

I. Newman's Views as an Anglican

The appeal to this principle, this source, helps to explain the astonishing continuity in Newman's thought, and how comparatively little it changed on his leaving the Church of England. 'I was not conscious to myself, on my conversion, of any change, intellectual or moral, wrought in my mind. I was not conscious of firmer faith in the fundamental truths of Revelation, or of more self-command; I had not more fervour ...' he stated in the *Apologia*, and Dr. Owen Chadwick has remarked recently about it, 'The book disclosed a powerful sense of continuity between his present mind and his Anglican past. Moreover he seemed to be grateful for what he owed to his Anglican past. He had learned his Catholicism within the Church of England and was willing to say so.'[4] That this was true of his devotion to our Lady Newman there tells us. Richard Hurrell Froude 'had a high severe idea of the intrinsic excellence of Virginity; and he considered the Blessed Virgin its great Pattern ... He fixed deep in me the idea of devotion to the Blessed Virgin.' This would have been when Newman was in his middle twenties, and before he became Vicar of St. Mary's. Later in the *Apologia* he wrote, 'I had a true devotion to the Blessed Virgin, in whose College I lived, whose altar I served, and whose Immaculate Purity I had in one of my earliest printed Sermons made much of.'[5] This was the sermon 'The Reverence due to the Virgin Mary,' first preached on 25 March 1832, more than a year before what is usually considered to be the beginning of the Oxford Movement. In it he asks, 'Who can estimate the holiness and perfection of her, who was chosen to be the Mother of Christ? If to him that hath, more is given, and holiness and Divine favour go together (and this we are expressly told), what must have been the transcendent purity of her, whom the Creator Spirit condescended to overshadow with His miraculous presence? What must have been her gifts, who was chosen to be the only near earthly relative of the Son of God, the only one whom He was bound by nature to revere and look up to; the one appointed to train and educate Him, to instruct Him day by day, as He grew in wisdom and stature? This contemplation runs to a higher subject, did we dare follow it; for what, think you, was the sanctified state of that human nature, of which God formed his sinless Son; knowing as we do, "that which is born of the flesh is flesh," and that "none can bring a clean thing out of an unclean." '[6] Newman goes on to note that everyone must feel some surprise that we are not told more about the Blessed Virgin in the Gospels. This is in mercy to our weakness. For, 'as to St. Mary, Christ derived His manhood from her, and so had an especial unity of nature with her; and this wondrous relationship between God and man it is perhaps impossible for us to dwell much upon without some perversion of feeling. For, truly, she is raised above the condition of sinful beings, though by nature a sinner; she is brought near to God, yet is but a creature, and seems to lack her fitting place in our limited understandings, neither too high nor too low. We cannot combine, in our thought of her, all we should ascribe with all we should withhold. Hence, following the example of Scripture, we had better only think of her with and for her Son, never separating her from Him ... nothing is so calculated to impress on our minds that Christ is really partaker of our nature, and in all respects man, save sin only, as to associate Him with the thought of her, by whose ministration He became our brother.'[7] In a later sermon in 1843, Newman compared our Lord's last feast with His apostles to that first one at Cana. There he had seemed to turn from His Mother's prayer while he granted it, because His hour was not yet come, implying 'that in that hour He should have to do with His Mother again.' At His last supper, He had told the Apostles about the future power of their prayers, 'Whatsoever ye shall ask the Father in My Name, He will give it you.' 'In the gifts then promised to the Apostles after the Resurrection, we may learn the present influence and power of the Mother of God.'[8]

Newman was not alone in speaking thus of our Lady. He had the warrant, to mention no others, of his spiritual counsellor, that traditional Anglican, John Keble. In his poem on the Annunciation, in *The Christian Year*, published in 1827, Keble writes:

Ave Maria! Mother blest,
To whom caressing and caressed,
Clings the Eternal Child ...
Ave Maria! thou whose name
All but adoring love may claim,
Yet may we reach thy shrine ...

In 1846 Keble brought out another volume of sacred poems, *Lyra Innocentium*, which Newman himself has described for us: 'The Virgin and Child is the special vision, as it may be called, which this truly evangelical poet has before him ...' After illustrating this, Newman continues: 'The feeling which is brought out into formal statement in these passages is intimated by the frequency and tenderness of expression with which the thought of the Blessed Virgin is introduced throughout the Volume. She is the "Blessed Mary" ... "the Virgin blest" ... "the Mother-maid" ... "Mother of God;" "the spotless Mother, first of creatures." ' And Newman concludes: 'If there be one writer in the Anglican Church who has discovered a deep, tender, loyal devotion to the Blessed Mary, it is the author of the *Christian Year*. The image of the Virgin and Child seems to be the one vision upon which both his heart and intellect have been formed; and those who knew Oxford twenty to thirty years ago, say that, while other college rooms were ornamented with pictures of Napoleon on horseback, or Apollo and the Graces, or Heads of Houses lounging in their easy chairs, there was one man, a young and rising one, in whose rooms, instead of these, might be seen the Madonna di Sisto or Domenichino's St. John—fit augury of him who was in the event to do so much for the revival of Catholicism.'[9]

II. Newman's Difficulties as an Anglican

If those were the terms in which Newman and his mentor spoke of our Lady, we almost begin to ask how he could have had difficulties about Roman Catholic teaching. What did he complain of? Let us take as the fairest statement, what he said in his article "The Catholicity of the Anglican Church," published in January 1840. He wrote of it to Keble, 'I seem to myself almost to have shot my last arrow against Rome,' and it represents his feelings right up to the time of his Anglican deathbed. This is Newman's charge: "In Antiquity, the main aspect in the economy of redemption comprises Christ, the Son of God, the Author and Dispenser of all grace and pardon, the Church His living representative, the sacraments her instruments, bishops her rulers, their collective decisions her voice, and Scripture her standard of truth. In the Roman schools, we find St. Mary and the Saints the prominent objects of regard and dispensers of mercy, purgatory or else indulgences the means of obtaining it, the Pope the ruler and teacher of the Church, miracles the warrant of doctrine. As to the doctrines of Christ's merits and eternal life and death, these are points not denied (God forbid!) but taken for granted, and passed by in order to make way for others of more present, pressing, and lively interest. That a certain change, then, in objective and external religion has come over the Latin, nay, and in a measure the Greek Church, we consider to be a plain historical fact; a change indeed not so great as is common Protestantism, for that involves a radical change of inward temper and principle as well, as indeed its adherents are not slow to remind us, but a change sufficiently startling to recall to our minds, with very unpleasant sensations, the words of the Apostle, about preaching any other Gospel besides that which has been received.'[10]

When he republished this article the year after the first Vatican Council, Newman added a note: 'Of these heads of accusation, the only one which will be allowed by Catholics is that "the Pope is the ruler and teacher of the Church." ' In particular, as to the accusation concerning the place of our Lady, he rejected it in the book he wrote as he was leaving the Anglican Church, his *Development of Doctrine*. He said: 'It must be observed, what is very important, that great and constant as is the devotion which the Catholic pays to the Blessed Mary, it has a special province, and has far more connexion with the public services and the festive aspect of Christianity, and with certain extraordinary offices which she holds, than with what is strictly personal and primary in religion.' Newman tells us that Cardinal Wiseman, on his reception as a Roman Catholic, 'singled out to me this last sentence, for the expression of his especial approbation.'[11] This point is so important for understanding Newman's teaching on our Lady, that it must be considered again later. Here it will be sufficient to note some of Newman's remarks in the *Letter to Pusey*: 'I say plainly, I never will defend or screen any one from your just rebuke, who, through false devotion to Mary, forgets Jesus.' He wanted it proved that devotion to our Lady did in fact throw our Lord into the shade. 'There is this broad fact the other way; he wrote—that, if we look through Europe, we shall find, on the whole, that just those nations have lost their faith in the divinity of Christ, who have given up devotion to His Mother, and that those on the other hand, who have been foremost in her honour, have retained their orthodoxy ... In the Catholic Church Mary has shown herself, not the rival, but the minister of her Son; she has protected Him, as in His infancy, so in the whole history of the Religion.' Further, Newman urges on Pusey, 'As you revere the Fathers, so you revere the Greek Church; and here again we have a witness on our behalf ... Is it not a very pregnant fact, that the Eastern Churches, so independent of us, so long separated from the West, so jealous for Antiquity, should even surpass us in their exaltation of the Blessed Virgin? ... What have the Latins done so bold, as that substitution of the name of Mary for the Name of Jesus at the end of the collects and petitions in the Breviary, nay, in the Ritual and Liturgy? Not merely in local or popular, and in semi-authorized devotions ... but in the formal prayers of the Greek Eucharistic Service, petitions are offered, not in "the name of Jesus Christ," but in that "of the Theotocos." '[12]

III. The Doctrine of the Immaculate Conception

Pusey's chief difficulty concerned the doctrine of the Immaculate Conception, and, in order to explain it, Newman turned, as he had said he would, to the early fathers of the Church. This explains how we already see the first lineaments of the doctrine in the Anglican sermons. Throughout his life the sources of revelation were for him one and the same. Indeed he was accused of holding the doctrine in that sermon of 1832 already quoted where he asked: 'What, think you, was the sanctified state of that human nature, of which God formed His sinless Son; knowing as we do, "that which is born of the flesh is flesh," and "none can bring a clean thing out of an unclean." '[12a] Here is what he says in the same sermon: 'In Mary was now to be fulfilled that promise

236

which the world had been looking out for during thousands of years. The Seed of the woman, announced to guilty Eve, after long delay, was at length appearing upon earth, and was to be born of her. In her the destinies of the world were to be reversed, and the serpent's head bruised. On her was bestowed the greatest honour ever put upon any individual of our fallen race. God was taking upon Him her flesh ... She of course would feel her own inexpressible unworthiness ... And she had moreover, we may well suppose, that purity and innocence of heart, that bright vision of faith, that confiding trust in her God, which raised all these feelings to an intensity which we, ordinary mortals, cannot understand.' Newman continues: 'Now let us consider in what respects the Virgin Mary is Blessed; a title given her by the Angel, and next by the Church in all ages ... I observe, that in her the curse pronounced on Eve was changed to a blessing. Eve was doomed to bear children in sorrow; but now this very dispensation, in which the token of Divine anger was conveyed, was made the means by which salvation came into the world! ... Therefore, instead of sending His Son from heaven, He sent Him forth as the Son of Mary, to show that all our sorrow and all our corruption can be blessed and changed by Him. The very punishment of the Fall, the very taint of birth-sin, admits of a cure by the coming of Christ.'[13] In a sermon of Christmas 1834 Newman says: 'All Adam's children are children of wrath; so our Lord came as the Son of Man, but not the son of sinful Adam. He had no earthly father ... He came by a new and living way; not, indeed, formed out of the ground, as Adam was at the first, lest He should miss the participation of our nature, but selecting and purifying unto Himself a tabernacle out of that which existed. As in the beginning, woman was formed out of man by Almighty power, so now, by a like mystery, but a reverse order, the new Adam was fashioned from the woman. He was, as had been foretold, the immaculate "seed of the woman," deriving His manhood from the substance of the Virgin Mary.' Newman repeats this in a later Christmas sermon, reminding us of the words 'Hail, thou art highly favoured, the Lord is with thee: blessed art thou among women.' 'He who is all purity came to an impure race to raise them to His purity. He, the brightness of God's glory, came in a body of flesh ...' 'He came by a new and living way, by which He alone had come, and which alone became Him.'[14]

The doctrine that our Lady was a new and second Eve Newman had found very explicit in the writings of the fathers, especially the earliest fathers of the Church. He quotes St. Justin, Tertullian and St. Irenaeus in the *Letter to Pusey*, and concludes: 'Now, what is especially noticeable in these three writers, is, that they do not speak of the Blessed Virgin merely as the physical instrument of our Lord's taking flesh, but as an intelligent, responsible cause of it; her faith and obedience being accessories to the Incarnation, and gaining it as her reward. As Eve failed in these virtues, and thereby brought on the fall of the race in

Adam, so Mary by means of the same had a part in its restoration.' Newman brings out the force of these testimonies as to the belief spread all over the Christian Church in her earliest days. 'No one, who acknowledges the force of early testimony in determining Christian truth, can wonder, no one can complain, can object, that we Catholics should hold a very high doctrine concerning the Blessed Virgin …'[15] Newman then shows how this doctrine carries within it that of the Immaculate Conception. The first Eve 'could not have stood against the wiles of the devil, though she was innocent and sinless, without the grant of a large grace. And this she had;—a heavenly gift, which was over and above and additional to that nature of hers, which she received from Adam, a gift which had been given to Adam also before her … This is Anglican doctrine as well as Catholic.' Newman then asks: 'Is it any violent inference, that she, who was to co-operate in the redemption of the world, at least was not less endowed with power from on high, than she who, given as a helpmate to her husband, did in the event but co-operate with him for its ruin? And this consideration gives significance to the Angel's salutation of her as "full of grace,"— and interpretation of the original word which is undoubtedly the right one, as soon as we resist the common Protestant assumption that grace is a mere external approbation or acceptance, answering to the word "favour" whereas it is, as the Fathers teach, a real inward condition … And if Eve had this supernatural inward gift given her from the first moment of her personal existence, is it possible to deny that Mary too had this gift from the very first moment of her personal existence?' This gift preserved her from that negative thing we describe as original sin. Newman insists that Mary shared our fallen nature and needed a Redeemer as we all do. 'We consider that in Adam she died, as others; that she was included, together with the whole race, in Adam's sentence; that she incurred his debt, as we do; but that, for the sake of Him who was to redeem her and us upon the Cross, to her the debt was remitted by anticipation …'[16]

There were a few Catholics who did not relish Newman's explanation. They had tried to maintain, by fine distinctions, that our Lady did not incur the debt of Adam. To one of these, who wrote to protest, Newman replied:'For myself, such subtleties touch neither my heart nor my reason. They don't seem to me to add one atom of honour to our Lady—they do but deprive her Son of subjects. I do but associate them with the loss of souls. It would not lead me to say with a clearer conscience "Per te, Virgo, sim defensus, in die judicii," to have the misgiving within me, that by my officious zeal for her honour, I had prevented my brethren from submitting to the Catholic Church, and enjoying the blessings of Catholic communion.'[17]

On the other hand, when expounding the Catholic doctrine of the Immaculate Conception to enquirers, as he not infrequently did, Newman always expressed surprise that they should find it a difficulty.

While still an Anglican he had felt it no obstacle, it seemed so natural. 'If I am asked for proof of the doctrine being held in the early Church, I answer that it seems included in the general belief that the Blessed Virgin was without sin ... but what to me is, and ever has been most striking, is the series of passages from the earliest Father in which Mary is contrasted to Eve, as typical contrasts ... when St. Irenaeus says, "mankind is surrendered to death by a *Virgin*, and is saved by a *Virgin*," he surely implies that as Eve was without sin, so was Mary. Why indeed is it difficult to suppose that Mary had at least the privilege of Eve?—And Eve had an immaculate conception and birth.'[18] To Robert Wilberforce he summed up the doctrine: 'We do not say that she did not owe her salvation to the death of her Son. Just the contrary, we say that she, of all mere children of Adam, is in the truest sense the fruit and the purchase of His Passion ... To others He gives grace and regeneration at a *point* in their earthly existence; to her, from the very beginning.' And Newman concludes: 'Many, many doctrines are far harder than the Immaculate Conception. The doctrine of Original Sin is indefinitely harder. Mary just has *not* this difficulty. It is *no* difficulty to believe that a soul is united to the flesh *without* original sin; the great mystery is that any, that many are born with it ... I say it distinctly— there may be many excuses at the last day, good and bad, for not being Catholics; *one* I cannot conceive: "O Lord, the doctrine of the Immaculate Conception was so derogatory to Thy grace, so inconsistent with Thy Passion, so at variance with Thy word in Genesis and the Apocalypse, so unlike the teaching of Thy first Saints and Martyrs, as to give me a *right* to reject it at all risks, and Thy Church for teaching it ... this is my plea for living and dying a Protestant." '[19] In fact, after reading the *Letter to Pusey*, Anglicans did exclaim, 'If this is the meaning of the Doctrine, there is no reason why all Christians should not hold it.'

IV. The Doctrine of the Assumption

What has Newman to say about the other 'Marian Dogma', her Assumption into heaven? In the *Letter to Pusey* he asks, 'What dignity can be too great to attribute to her who is as closely bound up, as intimately one, with the Eternal Word, as a mother is with a son? ... Is it surprising then that on the one hand she should be immaculate in her Conception? or on the other that she should be honoured with an Assumption, and exalted as a queen ...? Men sometimes wonder that we call her Mother of life, of mercy, of salvation; what are all these titles compared to that one name, Mother of God?' Newman goes on to show how soon this title arose, and how widespread its use. He begins with a quotation from Ignatius of Antioch, 'Our God was carried in the womb of Mary,' and ends with Athanasius, who 'engraved indelibly upon the imaginations of the faithful, as had never been before, that man is God, and God is man, that in Mary they meet, and

239

that in this sense Mary is the centre of all things.' Yet 'we have no proof that Athanasius himself had any special devotion to the Blessed Virgin; but he laid the foundations on which that devotion was to rest …'[20] As to the actual doctrine of the Assumption, writing on 10 September 1869 to a lady who wondered how it could be or become part of the Faith, of Revelation, Newman said: 'Not till the end of the fourth century did the Church declare the divinity of the Holy Ghost … *Of course* it was held by implication, since the Holy Trinity was believed from the first—but I mean the bare absolute proposition "the Holy Ghost is God—" and, as an illustration of what I mean, St Basil in the middle of the fourth century kept from calling Him God when his Arian enemies were on the watch. I say, kept silence on the point, and, when some Catholics found fault with him, St Athanasius took his part. The Assumption of our Lady is more pointedly and in express words held by all Catholics, and has been for a thousand years, than the proposition "The Holy Ghost is God" was held by the Catholic world in St Basil's time. There has been a gradual evolution of Apostolic doctrine or dogma, as delivered from our Lord to the Church. If the Assumption of Our Blessed Lady were now defined at the Vatican Council,' (Newman was writing just before the first Vatican Council), 'I should say that plainly it, as the Immaculate Conception, is contained in the dogma "Mary the Second Eve—" I have drawn out this argument as regards the latter doctrine in my Letter to Dr. Pusey—as to the Assumption, if Mary is like Eve but greater, then, as Eve would not have seen death or corruption, so while Mary underwent death because she was a child of fallen Adam, she did not see corruption because she had more than the prerogatives of Eve.'

Long before this, in a sermon for the Assumption in 1849, Newman drew out what told in favour of the doctrine, and how it fitted in with the rest of the Christian Faith: 'Who can conceive, my brethren, that God should so repay the debt, which He condescended to owe to His Mother, for the elements of His human body, as to allow the flesh and blood from which it was taken to moulder in the grave? Do the sons of men thus deal with their mothers? do they not nourish and sustain them in their feebleness, and keep them in life while they are able? Or who can conceive that that virginal frame, which never sinned, was to undergo the death of a sinner? Why should she share the curse of Adam, who had no share in his fall? "Dust thou art, and unto dust thou shalt return," was the sentence upon sin; she then, who was not a sinner, fitly never saw corruption. She died, then, as we hold, because even our Lord and Saviour died … She died … not … because of sin, but to submit herself to her condition, to glorify God, to do what her Son did; not however as her Son and Saviour with any suffering for an special end … but in order to finish her course, and to receive her crown. And therefore she died in private. It became Him, who died for the world, to die in the world's sight; it became the Great Sacrifice to be lifted up on high, as a light that could not be hid. But she, the Lily of Eden, who had always dwelt out of the sight of man, fittingly did she die in the garden's shade, and amid the sweet flowers in which she had lived. Her departure made no noise in the world. The church went about her common duties, preaching, converting, suffering; there were persecutions, there was fleeing from place to place, there were martyrs, there were triumphs; at length the rumour spread abroad that the Mother of God was no longer upon earth. Pilgrims went to and fro; they sought for her relics, but they found them not; did she die at Ephesus? or did she die at Jerusalem? reports varied; but her tomb could not be pointed out, or if it was found it was open ...'[21]

That may be called the rhetoric of a sermon, but in the *Letter to Pusey* Newman asks the very serious question 'whether the popular astonishment excited by our belief in the blessed Virgin's present dignity, does not arise from the circumstance that the bulk of men, engaged in matters of this world, have never calmly considered her historical position in the gospels, so as rightly to realize what that position imports.'[22] On the other hand, Newman did not see the need to *define* doctrines about which Catholics were agreed. Definitions were not a luxury but a painful necessity. And he doubted whether the definitions of the Immaculate Conception or the Assumption had led or would lead to an *increase* in *devotion*.

V. Our Lady's Services to Christian Faith and Life

Newman was not content merely to justify the dogmas concerning the Blessed Virgin Mary. He showed what great services she could perform for the followers of her Son, even though, as has already been made clear, they were generally outside 'what is strictly personal and primary in religion.'

In the first place, devotion to the Blessed Virgin is a great bulwark of the doctrine of St. John that 'the Word was made flesh', that God became man. The confession of Mary as the Mother of God is, says Newman, the safeguard of the doctrine that 'that which was from the beginning had appeared in the flesh.' 'It declares that He is God; it implies that He is man ... witnessing to the *process* of the union, it secures the reality of the two *subjects* of the union, of the divinity and of the manhood ... her grace and her glory are not for her own sake, but for her Maker's; and to her is committed the custody of the Incarnation ... As she was once on earth, and was personally the guardian of her Divine Child ... so now, and to the latest hour of the Church, do her glories and the devotion paid her proclaim and define the right faith concerning Him as God and man ... and hence the Church also addresses her in the Antiphon, as having "alone destroyed all heresies in the whole world." ' This explains why devotion to her only spread as the great heresies arose; 'He indeed had been from the very first proclaimed by Holy Church, and enthroned in His temple, for He was God ...' But 'when His name was dishonoured, then it was that she did Him service ... when heretics said that God was not incarnate, then was the time for her own honours. And then, when as much as this had been accomplished, she had done with strife; she fought not for herself ... she has grown into her place in the Church by a tranquil influence and a natural process.'[23]

This was a point Newman adverted to as he was writing his *Development of Doctrine*. The Arian controversy made it clear that no created being could be God. 'To exalt a creature was no recognition of its divinity.' Newman continues: 'Yet it is not wonderful, considering how Socinians, Sabellians, Nestorians, and the like, abound in these days, without their even knowing it themselves, if those who never rise higher in their notions of our Lord's Divinity, than to consider Him a man singularly inhabited by a Divine Presence, that is, a Catholic Saint,—if such men should mistake the honour paid by the Church to the human Mother for that very honour which, and which alone, is worthy of her eternal Son.' The Nestorian controversy completed the development. It, says Newman, 'supplied the subject of that august proposition of which Arianism had provided the predicate. In order to do honour to Christ, in order to defend the true doctrine of the Incarnation, in order to secure a right faith in the manhood of the Eternal Son, the Council of Ephesus determined the Blessed Virgin to be the Mother of God. Thus all heresies of that day, though opposite to each other, tended in a most wonderful way to her exaltation.'[24]

No wonder Newman was led, in the last of his *University Sermons*, to see in 'St. Mary our pattern of Faith, both in the reception and in the study of Divine Truth. She does not think it enough to accept, she dwells upon it; not enough to possess it, she uses it; not enough to assent, she develops it ... and thus she symbolizes to us, not only the faith of the unlearned, but of the doctors of the Church also, who have to investigate, and weigh, and define, as well as to profess the Gospel.'[25]

The second service that our Lady provides is a continuation of the first. It is especially when we think of her as already fully in glory, that we have strongly brought before us the next world, and those unseen realities, which are the essence of the Christian Religion. Thus people, whether inside the Roman Catholic Church or outside it, who did not for various reasons, welcome the papal definition of the Assumption, have rejoiced to see attention focussed upon a doctrine which is such an effective barrier against the attempts to secularise Christianity. In the *Letter to Pusey* Newman remarks: 'Christianity is eminently an objective religion. For the most part it tells us of persons and facts in simple words, and leaves that announcement to produce its effect on such hearts as are prepared to receive it ... It is in this way that the revealed doctrine of the Incarnation exerted a stronger and broader influence on Christians, as they more and more apprehended and mastered its meaning and its bearings.' Newman asks: 'Did not the All-wise know the human heart when He took to Himself a Mother? did He not anticipate our emotion at the sight of such an exaltation in one so simple and so lowly?' Clearly He 'meant her to exert that wonderful influence in His Church, which she has in the event exerted.' In another part of the *Letter* Newman writes: 'Even in the case of our Lord Himself, whose native home is the eternal heavens, it is said of Him in His state of glory, that He is a "priest for ever;" and when He comes again, He will be recognized by those who pierced Him, as being the very same that He was on earth. The only question is, whether the Blessed Virgin had a part, a real part, in the economy of grace, whether, when she was on earth, she secured by her deeds any claim on our memories; for if she did, it is impossible we should put her away from us, merely because she is gone hence ... and this surely she anticipated, when she said in her hymn that all "generations should call her blessed." '[26]

This suggests the third great service of the Blessed Virgin towards us, her power of intercession. In a private letter to Pusey on 3 February 1865 Newman wrote: 'The Blessed Virgin is the great pattern of prayer, especially intercessory. And in this age especially she ... is the *witness* against the prevailing theories ... that all things go on by fixed laws which cannot be broken; thus introducing a practical atheism.' He repeated this in the public *Letter*: 'She is the great examplar of prayer in a generation, which emphatically denies the power of prayer *in toto*, which determines that fatal laws govern the universe, that there cannot be any direct communication between earth and heaven, that God cannot visit His own on earth, and that man cannot influence His providence.'[27] Newman showed from the New Testament the very important part played by intercessory prayer in the life of the first Christians, and in preserving the unity of the Church amid persecution. Intercession was a first principle of the Church's life, and as an availing power, depended, according to the will of God, on the sanctity of those who prayed. He asked 'Was this spiritual bond to cease with life?' and again appealed to the New Testament for proof of its continuance. This was the conclusion: 'I consider it impossible then, for those who believe the Church to be one vast body in heaven and on earth, in which every holy creature of God has his place, and of which prayer is the life, when once they recognise the sanctity and dignity of the Blessed Virgin, not to perceive immediately, that her office above is one of perpetual intercession for the faithful militant, and that our very relation to her must be that of clients to a patron, and that ... the weapon of the Second Eve and Mother of God is prayer.'[28]

Newman noted, as will be emphasised in a moment, that Our Lady's power was indirect. Her prayers avail thanks to God, who is our all in all, and the Divine Presence is the intermediating power by which we reach her and she reaches us. Also, as an Anglican he had noticed; 'Invocations are not *required* in the Church of Rome; somehow, I do not like using them except under the sanction of the Church, and,' (he was writing more than a century and a quarter ago), this makes me unwilling to admit them in members of our Church.'[29]

There is a further service which Newman attributes to our Lady, one connected with her power of intercession with God. She is the pattern and the special intercessor for those who, in the midst of temptation, strive to preserve their innocence. Already in that Anglican sermon first preached in 1832, he draws attention to this. 'God gives His Holy Spirit to us silently; and the silent duties of every day (it may be humbly hoped) are blest to the sufficient sanctification of thousands, whom the world knows not of. The Blessed Virgin is a memorial of this; and it is consoling as well as instructive to know it. When we quench the grace of Baptism, then it is that we need severe trials to restore us. This is the case of the multitude, whose best estate is that of chastisement, repentance, supplication, and absolution, again and again. But there are those who go on in a calm and unswerving course, learning day by day to love Him who has redeemed them, and over-coming the sin of their nature by His heavenly grace, as the various temptations to evil successively present themselves. And, of these unde-filed followers of the Lamb, the Blessed Mary is the chief.' Thus 'the lesson which we gain from the history of the Blessed Virgin' is 'that the highest graces of the soul may be matured in private.'[30]

In one of the Sermons to Mixed Congregations, in 1849 he is much more explicit: 'And now, my dear brethren, what is befitting in us, if all that I have been telling you is befitting in Mary? ... if it became her to be free from all sin from the very first, and from the moment she received her first grace to begin to merit more; and if such was her beginning, such was her end, her conception immaculate and her death an assumption ⋯ what is befitting in the children of such a Mother, but an imitation, in their measure, of her devotion, her meekness, her simplicity, her modesty, and her sweetness? Her glories are not only for the sake of Her Son, they are for our sakes also. Let us copy her faith, who received God's message by the angel without a doubt; her patience, who endured St Joseph's surprise without a word; her obedi-ence, who went up to Bethlehem in the winter and bore our Lord in a stable; her meditative spirit, who pondered in her heart what she saw and heard about Him; her fortitude, whose heart the sword went through; her self-surrender, who gave Him up during His ministry and consented to His death.

Above all, let us imitate her purity ... O my dear children, young men and young women, what need have you of the intercession of the Virgin-mother, of her help, of her pattern, in this respect: What shall bring you forward in the narrow way, if you live in the world, but the thought and patronage of Mary ... She will comfort you in your dis-

couragements ... She will show you her Son, your God and your all ...
It is the boast of the Catholic Religion, that it has the gift of making
the young heart chaste; and why is this, but that it gives us Jesus Christ
for our food, and Mary for our nursing Mother? Fulfil this boast in
yourselves; prove to the world that you are following no false teaching,
vindicate the glory of your Mother Mary ... by the simplicity of your
deportment, and the sanctity of your words and deeds. Go to her for
the royal heart of innocence ... She is the personal type and representative image of that spiritual life and renovation in grace, "Without
which no one shall see God." '[31]

VI. Inviolable Truths

That was the peroration of an eloquent sermon, but it shows that
Newman always preserved a sense of the proper proportion of things.
He taught the firm deep foundations of devotion to our Lady, had a
warm devotion to her himself, but never allowed this to obscure fundamental truths, what is 'strictly personal and primary in religion.' In his
Development of Doctrine he remarked 'that the tone of the devotion
paid to the Blessed Mary is altogether distinct from that which is paid
to her Eternal Son, and to the Holy Trinity, as we must certainly allow
on inspection of the Catholic services.' Newman went on to show how
this applied also to Catholic devotional books, beginning with the
authoritative *Exercises of St. Ignatius*, founder of the Jesuits. 'In a
work so highly sanctioned, so widely received, so intimately bearing
upon the most sacred points of personal religion, very slight mention
occurs of devotion to the Blessed Virgin, Mother of God.'[32] Newman
insisted again on this in the *Letter to Pusey*. Mary did not obscure her
Son. Two of the saints most notorious for their devotion to her St.
Alphonsus and St. Paul of the Cross, 'have shown their supreme love
of her Divine Son, in the names which they have given to their respective Congregations, viz. that "of the Redeemer," and that "of the
Cross and Passion."[33]

It remained true, nonetheless, that some Italian devotions were not
suitable for England, and not in the tradition of the English Roman
Catholics. In the *Apologia* where Newman stated this, he went on:
'But, over and above England, my own case was special; from a boy I
had been led to consider that my Maker, and I, His creature, were the
two beings luminously such, *in rerum natura*. I will not here speculate,
however, about my own feelings. Only this I know full well now, and
did not know then, that the Catholic Church allows no image of any
sort, material or immaterial, no dogmatic symbol, no rite, no sacrament, no Saint, not even the Blessed Virgin herself, to come between
the soul and its Creator. It is face to face "solus cum solo", in all
matters between man and his God. He alone creates; He alone has
redeemed; before His awful eyes we go in death; in the vision of Him is

our eternal beatitude.'[34] Newman made the point once more, and as strongly, in the *Letter to Pusey*. When our Lord became man, 'He brought home to us His incommunicable attributes with a distinctiveness, which precludes the possibility of our lowering Him merely by our exalting a creature. He alone has an entrance into our soul, reads our secret thoughts, speaks to our heart, applies to us spiritual pardon and strength. On Him we sorely depend. He alone is our inward life; He not only regenerates us, but ... He is ever renewing our new birth and our heavenly sonship ... Mary is only our mother by divine appointment ... her presence is above, not on earth; her office is external to us. Her name is not heard in the administration of the Sacraments. Her work is not one of ministration towards us; her power is indirect. It is her prayers that avail, and her prayers are effectual by the *fiat* of Him who is our all in all. Nor need she hear us by any innate power, or any personal gift; but by a manifestation to her of the prayers we make to her ... and thus it is the Divine Presence which is the intermediating power by which we reach her and she reaches us.'[35]

Thus we are brought back to the supreme Christian privilege, the dwelling, the presence, and the activity of God within us. Justification, Newman tells us, in his *Lectures* on that subject, which some think the finest thing he wrote, consists in the Gift of the Holy Spirit, sent by our Lord to take his place. 'Whatever then is done in the Christian Church is done by the Spirit ... The Holy Spirit realises and completes the redemption which Christ has wrought in essence and virtue,' and He 'accordingly is the chief Agent in it.' Our Lord 'atoned in His own Person; he justifies through His Spirit.'[36] Nowhere has the presence and the activity of the Holy Spirit been more wonderful than in the Blessed Virgin Mary.

NOTES
1 *Difficulties of Anglicans* II, pp. 3 and 25. All references are to the uniform edition of Newman's Works.
2 *Apologia pro Vita sua*, p. 195.
3 *Difficulties of Anglicans* II, p. 24.
4 *Apologia*, p. 238; *Anglican Initiatives in Christian Unity*, London 1967, p. 82.
5 *Apologia*, pp. 24-5, 165.
6 *Parochial and Plain Sermons* II, pp. 131-2.
7 *Parochial and Plain Sermons* II, pp. 135-6.
8 *Sermons on Subjects of the Day*, pp. 36-7.
9 *Essays Critical and Historical* II, pp. 436, 438, 452-3.
10 *Essays Critical and Historical* II, pp. 74 and 8-9.
11 *Development of Christian Doctrine*, p. 428; *Difficulties of Anglicans* II, p. 93.
12 *Difficulties of Anglicans* II, pp. 90-3.
12a *The Letters and Diaries of John Henry Newman*, Vol. XIX, pp. 346-7.
13 *Parochial and Plain Sermons* II, pp. 128-30.
14 *Parochial and Plain Sermons* II, p. 31; V, pp. 91-2.
15 *Difficulties of Anglicans* II, pp. 35-6, 38-9.
16 *Difficulties of Anglicans* II, pp. 44-8.

17 *The Letters and Diaries of John Henry Newman*, Vol. XXII, 25 April, 1866.
18 *The Letters and Diaries of John Henry Newman*, XIX, p. 347.
19 *Meditations and Devotions*, pp. 117, 125-6.
20 *Difficulties of Anglicans* II, pp. 62-3 and 87-8.
21 *Discourses to Mixed Congregations*, pp. 371-3.
22 *Difficulties of Anglicans* II, pp. 52-3.
23 *Discourses to Mixed Congregations*, pp. 346-9 and 357.
24 *Development of Christian Doctrine*, pp. 144-5.
25 *Oxford University Sermons*, p. 313.
26 *Difficulties of Anglicans* II, pp. 86-7 and 52.
27 *The Letters and Diaries of John Henry Newman* XXI, p. 401; *Difficulties of Anglicans* II, p. 76.
28 *Difficulties of Anglicans* II, pp. 68-73.
29 *Apologia*, p. 231.
30 *Parochial and Plain Sermons* II, pp. 136-7.
31 *Discourses to Mixed Congregations*, pp. 374-6.
32 *Development of Christian Doctrine*, pp. 426 and 430.
33 *Difficulties of Anglicans* II, p. 93.
34 *Apologia*, p. 195.
35 *Difficulties of Anglicans* II, pp. 83-4.
36 *Lectures on Justification*, pp. 204 and 206.

Pope Pius XII and
the Blessed Virgin Mary

H.E. ARCHBISHOP H.E. CARDINALE, DD., J.C.D.

A strong personal relationship binds every true Christian to Christ with the over-riding aim that his Saviour may live and reign in his heart through faith, hope and charity. Thus rooted and grounded, he will have power with all the Saints to grasp the breadth and the length, the height and the depth of the love of Christ which surpasses all knowledge, and be filled with the fullness of God (Eph. 3.18-20).

The more he adheres to Christ, the more he will long to comprehend the unsearchable riches, the plan of the mystery hidden for ages in God and the manifold wisdom now to be made known even to the principalities and powers in heavenly places through the Church (Eph. 3.9-10). A Christian belonging to the Catholic tradition in the Roman allegiance will therefore turn instinctively for guidance to the Church. In her sacramental reality he will look for his Lord and Master. His search will not be in vain. As he seeks Christ, he finds him and adores him in his Mystical Body, where he lives and nourishes the faithful with his grace. He finds Christ and loves him in the Most Blessed Virgin Mary, Mother of God and of the Church, who bore the Son of the Eternal Father in the fullness of time "that we too might receive the adoption of sons" (Gal. 4.4-5). He finds Christ and obeys him in his Vicar, through whom he speaks and shepherds the people of God.

Pope Pius XII possessed in an eminent measure these three distinguishing marks so typical of a Catholic. His personal attachment to Christ was so real and apparent that it transfigured him in a way known only to those who had the honour of meeting him. This relationship sustained and guided him in his lofty responsibilities during one of the most trying periods of modern history. He sought and found Christ in all that was good and pure, and especially in his Mystical Body, in his Most Blessed Mother and in the office of Chief Pastor of the Church. From these three different realities, placed in the context of the Scriptures, and Tradition, he drew light in establishing the programme of his pontificate and strength in ensuring its realization.

"Pope Pius XII and the Blessed Virgin Mary" is the subject of this paper. He is often called the "Pope of Mary", and we shall try to see just how truly such a title is justified. Every pope, of course, could claim the same title. As Vicar of Christ, her Son, a pope cannot evade the influence of Mary, who surrounds him with her motherly care, enlightens him with her wisdom, and comforts him with her love. As Chief Bishop of the Church, he knows that Mary occupies a leading place among the members of the Mystical Body, who in various ways and degrees share in Christ's priestly mediation and kingly rule. As visible head of the Church he is aware of the typology of Mary with regard to the Church, which she once prefigured and on behalf of which she now exercises her role in the economy of salvation. She shines forth as a sign of sure hope and solace for the pilgrim People of God (*Lumen Gentium* ch. VIII).

Pius saw Mary playing her role in the great wedding of God and humanity in the sacrament of Christ and his Church (Eph. 5.21-23) in a most vivid manner. Hence with all right he can be called the "Pope of Mary" *par excellence*. His great love for the Mother of God urged him to delve into the hidden mysteries of the Church's treasure in order to elucidate the depths of Marian theology, intensify the fervour of Marian devotion and encourage the imitation of the Marian virtues. Mary for him was not an abstract of study, but a living person, highly favoured by God and powerfully intervening in our lives. He glorified her as Queen and Mother with a dogmatic definition, numerous addresses, new liturgical honours, and many moving prayers. It is dutiful for our Society to commemorate him as the "Pope of Mary" on the occasion of the thirtieth anniversary of his election to the Supreme Pontificate and the tenth anniversary of his death. And I am happy to be called upon to fulfil this duty, having been blessed by a close association with him during the last six years of his pontificate, when I served him as one of the privileged few admitted to his inner circle.

What were the guidelines followed by Pius in his study of the Blessed Virgin Mary? We have them from the Pope himself, as set forth in various documents. They are worth recalling in order to stress his theological approach to Mariology. His approach transcended the level of pious sentiment and was based on the solid ground of Scripture, tradition and history. Mariology, the Pope says, is not merely a separate dogmatic compartment in a structure without integration. It is part of the vital organism of theological mysteries in the midst of which Mary lives and moves, and from which she derives all her glory.

Since Mariology is included in the realm of theology it must first of all be based upon the solid foundation of theological doctrine. The more profound the investigation and the more accurately the truths of Mariology are compared and linked up with each other and with other truths of shared theology, the more necessary is this solid foundation. Research work even in mariological matters is safer and more rewarding to the extent that the Church's teaching authority is accepted by theologians who are called to investigate the deposit of the faith, as the immediate and universal standard of truth in matters of faith and morals. God has given this authority the duty to clarify and explain also those things that are contained in an obscure and implicit way in the deposit of faith.

In doing this work Scripture and Tradition must be carefully considered. The Old and New Testaments are filled with mystical portraits of the Virgin Mother. She is described there with lively colours either in prophecy or direct reference. The contents of the sacred books, however, must be explained properly by taking authentic traditions and the teaching authority of the Church into sufficient account. Positive theology cannot be considered as completely equivalent to historical sciences.

One must not ignore or make light of the teaching authority and the life and worship of the Church, as manifested over the course of the centuries, when investigating or explaining the documents of Tradition. Individual documents of antiquity, when considered only by themselves, sometimes give little enlightenment. But when put together and compared with the Church's liturgical life, and with the faith, devotion and piety of the Christian people, which the same teaching authority directs and sustains, they became magnificent testimonies for Catholic truth.

The Holy Spirit rules and guards the Church, and infallibly directs her to the knowledge of revealed truths not only in teaching and defining the faith, but also in regulating divine worship and in promoting the exercises of piety and devotion of God's people.

There has been much justified praise from all quarters for the clarity and balance which inspire the eighth chapter of conciliar constitution on the Church. It may be well to note in this connection that the presentation of Mary "as the foremost of all those who have shared in, and who still enrich the communion of Saints" (Dr. Albert C. Outler) and the necessary moderation required in the study of Mary, as put forward in that document, reflect Pius XII's own thoughts almost literally. The Pope, in fact, warns theologians and preachers to avoid straying from the right course by guarding against a twofold error. They must beware of unfounded opinions and exaggerated expressions which go beyond the truth. They must also watch for the excessive narrowness of mind of those who are filled with a kind of unreasonable fear of conceding more than they ought to the Blessed Virgin, as if they were withholding honour and confidence from the Divine Redeemer himself, when his Mother is honoured and invoked with filial reverence. (Pius XII's radio message of Oct. 24, 1954, and his encyclical "Ad Coeli Reginam", Oct. 11, 1954). Pius was no less anxious than the Council Fathers to stress that "as a descendant of Adam (Mary) has no privilege or grace which she does not owe to her Son, the Redeemer of the human race. Consequently, when we admire the Mother's eminent gifts and rightly praise them, we are admiring and praising the divinity, goodness, love and power of her Son." Indeed the Blessed Virgin is a member of the Church, but she is an entirely unique member.

Bearing these norms in mind and referring to the Pope's own word as faithfully as possible, we shall try briefly to sift from the Pope's impressive series of 1367 addresses, which he gave uninterruptedly for almost 20 years, some of his teachings regarding Mary, 1) in the theological perspective; 2) in relation to the Church; and 3) in relation to ourselves.

(1) Mary in the theological perspective

Pius XII's theological teaching regarding Mary may be included under a threefold heading: a) matters which have been already solemnly defined by the Church; b) a definition of his own; c) matters which have not been defined.

a) Matters which have already been defined

Among these the *divine motherhood* of Mary takes pride of place. Pius XII spoke of it as the source of all Mary's privileges, the origin of all her glories and the key to all her riches. But he did not see the divine motherhood as a static honour conferred on her by God for the sole purpose of giving birth to the Incarnate Word. He saw it rather as a personal dynamic and permanent relationship which began at the Incarnation and will continue for evermore, embracing the whole body of Christ, individual and mystical, as we shall explain later on.

From her union with Christ as his Mother, Mary attains a radiant eminence transcending that of any other creature. She receives the royal right to dispose of the treasures of the Divine Redeemer's Kingdom and she derives the inexhaustible efficacy of her maternal intercession before the Son of the Eternal Father ("Fulgens Corona").

Because of her divine motherhood, Mary, after Christ, not only possesses the highest degree of excellence and perfection but also shares in that influence with which her Son reigns over the minds and wills of men. For if the Divine Word performs miracles and gives graces through the humanity which he received from his Mother, and if he uses his sacraments and saints as instruments for the salvation of men, why should he not make use also of the role and work of his most holy Mother in imparting to us the fruits of redemption?

Mary responds generously to the mission God entrusted her with to be at once Mother of his Son and of all mankind. For she has no other desire but to lead men to Christ, and to introduce them to the heart of the central mystery of Christianity, that of redemption. She continues to give us the Son she brought into the world and to gather the whole family of Christ around the mystic Bread, symbol of unity, of peace and of the eternal joy of heaven (Radio Address to the Belgian National Marian Congress, Sept. 5th, 1954).

All she asks of us is to aspire to perfect Christian maturity of faith and fortitude, to assume full responsibility before God for our own moral lives, to have recourse to her motherly care, and to imitate her own intrepid readiness in obeying the voice of God.

If all Christians honoured and imitated their sublime Queen and Mother, concludes the Pope, they would realize that they are truly brothers. Then thrusting aside all envy and avarice, they would promote love among classes, respect the rights of the weak, and cherish peace. For to be a son of Mary, one must be like her, just, gentle and pure, and show a sincere desire for true brotherhood, whose aim it is not to harm and injure, but rather to help and comfort one's brethren ("Fulgens Corona").

It was precisely in view of her divine motherhood that Mary was proclaimed "full of grace" by the Angel, who set no restriction to the time and amount of that grace. The dogma of the *Immaculate Conception*, defined in 1854 by Pius IX and commemorated in 1954 by a Marian Year proclaimed by Pius XII, affirms no more nor less than this. Pius XII very often returns to the truth contained in this definition of the Immaculate Conception, which he sees as a prelude to all the glory that God could bestow on her at the incarnation of his Son. That the Mother of God was spotlessly pure from the first instant of her conception in no way restricts or belittles the universal range of Christ's redemption, by which men are delivered from the fatal consequences of original sin, and restored to divine friendship. For it was the same Saviour, her Son, who through the merits of his future sacrifice bestowed on Mary the singular grace and privilege of being redeemed in a more excellent manner by preserving her immune from all stain of original sin. Pius is well aware of the fact that many Christians, who are not of the Catholic tradition, find it difficult to accept this doctrine, because of their different approach to the problem of original sin. He therefore lays much stress on Mary's absolute integrity and perfect holiness, which has always been emphasized by the Eastern Churches. They do not hesitate to call Mary the *Panagia*—or the All-Holy—and to multiply liturgical services and feasts in her honour. The early Fathers of the Church teach that Mary's state of grace makes her holier than the Cherubim and the Seraphim. It fills her with so much holiness as to place her above all the Saints and to make limitless the difference between God's other servants and his Mother. One wonders then what other alternative is left to the human mind but to accept the doctrine of the Immaculate Conception in the clear terms of its definition? Some of its opponents often make little effort to understand this doctrine, perturbed as they are at the exercise of papal authority which the definition itself implies.

b) A definition of his own

The culminating point of the pontificate of Pius XII was undoubtedly the proclamation of *the dogma of the bodily Assumption of Our Lady into heaven*. By this act, in which the charism of papal infallibility was exercised for the first time since the First Vatican Council, the Pope integrated and gave significance to all the achievements of his pontificate. He brought himself to this definition in no light manner. He invoked the sure guidance of the Spirit of Truth by unceasing prayer and study, and consulted all the Catholic Bishops of the world. The original initiative of the definition was not his own. It came from the First Vatican Council (1870). In fact, after the proclamation of the dogma of the Immaculate Conception, the Holy See had been besieged with petitions for the definition of the dogma of the Assumption of Our Lady. Not a few Fathers gathered at Vatican One had made the same request of Pius IX. Since then and until the year 1941 the definition had been formally petitioned by 113 Cardinals, over 300 Archbishops and Bishops, some 32,000 priests and brothers, 50,000 religious women and more than 8,000,000 laymen. On May 1st, 1946—four years before the actual definition—a questionnaire was sent to all the Bishops of the Catholic Church, inquiring whether they, their clergy and their people judged that the bodily Assumption of the Blessed Virgin Mary could be proposed and defined as a dogma of faith. The reply was almost unanimously favourable to the definition. "Thus from the universal consent of the ordinary magisterium of the Church a certain and firm argument" was drawn in favour of the definition. In his apostolic constitution "Munificentissimus Deus" (Nov. 1st, 1950) Pius recalled the various testimonies, indications and traces of this accepted faith of the Church through the course of the centuries from the most remote periods. The belief of the faithful, the liturgy, the feast in the Western Church, the witness of the Eastern and Western Fathers and of the Doctors of the Church, the constant belief of the Church in a truth which was prefigured in the Scriptures, all this put together, served to build up a formidable and irrefutable argument in behalf of the definition. From all this evidence it is clear, therefore, that Catholics are not asked to believe in the Assumption because it has been defined; but that it has been defined because they had constantly believed in it.

Some of the terms of the definition are however studiously vague. They do not touch on the question of Mary's terrestrial end at all, but simply state that she was assumed when her earthly life was finished. Though not considering belief in the Assumption necessary for salvation, the well known Anglican theologian Dr. Eric L. Mascall admits that if it had to be defined, it could not have been done in more satisfactory terms.

Why then was it defined? Pius thought of the Church as something essentially dynamic, under the constant impulse of the Holy Spirit, who, as Christ had promised, would lead it into all truth (Jn. 16, 13) and preserve it from error (Mat. 16, 18). The Church therefore was to become progressively aware of the truths concealed in the "treasures of wisdom and knowledge that are hidden in Christ" (Col. 2, 3). Hence a dogmatic definition is not to be considered as an addition to the original deposit of faith that was committed by our Lord to the Apostles, but as an authoritative recognition—effected at the special time designed by the Holy Spirit—one of the many riches it contains. A static

253

concept of the Church, which does not move "as the Spirit blows wherever it wills" (Jn. 3, 18) is not a living body but a corpse. In proclaiming the dogma of the Assumption, Pius XII explained what he hoped would result from this definition. He said: "We have placed our pontificate under the special patronage of the Most Holy Virgin, to whom we have had recourse so often in times of grave trouble. We, who in public ceremonies have consecrated the entire human race to the Immaculate Heart and have time and again experienced her powerful protection, are confident that this solemn proclamation of the Assumption will contribute in no small way to the advantage of human society, since it redounds to the glory of the Most Blessed Trinity to which the Mother of God was united by singular bonds." He trusts that the definition will offer to the Church, rocked by adversity and threatened with tempest, another sure pledge of hope; to the faithful a glorious example of the full reward given in anticipation to a humble creature, whose whole life was dedicated to fulfilling the will of the Heavenly Father and to caring for the welfare of others; and to all men a solemn reminder of that deep respect we should feel for human life, having God destined both body and soul to such a lofty goal. Briefly, while increasing our devotion towards such an exalted member of the human race, faith in Mary's Assumption should make "our belief in the resurrection both stronger and more active", and prompt us to live good Christian lives.

c) Matters which have not been defined

Pius XII touched on a whole series of matters pertaining to Our Lady, which have not been defined and most likely never will be, but on which Catholics have concentrated much piety and thought over the centuries. These teachings are so numerous that we must be selective. All of them ultimately find their foundation in the principle of the divine motherhood and are directed to the glory of God.

Such is the *Queenship of Mary*, for the liturgical observance of which he set aside a special feastday to be kept on May 31st. He wrote a whole encyclical letter on the royal dignity of the Blessed Virgin Mary and the institution of her feast ("Ad Coeli Reginam", Oct. 11th, 1954). In it he explains that he is not introducing a new truth, since the title and the arguments on which Mary's queenly dignity are based have already been clearly set forth. They are found in the ancient document of the Church, in the books of sacred liturgy, in the testimony of the Fathers and the traditions of the Christian people. In all times and places, when Christianity was still undivided, and especially in the British Isles, Mary was greeted as the Queen of the World, the Queen of all creatures and the Sovereign of the Universe. The principal argument upon which Mary's royal dignity is based is beyond doubt her divine motherhood. She is a Queen because she bore a Son who, at the very moment of his conception, on account of the hypostatic union of his human nature with the Word, was also as man King and Lord of all things. So with complete justice St. John Damascene could write: "When she became Mother of the Creator, she freely became Queen of every creature." Mary's queenship is not a purely exterior and political attribute. It is a "supernatural reality which at the same time penetrates man's innermost heart and touches all that is spiritual and immortal in his very essence."

The role assigned to *Mary as Co-Redemptrix and Mediatrix of all graces*, is another of those ancient themes which were dear to Pius XII. Since the second century the Fathers of the Church spoke of Mary's part in the plan of redemption and, at least implicitly, of the dispensation of divine grace. They described the Virgin Mary as the new Eve, most intimately associated with the New Adam in the conflict of Satan. It is she who conceived the Saviour of the world, and the redemption of all. Through her divine motherhood Adam was delivered from his servitude and the heavenly powers were reconciled with the mortals.

Without speaking 'ex cathedra', popes of more recent times have dealt with these prerogatives of Mary in a more detailed manner, as they delved into the hidden treasures of the Church, especially since Pius IX concluded his constitution "Ineffabilis Deus" (1854) with an invocation of Mary as Conciliatrix and Mediatrix of the human race.

But while Mary is given the title of Mediatrix with no hesitation, one gathers the impression that papal documents are rather cautious about the use of the title Co-Redemptrix, though fully endorsing the truth expressed by that term. With regard to the use of this word, on June 26, 1913, the Congregation of the Holy Office praised the practice of adding to the name of Jesus the name "of his Mother, the Blessed Virgin Mary, as our Co-Redemptrix". Some six months later (January 22, 1914) it enriched with an indulgence a prayer in which the Blessed Virgin Mary was referred to as "Co-Redemptrix of the human race". Nevertheless, in my study of papal documents of the above mentioned period, I was able to find the term used only once and that was at the close of the celebration of the Holy Year (1933) when Pius XI invoked Mary publicly under the title of Co-Redemptrix.

In the concluding prayer of his encyclical on the Queenship of Mary (1954) Pius XII beautifully summarised the doctrine of Mary's mediation and her role in redemption. There is no doubt, he says, that only Jesus Christ, God and Maker, is King in the full, correct, and absolute sense of the word; but at the same time Mary shares also in that royal dignity, although by analogy in a limited degree. The Mother of God partakes both passively and actively in her Son's work of redemption in his struggle against his enemies and in the triumph which he has obtained over them all. The salvific effect of Christ's work of redemption, accomplished once and forever, continues to be applied to the end of time. Likewise Our Lady's cooperation in the redemption is not restricted to her past association with her Son, but goes on, as she

255

continues to live and rule with him in heaven, for the benefit of men of all times. But in all his utterances about Mary's mediatory and co-redemptive role, Pius XII was eager to stress that Christ alone is the Redeemer in the full extent of the term, that Marian mediation is not added to that of the "Unus Mediator", but participates in it. She is Mediatrix not so much *with* the Mediator as *in* him and *through* him. Hence it is "*per Mariam ad Jesum,*" *through Mary to Jesus,* and not *to Mary* as a term in herself that the faithful should approach the problem of their personal salvation. It is interesting to note that Pius XII, speaking officially of Mary's association with Christ and his redemption, never attributed to her the title of Co-Redemptrix. He wished thus to avoid all misunderstanding about the absolute oneness of Christ's redemptive action.

2) Mary's relationship to the Church

Our understanding of Mary's role in relation to the Church is much clearer today than it was in the past, thanks to the right direction authoritatively given to Marian theology by the Second Vatican Council. In fact chapter VIII on "The role of the Blessed Virgin Mary, Mother of God, in the mystery of Christ and the Church" was appended to the constitution on the Church, and not promulgated as a separate document according to the original plan. This was a deliberate action, and not the result of mere chance. The guidance of the Holy Spirit was evident at the time when the vote was taken at the Council. The balance which we note in that chapter between the tendency to emphasize Mary's unique connexion with Christ the Redeemer on one side and with the Church and all the redeemed on the other is easily detected in Pius XII's teachings on Our Lady.

These may be summarized as follows: Mary is the Mother of the Mystical Body. The source of this prerogative is the divine motherhood with which Mary was favoured by God above all creatures. The Word made flesh from her own flesh is also the Redeemer of mankind. As God Man, born of Mary, he acquired an individual body. As Redeemer of the human race he acquired a spiritual and mystical body, which is the Church, or the great gathering of those who believe in Christ. Through the same human nature he assumed from the Virgin Mary he became the Saviour of mankind. "Today," said the Angels to the shepherds, "there is born to you a Saviour" (Lk. 2.11). Thus Mary bore with her Son Jesus, the Saviour, all those whose lives were contained in his life, as "members of his body, made from his flesh and bones" (Eph. 5.30). "Mother of the head of the Mystical Body, Mary is also Mother of the members of Christ, who are we," says St. Augustine (de S. Virginitate, c.6). As Mother of God and of mankind, Mary undoubtedly makes every effort that Christ "the head of his body, the Church" (Col. 1.18) should infuse his gifts into us, his members, so that we may above all come to know him, love him and "live by him" (1. Jn. 4.9).

Pius's Marian doctrine on this point is beautifully summed up in the concluding prayer of his encyclical on the Mystical Body (June 29, 1943). There he says: "It was she who gave miraculous birth to Christ our Lord, adorned already in her virginal womb with the dignity of Head of the Church, and so brought forth the source of all heavenly life; and it was she who presented Him, the new-born Prophet, King and Priest, to those of the Jews and Gentiles who first came to adore Him. It was in answer to her motherly prayer 'in Cana of Galilee' that her Only-begotten worked the miracle by which 'his disciples believed in him.' She it was who, immune from all sin, personal or inherited and ever most closely united with her Son, offered Him on Golgotha to the Eternal Father together with the holocaust of her maternal rights and motherly love, like a new Eve, for all the children of Adam contaminated through his unhappy fall. Thus she, who was the mother of our Head according to the flesh, became by a new title of sorrow and glory the spiritual mother of all His members. She too it was by her most powerful intercession obtained for the newborn Church the prodigious Pentecostal outpouring of that Spirit of the divine Redeemer who had already been given on the Cross. She, finally, true Queen of Martyrs, by bearing with courageous and confident heart her immense weight of sorrows, more than all Christians 'filled up those things that are wanting of the sufferings of Christ, for His Body, which is the Church'; and upon the mystical Body of Christ, born of the broken Heart of the Saviour, she bestowed the same motherly care and fervent love with which she fostered and nurtured the suckling infant Jesus in the cradle."

Mary our Mother and our Mother the Church are linked together by a mysterious bond. Pius XII elaborated on this rapprochment in many of his speeches. He teaches, that as Mary brought forth nourished and raised the child Jesus with motherly care until he became a perfect man, so through baptism the Church gives birth to souls which are thus admitted to a mysterious sharing of the divine nature; nourishes them with the grace of the sacrament so that they may become "fully mature with the fullness of Christ himself" (Eph. 4,13); and stands at their side to help them all through their lives. Thus the Church and Mary are bound together as type and archetype according to the very ancient tradition which St. Ambrose appears to have been the first to record.

Mary realized in her own person the Church of the redeemed, experiencing in anticipation what the Church and its members will come to experience later. In this light one can more readily understand and accept the truth contained in the definitions of the Immaculate Conception and the Assumption. Accordingly Mary is redeemed in an excellent manner at the first moment of her conception, but always through the merits of her Son, from the wound of original sin. At the end she becomes the eschatological image of the Church in being configured to Christ in his death and resurrection, as all true believers are destined to be after the resurrection of the body and final judgment.

Mary played an important part in the life of the Church which in a way pre-existed in her from the beginning: at the Annunciation when she pronounced her humble "Fiat"; at the birth of Christ and his early trials; at the quiet life of Nazareth; at Cana and all through his public life; at the foot of the Cross and in the Cenacle at Jerusalem. Since the Pentecost she collaborated with the Holy Spirit in the mission of the Church, comforting and sustaining the faithful, who were aware of this, as witnessed by the paintings of her in the catacombs and the churches dedicated to her name. Her readiness to intercede for the Church in times of stress won her the title of Help of Christians and Queen of Victories. The history of the victories of the Church, says the Pope, is the history of the victories of Mary. To love Mary, then is to love the Church; and to love the Church is to love Mary, of whom she is, as he said speaking in a poetical vein, "*la divina Pastora*", the true import of which he explains by adding "*Madre comune e universale dei credenti*"—"the divine Shepherdess, common and universal Mother of the faithful"

As such, Mary is also centre of unity in the divided Christian family. She entreats us all to scrutinize more attentively the mystery of the one Church of her Son and leads us into the even deeper mystery of the one God in the Father, Son and Holy Ghost, reflected in the unity of the Church, by making us live more fully the life of the Mystical Body, which is the life of Christ. (Addresses to the Marian Congregations, April 26th, 1958, and to the Genoese pilgrimage, April 21st, 1940. Encyclical "Mystici Corporis").

3) Mary in relation to ourselves

Pius XII was eager to share with us his contemplation of the prerogatives of the Blessed Virgin; but he did not wish us to remain passive and inert in admiring them. Mary is not a lifeless figure, however beautiful, to be placed in a niche, surrounded by candles and incense. She is a living human being, a vital link between God and man. Her function, as we have already seen, consists in the special mission entrusted to her by God to lead all men to the knowledge, love and service of her Divine Son.

One of the great aims of Pius's pontificate was to bring about *a deep Christian renewal* in the world. This theme returns over and over again as a leit-motiv in his addresses, especially when speaking of Mary. If Christianity is life, growth and renewal in Christ, Christian life, growth and renewal come to us with the special help of Mary. "Devotion to Mary is the most abundant source of the renewal of Christian life". Divine Providence has seen fit to initiate this revival even in the darkest hours of materialism in the world. To bring it about, we must follow the teachings of the Gospel, and Mary offers us a striking and salutary example of their observance.

Renewal, of which today there is much talk as if it were one of our proud insights into the needs of the world, depends above all—in Pius's own words—on the interior renewal of Christendom itself "for only from Christian virtues may we hope to see the course of history take its proper orderly direction." Mary's motherly influence is "capable of remedying the world's ills, freeing it from its anguish and leading it toward the way of salvation." If we allow it to penetrate into our most intimate thoughts, she will strengthen our weak and infirm nature and bring it with herself to the level of the divine. But Mary does not change us by changing the world around us: rather she changes the world around us by first changing our inner lives if we invoke her help.

Christian renewal, then, to be effective, must shun externalism and superficialism, and concentrate on the interior consecration of the whole being to Christ. This is an arduous enterprise, but we need not despair. God has given us his Mother to be our example and our aid. She is above all an example of inner holiness and this is the source of her true glory and power. Mary's inner holiness is the result of the action of God himself. Finding her willing to cooperate with his grace, he took possession of her soul through a series of incomprehensible mysteries. Hence the Pope emphasizes the inner sanctity of the "*Virgo Sacrata*"—"the Holy Virgin"—even more than her most noble acts of virtue, which were its outward sign. In her inner holiness the mystery of Christ shines forth in its highest realization. Thus the Immaculate Conception is, in simple terms, Mary's full possession of holiness from the first moment of her existence. The Assumption is her complete and permanent association with the infinite holiness of God himself. It is to the attainment of inner and personal sanctity that Mary calls her children as they struggle against the powers of darkness in this vale of tears. (The encyclicals "Munificentissimus Deus", "Fulgens Corona", "Ad Coeli Reginam", and most of Pius XII's Marian addresses touch on the theme of renewal).

Conclusion

The concision of this essay and the limited time at our disposal have allowed us to do but little justice to Pope Pius XII's magisterium concerning the Blessed Virgin Mary. But I should feel less guilty if, with all its deficiencies, this paper has in some measure reached its aim. That was to show how seriously the Pope approached the subject of Mary and how much we too should strive better to know, love and imitate the Mother of God.

The well known 15th century ballad quoted by Pius XII to the Catholic soldiers of the British Isles, when they presented him with a beautiful figure of Our Lady of Walsingham in 1947, speaks of the shrine where "grace is dayly shewyd to men of every age". We of the Ecumenical Society of the Blessed Virgin Mary have no doubt that Mary still looks down with maternal love on these Islands and gives to those who turn to her, to use the Pope's own words, "a heavenly peace, born of childlike faith, which heals the heart and draws the veil from the vision of pure, unending joy." (H. M. Gillett, *Walsingham*, London, 1950, pp. 76-79).

VIII
DEVOTIONAL

Devotion to the Blessed Virgin at once raises the subject of intercessory prayer to the saints, and to her as greatest of all the saints. For Catholics, there has been an unbroken tradition of such intercession; for the Reformed Churches, it has been one of those issues that characterised their theology—that they insisted that there is but one mediator between God and man, Jesus Christ. Both traditions are reconcilable. Devotion also raises the subject of the Marian shrines throughout the world, of which surely the greatest is at Lourdes in the South of France: it is fitting, then, to end with a paper upon that great event which began in 1858, four years after the definition of the doctrine of the Immaculate Conception, and continues today and tomorrow.

The first lecture was given to the Society in London on 25 November 1969 by a member of the Epworth Press. He had already contributed to the Society's first publication (together with Dom Ralph Russell and Canon John de Satgé) with a paper entitled 'The Methodist point of view'. He has since become an Executive Co-Chairman of the Society.

The second lecture was given to the Society's Oxford branch in September 1978 by the Housemistress of Belmont Abbey School, Herefordshire. She had previously been engaged in work for the Red Cross. She is a Catholic.

Intercession

REV. GORDON S. WAKEFIELD, M.A., B.Litt.

Never was there an age in which Christians were so certain that if we are to pray at all we must pray for others and for mankind in its incessant torments and troubles; yet never was there an age in which Christians were less certain that their praying has any direct influence on what happens to others or to the course of history.

Let us begin by looking at the place and content of intercession in the various liturgical forms of Christendom. An Anglican scholar, E. C. Whitaker, in an invaluable little study of *The Intercessions of the Prayer Book*,[1] goes so far as to say that 'the Christian Sacrifice has never been offered up without prayer on behalf of all humanity'. Justin Martyr (c.150 or 160) in describing a primitive Eucharist says 'We send up prayers' and it is clear from his account of the Baptismal Lord's Supper that these were prayers for all men—'for themselves, for the newly baptised and for all men everywhere'. A little later Tertullian, from North Africa, writes that, at the Christian assemblies, prayers were made 'for the emperor and all in authority, for the condition of the world, for peace and for delay of the end of all things'. (This last seem strangely different from the earlier Christian liturgical cry 'Our Lord come!'). In Tertullian's treatise on Prayer, Christians are said to pray for their persecutors, for the departed, for the sick, the possessed and for prisoners.

The form of intercession was often a Litany with its succession of responses of many voices to one, rising and falling like the waves of the sea. Litanies are very ancient and probably derive from the synagogue. They give the people a continuous vocal part in prayer and are incompatible with the notion that worship is merely the performance of an individual leader however prophetic. Intercessions, above all, should be made the people's own.

The Liturgy of St. John Chrysostom, the normal rite of the Orthodox Churches, begins with a Great Litany, which has also been adapted for the Church of South India, though it occurs there at another place in the service:

Deacon: Bless, Master.
Priest (aloud): Blessed is the Kingdom of the Father and of the Son, and of the
      Holy Ghost; now, and always and world without end.
Choir: Amen.
Deacon: In peace let us pray to the Lord.
Choir: Lord have mercy.
For the peace that is from above, and for the salvation of our souls, let us pray to the Lord.

Lord have mercy

For the peace of the whole world, for the well-being of the holy Churches of God, and for the unity of them all, let us pray to the Lord ... and so on, for 'this holy house', for bishops and clergy, for kings and governments and armies, for cities and countries, for healthful seasons, for travellers, for the sick and the captives; and all in remembrance of Mary and the Saints.

The Orthodox liturgy is not content with this great comprehensive intercession at the start. The Western mind would give intercession its place in worship and get it over, passing on with due discipline to one of the other necessary elements. But the Eastern mind weaves each into a rich and variegated tapestry of bewildering colour and the shades repeat themselves in different parts of the whole. Or, to put it another way, the Eastern Church, having prayed for the world, does not forget but looks back constantly and makes intercession part of a continuing action with lesser Litanies every now and then interspersed.

The old Roman Mass was probably deficient in Intercessions, which is one reason why it has been reformed. But it did thrust them into the Canon—the solemn ritual of consecration—as though to bring them to the very heart of the sacramental mystery and presence of Christ. Thomas Cranmer in the Prayer Book of 1552 put the Intercession after the Offertory, partly to play down the latter, which, remember, was associated with the preparation of the bread and wine (the making ready of the sacrificial victim in medieval typology) rather than with finance. All the same, a good homiletical point can be made of it as Neville Ward does in *The Use of Praying*.[2] We offer not only our gifts and ourselves but 'the Church militant here in earth'. Perhaps this is a little restrictive unless one glosses it with the Maurician idea that through Christ all men are in some sense in the Church. But the Prayer Book also has Cranmer's stupendous, if somewhat dirge-like, Litany and Peter Gunning's *Prayer for All Sorts and Conditions of Men*.

The Protestant reformers and their Puritan successors thought the order of prayer important. William Gouge a Puritan who wrote in 1627, says that we should pray for people in the order in which we love them and this ought to be (note it well):

First, the saints i.e. the Church.
Second, Ministers of the Crown and Magistrates!
Third, Personal friends and families especially husbands and wives.
Fourth, Strangers i.e. 'all sorts …'
Fifth, Enemies. (Prayer for these Isaac Watts was later to call 'a noble singularitie of our religion'.)

Intercession constituted a problem for the Calvinist, a great case of conscience. Is it possible to pray for all men? The attempt to answer this led to some subtle distinctions in order that charity might prevail over logic. William Perkins, a Cambridge Puritan under Elizabeth I, concluded 'We may if all men or all mankind be taken distributively or severally. For there is no particular country, kingdome, towne, person but we may make prayers for it ... and though men bee devils incarnate, yet for anything we know they may belong to the election of God; except they sin against the Holy Ghost, which sin is very seldom and very hardly discerned of men ... We may not pray for all men if all men or all mankind be taken collectively, that is if all men be considered wholly together as they make one body or company and be taken as we say in grosse. For in this body or mass of mankind there be some whom God in his last judgment hath refused, whose salvation, by prayer, shall never be obtained'. William Gouge says that 'the ground of prayer is the judgement of charity, not certainty'. Even the Pope, as a man, may be prayed for! He quotes with approval the petition of Cranmer's Litany 'that it may please thee to have mercy upon *all* men'.[3]

There are still Christians who would regard such wrestling with conscience as more than the scrupulosity of devotion to a God less compassionate than men. I am not sure that the doctrine of election has by any means run its course yet. Racialism, the population explosion and technocracy may revive it in secular forms even if exclusive brands of Christianity do not prove to have more missionary success than the Catholic. But in the descendants of the major confessions, such doctrine is entirely out of fashion. The new Anglican and Methodist orders of Communion have large intercessions. The theological problems of prayer are very different for most of us from what they were for Calvinists.

There are, however, some details to be limned, in what we have perfunctorily sketched. By its stress on intercession in its public worship and in the central mystery of the Eucharist, the Church throughout the ages has recognised that prayer for the world and the needs of mankind is too great a burden for individuals to carry; indeed it may be too great a burden for the Church, hence the placing of intercessions in the eucharistic action which commemorates what God in Christ does and has done. But in all the liturgies we see the Church as a grand co-operative society, whose members exist to help each other and the world. And prayer is offered in the company not only of the visible fellowship and the unseen congregations far round the world but:

> Remembering our most holy, most pure, most blessed and glorious Lady, the Mother of God and ever-virgin Mary, with all the Saints, let us commend ourselves, and one another, and all our life to Christ our God.

In this co-operative society, the humblest shareholder has place and his intercessions rank equally with the celebrant's or preacher's. Ronald Knox put this, inimitably, in one of his sermons to schoolgirls about the old Latin Mass. In that part of the Canon called the Commemoration of the Living, the priest is allowed to think of the people for whose needs he personally wants this Mass to be an availing sacrifice.

265

I ask God to convert Stalin or whatever it may be. And immediately after that I go on to say *et omnium circumstantium*: "Please don't think I want you to listen to *me* more than to any of those horrible little creatures who are fidgeting behind me. *Quorum tibi fides cognita est, et nota devotio*—they do really believe in you, they are really quite pious, some of them, and each of them has her own intention that she's thinking about at this moment and it's just as good as mine. So please take it that this goes for Mary Jane's intention as well as mine. *Proquibus tibi offerimus;* I am offering this sacrifice for them just as much as for myself. *Vel qui tibi offerunt*, and they just as much as myself, are *offering* this Mass, so please don't convert Stalin if you would sooner convert Mary Jane's aunt. ···[4]

This sense is not as lacking from the Protestant tradition as one might expect. Some diaries and writings of the seventeenth and eighteenth centuries show an amazing familiarity with the saints in the household of God and give evidence of faith in a partnership of prayer which unites Abraham and the patriarchs to the leaders of the local congregation. Richard Baxter's hymn, *He wants no friends that hath thy love*, was written with the dispersed dissenting congregations in mind after the repressive laws of 1662. They who had once met together to worship God are scattered and assemble under grievous restrictions and not without danger, but:

In the communion of the saints
Is wisdom, safety and delight
And when my heart declines and faints,
It's raised by their heat and light!

As for my friends, they are not lost;
The several vessels of Thy fleet,
Though parted now, by tempests tost,
Shall safely in the haven meet.

In 1681, Baxter's wife, Margaret died. Almost thirty years younger than himself, she had been a sweet and restraining influence on his controversial temper and as close and congenial a companion as a man could wish. Now this hymn took on a deeper meaning: and the fellowship of those separated by earthly vicissitudes was affirmed beyond the gulf of death:

Still we are centred all in Thee
Members, though distant, of one Head,
In the same family we be,
By the same faith and spirit led.

Before Thy throne we daily meet,
As joint petitioners to Thee;
In spirit we each other greet,
And shall again each other see.

God has given us our friends and fellow-Christians to pray with us and for us and it is artificial to regard death any more than life as

266

making this impossible. Catholic and Orthodox Christians ascribe to Mary a supreme and for some Protestants embarrassing place in this community of prayer because she is seen as the first member of the Church, the link between the old Covenant and the new, bestowed on us by Christ with all the other saints to be our helpers and comrades in His Body the Church.

It would seem illogical to rule out prayer *to* the saints, if we accept prayer with them. Maurice Nédoncelle in his very important book on *The Nature and Use of Prayer* has shown that prayer may be from man to man and much of our conversation with other people is prayer. This may lead to idolatry, though properly understood, it could save us from that very danger.

> Prayer between human beings has a permanent place in any Christian teaching on prayer, that is, if it is true that the commandment to love our neighbour is akin to that of loving God. Its special place is in intercession and sacrifice ... is it not true that prayer between human beings is one of the possible climaxes of divine charity, and that it is the latter that confers its full value on the former? Is it not in the movement by which human prayer acquires its highest quality that it is led to discover its origins and horizons in God? Goethe felt this transition very keenly in that crisis of love which has left us the *Marienbad Elegy*: "In the pure centre of our soul there stirs the desire to give ourselves spontaneously and thankfully to some higher purer being, unknown to us, a desire decoding for itself the eternally unnamed being. This feeling we call piety. This is the blessed height I feel I have attained when I stand before her." (i.e. his beloved)[5]

But there is a liturgical form which though constantly repeated is no abra-cadabra nor empty convention but which at once serves as a safeguard from error and epitomises the whole theology of Christian prayer. It is customary to end 'through Jesus Christ our Lord'. We have the communion of the saints, living and departed, in Christ. It is through him, because of what he has done to overcome death and all that it means, to change the balance of spiritual forces in the universe, that we have a true relationship to one another wherever we are and may continue that conversation which is not only a mutual self-giving, a disclosure and a sharing of personalities, but a vast activity to carry on the work of love which he began. He is the one mediator, but in and through him we have all the saints too.

This, however, is not all. The perversions of belief in the communion of saints and their partnership in prayer are rightly seen to assail the uniqueness of Christ, to cast doubts on his adequacy, to imply that he is so intransigent and vengeful that we need Mary and the rest to plead for us with him. This makes nonsense of everything that has ever been understood by the Christian gospel. But sometimes our talk of the intercession of Christ himself may drive a wedge between the persons of the Godhead and depict Jesus as the one whose prayers and sacrifice are necessary to soften the heart and turn away the wrath of an implacable Father.

There is a well-known picture of Philippa of Hainault, Queen of Edward III, on her knees before the stern and angry king as she begs him to spare the lives of the condemned burghers of Calais, the ropes already round their necks. Medieval artists were as haunted by that scene as I, who have never forgotten it from *Highroads of History* forty-odd years ago. When they painted the Blessed Virgin, the Queen of Heaven, who prays for sinners, they give her Queen Philippa's face. But it is not only the thought of Mary interceding with a reluctant Jesus which is incompatible with Christianity, to regard Jesus himself as such an intercessor with a God whom he has to cajole and almost blackmail into mercy, is equally heretical. Rather we approach God 'through Jesus Christ our Lord' because in him there is the Divine fullness and the complete revelation of all that God is. The intercession of Jesus means simply that God himself is for us. This is clear from the great passage in the eighth chapter of Romans in which St Paul talks of Jesus who makes intercession for us, or, as the New English Bible has it 'pleads our cause'. The section begins 'If God is on our side, who is against us?' The intercession of Christ is the evidence that God loves us and supports us and wants to bring us into conversation with him and a relationship with one another that gives us overwhelming victory over all evil.

The starting point of Intercession is that great service from which our ancient examples were mostly drawn. Our prayers for one another and the world have their validity 'through Jesus Christ our Lord', as they are related to what he has done. The Eucharist is our remembrance of and our thanksgiving for this. And as we share in it we are caught up into the eternal activity of God's love in Christ.

But there is still more to be said. Intercession may now be defined as our co-operation with men and with God in a work which however perfectly seen in Jesus is not yet extended throughout the universe, or indeed to the heights and depths of our own being and therefore is still unfinished. This means that we may have to refine our notions both of the omnipotence and the impassibility of God, of what we understand by his power and his relationship to suffering. Both the belief that he is all-powerful and that he does not suffer are necessary in some form but only with many qualifications if we are at once to retain our Christianity and have a religion which is true to experience. What we are sometimes tempted to forget is that the Christian doctrine of the Incarnation means that God has limited himself, though the classical theologians have seen his self-limitation as the supreme act of his omnipotence; only the all-powerful can so limit himself as to become the all-loving too. Be that as it may, the God whom we see is the Christ on the Cross, the one whose agony in the garden and cry of forsakeness echo the groaning and travail of the whole creation and whose power will be revealed only at the end. Similarly the belief the God is impassable, does not suffer, safeguards the truth of his changelessness and of his Godhead. As David Jenkins has said,[6] nothing can put him off being God! It also assures us that God is not forever locked in the darkness and frustration of a cosmic Good Friday. But if his reality is love, and his unchangeability consists in this, then he must suffer. When Baron von Hügel attempted to resolve the dilemma by saying that while God could not suffer he did sympathise he was hoist with his own petard, for what is sympathy but 'suffering with'?[7] We understand more clearly perhaps than some of our predecessors that 'only a suffering God can help'. In some ways it is the result of the slow penetration of our religious thought by what Luther called the theology of the Cross rather than the theology of glory. Intercession is therefore further defined in Bonhoeffer's words as sharing the suffering of God in the world and kneeling beside Christ in Gethsemane.

Intercession does have an immediate effect especially if it is recognised as a corporate and eucharistic act before ever it is a personal and private one. To pray for our enemies is often the beginning of reconciliation. It can cast out hate. But it does need to be undertaken in the context of our recall of Christ and his forgiving death and probably also in the context of an attempt to discover more of the truth about the people and pressure-groups we dislike and to dare for some perilous moments to think as they think—perilous indeed if we are praying for enemies who happen to be the Klu-Klux-Klan!

One of G. K. Chesterton's Father Brown stories is called *The Hammer of God*. It tells of two brothers, the one a saintly parson, the other a libertine. The parson is always at his prayers, alone in his Church tower, but one morning he murders his brother by throwing down a hammer and crushing his skull. Father Brown solves what at first is a mystery because he knows the dangers of solitary prayer. Our fixations may become increased and if we seek to ascend to some high country of the spirit, we may take upon ourselves the vengeance of God. Christian prayer is not from a lofty tower by ourselves but as we kneel on the floor with other sinners. That is profoundly true and has been demonstrated in more than one tragedy of real life.

Yet sometimes there will be solitariness and struggle and to intercede will be like wrestling with God. Kierkegaard said 'True prayer is a struggle with God and man emerges victorious when God is the victor'. He was obviously thinking of the Old Testament myth of Wrestling Jacob, but, as Nédoncelle comments 'At the same time the combat is not so much to overcome God as to overcome ourselves by allowing him to convince us that we are understood by him'.[8] Friedrich Heiler's distinction between mystical and prophetic prayer is too sharp,[9] and yet there is a prayer which is not serene acceptance of the Divine will or for that matter gloomy submission or cheerful, triumphalist activism ('Thy will be *done* hurrah!'). An *intercession* in antiquity was an action by which an official could protest against or veto something which he deplored. It amazes me that in our time the *avant-garde* have not hailed this derivation with the glee they evinced when they realised that liturgy meant 'people's work'! Intercession is *protest* and it certainly was when the prophets argued with God and complained of his deceptions and injustice, when Jeremiah and Job and the Psalmists almost raised clenched fists to heaven or banners with slogans of doubt. There are those called to prayer for whom it will mean not only the green pastures and still waters of God's presence with his people but mortal combat, the dark night of desertions, the valley of the shadow of death—perhaps even of the death of God. Only such struggle, such sweat of blood, is adequate to the tragedy and glory of the world.

NOTES

[1] Published by SPCK in 1956. I am indebted to it for the substance of this paragraph.
[2] J. Neville Ward, *The Use of Praying* (Epworth Press 1967) p. 88.
[3] See G. S. Wakefield, *Puritan Devotion* (Epworth Press 1957) p. 75ff.
[4] Ronald Knox, *The Mass in Slow Motion* (Sheed and Ward 1948) p. 103f.
[5] Op. cit. (Burns Oates 1964) p. 66.
[6] David Jenkins, *The Glory of Man* (SCM 1967) p. 110.
[7] F. von Hügel, *Essays and Addresses*, Second Series (Dent 1926) p. 165ff.
[8] Op. cit. p. 79-80.
[9] Friedrich Heiler, *Prayer*, first published 1932, many editions.

Living Lourdes

MRS. A. G. C. KING

The Beginning

Roman Catholics are not *required* to believe that Our Lady appeared, in 1858, to a poor, sickly, ignorant peasant girl in the Pyrenean village of Lourdes – but many do. Bernadette Soubirous was, at the time, a timid girl of 14 who – as a result of an attack of cholera 3 years previously, and of a severe asthmatic condition – coupled with a life of great poverty – looked more like an eleven year old. Yet, despite her initial misgivings and the open opposition of the local parish priest and bishop, despite threats and rigorous cross-questioning, Bernadette held fast to her story and delivered the messages which she said that the Lady had given to her. Understandably, there were official attempts to hush the matter up and drive away curious visitors: but, ultimately, the Church authorities were forced to accept an embarrassing situation and make provision for the faithful who turned Lourdes into a place of pilgrimage.

It was on a cold February day that Bernadette and two other girls went to the grotto of Massabielle to collect firewood. Bernadette was not recollected in prayer when she first saw her vision: she was in fact taking off her shoes preparatory to crossing a stream that flowed into the river Gave. A sensible proceeding if she hoped to return home more or less dry-shod. She noticed a bush moving and then, quite suddenly, saw a young girl, dressed in white with a blue sash and, surprisingly, with a yellow rose on each foot. Bernadette described the golden roses as being 'of the same colour as the chain' on the lady's rosary. Her reaction was to put her hand into her pocket and draw out her own rosary beads; she tried to make the sign of the cross but found that she could not get her hand up to her forehead. 'It dropped down', she explained. One wonders if this was because the lady wanted to show her how the customary salute – which Catholics make before entering into a particular period of prayer – *should* be made: most of us are apt to get careless and slipshod. Bernadette describes how – in a graceful and dignified manner which she never afterwards forgot – the vision crossed herself. And she tells us that her own hand started shaking and she found that she was able to imitate the gesture. Bernadette started saying her rosary and she noticed that the lady's lips were still although her fingers moved over her beads. When Bernadette had reached the end of her rosary 'the vision disappeared all of a sudden'.

Meanwhile Bernadette's companions had seen nothing and had been busy collecting wood. When enquiries showed that they had not shared her vision she asked them to say nothing – but, of course, they could not keep quiet. Madame Soubirous was gravely disturbed and perhaps it was she who advised Bernadette to take holy water with her next time she went to the grotto. The girl collected it from her parish church and actually threw it towards the lady when she reappeared – but the lady merely smiled and bowed her head. Again the rosary was prayed and, as Bernadette finished, the lady disappeared. It was not until the third visit that the vision spoke and then, with the utmost courtesy, the lady asked: 'Would you have the goodness to come here for a fortnight?'. She also told Bernadette to ask the priests to build a chapel at the grotto; and she directed the girl to 'drink at the spring'. No spring was visible so Bernadette walked towards the river. 'Not there!' the lady corrected – and pointed with her finger. (I like that touch.) Bernadette could see only a small puddle of dirty water. She tried to scoop some up in her hand – and failed. She started to scrape at the earth with her fingers and 'then,' she says, 'I was able to get some. Three times I threw it away; the fourth time I was able to drink it. The vision disappeared and I went away.'

Every day for a fortnight the girl returned to the grotto and, with the exception of one Monday and one Friday, the lady appeared. She repeated her request for a chapel and asked Bernadette to go to the spring and wash, to eat some of the grass growing nearby, to pray for the conversion of sinners and to do penance. Over and again Bernadette asked the lady who she was but the vision only smiled until, one day, standing with both arms stretched downwards and with her eyes raised to the sky, she said in the Lourdes patois, 'I am the Immaculate Conception.' – 'Que soy era l'Immaculada Concepciou.' Bernadette tells us that she repeated the words over and again to herself as she walked home – so that he would not forget them. Clearly the expression was unfamiliar to her although even in this fairly remote part of France it is possible that priests interested in the new theological definition would have been discussing the concept.

For many centuries man has thought of God as being 'out there' – beyond the blue – beyond space and time, so when Our Lady raised her eyes to heaven as she proclaimed her title, she was, perhaps, acknowledging, in thanksgiving, the unearned grace – the free gift of God to man. In her case, prevenient grace anticipated the Incarnation and the Redemption in our time scale, for she was *born* fully towards God: she was infiltrated by the Holy Spirit from the moment of her conception, and her life began full of grace. To be born transparent to grace, without the least inclination towards sin is, for a human being, unique. It is what is meant by the angelic salutation which we variously translate as 'Hail, full of grace!' or 'Hail, highly favoured one!'. None of us can claim to have been born without any leaning towards sin but many Christians can accept that the woman who was to give birth to the Christ, the Son of God, would have been so favoured.

Today

The spring that Bernadette's scrabbling fingers released is still running 120 years later – though it is now channelled through pipes to taps and into bath cubicles which people either walk through or are dipped into in response to Our Lady's request to Bernadette, and as a traditional symbol of cleansing and renewal. If the original spring dried up and new sources of water were tapped the symbolic bathing would still continue as it has for over a century. Pilgrims also fill water bottles with Lourdes water, from taps in the grotto, and the variety of containers includes plastic madonnas with heads that unscrew. After the first shock of disbelief at such an idea one gets used to it – and obviously it is most attractive to many. Who made me the *arbiter elegantiarum*? Lourdes itself is set amongst beautiful hills and mountains: few of the buildings that have sprung up to cope with tourists are attractive and the shops and booths sell commercial atrocities of staggering gaudiness and doubtful piety. If you insist upon good taste and artistic merit you have to pay for it and nothing is cheap in Lourdes. But one becomes so fond of the place that even its vulgarities are lovable. Mercifully, trading is kept outside the Domaine – which contains the grotto, the three chapels, the underground basilica, the medical bureau and the 'Asile' hostel – renamed the 'Acceuil Notre Dame'. Candles only are on sale there: water is, of course, free. So far it has not been necessary for Christ to repeat His onslaught on the Temple traders.

For many of the pilgrims it is their one and only holiday away from home or hospital; for British pilgrims it may be their one glimpse of 'abroad' and much scraping, saving, love, longing and sacrifice will have gone into the preparation for just one week—or maybe a few hours—in Lourdes. It is the knowledge that, for so many, this is the holiday of a lifetime that makes the more fortunate amongst us anxious that nothing shall spoil it and that the pilgrims shall not be fleeced. The hoteliers are a mixed bunch but one is usually fortunate to discover and be accepted by hotels and boarding houses and hostels giving honest service and excellent food – as indeed the majority do. My sons will not forgive me if I do not here refer to *Hosanna House* – a wonderful venture which offers to the disabled all the joys and privileges of a retreat house and a holiday with Our Lady at Lourdes. It is near the sheepfold at Bartrès where Bernadette looked after her flock and, standing high above the town and looking into the Domaine, it is a place of refreshment and peace – a house of God. It is the Domaine Regina, offering a retreat-pilgrimage to groups of disabled people of every age, nation, creed or colour accompanied by their own helpers. In charge of the house are Sisters of the Franciscan Missionaries of Mary. If you want to know more about this venture – and I hope very much that you will – may I recommend the booklet *To Carry on Living*. Here you will find the authentic, unspoilt Lourdes.

One has to recognise that there are people who just can't 'take' Lourdes – for whom the sight of so much disfigurement and suffering collected into one place is unacceptable: there are those to whom the esoteric jokes and the gaiety and comradeship are anathema and the vocabulary – for which, initially, you almost need a glossary – is altogether too much. But in my limited experience these disenchanted pilgrims are relatively few. The vast majority of pilgrims enjoy themselves and will put up with any difficulty just because it is part of Lourdes and they set out with the idea of doing penance anyway. To them the sight of deformed people and the realisation of the constant suffering that some are called upon to endure throughout years and years is part of the shared burden of humanity and they see through the disfigurement to the glory within. Another aspect of this strange glory is the compassion called forth in those who care for the sick – not just in Lourdes but day in day out all over the world. To be part of that pushing, shoving multitude at Lourdes is to be part of the crowds that pressed around Our Lord in Palestine. Two thousand years ago in Judea and Galilee – or today in Lourdes – it is still the same: we clamour to be healed – and if we should, for a moment, think that we don't need the Physician – then we are sick indeed.

Miracles

Our Lady's message to Bernadette – which she faithfully passed on to her parish priest and bishop, and to us – is that we should pray for the conversion of sinners, do penance for our sins and also for the sins of others, and visit Lourdes in procession. *Prayer, Penance and Processions.* There was never, at any time, a promise of miracles; in any case, Our Lady doesn't work miracles – only God can do that. There was no physical miracle for Bernadette – no relief from her afflictions. Her asthma continued and the undermining effects of poverty and the attack of cholera left her an easy prey for tuberculosis. At the time of the apparitions the Soubirous family was living in one small room in the Cachot – the former town gaol converted into the nineteenth century equivalent of Part Three accommodation. Seven of them crowded into a dank, dark, place! One needs to visit that room to understand what it must have been like. Shortly before the appearances Bernadette had been sent, for six months, to her foster-mother in Bartrès where she could have better food and conditions than were possible at home. She had asked to be allowed to return to Lourdes in order that she might attend catechism classes. Until she was 15 she did not even know how to write. At 18 she almost died of pneumonia; at 22 she was allowed to take her vows as a nun in a convent far away at Nevers – she had not completed the novitiate but she was thought to be dying and an exception was made. At 35 she died, in great pain, her bones decayed by advanced tuberculosis. Our Lady had been perfectly frank. 'I do not promise to make you happy in this world,' she told Bernadette, 'but in the next.' And so it was.

Bernadette was insistent that neither she nor her brothers and sisters should accept gifts or make money out of Our Lady's visits and the fame that came to Lourdes. Her father had been a miller, owner of the Boly mill which he had inherited, but he was evidently no business man and when everything was lost the Soubirous had to depend on public charity. Bernadette loved her family and all that Lourdes meant to her yet when she entered the convent at Nevers she returned only once – to witness the consecration of the chapel which Our Lady had asked her to have built and which stands over the place were Our Lady appeared.

Although there had been no mention of miracles either by Our Lady or Bernadette, cures took place from the outset. For others than Bernadette there were physical miracles as well as the often experienced spiritual miracles of renewal and re-birth. It is through these latter that bitter and resentful patients and their families are enabled to discover within themselves the grace of acceptance, the ability to say: 'Thy will be done!' and to receive the miracle of grace that leads them to look beyond themselves and to *love*. As a nurse at Lourdes I have seen this happen. Any brancardier, handmaid, baths attendant – any priest, nun or layman – can tell of the miracles which were never suggested – still less promised – by Our Lady – but which, nevertheless, have happened. I have been introduced, at the Medical Bureau, to an elderly peasant woman with an entrancing smile, who rolled down her black wool stockings and raised her blue print dress in order to show me – as a nurse – the unmistakeable signs and scars of the rubber tubing which had formerly drained pus from many parts of her body. In the baths these had all fallen out and her flesh was instantly healed. It seems to be a token of the cure that some evidence is left behind.

I have made beds in the wards with an Italian woman who lost husband and son in the Second World War and who was wracked with bitterness and tortured by lack of faith. A priest said: 'There is only one thing for you to do – go to Lourdes!' – and he bundled her onto the next train. She found her pearl of great price – *peace* – and since then she has returned each year to Lourdes to work in the hospital throughout the busiest months, for those whose burdens are even greater than her own.

Physical cures are rare and, because of our modern understanding of psychosomatic disease and the pace at which science moves in discovering ever more powerful drugs and treatments, it is increasingly difficult to define a cure. Treatment is available to more people than ever before, and hospitals are loth to let their records, or even copies of their records, be made available to the international medical bureau set up at Lourdes. The stringent regulations governing the use of the term 'miracle' are there laid down and, unless a case meets all the conditions, it stands no chance of being defined as miraculous. These rules require, amongst other things, that the patient must previously have been diagnosed by independent medical opinions to be suffering from a condition for which there is, at present, no known cure. The patient must have produced incontrovertible evidence – medical reports, X-rays, scientific investigations carefully recorded to a high standard, that confirm the diagnoses of qualified doctors. The alleged cure must be instantaneous, complete and permanent; that is, a patient who has been bed-ridden for years must be able to get straight off a stretcher, or 'tronglot', or out of a chair and *walk* – and if you have ever had a bout of 'flu that left you feeling weak in the legs you will realise that it is quite remarkable for someone who has not walked for years to be able to do just that. A person with an essential part of the ear or eye destroyed must be able to hear and/or to see, although there is, on examination, no reason *why* they are able to hear or see. The patient has to return for re-examination at regular intervals for some years – and will be examined by doctors who may be sceptics and who, whether Christian or not, will be out for the truth. The patient must not have received within specified periods any drugs or treatment which might, conceivably, have had a delayed effect and brought about the alleged 'cure'. Finally, the patient – or former patient – must eventually die of quite another disease. Having said all this and ruled out a great many possible miracles and also the chance that a cure was merely a remission – one must add that it has never been known for an amputated or missing limb to be restored: but it has been known for unconscious patients to awake and discover themselves in Lourdes and to recover lost sight or the use of limbs which have been paralysed for years.

But the rare physical miracles accredited in the past and being investigated in the present are not important. The cures of the mind, heart and spirit – which are commonplace – are remarkable indeed. I shall never forget the agony of a young mother whose little boy was dying of a brain tumour. She kept on saying: 'He isn't ready to die! He's such a little heathen!' In Lourdes, this understandably petulant and difficult child became transformed. When he had died a few days after he was flown back home to England his mother told me how, in answer to her query about his poor swollen head, he replied: 'I'm all right. The thorns in Jesus' head and the nails in His hands must have hurt Him far more.' … I shall never forget how honoured I felt when a young couple asked me to take the wife – suffering from an advanced motor neurone disease – into the baths. I shall never forget the intensity with which we all prayed – nor the look on the husband's previously hopeful young face when we emerged and he could see for himself that there had been no physical cure: no miracle of bodily healing. Their love for each other was radiant and though it was already taking him an hour each morning to get her washed and dressed, one could see that theirs was a love that would survive and grow. Again, I shall never forget the young

276

woman, twisted almost into a knot, so that it took three trained nurses to lift her heavy body and turn her in bed. She was blind – I think from birth – and her hands were like claws. But, one day, when I had been treating her pressure points, she seized my hand and said: 'Nurse, I want to tell you something. Baby Jesus is here – beside me. Do you understand what I am saying? HE IS HERE.' She was not mad and she was not in the habit of making such unexpected statements as I discovered when I made discreet enquiries. Her illness affected her spine and the long bones and twisted her body. But the *happiness* in her face when she told me her great secret – invisible to me – was something that no nurse could forget. Imagination? self-deception? frustrated maternal instinct? brain disease? If you like. I only know that – with no reason on earth for happiness – she was happy. Then there was the tall negroid leper – his notes, of course, called it Hansen's disease and the disease was under control – burnt out – though it had left its legacy and he was scarred and maimed. He asked me to take him right into the grotto where a statue of Our Lady stands high up on a rock. I explained that this was impossible – the procession of the Blessed Sacrament was about to start and the grotto was officially closed. But he begged me to try, so I braved the fierce looking French 'Chef de Brancardiers' who looked more like a brigand than a pilgrim – and to my surprise, he said: 'Yes, if you hurry!'. My patient's black face beamed and he was able to reach up and touch the rock with his one hand. When we returned to the group he flung his remaining stump of an arm round my shoulder and kissed me. He was happy – and so was I. It has been said the true 'helpers' at Lourdes are not the fit and strong – but the sick. *They* are the *apostles* whose handicaps enable others to *see* and to *serve*.

Prayer and Processions

Prayer at Lourdes is like prayer anywhere – an extraordinary mixture. There is the prayer that is work, the run up to the hospital in the early morning – no pilgrims about – and the air cool and fresh as you hurry to get up to the wards to wash the patients and to do their dressings and give treatments. And then, thank God, the bliss of returning to your hotel for a delicious breakfast of steaming bowls of coffee and hot rolls. Prayer is the quiet group Mass or the precious ten minutes seized from the day in the hospital chapel: it is the Mass on the hospital balcony where the disabled priest officiates from a wheelchair and is surrounded by patients in beds and chairs and stretchers. It is the great liturgical celebration in the underground basilica where thousands are gathered together. Prayer is straining tired heart and sinews – pushing heavy patients up the way of the cross on the steep hillside and kneeling on the sharp pebbles. Some pilgrims do the climb in bare feet. Prayer is the daytime procession of the Blessed Sacrament and the

Blessing of the Sick. It is singing 'Gaude Jerusalem' and 'Benedictus qui venit' with heart and soul. Prayer is the torchlight procession at night: it is the Holy Hour, still beloved of the English, in the topmost of the three chapels built above Bernadette's grotto. Prayer is sinking exhausted onto a bench, or the hard stone floor, and thanking God for the chance to rest swollen feet and legs. Prayer is the silent contemplation down in the grotto around midnight, when only the soft shuffling of sandalled feet, the guttering of candles and the sighing of the night breeze can be heard. Under the stars there may be hundreds praying in the Domaine – 'saying goodnight to Our Lady'. There will be hundreds more in the hospitals, the hotels and hostels, in the quietening streets and even in the cafes where guitars are softly playing. In the house of prayer there are indeed many mansions.

When one hears – and joins in the intensive, repetitive prayers uttered in many languages: 'Lord, that I may see!' 'Lord, that I may hear!' 'Lord, that I may walk!' – one is caught up in a great communal exercise of faith and hope and intercession. Over and over again the pilgrims of many different nationalities join in crying out for cures of mind, heart, soul and body: it is Judea and Galilee all over again. And as in Palestine 2,000 years ago, there is the same delight in the incongruous, the same love of jokes and laughter. There is still, in Lourdes, some use of the traditional mediaeval devotion of the rosary though noticeably fewer pilgrims pray it these days. Hymns and folksongs with guitar accompaniment may be more to their liking.

Penance

I have said much about *Prayer and Processions* – but what about *Penance*? Bernadette had a tough time in this world and even in the convent at Nevers things were far from easy. Her fellow novices sometimes wanted to hear about her visions but she was told not to talk about them unless summoned to the parlour for the edification of a benefactor or visiting bishop. Plays and books have been written about the stern novice mistress who simply could not understand why God should choose an illiterate peasant for such favours: she wanted Bernadette to admit that her adolescent imagination had run away with her and that she had lied. The visions had led her into embarrassing situations from the start: scratching at the earth, scooping up and drinking muddy water and dirtying her face in consequence, eating grass, passing on awkward messages to resentful priests, annoying the police, and now – irritating her novice mistress. With Teresa of Avila, Bernadette could justly exclaim: 'No wonder, Lord, that You have so few friends!'

You don't need to look for penance at Lourdes – it seeks you out. All you have to do is to smile and laugh through whatever comes and think only of the happiness of someone else. In March or April the searing tearing winds can bite to the bone and send you home with a cold. In August heat, you can be sweltering and sweating one moment and, the next, soaked to the skin by rains of monsoon intensity. The nurses' wet hair may hang in rats' tails, their caps a sodden mess and their white overalls clinging like second skins as they push patients up the steep hill to the Sept Douleurs or Saint Frai hospital: but bedpans must be given, patients washed, changed, fed and made comfortable before stretcher bearers, doctors, nurses or handmaids can go off duty to change or have a meal. Queuing for the luxury of a shower – never mind a hot bath – and queuing for a meal in an over-crowded dining-room is part of the penance. So is sharing a bedroom with someone who snores or who has to get up early to nurse or to prepare breakfast for the sick. So is – for the patient – sleeping in an over-crowded ward with few chairs, no lockers and one pair of screens! Your clothing and possessions may be stuffed into your suitcase and kept under the bed – unless you are lucky! There are more modern hospitals and wards opening each year. For a nurse it is penance to work in a primitive 'hospital' – reminiscent of the worst wartime conditions – without either disposable dressings (other than those we bring with us) or facilities for sterilisation. Oddly enough there is no cross-infection in Lourdes and it is surely a miracle that even the handmaids and brancardiers who drink the filthy, greasy, grey water after the bathing of the pilgrims is over for the day – have not been known to suffer ill effects. By rights they should have septic throats and intestines. There are no flies in Lourdes – at least none that I have seen and perhaps it is as well! I have worked on a 30 bed ward where there was one gas ring and one kettle to cope with all aseptic dressing procedures: and where fulminating cancer of the breast was treated outside the lavatories in conditions of limited privacy or none at all. A humiliation shared by Christ on Calvary, of course. They say there is no humility without humiliation.

In the baths pilgrims – fit or well – undress or are undressed in the confined space of cubicles with the decency demanded by the fierce French and Italian contessas in charge! If only one of those in the cubicle is an overflowing peasant woman wearing layer upon layer of skirts and laced up corset it is an additional hazard. Towels are not used and one struggles to slide nylon tights over wet legs. The air is, in August, apt to be thick with sweating bodies, an absence of deodorants or – almost worse – a surfeit of 'Brut' or its feminine equivalent. But there is a glorious mixture of pilgrims and you may just as well be surrounded by expensive French scents and silk lingerie. Into the baths go pilgrims suffering from every ill known to man – from cancer to venereal disease. Open wounds, drainage tubes, sores that would disturb Job – and into the same grey greasy water – with faint heart barely overcoming repugnance – you entrust yourself. In the women's baths strong-armed handmaids seize hold of you and plunge you in, up to the neck; gasping with the sudden shock of cold and unable to join in the prayers, you are led to the end of the bath to kiss a crucifix or statue, then turned and helped up the step and out whilst the wet canvas robe is swept away and – in the same movement – a blue one flung over you: all decencies preserved and you go back through the curtain of your cubicle and dress whilst another is plunged into the water. All the time the prayers go on and outside, seated on benches awaiting their turn, pilgrims are praying the rosary. You go out of the bathhouse into the sunshine (where queues of waiting pilgrims are also reciting the rosary –) and you, who so hated the icy water, find you are walking on air and feeling marvellously refreshed. The drill I have tried to describe – which is meticulously observed in the women's baths – is something that seems to have grown up over the years and has nothing to do with Our Lady or Bernadette but a lot to do with protocol and custom. Outside the summer season it is all much more simple but the etiquette in high summer is remarkable. The privilege of being a handmaid working in the *Baths* is jealously guarded and, although there is a good sprinkling of aristocratic women amongst them, precedence and rank depends upon the number of years one has been working in this most testing of departments. Since I always shut my eyes tight on entering that icy water I could not have told you what happens had I not also been allowed to serve in the baths: and never was there a more stupid Englishwoman slower at picking up the correct way to pull off and wring out the heavy canvas robe with which modesty enshrouds female pilgrims!

Working in the Baths you may observe, with surprise, that the busy cheerful handmaid, alongside whom you work in the wards, has a huge mastectomy scar – or you learn of an active brancardier who has cancer or coronary disease. How dare *you* grumble – even in thought? When next you help to push a heavy patient up the hillside on the mountainous Way of the Cross, with its life size figures, and pause to wonder if you are not yourself a candidate for a coronary – if not for cardiac arrest – you think of the smiling man who knows that he carries within himself the beginnings of multiple sclerosis and that, in future pilgrimages, it will be he who rides in a wheelchair – his pushing days over. I hasten to reassure you that such diseases are not catching!

I have mentioned the dark side: finally I turn to the joy. It is typical of Lourdes that the Stations of the Cross on the flat land beyond the Baths have a fifteenth station – the Resurrection. There are, of course, many different versions of the Way of the Cross – but I like best the ones that end with *joy*. Joy at the end of the day, joy in the Cross, joy in the glorious resurrection. The risen Christ is at the heart of Lourdes. Through Bernadette His Mother asks for prayer, penance and processions – but, always, it is God Himself who is the centre and focus of our attention. We ask Our Lady to pray for us because we have a human conviction – amounting to certainty – that she must be the most precious person in His life. The Cana story suggests that her Son, who is God, listens to and accedes to her request. She who gave Him birth was the woman whom He gave to St John and to the world with His dying command: 'Behold your Mother!'. *That* is why, over and again in our various languages, we cry to her: 'Pray for us!' 'Priez pour nous!' 'Prega per noi!'. But it is to *God*, as Lord, that we cry: 'Lord that I may see!' 'Lord that I may walk!' and in so doing we are not necessarily asking for physical miracles – though hope underlies all the prayer. We know that Our Lady promised Bernadette happiness – not in this life but the next. And we know that Bernadette, despite illness and pain, found contentment and joy. When another nun asked her if it was not rather hard to have been at the centre of the exciting Lourdes revelations and then, later, hidden away – a nobody in a convent – she replied: 'What do you do with a broom when you have finished sweeping? Set it aside in the corner.' We must ask for her contented acceptance, the ability to come to terms with problems and disabilities, the willingness to be used.

Judged by our standards, God has chosen some very unlikely people to suit His purposes. He chose an unknown Jewish girl from Galilee to be His Mother. He chose a poor, sickly peasant girl to be His Mother's messenger and, ultimately, to bring together in the service of the sick and the search for the Holy Spirit – Christians, Jews, believers of all faiths. Agnostics and atheists go to Lourdes too – perhaps drawn by curiosity. Neither Mary nor Bernadette are the sort of persons whom most of us would have chosen to launch important ventures. But God chose them – and how effective! Lots of humility – lots of grace. Unbeatable combination. Lourdes lives!